Lake Superior

THE ULTIMATE GUIDE TO THE REGION
SECOND EDITION

First Edition: February 2010

LAKE SUPERIOR PORT CITIES INC.
P.O. Box 16417
Duluth, Minnesota 55816-0417 USA
888-BIG LAKE (888-244-5253) • www.lakesuperior.com
Publishers of *Lake Superior Magazine* & *Lake Superior Travel Guide*

5 4 3 2 1

Library of Congress Cataloging-in-Publication Data

Lake Superior : the ultimate guide to the region. – 2nd ed.
p. cm.
Includes index.
ISBN 789-0-942235-97-5
1. Superior, Lake, Region – Guidebooks. 2. Superior, Lake, Region – History, Local.
F552.L154 2010
977.4 '9–dc22 2009043236

Printed in China

Editors: Bob Berg, Konnie LeMay
Book Design: Randy Bauer
Inside Photos: *Lake Superior Magazine* (Paul Hayden, Bob Berg, Konnie LeMay)
Printer: Regent Publishing, Hong Kong

Cover: Ontario shoreline; Bayfield, Wisconsin; Minnesota's Split Rock Lighhouse (Lee Radzak); Pictured Rocks National Lakeshore (Gregg Bruff)

Back cover: Pictured Rocks National Lakeshore (Gregg Bruff); Duluth ship canal; Thunder Bay waterfront; Raspberry Island Lighthouse, Apostle Islands National Lakeshore

LAKE SUPERIOR

Contents

LAKE SUPERIOR Introduction

From the Thunder Bay, Ontario waterfront the profile of the Sleeping Giant can be seen on the distant Sibley Peninsula. It's one of the amazing discoveries found around Lake Superior.

For more than 30 years, we here at *Lake Superior Magazine* have written about the places, people and events in the Lake Superior region … and still we discover new things. That is why traveling to a destination in this region or taking on the entire Circle Tour can be so exciting; it's a choice you will treasure.

Having a great guide along the way enhances any journey, and we created this guide with that in mind. It brings you our accumulated knowledge of travel around the Big Lake and adds a dimension of history, insider suggestions and reminders of "must-see" attractions to help you get the most out of your trip.

In creating the text for this guide, we do not accept free food, lodging or other items that might sway our recommendations. We try to give you the same tips we would give as we send off any close relative on a Circle Tour adventure.

While we try to keep the information as up-to-date as possible, things do change. Please send us any of your observations or updates and watch for those of others at www.lakesuperior.com. You can also join our free Circle Tour Club there and get some free gifts.

Enjoy your travels!

Lake Superior The Big Lake

Behold the area that holds 10 percent of the world's surface fresh water. The entire Circle Tour route around Lake Superior totals about 1,300 miles.

Duluth to Thunder Bay = 195 mi. (313 km.)
Thunder Bay to Sault Ste. Marie = 440 mi. (708 km.)
Sault Ste. Marie to Duluth = 425 mi. (683 km.)

Statute Miles 0 10 20 30 40
Kilometers 0 10 20 30 40 50 60 70
Nautical Miles 0 10 20 30 40

LAKE SUPERIOR CIRCLE TOUR

Legend

- Shipwreck
- Lighthouse
- National Park or Lakeshore
- Provincial or State Park
- National or State Forest
- Waterfall
- Mountain peak
- International boundary
- State or Province boundary
- Other boundary
- Major highway
- Major road
- Other road
- Unimproved road
- Major trail
- Time Zone boundary
- Water depth
- ONTARIO — State or Province
- Duluth — City or town
- Isle Royale — Land feature

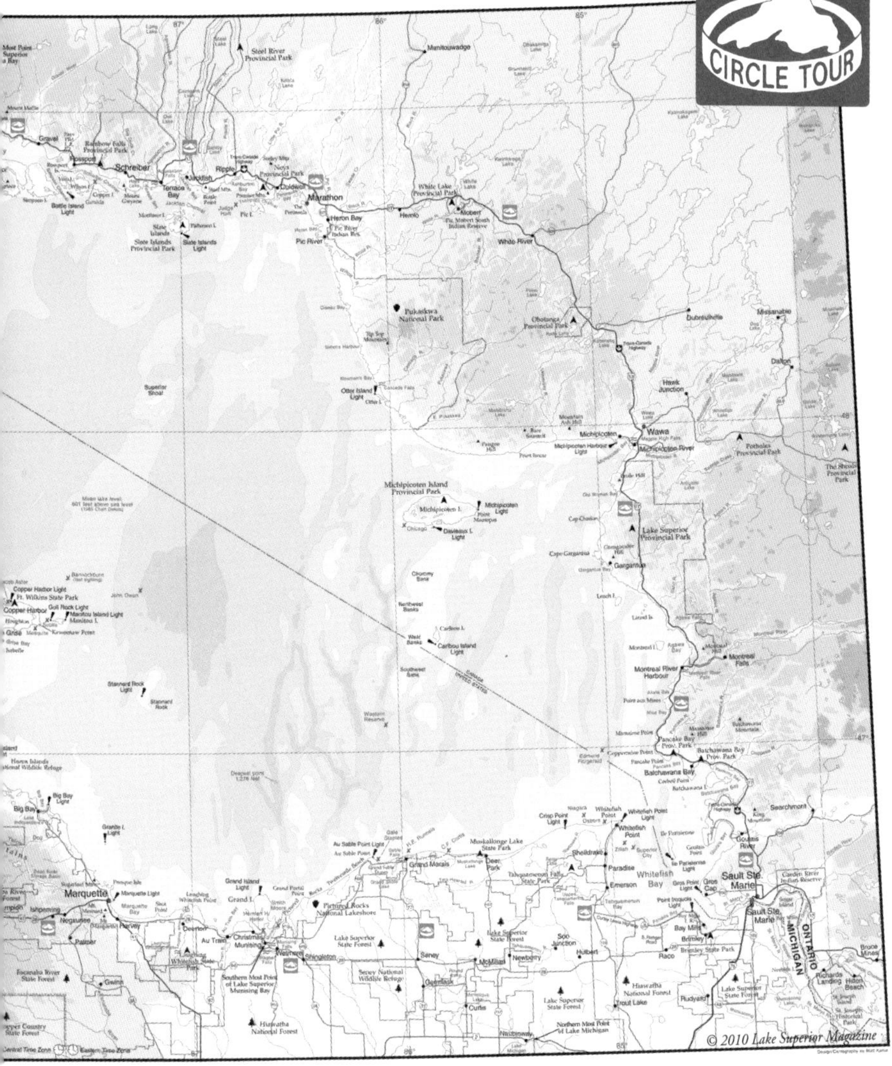

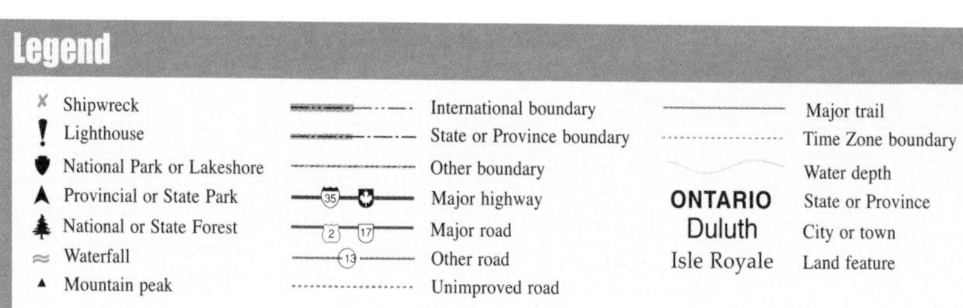

Using the Lake Superior Ultimate Guide

The beautiful Split Rock Lighthouse on Minnesota's North Shore is now run by the Minnesota Historical Society and is in a state park of the same name. (Lee Radzak / Split Rock Lighthouse)

Lake Superior can be – and has been – circled by just about any mode of transportation imaginable: by car, by kayak, bus, snowmobile, bicycle, motorcycle, horseback, powerboat, sailboat, canoe, on foot.

We know of kayakers who have taken two months to paddle around the edges of the lake and of one Iron Butt Association motorcyclist who completed the circle (legally) in 21 hours.

But traveling the full Lake Superior Circle Tour is certainly not the only way to enjoy and visit the Big Lake.

This guide is designed to enhance your trip whether you plan a one-night getaway, a couple of days at one location or a week or more enjoying a leisurely tour of the whole basin.

The region's cities and towns – along with many parks and public destinations – are listed alphabetically in their state or province. Many entries end with a directory of tourism bureaus and a few places to stay or eateries serving a local flavor; the lists are not comprehensive but highlight local operations. Icons for parks, camping, etc., will identify options. Larger towns have bus service and many have air service. Car rentals are readily available, and while most lake-area highways are two lanes, driving is extremely comfortable.

Throughout this section of the guide, you will find a series of maps, arranged

clockwise from the Head of the Lakes, Duluth. References within some individual listings direct you to those more detailed maps. You will also find a few suggested mini tours of specific regions and a fun section with a checklist of 50 lifetime lake experiences.

The opening section of this book also gives you a lake basin full of information, tidbits and tips for traveling or getting to know the lake region.

As you travel, remember, this is a safe and friendly part of the continent. Feel free to ask for help or directions if you need them.

Basics & Beyond

Area Codes

Thunder Bay/North of Superior, Ontario – Area Code 807.
Algoma Region/Sault Ste. Marie, Ontario – Area Code 705.
Michigan's Upper Peninsula – Area Code 906.
Northern Wisconsin – Area Code 715.
Northern Minnesota – Area Code 218.

Emergencies

All areas around the lake use 911 as the emergency call number. However, some cell phone services do not use that number. You should know the number used by your service in both the United States and Canada. Also, there remain many remote spots around the lake where cell phones do not work. All of the four major metropolitan cities around the lake, as well as some smaller cities, have excellent hospital coverage.

Time Zones

ONTARIO – All of Ontario near Lake Superior is in the Eastern Time Zone, however, the extreme northwestern part of the province, west of 90 degrees west longitude (Shebandowan on Highway 11), is in the Central Time Zone.
MICHIGAN – Most of the Upper Peninsula of Michigan is in the Eastern

Time Zone, however, the southwestern U.P. counties of Gogebic, Iron, Dickinson and Menominee are in the Central Time Zone.
MINNESOTA – The entire state is in the Central Zone.
WISCONSIN – The entire state is in the Central Zone.

ONTARIO TRAFFIC LAWS

SPEED LIMITS – All roads and highways, unless otherwise posted:
Passenger car – 80 km/h (50 mph) except on designated, signed Trans Canada routes or freeways – 90 or 100 km/h (56 or 62 mph);
Urban areas – 40 to 60 km/h (25 to 37 mph).
Safety belts – Required for everyone in the car. Children who are 1) younger than 8 or 2) weigh less than 36 kg. (80 lbs.) or 3) are shorter than 145 cm. (4 ft. 9 in.) must be in an age-appropriate safety seat.
Radar warning devices – Prohibited by law and cannot be in the vehicle, even if not in use, and might be confiscated.

U.S. TRAFFIC LAWS

SPEED LIMITS – All roads and highways, unless otherwise posted:
Passenger car – 55 mph (88 km/h) except on designated, signed rural freeways – 70 mph (104 km/h);
Truck – 55 mph (88 km/h);
School buses – 50 mph (80 km/h).
Safety belts – Required for everyone in the car. Children younger than 8 must be in an age-appropriate safety seat in all of the Lake Superior shore states. Height and weight modifications may apply by state.

LICENSES, PERMITS AND SUCH

To fish, hunt, camp or otherwise use a state or provincial park, various licenses

Metric Conversion

The Metric System is used in Canada and is applied to measurements and temperatures. The English System is used in the United States and is applied to measurements and temperatures. Use these simple conversions:

English	Metric
1 inch = 2.54 centimeters	1 centimeter = .039 inches
1 foot = 30 centimeters	1 meter = 3.28 feet
1 yard = 0.91 meters	1 meter = 1.09 yards (3.3 feet)
1 mile = 1.61 kilometers	1 kilometer = 0.62 mile
1 pound = 0.45 kilograms	1 kilogram = 2.2 pounds
1 pint = 0.47 liters	1 liter = 2.1 pints
1 gallon (U.S.) = 3.79 liters	1 liter = 0.26 gallons (U.S.)

To convert temperature:

Celsius to Fahrenheit: Degrees C x 9 ÷ 5 + 32 = degrees F.
Fahrenheit to Celsius: Degrees F -32 x 5 ÷ 9 = degrees C.

Common temperatures:

Water freezing – 32°F/0°C; Body temp – 98.6° F/37°C; Water boiling – 212°F/100°C
70°F = 21°C • 50°F = 10°C • –10°F = –23°C • –20°F = –28°C

or permits are required. If you're entering state or provincial parks, you can usually get one-day or multiday permits on-site. You can get a fishing license just about anywhere in season (ask at any convenience store), but hunting licenses require more effort. A license to hunt some animals, like bear, may require applying for a lottery. Regulations vary from state to state to province. So, if you want to hunt in the Lake Superior region, inquire at the local department or ministry of natural resources. If you are not hunting or fishing in your home country and plan to take home a trophy or meat from your catch, check with the border patrols before you go to find out about regulations and requirements for transporting such items.

Smoking Restrictions

Smoking is prohibited in restaurants and in most public places indoors around the lake. Our best advice: Ask about smoking laws before lighting up.

Crossing Borders

When traveling by car or boat between the United States and Canada, anyone 16 or older will need to satisfy travel document rules imposed by the United States by having a U.S. or Canadian passport, a U.S. passport card, a state- or province-issued enhanced driver's license (available in Michigan and Ontario), or a NEXUS, SENTRI or FAST/EXPRES card.

A passport is probably the best travel document to have (especially if flying is in your plans), but the U.S. passport cards are cheaper and work fine for driving to Canada and back. U.S. or Canadian children younger than age 16 traveling by land or water don't need a passport but should have a copy of their birth certificate, a Canadian Citizenship Card or other document. If you are traveling with children who are not your own, seek information before you go about what else might be required (such as a notarized permission letter from the parents).

For a breakdown of the U.S. requirements through Customs and Border Protection, go to www.getyouhome.gov; or for the Canada Border Services Agency, go to www.cbsa.gc.ca.

Pets in the Car

Dogs or cats older than 3 months need a veterinarian-signed certificate that shows vaccination against rabies at least 30 days, and no more than three years, prior to crossing the border. A pup younger than 3 months does not need proof of a shot, but any animal must appear in good health.

Some public areas, like Isle Royale National Park, don't allow pets in order to protect wildlife.

It's good to know:

Gasoline in Canada is sold by the liter rather than by the U.S. gallon. A liter equals about one quarter of a gallon. Be advised of this at the pump. You may also see reference to an "imperial gallon,"

Don't miss a chance to get out of the car and stretch on the many hiking trails like the Gitchi-Gami State Trail in Minnesota that hugs Silver Creek Cliff as it winds along the shore.

which is just less than U.S. gallon (0.83 of a U.S. gallon).

Returning from Canada after a 48-hour stay, you may be entitled to an $800 personal exemption on purchases in Canada that you bring back. A $200 exemption applies to stays of less than 48 hours. Keep your receipts and pack your purchases separately, especially if you're over the limit and expect to pay duty.

Canadians returning home after at least 48 hours may be able to claim up to $400 in goods without paying duties, or up to $50 in goods after a 24-hour stay.

Make Reservations in advance

The peak tourist season around much of Lake Superior is summer through fall colors (but winter sports enthusiasts flock to many parts of the lake to take advantage of the snow). So make reservations no matter the season.

Currency Exchange

Many businesses take U.S. and Canadian dollars, but not all do. Expect handling costs, however. To exchange money, try Ryden's Border Store in Minnesota (at the border) or the Ontario-run casinos in Thunder Bay or Sault Ste. Marie. All use the daily bank exchange rate without adding a fee.

Daily rates can be found at Bank of Canada: www.bankofcanada.ca.

Credit cards figure the exchange rate for you, but often add a fee. Bank/check cards may or may not have fees. Check with your companies before you go.

Gooseberry Falls State Park on Minnesota's North Shore is the most-visited park in the state.

Lake Superior Seasons

You might hear the phrase "colder by the lake" while you travel, and in many parts of the lake there is a near-shore temperature and an inland temperature. In Duluth, within the city limits, you might have 10°F difference from lakeside to hillside. The "colder by the lake" refers to summer months since it is "warmer by the lake" in winter.

• **Spring** generally starts in late April and is short and sweet. As the ice and snow melt and the world comes alive again, it's a perfect time for dedicated "birders" to hunt for their favorite feathered friends.

• **Summer** generally runs mid-June until September, yet weather depends where on the lake you are. On the southern shores, summers can get hot. The farther north you go, summer weather can range from hot to mild to chilly, especially at night. Even in summer, bring light gloves, just in case.

• **Fall** generally runs from September through mid-November and is a spectacular time around Lake Superior, with fall colors starting to appear in early September, and in some areas in late August. Many resorts and inns cater to "leaf spotters," and most weekends, especially in Michigan's Keweenaw Peninsula where some of the most awesome fall colors are found, are booked solid, sometimes months in advance.

• **Winter** generally runs mid-November (or earlier) into April (or later). The good news is that winter is beautiful here.

Winter Survival Guide

Cold temperatures and snow around Lake Superior are never trifling. Pay attention to storm warnings when driving and be aware of weather conditions. Don't be afraid to hold up until storms pass. Here is a list of survival tips to keep you safe, snug and warm.

• Dress appropriately. If you're planning on outdoor activities, make sure you've got a jacket, hat, mittens or gloves and boots made for this environment. Think goosedown or Thinsulate.

• Respect the temperature. If temperatures dip below zero Fahrenheit, take extra caution. Cover up fingers, ears, nose and cheeks on chilly days.

Winter Driving

Most times of the year, the roads around the Lake Superior region are highly driveable. But in winter, conditions can change quickly. Here are some tips:

• Is your car ready to travel in snow? Make sure it's tuned up and has good tires. Stock it with a scraper and brush, jumper cables in case your battery dies, a shovel and a bag of sand for traction in case you get stuck in the snow or on ice. Also, throw in a blanket and a working flashlight.

• Keep a survival kit in your trunk. In a clean coffee can (you can melt snow inside of it for water) place a candle with matches or a lighter, a red or white cloth to use as a distress flag, a first-aid kit and high energy, non-perishable foods.

• Front-wheel or four-wheel drive vehicles are most adaptable in tricky conditions, but even they can't handle blizzards and extremely icy conditions. (Local tow-truck drivers say they get the most calls from overconfident drivers of four-wheel-drive vehicles in the ditch.)

• Understand your vehicle's brake system – be it antilock or another – and what the best methods are for avoiding or driving out of a skid on ice.

• If you do get stranded, stay in your car. Run the engine for five minutes each hour, taking care to keep your exhaust pipe free of snow to avoid asphyxiation. Open the windows a bit to get fresh air.

• Some areas around Lake Superior have cell phone coverage, but not all do.

Local Flavor

When traveling around Lake Superior, there are some regional culinary specialties that you just shouldn't miss. Much of the traditional food comes from our immigrant forebears. Depending on where you are, you'll find strong Swedish, Norwegian, Finnish, German, Polish and Italian communities, and excellent examples of that cuisine in many local restaurants. These are closely held traditions of families sitting down together for dinner. If you see any of these regional specialties advertised or on menus, by all means, give them a try:

Wild rice: Wild rice is native to the cold rivers and lakes in Minnesota, Wisconsin and Ontario. It isn't a rice at all, but a long-grain water grass growing in shallow, marshy waters. Cooked and used like white or brown rice, wild rice has a nutty flavor that pairs well with many dishes. You'll find it in soups, breads and casseroles. Wild rice was a staple in the Native American diet in the region and is still harvested today using traditional methods. The temperamental grain has also been hybridized and farmed commercially. Wild rice aficionados prefer the naturally grown product.

Pasty: It's pronounced "PASS-tee," and is a Cornish-inspired hand-held meal popular in mining communities. This is a meat pie consisting of beef, potatoes, carrots, onions and sometimes rutabaga inside a flaky crust. Patsy preferences inspire a continuing debate over what to put in and on the pie. As sauce, some favor gravy, some butter; others slather on ketchup. You'll find several restaurants that serve pasties in Michigan's Upper Peninsula and on Minnesota's Iron Range.

Fish boil: Fish boils originated when Lake Superior was home to an armada of fishing boats and scores of people made their living fishing this inland sea. The men would bring home their catches, women would throw them in an outdoor cauldron of boiling water along with potatoes and other veggies on hand, and while the whole thing was boiling, people socialized. You'll find this tradition still alive around the lake, mainly on weekends during the summer.

Walleye: While Lake Superior doesn't have one regional specialty, this could be nominated for the title. People

Freighter Smokestacks

Algoma Central Corporation, St. Catharines, Ontario

American Steamship Company, Williamsville, New York

Great Lakes Fleet Inc., Duluth, Minnesota

Inland Lakes Management Inc., Alpena, Michigan

Interlake Steamship Company, Richfield, Ohio

Several places around Lake Superior, like Canal Park in Duluth by the north and south piers, provide great boat-watching spots for those interested in the maritime activity.

here love walleye, especially if they've caught it themselves.

Lefse: In Minnesota, lefse is a Scandinavian specialty, and it's fairly common around the holidays. Lefse, made from potatoes, is a cross between a pancake and a tortilla (and it's made on a griddle, not baked). It can be found in Scandinavian homes of which there are many in this region.

Lutefisk: Another traditional Scandinavian food, lutefisk is loved and hated with great passion in this region. It's fish soaked in lye. You won't find it on many menus, but if you do, try it once, just to say you've had it.

Tips for Watching the Big Boats

Big ships are a common sight on Lake Superior. Maritime activity generally runs from mid-March, when the Soo Locks open, to mid-January, when they close.

The freighters that stay on the Great Lakes are called *lakers*, and can reach more than 1,000 feet (308 metres). They carry coal, ore or stone. Oceangoing freighters are called *salties*, and are smaller because of the size limitation of the Welland Canal connecting Lake Ontario and Lake Erie. These ships often carry grain. Salties often carry cargo, while lakers mostly transport bulk commodities.

The best places to watch the ships are in the large ports of Duluth, Superior, Thunder Bay or Sault Ste. Marie. Witnessing one of these monster boats maneuver its way through the Soo Locks is quite a memorable sight, as is standing near the Duluth Ship Canal, watching an enormous ship slip by, almost close enough to touch.

When watching the big boats, common questions are: Which one is it? What's it carrying? There are ways for even novice maritime enthusiasts to answer some of the questions, and one way is to follow the smoke. That's because the smokestacks – and, though rarely used these days, ship flags – show the distinctive colors of the company operating the vessel. An easy way to track the ships, with all the detail you could ever want, is with a copy of *Know Your Ships*, a slender guide updated annually by Marine Publishing Co. of Sault Ste. Marie, Michigan. The book shows more than 150 different smokestack markings for domestic vessels that frequent the Great Lakes and St. Lawrence Seaway and 75 stacks from saltwater fleets.

At the Lake Superior Maritime Visitor Center, operated by the U.S. Army Corps of Engineers in Duluth's Canal Park, you'll find interactive video screens that give details about arriving ships, fleet smokestack colors and icons, and even the weather forecast.

Here are some very good spots for boat watching:

• In Duluth, in Canal Park by the Aerial Lift Bridge, or on a Vista Fleet cruise.

• In Two Harbors, Minnesota, at the Two Harbors Lighthouse or the ore docks.

• In Thunder Bay, head for the waterfront.

• In Sault Ste. Marie, Michigan, Soo Locks & Tours, or the Soo Locks Park. In Sault Ste. Marie, Ontario, there is also a lock next to a park; the lock is used for recreational vessels.

• Brimley, Michigan, the 18th hole, Wild Bluff Golf Course.

• Whitefish Point, Michigan, Whitefish Point Lighthouse.

• Marquette, the ore docks.

• Superior, Wisconsin, Connor's Point.

For information, the Boatwatcher's Hotline (218-722-6489) lists traffic for Duluth, Two Harbors and Superior. Or the Harbour Commission Vessel Location Line (807-345-1256) tracks vessels in Thunder Bay.

Rock Picking on the Shores

Okay, we admit it. Collecting rocks is an obsession for many people who live near (or love) Lake Superior.

You'll find them decorating many Lake Superior homes and businesses. People use them as literal touchstones to remind them of a favorite trip, an especially memorable excursion to the lake, or simply as a focal point for the spiritual pull Lake Superior has on many people who love it. These are the gray, flat, speckled or multicolored rocks you'll find on nearly any beach. But here's a quick rundown of more exotic rocks you might encounter:

Lake Superior agate – The official gemstone of Minnesota, an agate is a quartz with red, brown, gray and translucent bands. These stones are a favorite of collectors who slice and polish them into solid rainbows. Hot spots to check for agates: stream beds, gravel pits, gravel beaches and river mouths from Two Harbors through Grand Marais, Minnesota, and beaches in Michigan's Upper Peninsula. There were agate mines in Ontario as well.

Amethyst – This striking purple quartz adorns expensive jewelry and can be found along Minnesota's Gunflint Trail and Michigan's Isle Royale, but they're plentiful in Ontario. The province has five mines, and you can "pick your own" amethyst there like other people pick their own apples in an orchard. It's Ontario's provincial gemstone.

Isle Royale Greenstone – Greenstones are billions of years old and are aptly named. This dark green rock is the state gemstone of Michigan. The easiest place to look for them is Isle Royale, but be warned, it is not legal to take them from this national park.

JEFF KOPSI

Thomsonite – Thomsonite is a rare gemstone with many faces, colors, concentric bands and striped eyes. Pure Thomsonite is snow-white and sometimes translucent, says Lee Bergstrom of Thomsonite Beach Inn & Suites and Thomsonite Beach Jewelry Shop between Lutsen and Grand Marais, Minnesota. Common colors are pink, tan, white, red and brown. Those with green, gray or black backgrounds or green eyes are the rarest and most prized. Thomsonite is found only in a few spots around the world, including a limited stretch of Lake Superior shoreline and land adjacent to Lee's business. No Thomsonite picking is allowed on the shores of the inn, but guests can travel a half-mile to the cobblestone beach at Good Harbor Bay/Cut Face Creek Wayside Rest where they might find a piece.

LEE BERGSTROM

Lake Superior Wildlife

Much of the land around Lake Superior is wilderness, and there you'll encounter wildlife. The best time to see animals is from dusk to dawn. Catching

Lake Superior

- Contains 10 percent of the earth's surface fresh water and more than half of all the water in the Great Lakes combined. (Only 3 percent of the earth's surface water is fresh water.)
- Holds 3 quadrillion gallons of water. (Enough to flood North and South America under 1 foot of water.) It was filled with glacial melt 10,000 years ago.
- Is called "an ocean in a test tube" by some researchers because it often acts more like an ocean than a lake.
- Is about 601 feet above sea level.
- Averages a water temperature of 40 degrees Fahrenheit (4.4 degrees Celsius). Its bays and inlets can warm to 70 F (16 to 21 C). It can freeze "completely" for short periods (generally a few hours).
- Is considered "ultra-oligotrophic" by limnologists (lake scientists) because it has few nutrients, sediment and other material in its water.
- Has two major natural tributaries – Nipigon River in Ontario and St. Louis River at Duluth-Superior – plus a diverted source of water from Ontario's Ogoki and Longlac rivers that together almost equals the flow of each natural tributary.
- Anchors a basin 89 percent forest-covered and rich in resources. A wealth of minerals plus iron, gold, silver, copper, zinc and even diamonds have been found. Lake Superior has its "gems" – agates, amethyst, greenstone and Thomsonite.

Every shore brings stunning scenery. Pictured Rocks National Lakeshore, known for memorable multicolored cliffs, also has cobblestone-strewn beaches. (Gregg Bruff / National Park Service)

an unexpected glimpse of bears and moose is thrilling, but use caution.

Here's a list of some of larger animals you may encounter.

• **Black bears** are rarely encountered on a hike in the woods, but be prepared should you have such a chance meeting. Most black bears are wary of humans, but a mother with cubs can be dangerous – never get between them.

Some hikers wear a bell to avoid surprising a bear (and to give it time to leave). If you come face to face with a bear, do not run or panic. Talk loudly and back away slowly, making sure to leave the bear an avenue of escape. If it woofs, slaps the ground or bluff charges, continue backing away in a calm manner.

If a bear wanders into your campsite, make lots of noise. That will usually drive it off. Bears eat nearly anything and have learned to troll campsites for carelessly left food. Keep any food at your campsite high in a tree (at least 10 feet up) and away from the trunk, well out of a bear's reach. Use the special bear-proofed trash keepers found at most campgrounds. Never keep *any* food – even a candy bar – in your tent. Parks Canada advises never cooking in or near your tent to avoid lingering food odors.

• **Wolves**, a recovery success story, are now more plentiful in northern Minnesota and Ontario, and their numbers are up in Michigan and Wisconsin, but it's still rare to see one. (They don't want to see you.) If you encounter one of these magnificent animals, consider yourself fortunate. Wolves rarely attack humans, but have been known to kill unattended dogs. Keep your pet on a leash while hiking, especially in the spring when wolf pups are born.

• **Moose** are plentiful in many parts of the region. These shy, generally gentle giants gait through boggy terrain with poor eyesight. If you come upon a moose, remain still and it may continue with whatever it was doing without fleeing. In the fall during "rut," or mating season, exercise extreme caution around the bull moose especially. Locals say moose go a bit wacky in the fall and are more likely to charge humans – and even cars.

• **Cougars** or mountain lions have been seen in the Lake Superior region, but it is an extremely rare, probably once-in-a-lifetime, event. These great cats can be dangerous, especially if you're on foot in a remote area. If you find yourself face to face with a cougar, do not run and do not "play dead." Stand your ground, make yourself look as large as possible by opening your jacket and putting your arms above your head, wide. Pick up children or keep them close.

• Other animals you might encounter include skunks, raccoons, bobcats, lynx, badgers, fishers, porcupines, fox and lots of deer, not to mention the usual campground bandits, squirrels and chipmunks.

Deer in the Headlights

While most other large critters make rare appearances, you're virtually certain to find deer, oftentimes in great numbers. Deer are most active in the morning and at dusk, but you can find them nibbling the grass along the roadside at nearly any time of the day or night. They're gentle and fun to watch, especially as they leap and bound along.

Deer-car accidents are common, especially in wooded or rural areas. To avoid hitting one, scan the ditches on both sides of the road as you drive, especially at dusk and dawn. Seeing deer before they're in your headlights makes all the difference. Ask a passenger to act as a "deer spotter." If, despite your best efforts, a deer leaps into your path, do not swerve wildly to avoid it. Law officials say most human fatalities from deer-car accidents happen when people swerve, lose control and veer into oncoming traffic or roll down an embankment.

Lake Superior

• Covers about 31,700 square miles (82,103 square kilometers) – an area equal to Massachusetts, Connecticut, Rhode Island, Vermont and New Hampshire combined.

• Stretches 382 miles (615 kilometers) east-west and 160 miles (258 kilometers) north-south.

• Reaches to 1,279 feet (390 meters) deep, averaging 489 feet (149 meters).

• Totals 2,725 miles (4,385 kilometers) of shoreline on its edges and islands.

• Is the largest and deepest of the Great Lakes and could hold all the water of the other four, plus three more Lake Eries.

• Is head of an ancient river system we call "the Great Lakes." Duluth-Superior is "Head of the Lakes" and Thunder Bay is the "Lakehead" city. From there to the Atlantic Ocean on the St. Lawrence Seaway is more than 2,300 miles (3,700 kilometers) – seven days of travel for a typical shipping vessel.

• Takes 30 minutes for sunrise (and set) to arc east to west over the lake.

• Has a drainage area of 49,300 square miles (127,686 square kilometers).

• Has a periodic seiche (SAYSH) that sloshes water from side to side, rapidly raising water levels on one side while lowering them on the other. This shift is caused by rain, wind, barometric pressure and other natural phenomena.

• Turns over its water at a rate of 199 years. (The smallest Great Lake, Lake Erie, takes only about 3 years.)

Lake Superior Birds

Our bird-rich lake area attracts birders from around the world. Much of the excitement around birding comes when you spot one of the majestic raptors that soar here. There are some great flyway hot spots for birding around the Lake Superior region. Special spots include Whitefish Point, Michigan, Hawk Ridge in Duluth and Thunder Cape in Ontario. While great varieties of birds abound, here are some of the larger ones:

• **Bald eagles,** once threatened, have come back in great numbers. It isn't uncommon to look into the sky and see this enormous bird soaring. Better yet is to witness one diving into the lake for food.

• **Ospreys,** with their black and white feathers, are also highly skilled fishermen. Look for their huge nests in the treetops in remote areas generally around inland lakes.

• **Owls** live in the area, and also migrate from the north in winter. The region has seen large "eruptions" of the haunting snowy owls when food is scarce in Canada.

• **Hawks** of several types live and hunt in the region. Look for them sitting sentinel on top of telephone poles and in solitary branches on treetops. Peregrine falcons have recently nested in the cities of Duluth, Minnesota, Thunder Bay, Ontario, and Ashland, Wisconsin.

• **Loons** and their haunting laughter are true icons of Lake Superior wilderness. These black-and-white waterfowl live on large lakes throughout the region.

Recommended Drives

The many information centers around the lake are good launching points for scenic drives.

Circling Lake Superior, while a wonderful must-do experience, is but one way to make your lake visit. Following below are sections of the Circle Tour and region, any one of which would make a magical getaway for a few days or longer. These drives simply outline stretches of the larger Circle Tour that offer manageable shorter trips and sometimes give you a little bit of history to boot. Specifics for the towns and cities traversed by these drives can be found by checking the individual listings in the main body of this guide. So pack up the family and take to the road.

Minnesota's North Shore Scenic Drive

A scenic stretch of the Lake Superior Circle Tour follows Highway 61 into Minnesota's Arrowhead, beginning at the Lester River bridge within Duluth and running along Lake Superior to Canada's border, or southwesterly from the border to Duluth. For this description, begin at the eastern end of Duluth and stop at the little blue North Shore Information center overlooking the lake for a wealth of material. The center, near Lester River bridge on London Road and also close to Kitchi-Gammi Park at Brighton Beach, is actually operated by the Two Harbors Area Chamber of Commerce.

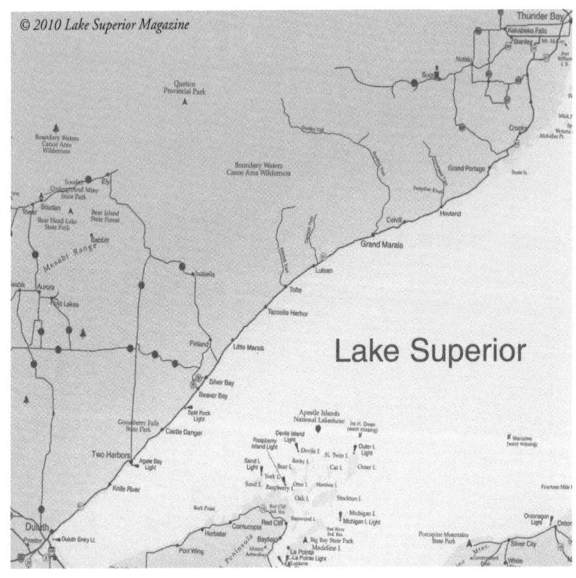

Minnesota's North Shore [Detailed Map Page 114]

west on the trail. At the top is the scenic overlook with interesting interpretive panels about the tunnel (a cool aerial photo of traffic using the old lake-side highway during tunnel construction). Or if you start from the west end of the trail, you'll be able to see a replica of the Silver Creek Cliff gateway that welcomed travelers in the early 1900s.

In the Lutsen-Tofte area, several former hiking trails have changed to accommodate multiple use by bikers and snowmobilers.

Of particular interest to bikers, hikers and inline skaters is the Gitchi-Gami State Trail, a non-motorized, 10-foot-wide paved route that eventually will extend 86 miles from Two Harbors to Grand Marais. Portions of the trail, a joint effort of the Minnesota Department of Transportation and the Department of Natural Resources with the Lake Superior Touring Trail Association, are completed, including a 13-mile segment from Gooseberry Falls State Park to Beaver River in Beaver Bay. Another segment connects Gooseberry Falls and Split Rock Lighthouse State Park. The former road bed for Highway 61 around Silver Creek Cliff was reconstructed to create a great trail around the new tunnel, on the lake side, providing hikers and bikers an outstanding panoramic lake view. Parking is available at Silver Creek Wayside Rest on the east side of Silver Creek Cliff Tunnel, allowing you to walk

Visitors in the winter months will be interested in the more than 900 miles of snowmobile trails and the equally impressive cross-country ski trail system along Minnesota's North Shore.

Kitchi-Gammi Park at Brighton Beach is a popular swimming and picnicking area with access just past the information stand at Lester River. Good skipping stones can be found along the beach.

The Minnesota shoreline of Lake Superior is targeted for a series of nonimpact camping and rest sites for canoeists and kayakers known as the Lake Superior Water Trail. A nonprofit volunteer organization hopes to eventually have sites in place all along the shore from Duluth to the Canadian border. More information is available from the Lake Superior Water Trail Association of Minnesota at Grand Marais.

Skyline Parkway in Duluth, the Superior National Forest Scenic Byway from Silver Bay to the Iron Range and the Gunflint Trail out of Grand Marais are all designated as State Scenic Byways. The entire North Shore route from Canal Park's Aerial Lift Bridge to the International Bridge at the Pigeon River is designated as an All-American Road by the U.S. Department of Transportation, one of only 27 such designated routes in the country.

For the first 20 miles (32 kilometers), the highway route splits into two roads. Minnesota 61 becomes a four-lane divided expressway one-quarter mile or more away from the view of the lake, although at intervals it has spurs down to the lakeshore. The expressway has no accommodations and the scenery is less enticing than the North Shore Scenic Drive closer to the lake.

Parallel to and above the scenic route and the expressway is the C.J. Ramstad Memorial North Shore State Trail, a multiuse recreation trail that runs from Duluth to Grand Marais. Primarily a snowmobile trail, it also offers opportunities for hiking in summer and cross-country skiing and dog sledding in winter. No motorized vehicles are permitted on the trail in summer.

County 61 runs right next to the lake, within yards of the shoreline, and is the preferred scenic route, having been designated the North Shore Scenic Drive. A marked bicycle route accompanies the entire Scenic Drive. Traveler pullouts are located conveniently close to Lake Superior. The Duluth Water Plant offers free cold and filtered water at the roadside pulloff adjacent to the plant. Access to the shore makes for a restful stop.

The North Shore Scenic Drive route has restaurants, lodging, great shops and many locations to stop and dip your feet in the cool water. It also passes over numerous streams that empty into the lake, most of which offer excellent fishing at all times of the year. The most popular are the Lester, French and Sucker rivers. Air conditioning, courtesy of the lake, is cheap, automatic and mechanically trouble-free. Ideal photographs can be made from almost any location.

Accommodations on Minnesota's scenic North Shore tend to fill up early in the day during summer and fall, so advance reservations are always recommended.

Businesses and residents on the route have planted thousands of flowering plants along the roadway as a showy welcome. Berry pickers are a common sight seeking wild strawberries, chokecherries and gooseberries in June, followed by raspberries in July and then the esteemed blueberries, which ripen in late July inland and early August along the shore.

The North Shore Scenic Railroad travels parallel to the North Shore Scenic Drive between Duluth and Two Harbors with shorter rides between The Depot in downtown Duluth and the Lester River area of the city.

Extensive stands of aspen from Lester River to Knife River are an indication that this area was once devastated by fire. This occurred in a series of forest fires in 1918. Aspen (poplar) and birch are referred to as "disturbance community" by foresters. Both trees begin new growth quickly after an area has been logged or burned.

Near Lakeview Castle is the McQuade Small Craft Harbor off North Shore Scenic Drive at McQuade Road. Powerboats, sailboats, canoes and kayaks can find protection from storms. Amenities include docks, fishing piers, breakwaters, walkway, restrooms and ample parking.

At the mouth of the beautiful French River just past Lakeview Castle, the Minnesota Department of Natural

Resources operates a modern cold water hatchery, the French River Fish Hatchery. Numerous species of fish such as sucker, walleye, steelhead and other strains of rainbow trout are incubated at the hatchery, using the cool, clear water available in this location to help ensure that the fishery continues to be healthy. Visitors are welcome for self-guided tours weekdays.

Along this route, two upscale dining options in relaxed contemporary settings with nice lake views are the New Scenic Café and Nokomis Restaurant and Bar.

Make time for gift shop browsing, since each store along the Scenic Drive has a unique personality. Tom's Logging Camp and Trading Post is a gift shop surrounded by a re-creation of an 1800s

North West Fur Company camp. Look for traditional gifts, clothing and footwear. There is a fee to enter the camp where there are tame deer and a trout pond.

A half-mile from Tom's is Stoney Point, site of several shipwrecks in the late 1800s and early 1900s. This jut of land is a dandy spot to watch large ships on their way to port.

The drive between Duluth and Two Harbors offers lodging opportunities, most with views of Lake Superior. Several new bed-and-breakfast inns and cabins have been added in recent years. And a couple of nice campgrounds offer additional overnight options.

Five miles (8 kilometers) northeast of the French River, a historic plaque commemorates the settlement of Buchanan, named after President James Buchanan (1857-61). Platted in 1856, the townsite was the home of the North Shore's first post office. The following year the first of the region's newspapers, the *North Shore Advocate*, was published here. Copper mining was the promise, but it never materialized, and the town was eventually abandoned and destroyed by fire.

At numerous locations along the North Shore route from Knife River to the Canadian border there is entry to the Superior Hiking Trail, planned eventually also to connect to Duluth, where the trail extends 39 miles. Earning high praise from hikers and hiking organizations, additional sections of the trail are being completed by volunteers, allowing free and easy access from many places of lodging along the way. More than 240 miles (386 kilometers) of trail are well-signed and maintained by volunteers to provide hikers with challenges at whatever level they desire. In fact, the Superior Hiking Trail has become a part of a lodge-to-lodge hiking system on the shore. Superior Shuttle service is available on Fridays, Saturdays and Sundays at many of the participating lodges, as well as numerous pickup and drop-off points along the trail from May to late October. Watch for the signs. Superior Hiking Trail Association has information at its office and store on Seventh Avenue in Two Harbors.

For information on specific areas of Minnesota's North Shore, turn to the listing for the various towns, but don't allow the border between the United States and Canada to stop you from continuing on the Circle Tour.

Canada has a range of rugged terrain presenting majestic views of Lake Superior, sandy beach access and excellent fishing experiences. Just across the border and the customs gate, you can obtain more current information about your trip into Canada at the Visitor Information Centre. Official maps and detailed brochures of locations in this region of Ontario are available at the center, which is open from mid-May through Labour Day.

Despite what you may have heard, crossing the border is not a big deal so long as you have the right documents. See the information in this section on crossing the border.

Ontario runs on the metric system, so road signs, speed and measurements might be a little strange if you're from the United States: kilometers per hour, litres instead of gallons. Also, radar warning devices are forbidden in Ontario, even if turned off and only transported in your vehicle. Police may confiscate such devices. The Lake

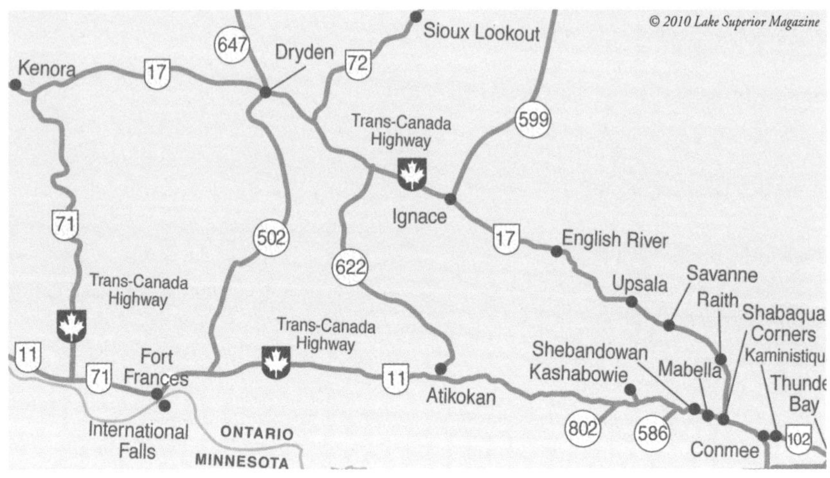

Sunset Country, Ontario

Superior area of Ontario is in the Eastern Time Zone.

Western Mesabi Iron Range, Minnesota

The Western Mesabi lies along Highway 169 between Hibbing and Grand Rapids, passing by or through the smaller mining towns of Keewatin, Nashwauk, Marble, Calumet, Bovey and Coleraine. Calumet is the unofficial gateway to the western Mesabi Range and home to the last intact iron ore pit mine in Minnesota that can be toured. Listed on the National Register of Historic Places, the Hill Annex Mine is a good history stop. (See the Calumet, Minnesota, listing.)

West of Calumet, winter skiers will want to visit Mont Itasca at Coleraine, which is designated as a U.S. biathlon training center and also offers ski jumping, snowboarding, downhill and cross-country trails. Coleraine was built as a model town for Oliver Iron Mining Company employees working in the mines and mining plants near the cities of Bovey and Coleraine.

The westernmost city on the Mesabi Iron Range is Grand Rapids, where timber and tourism have traditionally played a much more significant role than mining in the economy of the area. See details in the separate listing for Grand Rapids, Minnesota.

Sunset Country, Ontario

The Lake Superior Circle Tour follows Highway 61 northerly from the International Border at Pigeon River through Thunder Bay to Nipigon, but travelers with an extra day or two and a spirit of exploration may want to consider a round-trip side jaunt from Thunder Bay west to the twin border cities of Fort Frances, Ontario, and International Falls, Minnesota. Along the way, the landscape is dotted with fish-filled lakes and covered with thick boreal forest. This area is designated as Sunset Country for promotional purposes.

A short jaunt from Kakabeka Falls on

Highway 11/17 heading west from Thunder Bay brings you to Shebandowan, where the highway divides to become two routes into the far western haunts of Ontario. Highway 11 takes a southerly route and Highway 17 wends its way to the north.

The largest cities on the two routes are Fort Frances (population 8,000) on Rainy Lake and Kenora (population 16,500) on Lake of the Woods. This trip, we'll focus on the Highway 11 route.

LaVerendrye River Provincial Park occupies a large area to the south of the highway and is a complete wilderness area accessed from the Thunder Bay area by taking Highway 588 through Nolalu. Located between Lake Superior and the eastern boundary of Quetico Wilderness Provincial Park, the park is bounded on the south in the United States by the Boundary Waters Canoe Area Wilderness (BWCAW). LaVerendrye Park is undeveloped and, with no staff or campgrounds, open primarily for those hardy campers who desire a true wilderness experience. Crown land camping permits are required.

Quetico Wilderness Provincial Park is a wilderness area of lakes, streams and woods that has changed little since the voyageurs paddled the waters three centuries ago.

The park covers 475,782 hectares, including more than 1,400 kilometers (870 miles) of canoe routes. The park is adjacent to the U.S. Boundary Waters Canoe Area Wilderness and many visitors enjoy both parks in one trip. Due to the popularity of backcountry travel, reservations to paddle the interior are advisable well in advance. Use of Quetico's interior is by permit based on a quota per entry point. The park regulates what can be taken into Quetico (bottles and cans are banned) and how to handle disposable waste. Visitors entering the park via water from the U.S. side must obtain a Remote Border Crossing Permit from Immigration Canada and register with the park.

Quetico offers canoeing, hiking, picnic areas, campgrounds, beaches and summer interpretive programs at its Dawson Trail Campground (accessed from Highway 11). In winter, hardy skiers and snowshoers share Quetico with the wolves and moose. The park contains the largest concentration of pictographs between Lake Superior and Manitoba, with 30 known sites.

The campground features two yurts to rent year-round. They are tentlike dwellings on wooden platforms. Each offers bunk beds to sleep six, table and chairs, heating and outdoor barbecue. Dawson Trail Campground is 148 kilometers (92 miles) west of Thunder Bay or 48 kilometers (30 miles) east of Atikokan. The campground offers tent and trailer camping from mid-May to mid-October.

Atikokan (population 3,400), just north of the park on Highway 11, has complete services for park visitors. Numerous outfitters and stores stock everything that canoeists, backpackers, anglers and campers need.

For those who prefer conveniences, there are hotels and restaurants. The town is a jumping off point to deeper wilderness – it's the Canadian equivalent of Ely, Minnesota.

At the western terminus of our side trek is Fort Frances. Just across the Rainy River, International Falls, Minnesota, (population 5,906) joins its Canadian twin in producing a huge volume of paper products. This is also prime fishing and water recreation country, with the Rainy River and Rainy Lake serving as a boundary between the United States and Canada and Lake Kabetogama in the back yard.

To return to our Lake Superior Circle Tour, either retrace your track coming in, or, about 32 kilometers (20 miles) northeast of Fort Frances, take Highway 502 northward to visit Dryden and Ignace, then back to Thunder Bay by way of Highway 17. There are several other worthwhile stops and points of interest along the way. Highway 11/17 brings you into the western part of Thunder Bay.

Ontario's Shore

Near Pearl on Trans Canada Highway 11/17 between Thunder Bay and Nipigon, keep a sharp eye out for signs pointing the way to amethyst mines. Amethyst is Ontario's official gemstone, as well as the February birthstone. The semiprecious gem can be found at the Blue Points Amethyst Mine, Ontario Gem Amethyst Mine, which has a gift shop, and the Amethyst Mine Panorama, the largest amethyst mine on the continent.

A visit to Ouimet Canyon Provincial Park is well worth the visit. The park features walls that stand 150 meters (492 feet) apart and 100 meters (328 feet) high and face each other for 3 kilometers (1.8 miles). Ouimet is a day-use only park, with hiking trails along the canyon rim. A barrier-free boardwalk to viewing platforms makes this area more accessible for visitors. Two spectacular viewing pods overlook the canyon's edge and feature interpretive signs. On the canyon floor, plants native to the arctic tundra grow where the lower temperature and shadows are untenable for indigenous regional plants. Thus, access to the canyon floor is not allowed, so that the fragile plants are protected.

The parking area is 11 kilometers (7 miles) off Highway 11/17. Open mid-May to mid-October. A donation made to the Friends of Ouimet Canyon Provincial Park by day-use visitors provides funds to assist this volunteer group with operations and maintenance.

We're reaching the top of the lake as we travel toward Red Rock and Nipigon. Don't blink or you'll pass the Dorion Loop taking you to the village of Dorion, home of Ontario's largest fish hatchery and Canada's largest wildlife mural on the walls of the Canyon Country Store. There's a Fall Fair and Festival.

Hurkett Cove Conservation Area lies just 3 kilometers (2 miles) east of the Wolf River and south of the highway and is home to a variety of songbirds, waterfowl and other wildlife.

The community of Hurkett is situated on Black Bay. Take the Hurkett Loop from Highway 11/17. If you're not in a hurry, this little side trip should yield some interesting photo opportunities.

You're now in what is called North of Superior and the most northerly point on Lake Superior.

To the east is Algoma Country and the twin cities of Sault Ste. Marie, Ontario and Michigan. This entire stretch of the Circle Tour is the northern part of the Great Lakes Heritage Coast under an Ontario Ministry of Natural Resources initiative.

En route, you'll have the opportunity to see lots of wildlife, papermaking and gold mining and also visit numerous provincial parks, many with campgrounds, and a national park.

This portion of Lake Superior is home to some of the most dramatic coastlines and waterscapes, yet you'll seldom be more than a few kilometers from good food, lodging, stores and gift shops, fuel or anything else you need.

Lake Nipigon, Frontier Trail, Ontario

From Nipigon, Trans Canada Highway 11 heads northeastward and is called the Frontier Trail-Circuit du Nord Tourist Route.

This side trip takes a lazy arc up the Clay Belt and across the northern spruce bush, opening the north to thousands of anglers, hunters and other outdoor enthusiasts. This is a vast watershed area for Lake Superior, with Lake Nipigon, the Nipigon River and the Longlac Water Diversion project providing the greatest source of flow into the big lake.

Take the 50-kilometer (31-mile) drive from Nipigon up to Orient Bay on Lake Nipigon, where the rocks of the Canadian Shield are called the Pititawabik Palisades.

Many of the Lake Nipigon beaches consist of black sand that has been eroded from Lake Nipigon's basaltic cliffs and gathered by wave action on the shorelines.

The southeast corner of Lake Nipigon/Orient Bay has many waterfalls that freeze in the winter and attract hearty visitors interested in climbing the icy precipices. An annual Ice Fest in March celebrates the phenomena.

Southern Upper Peninsula, Michigan

From Sault Ste. Marie, you can continue directly on the Lake Superior Circle Tour route, but you might want to consider a slight detour, if you have time. An interesting side trip from the Sault area is toward St. Ignace and the Mackinac Bridge (MACK-i-naw).

You can drive directly south for about 45 minutes on Interstate 75 from Sault Ste. Marie to St. Ignace and the bridge, which connects the Upper and Lower peninsulas of Michigan. A nice alternate route east from the Soo on M-129 opens the eastern U.P. for exploration.

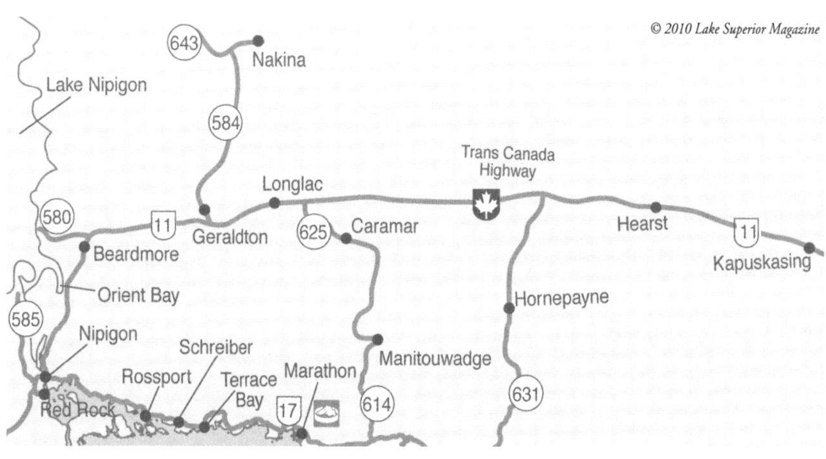

Lake Nipigon Frontier Trail, Ontario

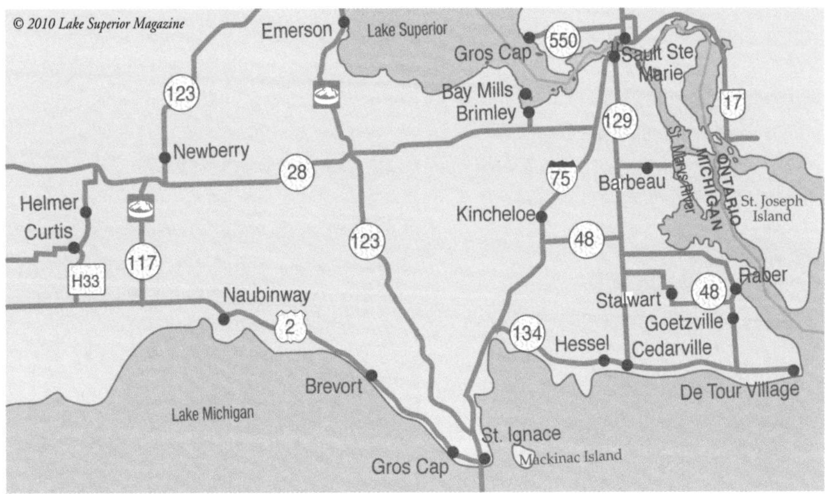

Southern Upper Peninsula, Michigan

While the southern U.P. trip can go either west to east or vice versa, we will describe the trip from east to west here, with some towns also being referenced in their own listing in the Michigan section.

From the Sault area, Michigan 129 gives access to Sugar, Neebish and Drummond islands on the U.S. side of the St. Marys River waterway. A fourth island in the chain, St. Joseph, lies on the Canadian side of the border.

Sugar Island is accessible from Sault Ste. Marie. To reach Neebish Island, stop at Barbeau, where a car ferry takes the visitor across the channel. The island sits between Lake Nicolet and Munuscong Lake; both offer recreational opportunities. At Barbeau, Cozy Corners restaurant offers good food for hungry travelers.

Before reaching the last island, you'll pass the Raber Bay area, which includes the small towns of Stalwart, Goetzville and Raber. This is an area of fine lodging and restaurants and our route is now along a portion of the Lake Huron Circle Tour.

The third island is Drummond Island, the largest of the group, which is accessed by ferry from De Tour Village on Highway 134 at the very eastern tip of the U.P.

From De Tour, M-134 takes you to Cedarville and Hessel in the Les Cheneaux Islands area. There are 36 islands in the group, with marinas, beaches and waterfront walks to delight the visitor. Visit the Les Cheneaux Historical Museum for insight into the lake-oriented culture of the region. On the second Saturday in August, attend the Antique Boat Show, Art Festival and Regatta in Hessel. Cedarville's annual Les Cheneaux Snowfest in February is also famed for its festive nature. Golfers will want to try out Hessel Ridge Golf Course. From here, we head for a junction with I-75 to visit St. Ignace, Mackinac Island (see separate listing) and the Mackinac Bridge, described in the St. Ignace section. Take U.S. Highway 2 west from St. Ignace toward Gros Cap. The Gros Cap Church was built in 1918. Brevort has several campgrounds and offers access to Lake Michigan's dunes. Lake Michigan's shorelines are nearly all sandy, with dunes as a common feature.

You'll pass communities steeped in the traditions of fishing. Naubinway is known as the "Land of Echoes" and has a marina, complete with charter fishing. The Fishermen's Memorial honors local fishermen who lost their lives on Lake Michigan. Naubinway is also home to Garlyn Zoological Park right on Highway 2, featuring the U.P.'s largest variety of live animals, all in a natural setting. Open daily April through October, and weekends in November and March.

If you want to return to the Lake Superior Circle Tour, a number of routes turn north off Highway 2 and allow you to rejoin the Lake Superior route wherever you choose. In this particular area, Highway 117 is a straight shot to Highway 28 just west of Newberry.

For a more scenic route, County Road H-33 at the junction in Gould City heads north to Curtis and the Manistique Lakes area for excellent recreation.

A bit farther north on H33, Helmer is home to the Helmer House Inn, a historic bed-and-breakfast inn and restaurant that you'll want to put on your agenda. After renovation in 1982, it is a favorite destination for those who want to escape the cares of the world. The restaurant specializes in fresh-caught whitefish. One of Lake Superior's best places to eat and stay. Open May through October.

U.S. Highway 2 travels nearly straight west from Naubinway past Gould City and Blaney Park, before bearing southwest toward Gulliver. The sights at Gulliver are described in the town's listing.

Traveling Highway 2 west from Gulliver, the shoreline city of Manistique offers a good selection of lodging facilities, including several state or private campgrounds, and dining for whatever your taste may be. (See separate listing.)

At Garden Corners on Highway 2 in Michigan's southern U.P., catch vistas of Big Bay de Noc as you pass the small towns of Isabella, Nahma Junction and Ensign to Rapid River at the north end of Little Bay de Noc. Follow Highway 2/41 along the shoreline southwesterly to Gladstone (population 5,067) and Escanaba (population 12,214). See the Escanaba listing for more detail on this area.

On Highway 2/41 through the southern U.P. west of Escanaba/Gladstone, you pass through several small towns, but will want to watch for signs to Island Resort and Casino about 13 miles (21 kilometers) west of Escanaba at Harris, with 113 rooms, RV park, restaurants and gaming. It's operated by the Hannahville Tribe on the Potawatomi Reservation.

On Highway 2/41 about midway between Escanaba and Iron Mountain, watch for Hermansville to visit the IXL Historic Museum, housed in the 1882 headquarters of the Wisconsin Land and Lumber Company. Open Memorial Day through Labor Day, with group tour arrangements during the off-season. See the separate listing under Hermansville.

You are far from both Lake Superior and Lake Michigan at this point, heading for the western U.P. where iron ore mines once fostered an abundant economy. Although the mines are long depleted, many of the smallish communities you pass were mining locations where the families of employees lived, worked and did most of their day-to-day business.

Plan to stop at Vulcan for an underground tour by train of the Iron Mountain Iron Mine, where you'll travel 2,600 feet (792 meters) through the drifts and stopes (tunnels and roomlike areas) of the mine.

Nearby in Norway (population 2,821), Jake Menghini Historical Museum is in a historic log cabin that once a carriage stopping place. The museum is open free of charge Memorial Day through the Saturday prior to Columbus Day in October, although donations accepted.

Waterfall aficionados can check out Piers Gorge in Norway, where white water tumbles over 10-foot falls and roars wildly through canyon walls. A bit farther on Highway 2, a roadside at Quinnesec Park has tables, water and toilets as well as a nice view of Fumee Falls.

Iron Mountain snuggles into a large bend of the Menominee River that forms the boundary between Michigan and Wisconsin. Like a mother hen with chicks, a number of smaller towns in both Wisconsin and Michigan surround Iron Mountain. See Iron Mountain listing for more details.

Highway 2/141 jogs into Wisconsin for a brief sojourn just west of Iron Mountain and passes through two small towns, the interestingly named Spread Eagle and Florence, before re-entering Michigan in Iron County.

A 15-minute drive brings you to Crystal Falls, the Iron County seat and a crossroads community where you can catch Highway 141 north to rejoin the Lake Superior Circle Tour. See the listing under Crystal Falls for details.

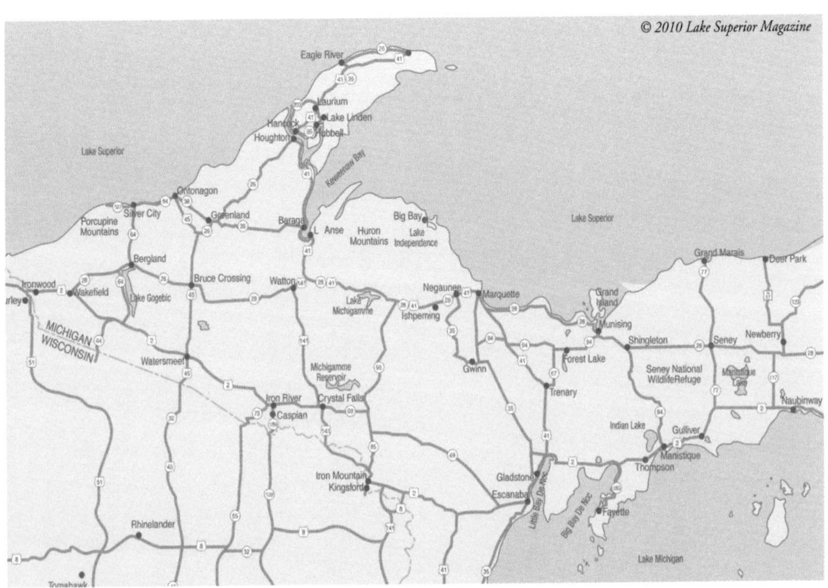

Upper Peninsula of Michigan & Northeast Wisconsin

Another hen-and-chick community, with the former mining locations of Gaastra, Caspian, Stambaugh and Mineral Hills nearby, Iron River offers travelers a number of lodging, shopping and dining options.

In nearby Caspian, the Iron County Historical Museum features 20 pioneer buildings reflecting logging, mining, transportation and other aspects of settling the area. See Iron River, Michigan, listing for details.

Wisconsin Indianhead Region

As you again head westward, traveling through the Ottawa National Forest, a huge area of the western U.P. set aside for multiple use. The Ottawa Visitor Center in Watersmeet can provide full information on recreational facilities within this wonderfully scenic area. See the Watersmeet listing for detail.

The route westward along Highway 2 is now well into Big Snow Country, heading for Wakefield, Bessemer and Ironwood.

Indianhead Region, Wisconsin

From U.S. Highway 2 at Brule we recommend an interesting side trip south via Highway 27. If you have time, turn east on County N to visit Barnes and Drummond, which has an interesting museum of local history.

Continuing south on Highway 27 leads to Hayward, the home of the National Fresh Water Fishing Hall of Fame, documenting the exploits of noteworthy anglers and their prize-winning catches. This is also home to the World Lumberjack Championships. Just east of town, the Lac Courte Oreilles Band of Ojibwe operates Lac Courte Oreilles Casino, Lodge and Convention Center, offering many amenities and gaming fun.

From Hayward, catch Highway 77 westward through areas dotted by inland lakes and interesting towns to reconnect to the Circle Tour via Highway 35. Just to the south of the junction with Highway 35, Forts Folle Avoine Historical Park between Webster and Danbury is a worthwhile stop, recreating an early fur trading post. Area lodging information is available from Burnett County Resort and Campground Association. Also in the area is Hole in the Wall Casino for gaming fun, a hotel and pool. There are several good good restaurants in Danbury.

A Suggested Itinerary

Allow some flexibility in your schedule for interludes like a scenic walk around Silver Creek Tunnel on Minnesota's North Shore. At the top is a lookout with a cool interpretive panel.

What if you only have five, seven or 10 days to do the Circle Tour?

The answer varies as much as a traveler's desires. Are you a shopper or a hiker? A boat nerd or a music lover?

That said, here you will find a suggested itinerary – basically mile by mile – for travel around Lake Superior. We consider these "must see" places or experiences. If you don't have many days, we strongly urge you to plan a "semi-Circle Tour" and return again.

Here are basics to consider with any Circle Tour:

• The full circle by land is about 1,300 miles; you need to divide that number by the number of days you are driving to get a sense of where to end up at the end of each day.

• There is a big difference between *driving* the circle and *seeing* the region. Do schedule time to stroll beside the lake.

• Finally, it's good to see how others enjoyed their Circle Tour. Read their advice at **www.lakesuperior.com** and click on the Circle Tour logo.

Minnesota

- Duluth
  Aerial Lift Bridge
  Lake Superior Maritime Visitor Center
  Canal Park shopping, eating
  Downtown shopping, eating
  Great Lakes Aquarium
  Skyline Parkway
  William A. Irvin museum boat
  Enger Tower
  Rose Garden (in season)
  Lakewalk
  Glensheen Historic Congdon Estate
  Harbor boat tour
- Scenic North Shore Drive
- Two Harbors
  Lighthouse/*Edna G.*
- Gooseberry Falls State Park
- Split Rock Lighthouse
- Eat pie somewhere between Duluth and Thunder Bay
- North Shore Commercial Fishing Museum (Tofte)
- Grand Marais shopping, eating
- Grand Portage National Monument

Ontario

- Ontario Parks
  Here are a few of our favorites:
  Sleeping Giant
  Ouimet Canyon
  Neys Provincial Park
  Pukaskwa National Park
  Lake Superior Provincial Park
- Thunder Oak Cheese Farm
- Founders Museum & Pioneer Village
- Thunder Bay
  Hoito Restaurant
  Fort William Historical Park
  Waterfront
  Downtown shopping
- Kakabeka Falls
- Terry Fox Monument
- Amethyst mines
- Nipigon murals, beach
- Rossport
- Schreiber
  Canadian Pacific Depot
- Terrace Bay
  Aguasabon Falls & Gorge
- Marathon shopping, beaches
- White River
  Winnie-the-Pooh statue
- Wawa
  The Goose
  Young's General Store
- Lake Superior Provincial Park
  New visitor center
- Sault Ste. Marie
  Canadian Bushplane Heritage Centre
  Canadian Lock
  St. Marys River Boardwalk
  Algoma Central Railway trip
- International Bridge

Michigan

- Sault Ste. Marie
  Soo Locks & lock boat tour
  Tower of History
  Downtown shopping
  Valley Camp museum boat
- Point Iroquois Light Station
- Paradise shopping, eating
- Whitefish Point
  Great Lakes Shipwreck Museum
  Whitefish Point Bird Observatory
- Tahquamenon Falls
- Newberry shopping, eating
- Pictured Rocks National Lakeshore
- Munising
- Pictured Rocks boat tours
- Marquette
  Presque Isle Park
  Downtown shopping, eating
- Hancock/Houghton
  Quincy Mine
  Isle Royale National Park headquarters
  Shopping, eating
- Calumet
  Keweenaw National Historical Park
  Calumet Theatre
- Copper Harbor
  Copper Harbor Lighthouse
  Fort Wilkins State Park
  Shopping, eating
- Brockway Mountain
- Ontonagon
- Porcupine Mountains Wilderness State Park & Lake of the Clouds

Wisconsin

- Ashland
  Murals
  Northern Great Lakes Visitor Center
- Washburn
- Bayfield
- Apostle Islands boat tours
- Madeline Island
- Highway 13
- Superior
  Fairlawn Mansion
  Barker's Island
  Wisconsin Point

Lake Superior Experiences Top 50

In Bayfield, Wisconsin, sailboats help define the popular town, much like the local apples do.

We find every moment by the Big Lake is a great experience, but for these pages, we narrow to a manageable 50 our picks for Lake Superior experiences of a lifetime.

1 Do the Circle Tour – Clockwise or counterclockwise? Car, bicycle, motorcycle or shoes? Who cares! Just circle the entire lake at least once in your life.

2 Sail, cruise or paddle – In a kayak, a powerboat or under a sail, the lake is different from on the water. Don't have a boat? Try options like Vista Fleet in Minnesota; Pictured Rocks Cruises and Shipwreck Tours in Michigan; Soo Locks Tours in Sault Ste. Marie, Michigan; or the Madeline Island Ferry Line and Apostle Islands Cruise Service in Wisconsin.

3 Take a trip to an island – Pick an island, any island. Try an Apostle in Wisconsin for a short ferry ride or Isle Royale in Michigan for a long excursion. Or head to Ontario to a wilder island.

4 Attend a festival – How can you say you've truly "done" the region without at least one "fest" on your itinerary? Celebrate blueberries and apples or hail winter, St. Urho, fish boils, blues music, theater and the Fourth of July.

5 Swim or dip your toes in the water – There's nothing quite like a swim in the biggest freshwater lake in the world. It's not that cold, Really.

6 Watch a storm – Marvel at the awesome power of wind and the waves. A waterfront resort, cabin or hotel gives comfortable views for gales.

7 See the northern lights – If you don't believe in magic, the spectral aurora borealis on a crisp evening will change your mind.

8 Visit in all four (some say seven) seasons – Cross-country ski in winter, hike in spring, paddle in summer, take a leaf tour in fall or hang out as each season unveils its qualities. It is, after all, a lake for all seasons.

9 Tour a lighthouse –Lighthouses once served mainly as aids to navigation (and still do), but now they are time machines into the lake's history. Some are historic sites, some are bed-and-breakfast inns, all are marvelous reminders of the past.

10 Listen to a lighthouse – Is it the sound of the signal, the fog itself or the combination that creates the unsettling effect both comforting and chilling when the fog signals sound at the lighthouses?

11 Watch a ship come in – Check out the mighty freight-carrying lakers or oceangoing salties in Thunder Bay, Ontario; the Sault Ste. Maries; Marquette, Michigan; and Duluth, Two Harbors and Silver Bay, Minnesota, and at various other points around the lake.

12 Watch a sunrise or a sunset over the lake – Oranges and reds on the water are an awesome sight.

13 Or watch a full moon rise – An enormous orange moon suspended over the calm lake creating a trail of light. There's a memory.

14 Savor regional specialties – Lake trout, wild rice, cranberries ... pasties. Heck, you may want to try a lutefisk church dinner … maybe.

15 Stroll along a waterfront – Small and large towns created paths along the water. Sault Ste. Marie, Ontario's riverwalk features funky statuary while Duluth's lakewalk has hiking, biking and skating.

16 Seek out wildlife – Bear, fox, moose, deer, caribou or birds (especially geese and gulls) abound. Many trails offer wildlife watching. Bird migrations can be witnessed at Hawk Ridge in Duluth, Whitefish Point in Michigan or near Thunder Bay.

17 Seek out a really BIG critter – like the goose at Wawa or the Winnie-the-Pooh at White River, both in Ontario. Or how about that huge muskie hanging out at the National Fresh Water Fishing Hall of Fame in Hayward, Wisconsin.

18 Sit on a beach at night and listen to the waves – Whooosh, whooosh, whooosh.

19 Beachcomb – Pick rocks (agates are in there somewhere); find treasures flung up by the lake or left by beach visitors; feel the sand between your toes; roam freely.

20 Skip rocks on the lake – If you've never found a flat skipping rock, hefted it for the right balance and then launched it across the water for one, two, three, maybe four or more skips, well, then you just haven't.

21 Hike, bike, inline skate, cross-country ski or snowmobile on any trail – Hundreds of miles of rustic or paved trails exist around the lake. Make friends with them; take friends on them.

22 Rent a lakeside cabin – Just for a week or a weekend, pretend it's yours and get to know the lake like a local (except for not having to go to work).

23 Camp lakeside or north woods – It's an intimate way to get up close and personal with the lake … and maybe a moose.

24 Stay for a week in one spot – Sample the variety of accommodations – big lodge, family-run resort, small motel or fancy hotel. Plan time to explore, to get to know the staff and feel the real flavor of the area.

25 Visit a waterfall – So many waterfalls, so little time. Almost every direction has a waterfall in there somewhere.

26 Watch a dog sled, dragon boat, snowmobile, snowshoe or running race. Or better, volunteer to help – Check out race dates at www.lakesuperior.com. There's something about watching folks go, go, go that reflects life on our lake.

27 Bring your dog to the lake – Don't be selfish with your lake time; bring the pup to the world's largest water dish.

28 Visit the Great Lakes Aquarium – Have an environmental Circle Tour of Lake Superior in a couple of hours. It's the biggest freshwater aquarium in the world.

29 Tour the locks at Sault Ste. Marie, Ontario & Michigan – You simply have to see what opened Lake Superior to the world in 1855. You can practically touch a boat as it goes by.

30 Take a walk in the fog – Definitely a lake experience. Pick the right, safe path (not a road). If it's too thick to walk, sitting by the lapping lake will suffice.

31 Travel a side road – Get off the well-beaten paths. In parts of Ontario, the only way to reach the lake is on a side road.

32 Slow down to lake time – If you plan to visit for one day, take two. Don't rush in the car; don't rush in general. If you're counting, you'll notice fewer stoplights and traffic jams than you might be used to.

33 Stop at a visitor center – Get directions, pick up brochures, talk to folks about what to do and see. You can relive the lake experience with those brochures later.

34 Picnic on the lakeshore – Pack your own or pick up something (like smoked fish) en route. Food tastes better garnished with lake breezes and splashing waves.

35 Experience winter in Big Snow Country – Just once, learn what it really means to be snowed in.

36 Charter a fishing boat – Find an experienced guide and get out there to fish or cruise. Visitor information centers can direct you to the local charters.

37 Ride a scenic train – Several lake spots connect to the rails. Try at Sault Ste. Marie and White River, Ontario, and Spooner, Wisconsin. Duluth, Minnesota, hosts two scenic trains.

38 Simply find a view to enjoy and enjoy it – 'Nuff said.

39 Visit a national, state or provincial park – With more than 50 parks, public forests or wildlife refuges, there is one around every Lake Superior corner.

40 Do the tour with someone special – It's one thing to have great experiences; it's a better thing to share them with someone.

41 Create memories for your children – Lake and northwoods holidays should mean no stuffy can't-touch-can't-talk-just-can't-only-for-grown-ups activities.

42 Breathe it all in – The sense of smell is the best memory trigger. Go to places where you'll remember campfire smoke, fresh lake air or moist deep-woods vegetation.

43 Shop a local specialty store – Need a mini moose for the mantel, a jar of lingonberries to take home, a regional book or local art? Check out the shops that feature local foods, artists and trinkets.

44 Get to know some locals – We're very friendly. Feel free to say "Hi" and chat at a walkway or in a local eating establishment. Conversing with clerks is cool. Knowing us helps you know the lake region.

45 Visit a historic re-enactment or a local museum – Try Fort William Historical Park in Thunder Bay and Fort Wilkins in Copper Harbor, Michigan, or visit a small museum like the one on Madeline Island, Wisconsin.

46 Tour a lakeside mansion – We've got some great past lifestyles of the rich and famous. Check out Glensheen The Historic Congdon Estate in Duluth, Minnesota; Fairlawn Mansion & Museum in Superior, Wisconsin; or bed-and-breakfast inns like Laurium Manor Inn in Laurium, Michigan, or Rittenhouse Inn in Bayfield, Wisconsin.

47 Cross the border – Going north or going south, it's a lake experience to see both countries and realize the differences and the similarities.

48 Sample a marine museum – Several reveal our maritime heritage. Try Great Lakes Shipwreck Museum at Whitefish Point, Marquette Maritime Museum in Michigan or the Lake Superior Maritime Visitor Center in Duluth.

49 Do something nostalgic – Sure, you can do these anywhere, but by the lake is better. Eat at a diner or family restaurant. Go to a northwoods resort where the kids can learn to paddle a canoe. Get a fishing license and drop a line into the water. Your childhood memories will steer you.

50 What's on your list – Consider this one for the road … fill it in with your own lifetime experience on Lake Superior.

Lake Superior **Michigan**

The lookout at Lake of the Clouds is one of many outstanding features at Porcupine Mountains Wilderness State Park, near Silver City.

Michigan is known for Pictured Rocks National Lakeshore and sandstone cliffs of stunning color, waterfalls and beaches. Yet from Ironwood to Copper Harbor, Brockway Mountain to Marquette and Sault Ste. Marie, the Upper Peninsula is a traveler's delight. It has big state parks – Porcupine Mountains Wilderness State Park and Tahquamenon Falls State Park – to lure hikers, cross-country skiers and snowmobilers. Or how about a visit to the splendid Great Lakes Shipwreck Museum at Whitefish Point? Or a trip to Isle Royale National Park on the largest ship operated by the National Park Service?

Travel Michigan
888-784-7328
www.michigan.org

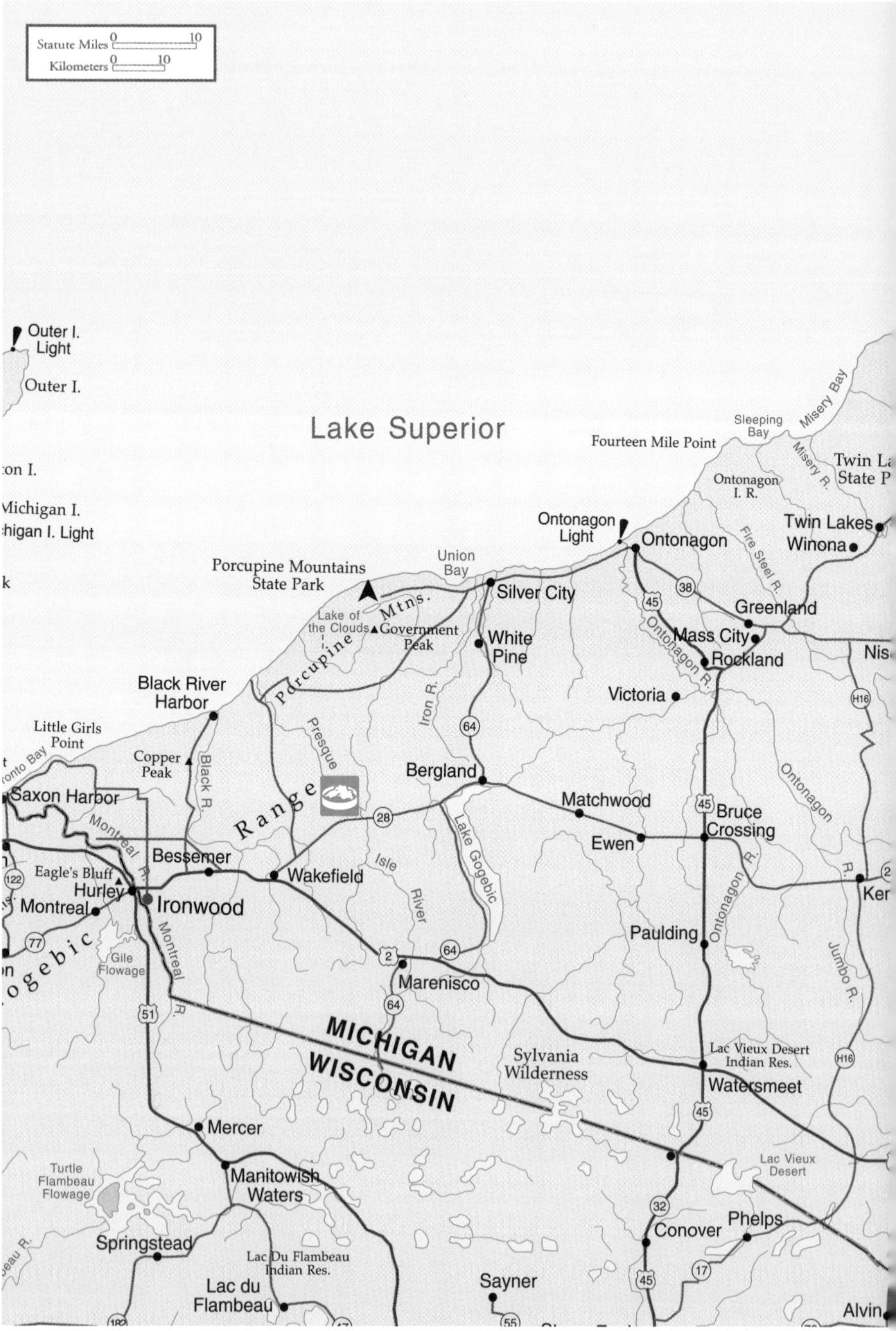

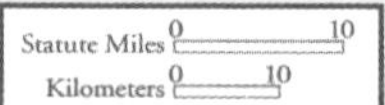

Michigan's Upper Peninsula – West

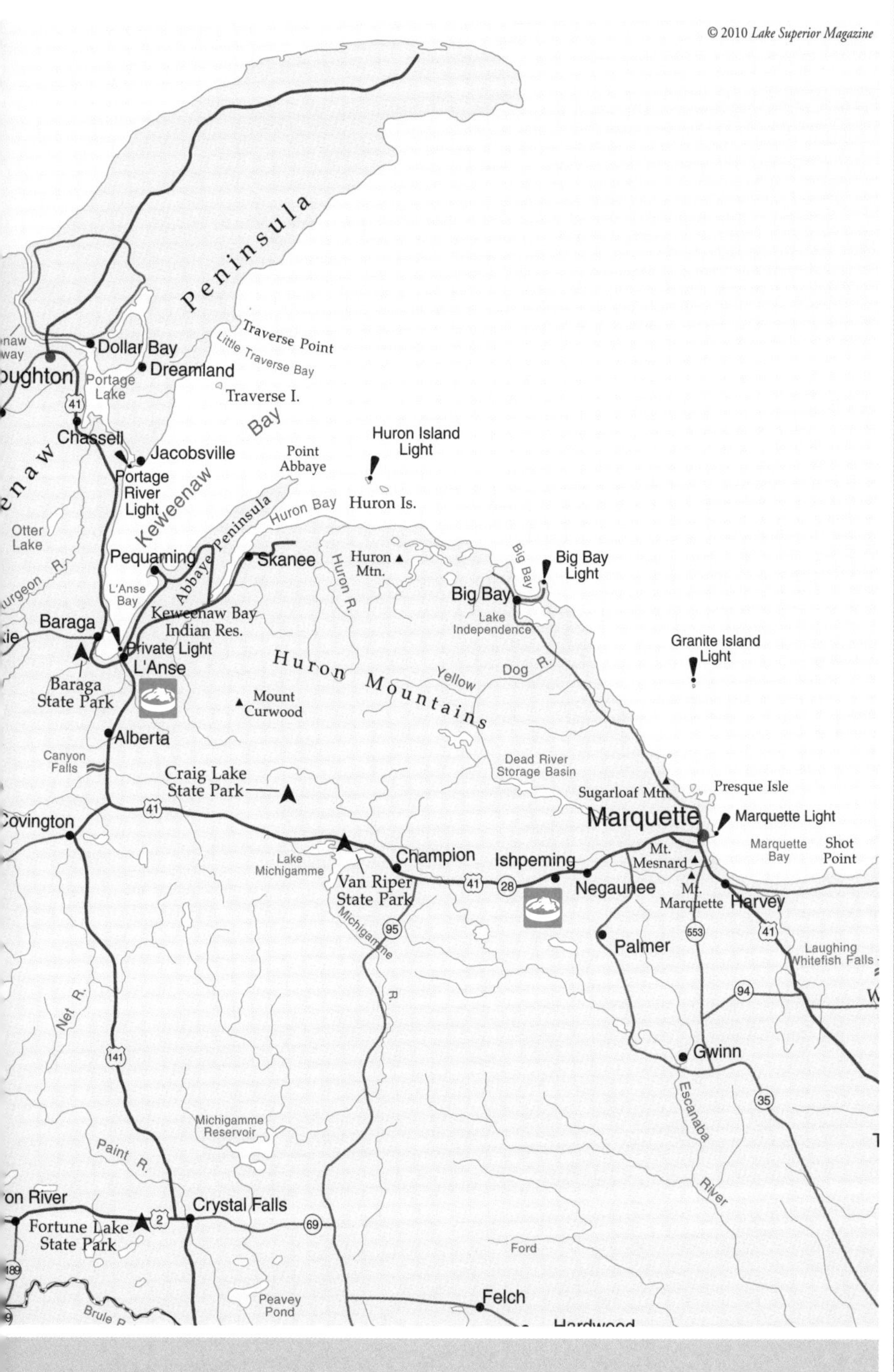
© 2010 Lake Superior Magazine
Peninsula
Traverse Point
Little Traverse Bay
Dollar Bay
Dreamland
Portage Lake
Traverse I.
Bay
Chassell
Jacobsville
Portage River Light
Point Abbaye
Huron Island Light
Huron Is.
Huron Bay
Keweenaw
Otter Lake
Pequaming
Abbaye Peninsula
Skanee
Huron Mtn.
Huron R.
Big Bay
Big Bay Light
Big Bay
Lake Independence
L'Anse Bay
Baraga
Keweenaw Bay Indian Res.
Private Light
L'Anse
Baraga State Park
Huron Mountains
Yellow
Dog R.
Granite Island Light
Mount Curwood
Alberta
Canyon Falls
Craig Lake State Park
Dead River Storage Basin
Sugarloaf Mtn.
Presque Isle
Marquette
Marquette Light
Covington
Lake Michigamme
Champion
Ishpeming
Van Riper State Park
Mt. Mesnard
Marquette Bay
Shot Point
Negaunee
Mt. Marquette
Harvey
Michigamme R.
Palmer
Laughing Whitefish Falls
Net R.
Gwinn
Escanaba River
Michigamme Reservoir
Paint R.
Crystal Falls
Fortune Lake State Park
Ford
Peavey Pond
Felch
Hardwood
Brule R.
41
28
95
553
94
35
141
2
69
189

Michigan's Upper Peninsula – East

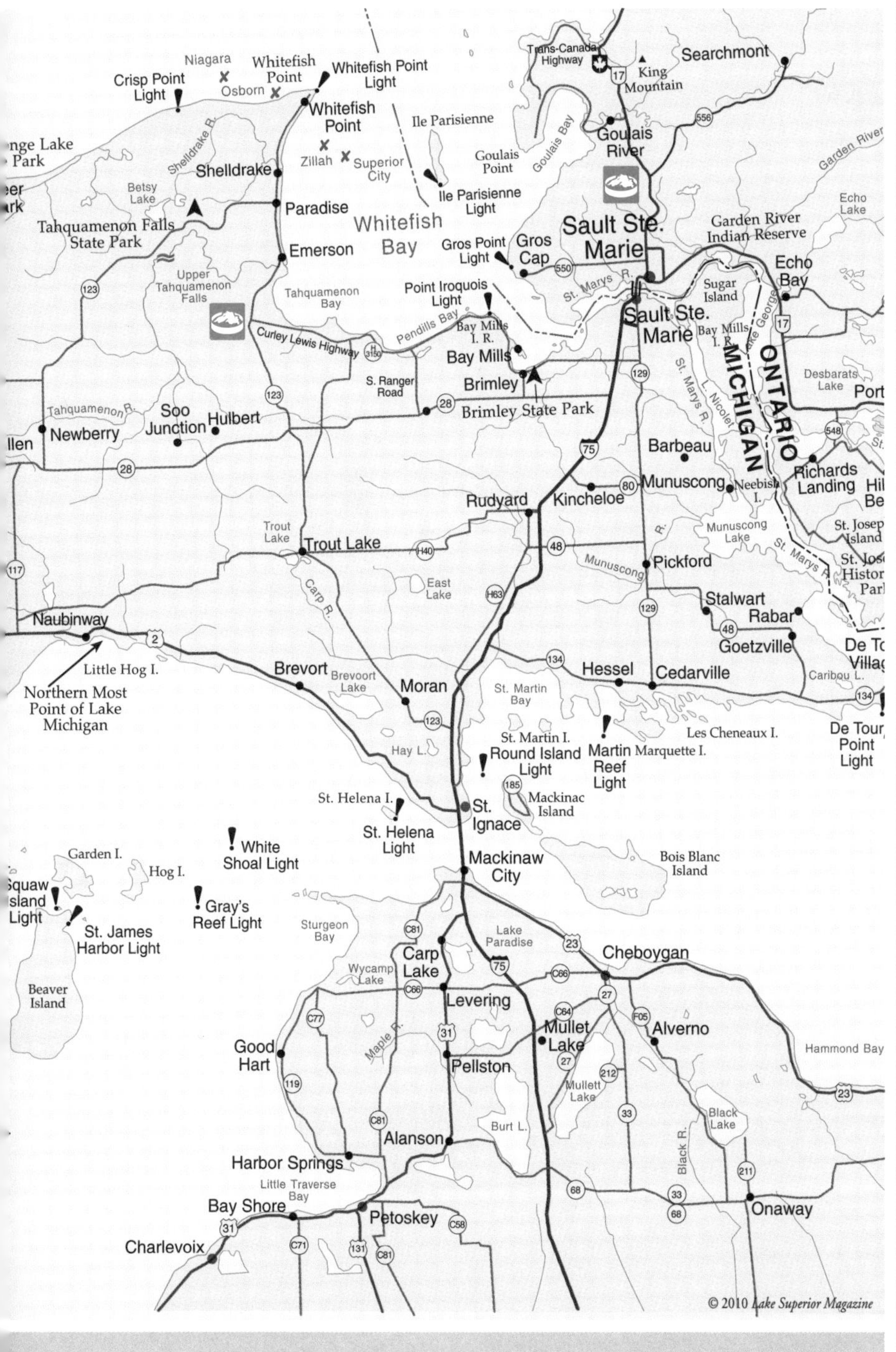
Niagara
Whitefish Point
Whitefish Point Light
Crisp Point Light
Osborn
Whitefish Point
Ile Parisienne
Trans-Canada Highway
King Mountain
Searchmont
Shelldrake R.
Shelldrake
Zillah
Superior City
Goulais Point
Goulais Bay
Goulais River
Garden River
Betsy Lake
Paradise
Ile Parisienne Light
Echo Lake
Tahquamenon Falls State Park
Whitefish Bay
Sault Ste. Marie
Garden River Indian Reserve
Emerson
Gros Point Light
Gros Cap
Echo Bay
Upper Tahquamenon Falls
Tahquamenon Bay
Point Iroquois Light
St. Marys R.
Sugar Island
Pendills Bay
Bay Mills I. R.
Sault Ste. Marie
Bay Mills I. R.
Lake George
Curley Lewis Highway
Bay Mills
ONTARIO
MICHIGAN
Desbarats Lake
Port
S. Ranger Road
Brimley
Tahquamenon R.
Soo Junction
Hulbert
Brimley State Park
St. Marys R.
L. Nicolet
Newberry
Barbeau
Richards Landing
Munuscong
Neebish I.
Rudyard
Kincheloe
Trout Lake
Trout Lake
Munuscong Lake
St. Joseph Island
Munuscong R.
Pickford
St. Marys R.
St. Joseph Historic Park
Carp R.
East Lake
Stalwart
Rabar
Naubinway
Goetzville
De Tour Village
Little Hog I.
Brevort
Brevoort Lake
Hessel
Cedarville
Caribou L.
Northern Most Point of Lake Michigan
Moran
St. Martin Bay
Les Cheneaux I.
De Tour Point Light
St. Martin I.
Round Island Light
Martin Reef Light
Marquette I.
Hay L.
Mackinac Island
St. Helena I.
St. Ignace
St. Helena Light
White Shoal Light
Garden I.
Hog I.
Mackinaw City
Bois Blanc Island
Squaw Island Light
Gray's Reef Light
St. James Harbor Light
Sturgeon Bay
Lake Paradise
Carp Lake
Cheboygan
Wycamp Lake
Beaver Island
Levering
Mullet Lake
Alverno
Maple R.
Good Hart
Pellston
Hammond Bay
Mullett Lake
Black Lake
Burt L.
Alanson
Black R.
Harbor Springs
Little Traverse Bay
Bay Shore
Petoskey
Onaway
Charlevoix
© 2010 Lake Superior Magazine

Alberta

The museum village of Alberta and the Ford Forestry Center are part of Michigan Technological University in Houghton. The site, about 9 miles south of L'Anse on U.S. 41, encompasses nearly 2,000 acres of forest around the original townsite, which now serves as a research facility and conference center of MTU. An integral part of the site is the Ford Historic Sawmill, operated as an exhibit by the Alberta Village and Museum Board, with a guided tour following the path of lumber from logs to finished boards. A house nearby is also open for tours. A gift shop welcomes visitors seeking a memento of their visit. Open Mondays, Tuesdays and Fridays.

Travelers picking up M-28 to the east or west will find the intersection with U.S. 41 about 4 miles south. To visit L'Anse, take the highway north about 9 miles.

A Bit of History

To ensure a steady supply of hardwood lumber needed in manufacturing cars by his company, Henry Ford established five sawmill sites in the northern Upper Peninsula, with Alberta being established last in 1935 as a satellite mill to his larger operation in L'Anse. The site was cleared in dense forestland, and a village, steam-powered sawmill and a dam for a mill pond were constructed. While not grand by today's standards, the homes were comfortable and workers and their families were apparently quite happy to have both good jobs and decent housing and schools. The mill was a model of its time – clean, safe, efficient and pleasant to work in with good lighting, a varnished interior and painted floors with clearly marked pathways. Converted to electrical power after the site was donated to Michigan Technological University, the mill operated part time as a teaching site for forestry students until about 1980. It is now an interesting look at how logs were turned into 15,000 board feet of lumber per day in the 1930s.

Today

The public is welcome to stop by and partake of the trails, wander through the model townsite that housed workers at the sawmill, tour the mill and view the historic memorabilia. A trail takes you from the townsite to Canyon Falls and another circles Plumbago Lake, a pleasant way to spend an hour or so.

What to See and Do

Near Alberta is Canyon Falls, the Grand Canyon of the Upper Peninsula. Look for the signs for the Sturgeon River Roadside Park off Highway 41, which has a 10-minute self-guided hiking trail to the gorge and waterfalls. There is also a hiking trail to the falls from Alberta Village.

The museum holds a "Tin Lizzie" show in early summer and an art sale and music festival in August.

What's Next

From Alberta Village, U.S. Highway 61 heads 8 miles north toward L'Anse or south about 5 miles to a junction with Michigan Highway 28/141.

Au Train

Population 570

Au Train River generously scoops patterned pools in the sand at its access to Lake Superior between Marquette and Munising. Here, you are in the central Upper Peninsula. A half-mile east of Au Train is a beachside picnic park with Scott Falls, a low waterfall, across the

A short jaunt east from Au Train in Lake Superior is Grand Island and its East Channel Lighthouse. You can visit the island from a boat tour out of Munising.

highway. At Au Train Campground, wander down the Song Bird Trail for a live concert along an interpretive path. A campground is on U.S. Forest Service Road 2276, south of M-28 about 6 miles (10 kilometers) on County Road H-03. Open from late spring into October. Those desiring indoor accommodations will want to contact Pinewood Lodge Bed & Breakfast. Nearby, the Brownstone Inn offers a tempting array of homemade entrees, handcut steaks and fresh fish.

What's Next

Along M-28 to the east you'll come to Munising. To the west there are several scenic lakeshore turnoffs between Au Train and Marquette.

INFO & OPTIONS

Brownstone Inn
M-28 West
Au Train, MI 49806
906-892-8332
www.brownstoneinn.net

Au Train Lake Campground
Call for directions: 906-387-2512 (Munising Ranger District)

Baraga

Population: 1,285

On Highway 41 east of Houghton and west from L'Anse, Baraga (BEAR-a-ga) sits snugly in the southeast corner of Keweenaw Bay. Named for Catholic missionary Bishop Frederic Baraga, who ministered to Native Americans from 1831 to 1868, often on snowshoes, his memory is preserved at the Shrine of the Snowshoe Priest, an impressive 35-foot (11-metre) copper statue overlooking Keweenaw Bay from a 25-foot (8-meter) pedestal atop Red Rock Bluff between L'Anse and Baraga. There is a nice gift shop offering mementos.

Most visitors never seem to tire of looking out over Keweenaw Bay, and the town seems to agree, with much of it located either on the waterfront or on the gently rising hillside to the west that presents panoramic views of the shore.

A Bit of History

The early history of Baraga mentions fur trading outposts in the area, but it was the 1881 arrival of Thomas Nestor and his construction of a huge modern sawmill that spurred development in the area. Capable of producing 46 million board feet of timber products per year, Nestor established his own fleet of lumber barges. The company became Estate of Thomas Nestor after his death in 1890 at Baraga, and logging by that peculiarly named lumber company continued until the surrounding pinery was depleted. Subsequently, the Detroit-based company bought huge stands of pine in Wisconsin and in the Gooseberry River watershed in northeastern Minnesota, rafting logs to Baraga until about 1910, when those western pineries were gone.

During the same period, commercial fishing became important in the Baraga area and remained a source of income for many fishermen until the invasion by lamprey eels caused fish populations to dramatically decrease by the 1970s. Farming was also possible in the area and histories record that several large cheese factories were located in the surrounding area. By that time, tourists began to visit and became an economic factor that remains important to the present.

Today

The Keweenaw Bay Indian Community's development of Ojibwa Casino along with other visitor amenities became an important employer in the latter 1900s and remains important to the area's economy.

Baraga

What to See and Do

A fun activity is the Ojibwa Casino Resort on M-38 with the latest Las Vegas-style games, Big Bucks Bingo, lodging, a restaurant and other amenities. The tribe operates another casino near Marquette.

There are various routes to Sturgeon River Gorge, one of the Upper Peninsula's most spectacular rustic scenic lookouts. A comparatively easy route follows M-38 west to Prickett Dam Road, then 9 miles (14 kilometers) south along the Sturgeon River to the gorge, falls and Silver Mountain. Silver Mountain Trail leads to moss-covered boulders through deep forests to a scenic view of the western Upper Peninsula with falls at the bottom. Don't stray too close to the edge. This is a wilderness setting. It is not handicapped accessible.

Notable Museums

Baraga County Museum is on the Lake Superior waterfront, displaying interesting prehistoric culture and recorded history from the Ice Age forward. Open May to mid-October, Tuesday through Sunday.

At Arnheim, turn left for 6 miles (10 kilometers) to visit the Hanka Homestead, a living outdoor Finnish museum that takes you back to the 1920s. Fee.

Parks and Public Areas

Baraga State Park has modern campgrounds across U.S. 41 from the head of Keweenaw Bay and the boat launch site. Fishing, swimming, hiking, picnicking. Admission by park permit.

Notable Events

• Keweenaw Bay Indian Community hosts a major powwow, open to the public, in the county park each year on the fourth weekend in July.

Campers will want to check the Ojibwa Campgrounds, also operated by the Keweenaw Bay Indian Community.

What's Next

If your direction of travel is west from Baraga, M-38 travels past Nisula and across the Keweenaw, ending in Ontonagon. Our recommended Circle Tour route follows U.S. 41. For several miles north of Baraga, the highway hugs the sandy shoreline of Lake Superior. To the east, it's about a 5-mile drive to L'Anse.

INFO & OPTIONS

Baraga County Convention & Visitors Bureau
755 East Broad St.
L'Anse, MI 49946
800-743-4908
www.baragacountytourism.org

Eagle's Nest Migizi Wadiswan
16449 Michigan Ave. (M-38)
Baraga, MI 49908
906-353-4494
www.ojibwacasino.com

Best Western Baraga Lakeside Inn
900 South U.S. 41
Baraga, MI 49908
(906) 353-7123
www.bestwesternmichigan.com

Ojibwa Casino Resort
16449 Michigan Ave. (M-38)
Baraga, MI 49908
800-323-8045
www.ojibwacasino.com

Baraga State Park
1300 U.S. 41 South
Baraga, MI 49908
906-353-6558
michigan.gov/baraga

Ojibway Casino RV Park
16449 Michigan Ave. (M-38)
Baraga, MI 49908
800-323-8045
www.ojibwacasino.com

Bergland & Lake Gogebic

Population 440

At the junction town of Bergland, where M-28 is crossed by M-64 from the north, the nearly 14,000 acres of Lake Gogebic provide year-round recreation.

Lake Gogebic State Park borders its western shore. The lake sits about 1,300 feet (400 meters) above sea level. Above the lake, Gogebic Ridge Hiking Trail offers spectacular views. To the south is the Sylvania Recreation Area of Ottawa National Forest. A number of resorts, lodgings and campgrounds are on the lake.

What's Next

To the west, Highway M-28 heads for Wakefield, Bessemer and Ironwood. Easterly lies Bruce Crossing and the junction with U.S. Highway 45. Depending on your route, we recommend taking Highway 64 north from Bergland to Silver City, the Porcupine Mountains and Ontonagon.

INFO & OPTIONS

Walleye Lodge Motel & Resort
35131 Hwy. M-28
Bergland, MI 49910
866-464-3242
www.walleyelodge.com

Bessemer

Population 2,145

Bessemer is located on M-28/U.S. Highway 2 midway between Ironwood on the west and Wakefield to the east.

Settled when iron ore mining opened on the Gogebic Range in the 1880s, Bessemer experienced the boom of both logging and mining. The logging played out relatively quickly as available stands of timber were depleted, but mining continued until the early 1950s, when many Gogebic Range mines ran out of ores. As the population dwindled in area cities, it seemed the importance of the area would likewise wither, until the development of ski resorts in the nearby mountains resurrected the area.

With consistently excellent snow, it's no wonder that this became the Upper Peninsula's skiing heartland. Major resorts in the iron mountains include Blackjack, Big Powderhorn and Indianhead ski areas. Several other skiing opportunities are located in close proximity, including Porcupine Mountains and Whitecap Mountains in nearby Montreal, Wisconsin (both discussed elsewhere in listings). Check for combination lift tickets that allow you to ski several or all of the hills. All offer instruction and equipment rentals. Big Powderhorn, a pioneer ski operation in the Midwest, is now in its fourth decade as a major ski area.

What to See and Do

Take County Road 513 from Bessemer to the Copper Peak Ski Flying Hill, the world's highest artificial slide with a 610-foot (186-meter) steel ski-flying tower. Open daily, June 15 through Labor Day, and weekends during fall colors. Admission fee for chairlift and elevator. The present hill jump record is 512 feet, set by Vasko Stanislav of Czechoslovakia. The jump is expected to reopen with upgrades within a year or two.

Continue on County Road 513, now designated as the Black River Scenic Byway, to Black River Harbor (population 19) and five scenic waterfalls with trails and overlooks, an excellent forest campground, marina, beach and swinging suspension bridge. Fishing charters are available. Beachcombing is a favorite here as is the Labor Day fishing derby.

Hundreds of area streams provide excellent fishing.

Notable Events

• Bessemer holds a Pumpkinfest in October with pumpkin carving to seed spitting and a pie social. The city also has a nice July 4 celebration.

What's Next

To continue the Circle Tour route, take U.S. Highway 2 either east to Wakefield or west toward Ironwood. At Wakefield, Michigan, Highway 28 heads northeasterly toward the Keweenaw Peninsula and Highway 2 bends southeast into the southern Upper Peninsula toward Lake Michigan's north shore.

INFO & OPTIONS

Bessemer Area Chamber of Commerce
U.S. Hwy. 2
Bessemer, MI 49911
906-663-0026
www.bessemerchamber.org

Black River Falls Harbor & Campground
15 miles north of Bessemer, County Rd. 513
906-932-7250

Big Snow Country

When it comes to snow, Big Snow Country in the western Upper Peninsula is well named. It annually averages 200 inches of the white stuff. For those seeking recreation, it means snowmobiling, skiing, snowboarding and other activities on well groomed trails and terrain parks, with five major facilities concentrated between the Porcupine Mountains Ski Area to the northeast and Whitecap Mountains Ski Area southwest of Ironwood-Hurley, Wisconsin. Other major Big Snow Country resorts include Indianhead, Blackjack and Big Powderhorn, clustered near Bessemer. Nearby national and state forest areas also present many other winter recreational opportunities, from snowmobiling to cross-country skiing and snowshoeing.

Summer is also a grand time in Big Snow Country. The natural wilderness conditions are a huge attraction. More than 900,000 acres of the Ottawa National Forest are spread through the area. Nearly 400,000 visitors annually tour it by car. Close to 600,000 others come to hike, hunt, canoe, fish or enjoy other summer outdoor activities. More than 35 waterfalls are accessible by roads and woodland trails.

Point Iroquois Lighthouse north of Brimley has a ghostly history and nice gift shop.

Big Bay

Population 200

A pleasant 25-mile (40-kilometer) drive north on County Road 550 from Marquette through the forests leads to the village of Big Bay, where delightful Perkins Park has access to Lake Independence, with a boat launch, docks, camping, fishing, swimming and picnic area.

The Thunder Bay Inn, once owned by Henry Ford, was built in 1911 as a general store. Ford renovated it in 1940 to house executives visiting the Ford Retreat in the Huron Mountains. It was later used in the filming of the movie "Anatomy of a Murder." Today the inn has been renovated, with charming antique-filled rooms and a friendly tavern/restaurant.

The Big Bay Point Lighthouse is a bed-and-breakfast inn in a 100-year-old active lighthouse. The atmosphere is laid-back and casual, but be on the alert for a ghostly encounter that has been reported.

What's Next

Return on County 550 to Marquette, where you can continue your Circle Tour east or west on Michigan Highway 28.

INFO & OPTIONS

Big Bay Point Lighthouse Bed and Breakfast
3 Lighthouse Rd.
Big Bay, MI 49808
906-345-9957
www.bigbaylighthouse.com

Perkins Park Campground & Picnic Area
County Rd. 550
Big Bay, MI 49808
906-345-9353

Brimley

Area Population 950

Brimley is a few miles west of Sault Ste. Marie. If traveling M-28 from the west, watch for County 221 north a few miles before the junction with I-75 at Dafter. From Sault Ste. Marie, the Lake Superior Circle Tour route that we recommend takes either Business Interstate 75/County H-63 or Highway 129 south to Six Mile Road and turn right. If traveling the Circle Tour to the west, this route will take you closer to the shoreline and cut off several miles of travel. Information is available on the way out of the Soo at the Soo Chamber Office on I-75 Business Spur.

What to See and Do

Famous at the height of logging days, Brimley is the home of the Bay Mills Indian Community, which operates the King's Club Casino, the first tribally run blackjack casino in the United States. The Bay Mills Resort and Casino is on Waishkey Bay, with two floors of hotel rooms, theme suites, lounge, restaurant, convention center and the excellent Wild Bluff Golf

Course. The Bay Mills Ojibway tribe also runs a 75-site RV park; 30 sites offer water, sewer, electricity and cable.

Notable Museums

Wheels of History Museum, operated by the Bay Mills-Brimley Historical Research Society, displays items from the early lumbering, fishing and railroading. It is in a rebuilt wooden passenger coach. A gift shop and tourist information center is in Detroit and Port Huron Railroad Caboose *No. 52.*

Parks and Public Areas

Brimley State Park (151 acres) has sand beaches, campgrounds, a picnic area and swimming. Admission by park permit.

Point Iroquois Light Station is north of Brimley and has been on the National Register of Historic Places since 1975, operated by the Bay Mills-Brimley Historical Research Society and the U.S. Forest Service. Iroquois warriors were killed there by the Ojibway in 1662. It is one of the few lighthouses where visitors can climb the 65-foot (20-meter) tower for a spectacular view of Lake Superior and the bay. The museum has a gift shop, but don't stay too late. Rumors are a ghost lives at the lighthouse. Open mid-May to mid-October. Free, donations welcomed.

What's Next

Leaving Brimley to the east, a short drive brings you to I-75 from the south, which leads to Sault Ste. Marie. About a 3-mile trip south from Brimley on Highway 221 leads to Michigan Highway 28.

West and north, Curley Lewis Memorial Highway (Shore Drive) is Forest Road 3150 and follows a scenic lakeside route from the Sault to Brimley and on to M-123 that takes you to Tahquamenon Falls State Park and Paradise. This is a drive of beauty, especially spectacular in the fall when leaves have achieved their full color. Eastward travelers will take the route described above to Sault Ste. Marie.

Worthwhile westbound stops: Old Mission Indian Cemetery, the U.S. Forest Service Bay View Campgrounds and picnic area at Big Pine, and guided tours at Pendills' Creek National Fish Hatchery, where lake trout are reared to replenish local stocks. A scenic overview at Mission Hill Cemetery (watch carefully for the area) is the burial site for the crew of the shipwreck *Myron*, which sank nearby in November 1919. The U.S. Forest Service campground at Monocle Lake has fishing, hiking and swimming. There are private campgrounds in the area.

The forest service road intersects with Michigan Highway 123 about 5 miles (8 kilometers) south of the Rivermouth Unit of Tahquamenon Falls State Park, which includes a campground and Lake Superior access. The eastern Upper Peninsula branch of the North Country Trail enters the area at this point from St. Ignace and extends west, with a number of other segments completed across the region. Check with local information centers.

You'll pass the old townsite of Emerson, once home of the Chesbrough Lumber Company and a hub of lumbering famous for pine, but that ceased in the early 1910s. This area is now a center for fishing.

INFO & OPTIONS

Bay Mills Resort and Casino
11386 West Lakeshore Dr.
Brimley, MI 49715
888-422-9645
www.4baymills.com

Brimley State Park
9200 West Six Mile Rd.
Brimley, MI 49715
906-248-3422

Bruce Crossing

Area Population 1,115

Bruce Crossing is a wonderful crossing of roads where U.S. 45 and M-28 meet almost exactly in the center of the western Upper Peninsula. If you have the hungries or need lodging, check at Tulppo's Restaurant and Motel at the crossroads. During the winter, snowmobilers and cross-country skiers are within one hour of any area in Big Snow Country (see separate listing).

To the south of Bruce Crossing, off Highway 45 at Paulding, you can visit Bond Falls. Nearby are hiking trails, fishing and camping facilities. Paulding is also home to the mysterious Paulding Light, which has gained the burg a great deal of attention. (See details under Paulding listing.)

Brockway Mountain

From Copper Harbor or Eagle Harbor, take M-26 to experience the 9.5-mile (15-kilometer) drive over Brockway Mountain with many scenic overlooks at regular intervals. The scenic vista at the top is more than 700 feet (213 meters) above Lake Superior, with a view that stretches from Keweenaw Point in the east to Eagle Harbor in the west. The Skytop Inn on the summit offers shelter from the wind on blustery days and a selection of gifts.

Brockway Mountain is a major birding site for the spring and fall migration of hawks and other raptors.

From Bruce Crossing there are several travel options. M-28 is the east-west route. North on U.S. 45 takes the traveler to Ontonagon.

Calumet

Population 880

The name Calumet generally translates to "Peace Pipe." Steeped in copper mining history, the village is a focal point of the Keweenaw National Historical Park, authorized in 1992. Calumet Theatre, the fire hall and Calumet's magnificent churches are among the historic sites. Maps of the Quincy and Calumet units, and a regional district map, can be found in the park newspaper, at park headquarters or online.

What to See and Do

Calumet Theatre opened in 1900 and is still active, hosting 60 to 80 events each year. This beautiful showplace was the first municipally owned theater in America. The worthwhile guided tours are Monday through Friday summer and fall; self-guided tours are available year-round.

Stop at Shute's 1890 Bar, long a popular Calumet watering hole, next to the Calumet Theatre. It's Michigan's oldest-known original tavern, with antique fixtures and a magnificent bar.

If you golf, try Calumet Golf Course, which has 9 holes just south of town off U.S. 41. Take Highway M-203 from Calumet to the lakeshore to watch sunsets from 43-acre Calumet Township Park.

Notable Museums

Coppertown USA Mining Museum on Red Jacket Road traces the area's copper mining history through its days of fame as the Calumet and Hecla Consolidated

Copper Company. Small fee. Open June to mid-October, Monday through Saturday (plus Sundays in July and August).

Upper Peninsula Fire Fighter's Memorial Museum honors those who have been on the job over the last century. Housed in the 1900-era Red Jacket Fire Station with three floors of equipment and displays. Open afternoons daily, late June to late August.

The Keweenaw Heritage Center is at St. Anne's Church and contains many interesting displays. Opens daily afternoons, July and August. Free, donations welcome.

Parks and Public Areas

In 1913, during a bitter miners' strike, someone yelled "fire" at a Christmas party at Italian Hall, causing a stampede and killing 73 people, mostly children. Italian Hall Memorial Park honors the victims. The tragedy created a national sensation and triggered changes in mining labor and free speech laws.

The Pine Mountain Music Festival's specially commissioned opera, "Children of the Keweenaw," based on the Italian Hall tragedy, appropriately premiered at the Calumet Theatre, which served as a temporary morgue after the disaster.

Continue on Highway M-203 nearly to the Keweenaw Waterway to find the 401-acre F.J. McLain State Park on Lake Superior and Bear Lake. It features modern campgrounds, beaches, an excellent day-use area, refreshments, swimming and agate hunting. Some mini-cabins are available. Admission by park permit.

Notable Events

- Calumet hosts the Portage Health Great Bear Chase Cross-Country Ski Race in March and a late August Heritage Celebration.

Where to Shop

Copper World has copper items, lighthouse collectibles, T-shirts and local history books for sale. Next door, check out the stock of goodies and collectibles at Calumet Mercantile and General Store on Fifth Street.

Mine Street Station offers shopping and lodging on land once owned by the Calumet and Hecla mining company.

What's Next

If your route is to the north toward Copper Harbor, stay on U.S. Highway 41, but we recommend catching South Shore Drive at Fulton to take a scenic tour of the Keweenaw's eastern shoreline and the small towns of Gay and Lac La Belle (see separate listings). If you're returning from Copper Harbor, continue on Highway 41 to Hancock and Houghton.

INFO & OPTIONS

AmericInn of Calumet
56925 South Sixth St.
Calumet, MI 49913
800-396-5007
www.americinn.com

Gratiot River Recreation Area
Five Mile Point Rd.
Ahmeek, MI 49901
906-337-0782
www.northwoodsconservancy.org

Sunset Bay Campground and Cabins
2701 Sunset Bay Beach Rd.
Ahmeek, MI 49901
906-337-2494 (summer)
941-232-4832 (winter)

Central

Central, a small village on U.S. Highway 41 some 25 miles north of Houghton-Hancock on the Keweenaw Peninsula, is a good look at all that remains of a bustling 1800s Keweenaw Peninsula copper mining community. Each July, the town hosts the annual Central Mine reunion of descendants of original settlers in the area at the Central Church.

Just north on Highway 41, plan a stop at Delaware Mine Tour for an underground, self-guided walk in one of the oldest mines on the Keweenaw, where you'll see exposed veins of copper. The mine is not handicapped accessible. A variety of friendly animals for the kids has been added at the grounds, which feature rides and exhibits of owner Tom Poynter's extensive collection of scale model railroad equipment. Many visitors say that the highlight is meeting Oreo the pet skunk, the official greeter and mascot. Open mid-May through mid-October. Admission fees.

North from nearby Phoenix, U.S. 41 approaching Copper Harbor is a designated Scenic Highway and an exceptionally lovely drive, with tunnels of pine and hardwood trees that are especially spectacular in fall color.

Chassell

Population 1,829

On the eastern edge of the Keweenaw Peninsula at Chassell, watch for roadside strawberry stands in season. Strawberries grown here are huge and juicy. Come in July for the Chassell Strawberry Festival.

Amenities in town include a motel, cabins, a bed-and-breakfast inn, bakery and restaurant and a nice bayside park.

What to See and Do

The Sturgeon River Wilderness Area bird sanctuary reaches across the highway east of the village. There is a turnoff and observation platform in the wetland sloughs. The DeVriendt Nature Trail is part of the sanctuary, off U.S. 41. The 1.5-mile (2.4-kilometer) loop combines a boardwalk through the slough and chipped trails through the woods. Many waterfowl nest here.

Just south of Chassell, watch for the turn-off to Keweenaw Berry Farm, a fun family stop with a nice farm animal collection for kids to pet and some of the tastiest piping hot pasties we've found.

On the Portage Entry Road, there is a marina, boat docking area and a launch. This is a good spot to see fishing boats.

A pleasant way to pass the time is at Einerlei on U.S. 41, a shop with books, furnishings, regional art, casual clothing, gourmet kitchenware and interesting gardens. Events are regularly scheduled.

Chassell has a nice park, a swimming beach, playground, boat launch and fishing dock. It's a great place for small sailing craft and kayakers and canoeists to put in.

Notable Museums

Chassell Heritage Center in the old elementary school has displays of Chassell Township history, showcasing logging, milling and strawberry farming. The center, home to the Friends of Fashion, houses the most extensive vintage clothing museum collection in the U.P. Thursday evenings in the summer, local and regional artists, researchers and musicians present programs at the Heritage Center at 7 p.m. In July and August, it's open 1-4 p.m. Tuesdays and 4-9 p.m. Thursdays.

The heritage center is at the head of the Chassell Classic Cross Country Ski Trail, a 10-kilometer picturesque skiing trail that winds through the forest and uphill from Chassell. Chassell's Old-Fashioned Christmas celebration is held annually on the second weekend of December. Festivities include a house tour, craft show and free sleigh rides.

Notable Events

• In January Chassell hosts the Chassell Bay Ice Fishing Derby and Copper Island Classic X-C Ski Race.

• The Carl Olson Memorial Adventure Trail Run occurs in June.

• July sees the Strawberry Festival.

• Old Fashioned Christmas is held in December.

What's Next

If traveling westward, follow Highway 41 along Portage Lake to explore another of Lake Superior's "twin cities," Houghton and Hancock separated by Portage Lake. If your line of travel is to the east, stay on Highway 41 heading for Baraga and L'Anse.

Copper Harbor

Population 100

At the very northern tip of the Keweenaw Peninsula, Copper Harbor is a beautiful village destination more than 150 years old. A marvelous year-round haven that caters to visitors, the village offers an abundance of shops, a marina, great lodging and delicious food. If you're arriving by boat, the marina is a short walk from town. Most businesses in the area belong to the Copper Harbor Improvement Association and will be happy to provide details on almost anything you might seek.

What to See and Do

Average annual snowfall in the Keweenaw Peninsula is more than 250 inches. A good photo stop en route to Copper Harbor is the tall snowfall measuring gauge, which records annual snowfalls of note. A record 390.4 inches was measured in the winter of 1977-78. Snow means winter fun, and the upper Keweenaw is criss-crossed with more than 250 miles of snowmobile trails. Copper Harbor has 20 kilometers of cross-country ski trails, including 10k of classic ski trails at the Keweenaw Mountain Lodge.

Copper Harbor is a hiker's paradise. Estivant Pines Nature Sanctuary is a patch of old-growth forest that escaped the axe. The 2-mile loop weaves by 500-year-old giant white pines more than 300 feet tall (91 meters) and up to 6 feet (1.8 meters) in diameter. Hunter's Point has new trails on the inner and outer side of Copper Harbor. This narrow finger of land provides natural protection for the harbor and has been designated as a park.

Keweenaw Adventure Company conducts sea kayak tours, lessons and rentals, and offers mountain bike rentals, service and backcountry tours.

Isle Royale Queen IV, which offers transportation to and from Isle Royale National Park, welcomes passengers for nightly sunset cruises from July Fourth through Labor Day. Operated by the Royale Line Inc.

Copper Harbor's school is the state's last operational one-room schoolhouse. Its viewing room allows you to peek in on the elementary classes.

The 9.5-mile (15-kilometer) drive over Brockway Mountain has scenic overlooks at regular intervals. The scenic vista at the top is more than 700 feet

(213 meters) above Lake Superior, with a view that stretches from Keweenaw Point west to Eagle Harbor and on the lake as far as the passing ships. Skytop Inn on the summit offers a selection of gifts and souvenirs. Local birdwatchers credit Brockway Mountain as a major viewpoint to track the spring and fall migration of hawks and other raptors, since a flyway brings the birds almost directly overhead.

Notable Museums

A must stop for history is the Copper Harbor Lighthouse and Museum at the entrance to the harbor facing the village. Emphasis is on Lake Superior maritime history, with access to the keeper's quarters and the remains of the shipwreck of the *John Jacob Astor*, driven ashore in an 1844 gale. Accessible only by Lighthouse Tour boat (*Spirit of America*), which departs hourly from the Copper Harbor Marina, Memorial Day through mid-October, with limited spring and fall tours. Some evening cruises are offered, and there's a gift shop.

Another good stop for a taste of the area's past is the Astor House Museum at Minnetonka Resort. Loaded with regional artifacts, including dolls and mining equipment, it is well worth a visit.

Parks and Public Areas

Fort Wilkins State Park re-enacts life on the 199-acre site of an Army post established in 1844, ostensibly to protect rowdy copper miners from local Indian people. Abandoned in 1870, the fort has been restored, with interpretive actors during the tourism season. Admission by permit. Camping reservations mid-May to mid-October. Lake Fanny Hooe Resort and Campgrounds has a swimming beach and lodging on Lake Fanny Hooe.

Notable Events

- Brockway Mountain Challenge X-C Race in February challenges skiers with some of the most striking scenery around.
- Longest Day Fishing Tournament in June is a chance for anglers to spend the long daylight hours fishing for worthwhile prizes.
- Copperman Triathlon in August establishes bragging rights for winners and non-winners alike.
- Art in the Park in August is an chance for artists and craftspeople to show their works to an appreciative public.
- Fat Tire Festival in September challenges mountain bike enthusiasts.

Where to Shop

There are shops galore, some with imaginative names and gifts.

Laughing Loon Gifts & Crafts of the Northwoods is loaded with tantalizing gifts, many made from native copper. Owner Laurel Rooks, an excellent source of local knowledge, operates Patchwords Books under the same roof. Another choice for books is the delightful Grandpa's Barn, where owner Lloyd Wescoat says her unusual name is an inheritance from her family.

Country Village Shops offer gifts, Christmas decorations and interesting food items, including fudge and the local favorite, thimbleberry ice cream sundaes.

Check out Sugar Plum Shop for candy and Christmas items, the T-Shirt Gallery or Shea's Tees and Treasures, all near the historic one-room schoolhouse.

Minnetonka Resort in the middle of town has a well-stocked gift store where you're sure to find just the right souvenir or memento of the area.

A view above the town shows Copper Harbor nestled into the woods near the northern most point of the Keweenaw Peninsula looking into Lake Superior.

What's Next

You'll arrive and depart Copper Harbor by either U.S. Highway 41 or Michigan Highway 26, depending on your intended route. U.S. 41 is a direct route to Houghton-Hancock, while M-26 follows the Keweenaw's western shoreline through Eagle Harbor and Eagle River, before joining U.S. 41 at Phoenix. Take U.S. 41 to Delaware and turn southeast, if you plan to travel the eastern side of the peninsula back to Houghton-Hancock.

INFO & OPTIONS

Keweenaw Convention & Visitors Bureau

56638 Calumet Ave.
Calumet, MI 49913
906-337-4579
www.keweenaw.info

Brockway Inn

840 Gratiot St.
Copper Harbor, MI 49918
906-289-4588
www.brockwayinn.com

Harbor Haus
77 Brockway Ave.
Copper Harbor, MI 49918
906-289-4502
www.harborhaus.com

Harbor Lights Inn
U.S. Hwy. 41 & Fifth St.
Copper Harbor, MI 49918
906-289-4741
www.harborlightsinn.biz

Keweenaw Mountain Lodge
U.S. Hwy. 41
Copper Harbor, MI 49918
888-685-6343
www.atthelodge.com

King Copper Motel
447 East Brockway Ave.
Copper Harbor, MI 49918
800-833-2470
www.kingcoppermotel.com

The Mariner North Resort
245 Gratiot St.
Copper Harbor, MI 49918
888-626-6784
www.manorth.com

Fort Wilkins State Park
P.O. Box 71
Copper Harbor, MI 49918
906-289-4215

Lake Fanny Hooe Resort & Campground
505 Second St.
Copper Harbor, MI 49918
906-289-4451

Crystal Falls

Population 1,965

Crystal Falls on U.S. Highway 2 in Michigan's southwestern Upper Peninsula is the Iron County seat and a crossroads community where we can catch Highway 141 north to rejoin the Lake Superior Circle Tour as it wends east or west.

Crystal Falls was named for a waterfall on the Paint River where a dam now stands. Locals claim that the distinction of being the county seat was moved from Iron River to Crystal Falls in the dark of night during an 1880s poker game. Notwithstanding this questionable origin, the Iron County Courthouse is a proud structure atop the hill, offering a wonderful vista of the surrounding territory. Crystal Falls is home to the "Humungus Fungus," which is mostly underground but produces above-ground mushrooms. It inspired the Humungus Fungus Fest in August.

Visitors can pick up an Iron County Heritage Route brochure and other informational materials at various businesses in Crystal Falls. There are lodgings in town and an AmericInn Lodge and Suites is 16 miles west in Iron River.

What to See and Do

Interesting sites worth visiting in town are the Harbour House Museum on Fourth Street (fee), and Fortune Pond a couple of miles out of town where nature has healed the scars of mining and turned the former iron ore pit into a lake.

East of Crystal Falls on M-69, take Mansfield Cutoff Road 7 miles north and travel another mile north on Stream Road to a National Historic landmark. Marking the 1893 flooding of the Mansfield Mine in which 27 miners died, the Mansfield Location and Pioneer Church site includes original landmarks and artifacts of that era.

Parks and Public Areas

West on Highway 2 takes us past Be-Wa-Bic State Park, an entry point to the Pentoga Trail and Larson Park, inviting inspection of their scenic settings. Larson Park was the first roadside picnic site in the state and possibly the country.

What's Next

Staying on U.S. 2 to the west, you're heading for Big Snow Country (see separate listing under Ironwood) in the western Upper Peninsula. Eastward, U.S. 2 heads for Escanaba and an encounter with Lake Michigan's northern shore.

Drummond Island

Population 990

Drummond Island is the largest of three U.S. islands (Sugar and Neebish, too) in lower St. Marys River. Catch the ferry from De Tour Village on Highway 134 at the eastern tip of the U.P. Visitors will find a museum, good restaurants and lodging. Called the Gem of the Huron, the island offers opportunity to photograph another Great Lake. Potagannissing Bay is to the north, but Lake Huron surrounds the rest.

INFO & OPTIONS

Drummond Island Information Center
P.O. Box 200
Drummond Island, MI 49726
800-737-8666
www.drummondislandchamber.com

Moosehead Lodging
18354 East North Caribou Lake Rd.
DeTour, MI 49725
888-870-1118
www.mooseheadlodging.net

Drummond Island Resort and Conference Center
33494 South Maxton Rd.
Drummond Island, MI 49726
906-493-1000
www.drummondisland.com

Eagle Harbor

Township Population: 281

The small village of Eagle Harbor was once an important port in the early days of the copper boom, but that importance subsided as ships grew larger and the harbor became difficult for the ships to navigate.

What to See and Do

The rules and bylaws for the international charitable, benevolent and fraternal Order of the Knights of Pythias were written in 1858 in this lakeside village by school teacher Justus Rathbone, for whom the schoolhouse was later named. A convention of the Pythian Sisters women's auxiliary still convenes at the Rathbone School each summer.

The oldest Catholic church in use in the Upper Peninsula is Holy Redeemer Church. Built in 1852, it is still used today, a memorial to Bishop Frederic Baraga. Open daily, mid-June through September.

Notable Museums

The former U.S. Life-Saving Station at Eagle Harbor, once an important facility for maritime safety, serves as the public marina. Keweenaw County Historical Museum is housed in the former Eagle Harbor Lighthouse, with many exhibits of earlier times on display including the Signal House. Open daily, mid-June through September.

What's Next

As you travel the west side of the Keweenaw Peninsula stop and search for agates, greenstones and driftwood on the public beaches along M-26.

Heading north from Eagle Harbor on M-26 takes you to Copper Harbor. Heading south, there are nice scenic turnouts and agate beaches between Eagle Harbor and Eagle River, notably Cat Harbor and Great Sand Bay. Be sure to make a stop at Jacob's Creek Falls at Great Sand Bay for a photo. Watch for it

Between Eagle River and Eagle Harbor, visitors will see an onion-domed monastery and church on Highway M-26. This is home of the Society of St. John, and the brothers operate the Jampot store.

from the car window. And while you're there, sample some of the most sumptuous treats imaginable at the Jampot, operated by the good brothers of the Society of St. John. The Jampot is open Memorial Day until mid-October, Monday through Saturday. Visitors cannot help but notice the new onion-domed monastery and church on the lake side of the highway about a quarter-mile from the Jampot.

INFO & OPTIONS

Dapple Gray Bed & Breakfast
13640 Hwy. M-26
Eagle Harbor, MI 49950
866-909-1233
www.dapple-gray.com

Eagle Harbor House
413 Front St.
Eagle Harbor, MI 49950
906-289-1039

Eagle Lodge Lakeside
13051 M-26 (Lakeshore Drive)
Eagle Harbor, MI 49950
888-558-4441
www.eaglelodge-lakeside.com

Shoreline Resort
122 Front St.
Eagle Harbor, MI 49950
906-289-4441
www.shorelineresort.com

Eagle River

Township Population 204

Eagle River has the oldest courthouse

in Michigan and is the county seat of Keweenaw County. M-26 crosses the Eagle River, with 60-foot (18-meter) Eagle River Falls visible upstream from the bridge. The village's old highway bridge has been turned into a walking bridge, replaced by a modern structure, which is made primarily of wood. On the outskirts of the village is the Evergreen Cemetery, with only weathered headstones left to tell the story of the rough early mining days.

In nearby Phoenix, the Phoenix Church, built in 1858 in Cliff, dismantled and reassembled in Phoenix, is operated by the Keweenaw County Historical Society as a museum. The Bammert Blacksmith Shop opens daily, mid-May through early October.

From Phoenix, take Highway 41 to return to Hancock/Houghton.

INFO & OPTIONS

Fitzgerald's Restaurant (Eagle River Inn)
5033 Front St.
Eagle River, MI 49950
906-337-0666
www.eagleriverinn.com

Eagle River Inn
5033 Front St.
Eagle River, MI 49950
906-337-0666
www.eagleriverinn.com

Escanaba

Population 12,297

Although not part of the official Lake Superior Circle Tour route, there is much to recommend a side trip or alternate route on U.S. Highway 2 to take in Michigan's southern Upper Peninsula. The highway is the northern leg of the Lake Michigan Circle Tour. Westbound travelers should watch for Rapid River at the north end of Little Bay de Noc to follow Highway 2/41 along the shore southwesterly to Gladstone (population 4,565) and Escanaba. Eastbound travelers on Highway 2 from Iron Mountain and Big Snow Country in the western U.P. will note the junction where Highway 41 joins U.S. 2 from the south about 20 miles west of Escanaba.

A Bit of History

Protected from the storms of Lake Michigan in virtually every direction, Escanaba is a commercial and iron ore harbor and was once the shipping destination for the huge tonnages produced by the many iron mines to the west on the Menominee Range.

Incorporated in 1866, by the early 1880s Escanaba had grown to city status and the waterfront was lined by docks shipping not only iron ore but lumber and other products. It has served as the county seat of Delta County virtually since the county was formed.

Today

Unlike ports on Lake Superior that are dependent on the Soo Locks, this harbor can ship iron ore well into the winter season, making it especially important after the Soo Locks' annual shutdown in mid-January. Today, ore cargoes originate on the Marquette Iron Range and are shipped to the Escanaba docks by the Canadian National Railway.

What to See and Do

A number of parks offer seasonal recreational opportunities.

Five 18-hole and two 9-hole golf courses within a few miles will challenge your skills. If you're traveling with kids, a stop at the Family Fun Park on Third

Michigan

Avenue North will be welcome, with miniature golf, go-karts, bumper boats and other fun activities.

Art enthusiasts will want to check the schedule at William Bonifas Fine Arts Center downtown to view exhibits by local, regional and international artists, as well as any performing arts events.

U.P. State Fairgrounds host the fair in August. The fairgrounds are busy throughout the year with a variety of activities like craft sales, sports shows and other events. Information is available at the fairground office.

Island Resort and Casino is about 13 miles (21 kilometers) west of Escanaba at Harris. Offering a 113-room hotel, an RV park, restaurants, convention and banquet facilities, a pool and a variety of gaming, it's operated by the Hannahville Tribe on the Michigan Potawatomi Reservation.

What's Next

Leaving Escanaba on Highway 2/41, we head either west through a number of towns of the Menominee Iron Range toward Big Snow Country or north and then east on Highway 2 toward St. Ignace and the Mackinac Bridge.

INFO & OPTIONS

Bays de Noc Convention and Visitors Bureau
230 Ludington St.
Escanaba, MI 49829
800-533-4FUN (533-4386)
www.travelbaysdenoc.com

Hereford and Hops
624 Ludington St.
Escanaba, MI 49829
906-789-1945
www.herefordandhops.com

House of Ludington
223 Ludington St.
Escanaba, MI 49829
906-786-6300
www.houseofludington.com

House of Ludington
223 Ludington St.
Escanaba, MI 49829
906-786-6300
www.houseofludington.com

Ewen

Township Population 670

Just west of Bruce Crossing and 15 miles (24 kilometers) east of Bergland on the Highway 28 Circle Tour route, pause in Ewen, home of the 1893 World's Fair Load of Logs – a replica was displayed here for many years before deterioration forced it to be disassembled. An townwide Log Jamboree celebration in mid-September commemorates the area's logging history.

If you need a meal or a bed, check TJ's Restaurant and Motel right on the highway.

Gay

Township population 60

This little burg's Gay Bar is has become a must stop on the south shore of the Keweenaw Peninsula on Keweenaw Bay. Opens at lunchtime during the week and Saturdays. Everyone should have a souvenir T-shirt or cap. To find Gay, catch South Shore Drive from M-26/U.S.-41 out of Fulton-Mohawk. This is an excellent alternate scenic route to Lac La Belle past Point Isabelle.

Gay's annual Fourth of July Parade is a fun event for upward of 4,000 viewers in the area. Lasting from four to 15 minutes, the "just for fun" parade starts promptly at 2 p.m. on Main Street. It's reported that the old smokestack nearby actually billows smoke for the event.

WHAT'S NEXT

If you're heading up the Keweenaw, the route from Gay to Lac La Belle along Lake Superior is a marvelous experience, through heavily wooded forests and then, closer to Point Isabelle, right beside the water. You'll pass through a nice year-round residential grouping of homes called Little Betsy at Betsy Bay. If traveling southward, you can continue to Highway 26 just north of Lake Linden, or follow South Shore Drive to Fulton-Mohawk to rejoin Highway 26/41.

Grand Marais

Population 450

The quaint village of Grand Marais (Mah-ray) is snuggled in a natural harbor. You'll find it by taking Michigan Highway 77 north from M-28 at Seney. An alternate route preferred by many travelers is to catch Highway 58 to the west in Munising and travel about 40 miles through Pictured Rocks National Lakeshore (see listing under Pictured Rocks).

There are docks, a lighthouse, a park and a scattering of shops and delicious restaurants. The site first served as a harbor of refuge for early voyageurs and was settled as a fishing village. It later served as the sawmill headquarters site for the huge Alger Smith Lumber Company, which logged as far away as Seney, Germfask and Curtis and operated the 78-mile Manistique Railroad to serve its camps and mill. The county is named for General Russell Alger, a partner in the company, who served as governor and senator for Michigan and was secretary of war during the Spanish-American War.

This small town is a hotbed of journalistic efforts as two newspapers, *Grand Marais Gazette* (focusing on "hard" news) and the *Great Lakes and Grand Marais Pilot* (with more of an eye to history) both operate here.

WHAT TO SEE AND DO

Grand Marais hosts the historic Pickle Barrel House, given to the town by Bill Donahey, creator of the "Teenie Weenies" comic strip from the 1920s and '30s. The Grand Marais Historical Society had the cottage restored to its original condition.

NOTABLE MUSEUMS

The Grand Marais Historical Museum, next to the pier, features local history. A monument to area commercial fishermen is adjacent.

The Grand Marais Maritime Museum is run by Pictured Rocks National Lakeshore.

The new museum of Grand Marais history is in the newly renovated, five-sided Old Post Office, which served as the Grand Marais Post Office for more than 70 years.

NOTABLE EVENTS

• The town hosts the Great Lakes Sea Kayak Symposium and its annual Fly-In in July and the Grand Marais Music Festival in August.

WHAT'S NEXT

To leave Grand Marais, take either M-77 south to pick up M-28 at Seney or catch H-58 to the west and the Pictured Rocks.

INFO & OPTIONS

Grand Marais Chamber of Commerce
P.O. Box 139
Grand Marais, MI 49839-0139
906-494-2447
www.grandmaraismichigan.com

Au Sable Light Station just west of Grand Marais at Pictured Rocks National Lakeshore is open in the summer. Visitors go to the top of the 87-foot lighthouse to see the 6-foot-high Fresnel lens and get a great view of the lake. (Gregg Bruff / National Park Service)

Grand Sable Visitor Center
East 21090 County Rd. H-58
Grand Marais, MI 49839
www.nps.gov/piro

Woodland Park Campground
906-494-2613 (April-October)
www.grandmaraismichigan.com

Greenland

Population 160

At the junction of M-38 with M-26 southeast of Ontonagon, pause at the community of Greenland for an excellent tour of one of Copper Country's historic underground mines. Adventure Mine has been the site of mining activity for 5,000 years or more, but hit the big time during the mid-1800s copper boom. Adventure Mining Company is operated by Matthew and Victoria Portfleet and offers a variety of extensive guided underground and surface tours, with a wide panorama of forests and countryside from one of the mine's adits (openings) high on a "backdoor" hillside as a bonus during the tour. Knowledgeable guides bring the history and 1800s' mining technology to life as they lead the way through the drifts (shafts) and stopes (rooms) of the mine. A gift shop offers handcrafted copper items. Adventure Mine is open late May through mid-October.

Gulliver

Population 840

A must-stop just a bit off the highway at Gulliver and past McDonald Lake is the 1895 Seul Choix Point Lighthouse Museum, which maritime historian Frederick Stonehouse rates as one of the most haunted sites on the Great Lakes. Once dilapidated but now restored, Seul Choix (locally pronounced SIS-Shwa) is said to be haunted by a cigar-smoking ghost of a former keeper, along with other "shades of the past." Museum personnel are comfortable discussing ghostly encounters and can point to any number of phenomena and recordings documenting the haunts.

What's Next

Gulliver is in the central southern Upper Peninsula on U.S. Highway 2, which follows an east-west track around Lake Michigan's northern shoreline. Traveling Highway 2 west from Gulliver, the shoreline city of Manistique offers a good selection of lodging facilities, including several state and private campgrounds, motels, resorts and bed-and-breakfast inns, and dining for whatever your taste may be. If traveling east, you'll pass through a number of small towns while heading for St. Ignace and the Mackinac Bridge.

Hancock

Population 4,325

Hancock is on the upper side of the Portage Lift Bridge that connects the city to Houghton. In a nod to Hancock's sizable Finnish community, some street signs are in both English and Finnish.

Hancock is smaller than its twin across Portage Lake, but it has good shopping on Quincy Street. Part of the downtown is on the National Register of Historic Places. A brochure at many locations guides you along historic streets and past significant buildings and classic homes.

This is the home of Finlandia University, the only Finnish university in America. On campus is the Finnish-American Heritage Center, housed in a remodeled Catholic church built in 1885. Inside is a museum, art gallery and theater. Open weekdays. North Wind

Books is also at the university. Open year-round, Monday through Saturday.

All of the shopping is within walking distance from the 54-slip, full-service Houghton County Marina on the Waterway in Hancock. Lovers of copper artworks will want to visit Eric Walli's Copper Arts Studio just north of the Quincy Mine Hoist on U.S. 41.

What to See and Do

Copper Country Community Arts Council on Quincy Street features three galleries with monthly exhibits and classes. Open Tuesday through Saturday.

In winter, take advantage of Mont Ripley ski hill, which long served as the only alpine ski facility in the Keweenaw, but is now joined by Mount Bohemia Ski Hill at Lac La Belle. (No beginners are allowed on Mount Bohemia.)

On U.S. 41 heading north, stop at the roadside park on Quincy Hill, which overlooks Hancock, Houghton and the deep valley of the Keweenaw Waterway.

A quarter-mile north on U.S. 41 is Quincy Mine and tours of the Nordberg, the largest steam hoist ever built. It operated from 1921 to the mid-1930s, lowering and raising men and copper from the 9,260-foot-deep (2,822-meter; 1.5- mile) shafts, at a maximum speed of 3,200 feet (975 meters) per minute, or 36.4 miles per hour. An inclined cog-railway tram shuttles visitors to one of the old copper mines for visits to the underground diggings. Also displayed is a 17-ton copper boulder discovered in Lake Superior off the Keweenaw and a G-scale model railroad. Incredibly detailed, it won the Bert Boyum Historic Preservation Award. Open late April to late October. Fee.

Notable Museums

Pewabik House and Museum on Hancock Street is a resource on the history of the area and the life and work of potter Mary Chase Stratton (founder of Pewabic Pottery).

Notable Events

• Hancock hosts the Heikinpaiva Mid-Winter Festival in mid-January.

• Bridgefest and the Keweenaw Chain Drive Festival are held in mid-June.

• Keweenaw Trail Running Festival challenges competitors in wonderful surroundings in July.

• Houghton County Fair occurs near the end of August.

What's Next

Beyond Houghton/Hancock, the Keweenaw Peninsula offers hikers trails of varying length and difficulty in sanctuaries owned and managed by the Michigan Nature Association. Head north on U.S. 41 from the Quincy Hill park to pass numerous abandoned mine sites and ghost towns. The area is designated as Keweenaw National Historical Park, established to preserve the area's mining history and traditions. For details, contact the park (906-337-3168) in Calumet on Red Jacket Road or the Keweenaw Convention and Visitors Bureau on U.S. Highway 41 between Calumet and Laurium.

Going north from Hancock, there's an alternate route heading into the Keweenaw Peninsula proper. Take M-26 to the east through Ripley, Dollar Bay, Hubbell and Lake Linden on the way to Laurium. Dollar Bay is home to Horner Flooring, the world's top producer of wooden basketball and dance floors. Tours for groups available. At Hubbell, where the famed Calumet and Hecla Copper Company

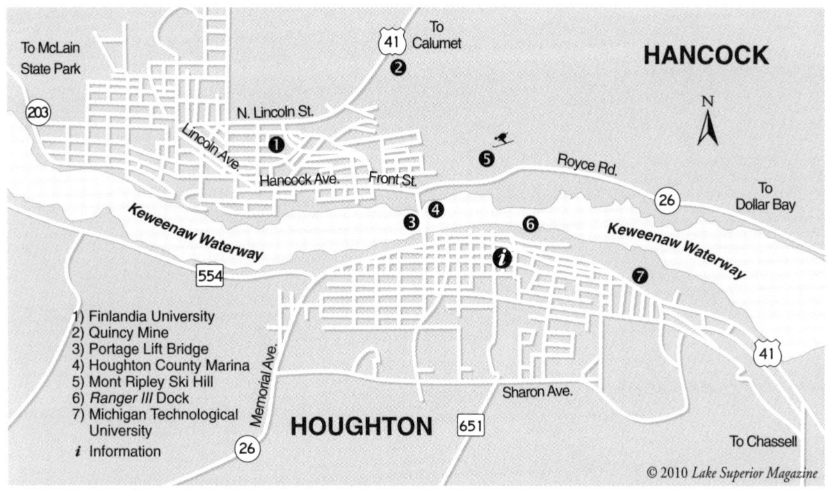

processed its copper ore, take Sixth Street and several turns to Upper and Lower Hungarian Falls. Trails rated: moderate.

INFO & OPTIONS

Gemignani's Italian Restaurant
512 West Quincy St.
Hancock, MI 49930
906-482-2920
www.gemignani.com

Best Western Copper Crown Motel
235 Hancock St.
Hancock, MI 49930
800-925-7144
www.bestwesternmichigan.com

Ramada Inn Waterfront
99 Navy St.
Hancock, MI 49930
877-482-8400
www.ramadahancock.com

Hancock Recreational Boating & Camping Facility
On M-203, 1 mile west of Hancock
906-482-7413 or 906-482-2720
www.cityofhancock.com

F.J. McLain State Park
Rt. 1 Box 82, M-203
Hancock, MI 49930
906-482-0278

Helmer

Township Population 900

South on H-33 from Seney on the M-28 Circle Route, Helmer is home to a fascinating historic bed-and-breakfast inn and restaurant that you'll want to put on your agenda. Originally the Helmer House was the home of a Presbyterian minister and eventually became a general store and hotel. After renovation in 1982, it has become a favorite destination for those who want to escape the cares of the world. Five rooms are available. The restaurant specializes in fresh-caught whitefish. One of Lake Superior's Best. Open May through October.

Helmer is also the gateway city to the Manistique chain of lakes, with plenty of recreational opportunities.

The quarter-mile-long Portage Lift Bridge across the Keweenaw water way links Houghton with Hancock, on the right, and is a landmark of the two cities.

Hermansville

Township Population 1,050

On Highway 2 about midway between Escanaba and Iron Mountain, keep an eye out for Hermansville to visit the IXL Historic Museum, housed in the 1882 headquarters building of the Wisconsin Land and Lumber Company. Rooms of elegant period furnishings, wonderfully elaborate woodwork, pictures, records and tools of the 1880s document the time when IXL Hardwood Flooring Company revolutionized the lumber industry and became the largest hardwood flooring manufacturer in the country. A National Register of Historic Places site, it's open Memorial Day through Labor Day. Fee.

Houghton

Population 6,630

Houghton is the largest city in the Keweenaw Peninsula and all of Copper Country. It is accessed on highways U.S. 41 or Michigan 26 north from Highway 28. (See city in Hancock listing.)

A Bit of History

The word "Keweenaw" is said to mean "portage" in Ojibway. Portage Lake always provided a natural water pathway across most of the Keweenaw Peninsula, but the complete water path was blocked at the north end by a rocky highland that required a portage. This is what was called Keweenaw. In the late 1800s, a canal was opened through this area, connecting Lake Superior with itself and creating a shortcut for lake vessel shipping. In essence, most of the Keweenaw Peninsula became an island above the completed waterway.

Here in the heart of Copper Country, King Copper as they call it, copper has been found throughout the western end of Upper Michigan and into the Keweenaw from earliest times. There's a copper color in almost everything. Copper has been responsible for much of the prosperity that the region has experienced. From 1870 to 1910, this was considered one of the wealthiest regions of North America. All copper mining activity, with the exception of the Copper Range Company at White Pine to the southwest, ceased decades ago. Today, tourism is a major economic factor in the area.

What to See and Do

Houghton is home to the 7,000-student Michigan Technological University. U.S. 41 cuts through the campus. MTU's world-class A.E. Seaman Mineral Museum displays about 30,000 specimens of rocks and gemstones from around the world. It has excellent exhibits and an extensive archive of minerals located on the fifth floor of the Electronic Energy Resources Center building. Handicapped accessible.

Come in the winter for Michigan Tech's Winter Carnival with snow statues in early February. The Keweenaw Symphony Orchestra at MTU plays in the $20 million Rozsa (Roh-zay) Center for the Performing Arts. Featuring the largest stage north of Midland, Michigan, the stage seats a full orchestra. It features nationally recognized performers. Also at Michigan Tech, J.R. Van Pelt Library houses the Copper Country Archives, an important resource for scholars.

The city's Nara Park trails have been linked with the Michigan Tech University trail system – formally called Recreational Forest & Nordic Ski Trails – to provide a total of 35 kilometers of trails. The linkup was completed in 2008, with specific posted trail segments for mountain biking and cross-country skiing or snowshoeing in winter. The trails are open to hikers when free of snow; and look for certain trails that even allow dogs (best to check in advance). Also new is the city chalet building that's open year-round off Highway 41 at the Pilgrim River east of Houghton at the Nara Nature Center. Not only does it offer a place to warm up, but it contains showers and changing rooms. Trail maps and other details are available through Michigan Tech's website. Other improvements to the MTU nordic trails include the addition of 7 kilometers of lighted trails, and efforts have been made to help people with disabilities enjoy the trails.

The double-decker, quarter-mile-long Portage Lift Bridge joins Houghton and the Circle Tour with Hancock and the rest of the peninsula at Portage Lake. Completed in 1959, it is believed to be the heaviest lift bridge in the world and is certainly the largest lift bridge on Lake Superior, surpassing even the Duluth Aerial Bridge. In Michigan, it is second only to the Mackinac Bridge for largest bridge honors. The upper level is a four-lane highway, and the lower level is a rail bridge. The span is raised and lowered like an elevator for passing watercraft. Average openings per year is 700. A Bridgefest Celebration is held annually on Father's Day weekend, complete with parade, races, dances, seafood and more.

For opera, symphonic and chamber music, the Upper Peninsula's annual Pine Mountain Music Festival in June and July engages world-class artists to perform in and around Houghton, Hancock, Calumet, Lake Linden, Iron Mountain, Marquette and Land O' Lakes. The festival has been feted in articles in major newspapers, including London's *Financial Times*, and has won Michigan's top arts awards.

Houghton is headquarters for Isle Royale National Park and its *Ranger III*, which twice weekly ferries visitors to Rock Harbor on the nation's first island national park. Books about the park are available at the visitor center. (See separate Isle Royale National Park listing and the Copper Harbor, Michigan, listing.)

Keweenaw Water Trail Association has developed maps and associated information for silent watercraft boating along the waterway and around the Keweenaw Peninsula. Contact the association through the Keweenaw Convention and Visitors Bureau in Calumet.

Portage Lake Golf Course is on U.S. 41 south of Houghton, offering an18-hole challenge.

Where to Shop

Shopping in downtown Houghton means moving among quaint shops, with always a surprise a few steps on. The downtown is accessible in all kinds of weather through its skyways, which bridge between buildings. Stop in at Down Wind Sports on Shelden Avenue for great outdoor accessories. Surplus Outlet has something for the adventurer in you.

On Memorial Drive, the Keweenaw Gem and Gift shop has marvelous examples of local gems. Its building simulates a "headhouse," the structure covering the top of a mine shaft. The Copper Country Mall has a collection of stores for those who feel the urge to splurge.

What's Next

Across the Portage Lift Bridge, Hancock sits nicely on the hill overlooking Houghton and the waterway.

North on U.S. 41, the Keweenaw Peninsula beckons travelers with its wonderful scenery and interesting activities. Southbound travelers can take U.S. 41 to a junction with Michigan Highway 28 to travel either east or west. Southwest from town, M-26 is the logical route for those traveling westerly on the Circle Tour deeper into Copper Country, winding through Atlantic Mine, South Range, Trimountain and Painesdale, villages surviving the closing of their copper mines. The Copper Range Historical Museum is in South Range in the old bank. Open Monday through Saturday, June to mid-October. Just off M-26 at Painesdale, the restored Painesdale Mine and Shaft offers tours of the hoist and shaft house by appointment.

Twin Lakes State Park (Roland and Gerald lakes) offers 175 acres of heavily wooded wilderness, with campgrounds, hiking, fishing, swimming and boating. Admission by park permit. Play the 9-hole Wyandotte Hills Golf Course, where Wyandotte Hills Resort also offers new resort cabins for visitors. Another quiet place to stay, with a good sand beach, is under the pines at Twin Lakes Resort. Nearby is Krupp's Resort, which also has cottages.

After Winona, the Circle Tour enters Big Snow Country, turning toward the lake and Ontonagon at M-38.

INFO & OPTIONS

Keweenaw Peninsula Chamber of Commerce

902 College Ave.
Houghton, MI 49931
866-304-5722
www.keweenaw.org

Isle Royale National Park

800 East Lakeshore Dr.
Houghton, MI 49931-1896
906-482-0984
www.nps.gov/isro

Ranger III, the official National Park Service vessel servicing Isle Royale National Park, is based in Houghton and takes passengers and freight to the islands.

Isle Royale Natural History Association
800 East Lakeshore Dr.
Houghton, MI 49931
800-678-6925
www.irnha.org

The Ambassador
126 Shelden Ave.
Houghton, MI 49931-2132
906-482-5054

Kaleva Café
234 Quincy St.
Houghton, MI 49931
906-482-6001

The Library Bar and Restaurant
52 North Isle Royale St.
Houghton, MI 49931
906-487-5882

North Shore Grill & Pub
820 Shelden Ave.–7th floor
Houghton, MI 49931
906-482-4882
www.northshoregrill.com

Suomi Home Bakery & Restaurant
54 North Huron St.
Houghton, MI 49931
906-482-3220

Best Western Franklin Square Inn
820 Shelden Ave.
Houghton, MI 49931
888-487-1700
www.houghtonlodging.com

Budget Host Inn
46995 U.S. Hwy. 41
Houghton, MI 49931-9019
906-482-5351
www.bhihoughton.com

Country Inn & Suites
919 Razorback Dr.
Houghton, MI 49931
800-596-2375
www.countryinns.com

Isle Royale National Park
800 East Lakeshore Dr.
Houghton, MI 49931-1896
906-482-0984
www.nps.gov/isro

Isle Royale Natural History Association
800 East Lakeshore Dr.
Houghton, MI 49931
800-678-6925
www.irnha.org

Rock Harbor Lodge (Summer season)
P.O. Box 605
Houghton, MI 49931
906-337-4993

City of Houghton RV Park
West Lakeshore Dr.
Houghton, MI 49931
906-482-8745, 906-482-1700
www.cityofhoughton.com

North Canal Township Park
Houghton Canal Rd.
Houghton, MI 49931
906-482-8319

Iron Mountain

Population 8,525

Iron Mountain snuggles into a large bend of the Menominee River that forms the boundary between Michigan and Wisconsin. Like a mother hen with chicks, a number of smaller towns in both Wisconsin and Michigan surround Iron Mountain.

The city offers a good selection of lodging (especially on Stephenson Avenue) and dining and is interesting for the number of good museums and visitor sites.

You are well away from the shores of both Lake Superior and Lake Michigan at this point on Highway 2 in the southern Upper Peninsula. Nearby iron ore mines once fostered an abundant economy here, but that boom ended decades ago. Although the mines are long since depleted, many of the small communities you pass were mining locations where the families of employees lived, worked and did most of their day-to-day business.

Before leaving Iron Mountain, shoppers should check out the various antique, gift and specialty stores for that perfect gift from the north country.

What to See and Do

The city is home to the Festival of the Arts for eight weekends of music, drama, art and dance from mid-June to mid-August. Some of the events are sponsored by Pine Mountain Music Festival and scheduled at the Community Performing Arts Center on East B Street. The Dickinson County Council for the Arts is an umbrella for many artistic and performing events.

Pine Mountain Ski Jump is ranked as the "world's highest artificial ski jump" (as opposed to Copper Peak's claim as the highest artificial ski slide, where ski flying is performed).

Timber Stone Golf Course is ranked as a premier 18-hole challenge by *Michigan Golfer Magazine* and offers golf packages through a number of local lodging facilities. There are nine other golf courses of varying degrees of difficulty within easy commuting distance.

Notable Museums

The Cornish Pump Museum houses the largest mine pump ever built. Located west of U.S. 2 on Kent Street, it is open daily, Memorial Day to Labor Day, with reduced hours in spring and fall. Small entry fee.

Menominee Range Historical Foundation Museum has more than 100 exhibits that document mining and other aspects of early days in the area. Monday-Saturday, Memorial Day to Labor Day. Entry fee.

What's Next

Continue on your southern Upper Peninsula trip either to the west by departing on Highway 2/141, which enters Wisconsin for a brief sojourn just west of Iron Mountain and passes through two small towns, the interestingly named Spread Eagle and Florence, before re-entering Michigan in Iron County. If traveling east on Highway 2, you'll quickly spy Kingsford, Norway and Vulcan on your way to Escanaba and an encounter with the northern leg of the Lake Michigan Circle Tour route.

Just east of Iron Mountain on Highway 2, a roadside park at Quinnesec has tables, toilets and water and gives a nice view of Fumee Falls.

If time allows, pause in Norway at the Jake Menghini Historical Museum, housed in a historic log cabin that once served as a carriage stopping point. Displaying artifacts from Jake's personal collection, as well as exhibits that change yearly, the museum is free of charge, although donations are accepted. Open Memorial Day through the Saturday prior to Columbus Day in October. Also at Norway, waterfall aficionados can check out Piers Gorge, where white water tumbles over a 10-foot falls and roars wildly through canyon walls. It is among the fastest moving water flows in the state.

In Vulcan, plan to take an underground train tour at the Iron Mountain Iron Mine, where you'll travel 2,600 feet (792 meters) through the drifts and stopes (tunnels and roomlike areas) of the mine.

INFO & OPTIONS

Dickinson County Chamber of Commerce – Iron Mountain
600 South Stephenson Ave.
Iron Mountain, MI 49801
906-774-2002
www.dickinsonchamber.com

Upper Peninsula Travel and Recreation Association
P.O. Box 400
Iron Mountain, MI 49801
800-562-7134
www.uptravel.com

Dobber's Pasties
1402 South Stephenson Ave.
Iron Mountain, MI 49801
906-774-9323
www.dobberspasties.com

Comfort Inn of Iron Mountain
1565 North Stephenson Ave.
Iron Mountain, MI 49801
906-774-5505
www.comfortinn.com

Executive Inn Iron Mountain Motel
1518 South Stephenson Ave.
Iron Mountain, MI 49801

Pine Mountain Hotel & Resort
North 3332 Pine Mountain Rd.
Iron Mountain, MI 49801
877-553-7463
www.pinemountainresort.com

Iron River

Population 2,425

Another hen-and-chick community on Highway 2 in the southwestern Upper Peninsula along with the Iron Mountain area, Iron River is surrounded by the former mining locations of Gaastra, Caspian, Stambaugh and Mineral Hills. Here winter travelers will find wonderful terrain for snowmobiling, cross-country skiing and other outdoor cool weather recreation.

Accommodations range from camping to deluxe American-plan resorts.

What to See and Do

Downhill skiers will want to check out Ski Brule. A number of year-round resorts and lodging facilities are located on trails or within minutes of a good starting point for a day of outdoor fun.

Iron River is the home of the U.P. Championship Rodeo, which has been held each July since 1967.

West of Iron River is Ottawa National Forest, a huge chunk of the western U.P. set aside for multiple use. Ottawa Visitor Center in Watersmeet can give information on its 27 campgrounds, hiking and biking, fishing, canoeing, hunting or other recreational activity in this scenic area. Southwest of Watersmeet, the 19,000-acre Sylvania Wilderness Area and Sylvania Recreation Area provide more opportunities for outdoor recreation.

Notable Museums

Iron County Historical Museum in nearby Caspian features 20 pioneer buildings reflecting logging, mining and transportation. Nearby Lee LeBlanc Wildlife Art Gallery has more than 200 works. The Midwest's oldest steel headframe (the structure above the shaft attached to the lifting equipment) towers over the site, which includes 100 major exhibits and the largest miniature logging exhibit in the world. Open June through September daily. Fee.

INFO & OPTIONS

Iron County Chamber of Commerce
50 East Genesee St.
Iron River, MI 59935
906-265-3822
www.iron.org

Americinn Motel & Suites
40 East Adams St.
Iron River, MI 49935
800-396-5007 (Reservations)
www.americinn.com/hotels/MI/IronRiver

Ironwood

Population 6,295

Ironwood was founded on iron mining. Called the Western Gateway City to the Upper Peninsula, Ironwood sports a Michigan Visitor Center on the U.S. 2 Circle Tour route at the state border with Wisconsin at the Montreal River, with tons of brochures, travel information and complete rest facilities.

What to See and Do

Downtown on Houk Street, a 52-foot (16-metre), 16,000-pound fiberglass statue of Hiawatha in formal headdress holds his peace pipe, extending a hand of welcome over the city and the great "Gitche Gumee." In an area near the statue are several mining artifacts, with an informational plaque describing them.

The renovated Ironwood Theatre (circa 1928) and the Gogebic Range Players offer community theater productions throughout the year. The theater also offers a schedule of varied entertainment. It is on the National Register of Historic Places.

Notable Museums

Old Depot Park Museum, in the railroad depot downtown, is operated by Ironwood Area Historical Society. Open afternoons, Memorial Day through Labor Day. No fee, but donations welcome.

Notable Events

• Gogebic County Airport Fly-In in June gives non-pilots a chance to see neat airplanes and get to know the pilots.

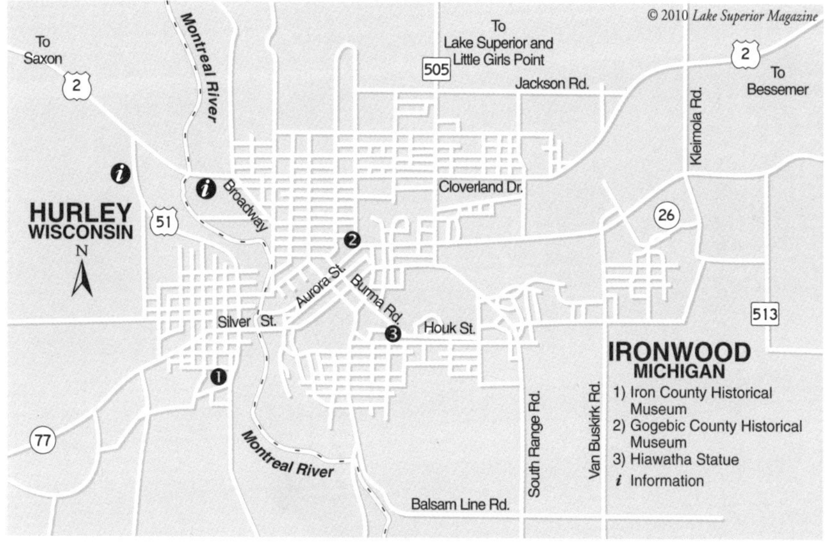

Ironwood, Michigan & Hurley, Wisconsin

• Upper Lakes Renaissance Faire in July is a fun event based on the Middle Ages.

• Festival Ironwood in July celebrates the heritage and history of the city.

• Gogebic County Fair is held in August at the fairgrounds in the western edge of the city.

• Jack Frost Festival of Lights Parade is the traditional kickoff of the holiday season in early December.

What's Next

Ironwood's twin city, across the state border of Wisconsin and Michigan, is Hurley, Wisconsin, (see separate listing) which is part of Big Snow Country, and just over the Montreal River Bridge on Highway 2. If your route takes you east, you'll follow U.S. 2 through Bessemer to Wakefield, where you have the option of following the Lake Superior Circle Route on Michigan 28 or on Highway 2 for a trip through the southern Upper Peninsula.

A more attractive route is to follow the alternate Lake Superior Circle Tour sign at Lake Street, traveling 17 miles (27 kilometers) north of Ironwood on County Road 505 to Little Girls Point, named for an Ojibway girl who died there in the 1800s. A sweeping lake view can be seen from this elevated point, which is in County Park and Campgrounds. Just before the border on the Michigan side (5.5 measured miles from Little Girls Point), an unmarked cutoff toward the lake affords a spectacular view of Superior Falls on the Montreal River as it falls toward the lake. When the morning sun is right, this spot is ideal for pictures. The lower trail leads to a cliff overlooking Lake Superior. A rather steep trail takes hikers to the river's mouth, but it's tough to climb back up. Rated: difficult.

From here you can continue west on County Road 505, which joins Wisconsin 122 near Saxon Harbor and picks up Highway 2 at Saxon, or you can backtrack to Ironwood to continue east.

The wacky Da Yoopers outside Ishpeming, with its many oversized displays, celebrates U.P. (Yooper) wit and culture. The self-proclaimed tourist trap must be visited tongue in cheek.

INFO & OPTIONS

Ironwood Chamber of Commerce
Old Depot Museum
150 North Lowell St.
Ironwood, MI 49938
906-932-1122
www.ironwoodmi.org

Ironwood Tourism Council
648 West Cloverland Dr.
Ironwood, MI 49938
906-932-1000

Ottawa National Forest Information
East 6248 U.S. Hwy. 2
Ironwood, MI 49938
906-932-1330
www.fs.fed.us

Western U.P. Convention and Visitors Bureau
P.O. Box 706
Ironwood, MI 49938
800-522-5657
www.westernup.info

Don and G.G.'s Food and Spirits
1300 East Cloverland Dr.
Ironwood, MI 49938
906-932-2312

Elk and Hound
North 10233 Country Club Rd.
Ironwood, MI 49938
906-932-3742

Joe's Pasty Shop
930 East Cloverland Dr. and 116 West Aurora St.
Ironwood, MI 49938
906-932-4412
www.joespastyshop.com

AmericInn Motel and Suites
1117 East Cloverland Dr.
Ironwood, MI 49938
800-396-5007
www.americinn.com

America's Best Value Inn – Ironwood
160 East Cloverland Dr.
Ironwood, MI 49938
906-932-3395
www.americasbestvalueinn.com

Curry Park
U.S. Hwy. 2/West Cloverland Dr.
Ironwood, MI 49938
906-932-5050

Ishpeming

Population 6,685

In Ojibway, the name of the iron mining city Ishpeming means "on high ground" or "in heaven." This is the heart of the Marquette Iron Range, the only range in the Upper Peninsula still producing iron ore. Architecture reflects the days of mine captains and miners.

What to See and Do

Tilden Iron Ore Mine offers tours June through August, Tuesday-Saturday, leaving the Marquette Chamber office at noon, and the Ishpeming-Negaunee Chamber office at 12:30 p.m. Reservations needed.

A cast-iron statue of a Native American man stands on an island at converging streets in the small downtown business district. Known locally as "Old Ish," the statue is a favorite of residents, keeping watch over the city since 1884.

Al Quaal Recreation Area in North Ishpeming offers year-round outdoor activities, with a 1,500-foot (457-meter) iced toboggan run, downhill and more than 18k of cross-country skiing, some lighted for night skiing or snowshoeing. Summer choices of tennis, hiking, swimming or canoeing on Teal Lake.

Notable Museums

Ishpeming is an appropriate site for the U.S. National Ski and Snowboard Hall of Fame and Museum. Skiing in America was born here when Scandinavian miners brought the sport along when they came to work the mines. Inductions held annually. On U.S. 41 between Second and Third streets. Open Monday through Saturday year-round. Free. This is home to the Ishpeming-Negaunee Chamber of Commerce and Information Center.

Iron Range Mining Heritage Theme Park is in a former mine building on Euclid Street. One eye-catching exhibit is a slab of native copper 6 feet tall and 3 feet wide.

Where to Shop

Ishpeming-Negaunee offer virtually anything a shopper needs, from groceries, convenience items, gifts and souvenirs to gas and vehicle servicing. Nearby, Marquette to the east is certain to be able to fill all needs.

Downtown, the historic Butler Theatre has been extensively renovated and hosts antique dealers that each feature a distinct line of products. The interior of the 90-year-old Butler Theatre Antique Mall building replicates the art deco wall flowers and retro floor of the original theater, and the products will entice antique enthusiasts.

Da Yoopers Tourist Trap and Museum outside of Ishpeming will improve your mood. Recording artists Da Yoopers are headquartered at You Guys Records in Ishpeming. Their satirical, bawdy hits include "Second Week of Deer Camp," "Rusty Chevrolet" and "Smelting U.S.A." Their gift shop and separate rock shop reflects their "different" outlook on life and highly questionable taste, but we still love it.

Notable Events

- Noquemanon Cross-Country Ski Race in late January challenges skiers in the area where American skiing was born.
- Pioneer Days in early July celebrates the history and heritage of this multi-ethnic area.
- Renaissance Festival in late July is a romp that celebrates the Middle Ages.
- Ore to Shore Mountain Bike Epic in early August has pedallers vying for honors in awesome surroundings.

INFO & OPTIONS

Ishpeming-Negaunee Chamber of Commerce
Marquette County/Ishpeming Office
119 West Division St.
Ishpeming, MI 49849
888-578-6489
www.marquette.org

Country Kitchen
850 U.S. Hwy. 41
Ishpeming, MI 49849
906-486-1074
www.countryvillageresort.com

Jasper Ridge Brewery
1075 Country Ln.
Ishpeming, MI 49849
906-485-6017
www.countryvillageresort.com

Best Western Country Inn
850 U.S. Hwy. 41 West
Ishpeming, MI 49849
800-780-7234
www.bestwesternmichigan.com

Jasper Ridge Inn & Vacation Homes
1000 River Pkwy.
Ishpeming, MI 49849
866-875-4312
www.countryvillageresort.com

Country Village Resort
1200 Country Ln.
Ishpeming, MI 49849
906-486-0300
www.countryvillageresort.com

Squaw Lake State Forest Campground
4 miles northwest of Witch Lake
906-346-9201

Isle Royale National Park

Copper Harbor and Houghton, Michigan, and Grand Portage, Minnesota (see individual listings), are the three departure points to Isle Royale National Park, the largest island in Lake Superior. The *Isle Royale Queen IV* makes round trips to the island from mid-May to late-September. Reservations are required. The National Park Service operates the double-decked *Ranger III* from Houghton during summer, departing on Tuesdays and Fridays and returning the following day.

Isle Royale National Park is 50 miles (80 kilometers) from Upper Michigan's Copper Country and 18 miles (29 kilometers) from the nearest point on the Minnesota shore. The island is about 45 miles long (72 kilometers) and 9 miles wide (14 kilometers), a land area of 210 square miles (544 square kilometers). It became a national park in 1940 and is one of five National Park Service sites on Lake Superior. The island is closed November 1 and reopens in April.

Isle Royale is classified as a "national biosphere." To protect native wildlife, no pets are allowed. This is strictly enforced. There are no roads or private vehicles on the island, but parking is available at embarkation points on the mainland.

Isle Royale National Park charges user fees for adults; children 12 and younger are free. Isle Royale can be a day trip, but plan to stay for a few days. Most people hike and camp; there are more than 160 miles of trails and many campgrounds. Sturdy hiking shoes and rain gear are a must for any trip to Isle Royale. And bring a camera. The island's population of moose, wolves, beaver, fox and other wildlife is sure to make your visit worthwhile. Trout fishing among Isle Royale's reefs can yield some lunkers.

Unless you intend to camp or arrive in your own boat, you will need to stay at Rock Harbor Lodge on the shore of Rock

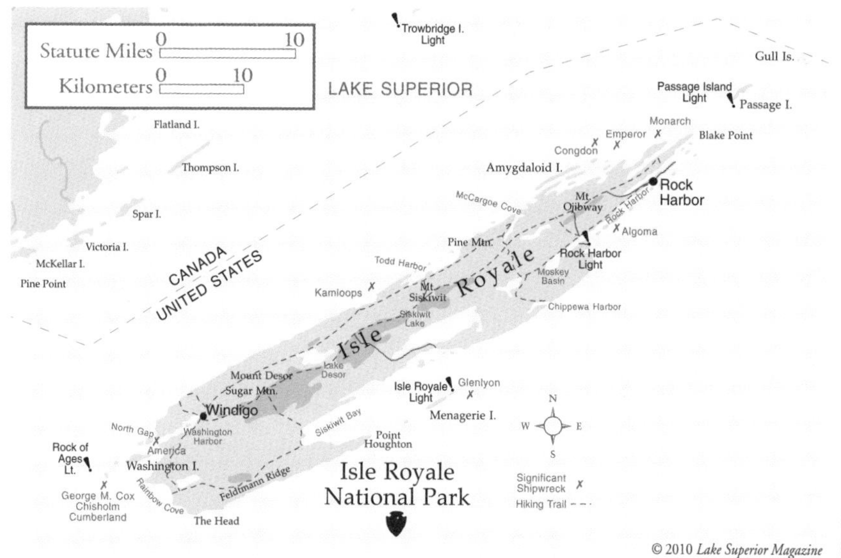

Isle Royale National Park

Harbor. Make reservations before you go. Open late May to early September, the lodge has a gift shop, dining room and marina store. Laundry and showers are available, as are fishing tackle, charters, sightseeing tours and gear from the concessionaire, Forever Resorts.

Boats up to 65 feet (20 meters) can be accommodated at the Rock Harbor Marina with 450 feet (137 meters) of dock space. Fuels, AC electrical, pump-out and freshwater hookups are available, as are boat and canoe rentals, by the day or week, and fishing charters.

Windigo at Washington Harbor on the southwestern end of Isle Royale is a perfect starting point for camping, hiking or trout fishing. There are no overnight facilities at Windigo, but campsites are available on Washington Creek. A grocery has cold sandwiches, freeze-dried foods, canned goods and soft drinks. Fishing tackle, licenses, laundry and showers available.

Royale Air Service offers flights from Houghton to Rock Harbor and Windigo by float plane.

On the island, cruises and walks visit Lookout Louise, Daisy Farm, Rock Harbor Lighthouse and Edisen Fishery, Passage Island and Raspberry Island.

Isle Royale is a popular destination for scuba divers. Among the more noteworthy wrecks in this underwater preserve are the *America, Emperor, Cox, Kamloops, Algoma, Congdon* and *Monarch*. Isle Royale and Keweenaw Parks Association, at park headquarters in Houghton and with Windigo and Rock Harbor stores, offers park-related books.

Lac La Belle

Township Population 175

Although technically not on the Circle Tour route, we recommend taking wonderfully scenic South Shore Drive at Mohawk through Gay and Point Betsy to visit Lac La Belle. If you're driving U.S. 41 farther north on the Keweenaw Peninsula, turn east just north of Delaware for the 5-mile (8-kilometer) trip to Lac La Belle.

Nearby are the remains of an old stamp mill used to crush copper-bearing rock from nearby mines in the 1800s. It is here that the first electricity in Keweenaw County was used – to light the Lac La Belle stamp mill. This is a major bird migration flyway in April and May.

In the winter, the area is a favorite destination for skiers and snowmobilers and 270 inches of average snowfall per winter nearly guarantees excellent conditions for any type of outdoor winter activity.

What to See and Do

Lac La Belle is especially scenic in autumn, when the multicolored hillsides around the lake catch the sun and reflect in the water.

At Lac La Belle, stop at the easily accessible Haven Falls in Haven Park, with a drop of 38 feet (11.5 meters).

Near Lac La Belle, Mt. Bohemia has been developed into a major midwestern downhill ski facility that is billed as "the Rocky Mountains of the Midwest." Its 900-foot (274-metre) vertical drop, steep terrain, gladed runs and even cliffs provide a westernlike ski and snowboard experience unlike anything else in the Midwest. Slope difficulty ranges from intermediate to expert, but with no beginner hill. The resort has a limited number of ski-in, ski-out cabins.

Parks and Public Areas

Three miles beyond the village of Lac La Belle is Bete Grise (BAY-ta GREE), location of the breakwater and harbor entrance to Lac La Belle (the lake) through the Mendota Ship Canal. The old Mendota Lighthouse has been extensively restored and is privately owned.

Keystone Bay is part of the Keweenaw Underwater Preserve, a 103-square-mile area that protects the waters and shipwrecks around the peninsula.

In December 1989, the U.S. Coast Guard cutter *Mesquite* went aground off Keweenaw Point. In July 1990, the 180-foot (55-metre) vessel was removed from the hazardous reefs, moved about 2 miles to the southeast of Keweenaw Point and then sunk in Keystone Bay in 80 to 120 feet (24-37 meters) of water. Today, the vessel is an underwater attraction, the perfect shipwreck for the curious scuba diver.

Other vessels in the Keweenaw Underwater Preserve include the *Langham* at Bete Grise, *Scotia* at Keweenaw Point, *Wasaga* at Copper Harbor, *City of St. Joe* at Little Grand Marais Harbor, *Traveller* at Eagle Harbor and the *Moreland* at Sawtooth Reef, Eagle River.

To depart Lac La Belle, travel either westerly 5 miles to pick up M-26 or take South Shore Drive to rejoin Highway 41 at Mohawk.

INFO & OPTIONS

Lac La Belle Lodge
11627 Superior St.
Lac La Belle, MI 49950
888-294-7634
laclabellelodge.com

Lake Gogebic & Bergland

Population 440

Bergland is at the junction of Michigan highways 28 and 64 in the western Upper Peninsula. The town sits on the north end of the nearly 14,000-

acre Lake Gogebic, which provides year-round recreation. Lake Gogebic State Park borders its western shore. The lake sits about 1,300 feet (400 meters) above sea level. Above the lake, Gogebic Ridge Hiking Trail offers spectacular views. To the south is the Sylvania Recreation Area of Ottawa National Forest and there are a number of resorts, lodgings and campgrounds on the lake.

Lake Linden

Population 1,080

At Lake Linden north of Houghton/Hancock on M-26, stop at Lindell's Chocolate Shop, an old-fashioned ice cream parlor, for a trip into the past. For campers, the Lake Linden Village Park and Recreation Area is on Torch Lake, with a picnic area, tennis, horseshoe and basketball courts. It is open Memorial Day through September.

Houghton County Historical Society's Museum Park is a 15-acre mill site of the Calumet and Hecla Copper Company, including the historic red schoolhouse, church and museum building, the Copper Country Railroad Heritage Center and the Lake Linden & Torch Lake Railroad, 3-foot gauge railroad on the grounds. Open daily mid-June through September. Fee. The Copperland Arts and Crafts Shop is next to the museum, specializing in handcrafted copper gifts and artworks.

INFO & OPTIONS

Schoolcraft Township Rustic Campground

Mink Farm Rd.
Lake Linden, MI 49945
906-296-8721

Lake Michigamme

Population 290

The M-28/U.S. Route 41 Circle Route follows the forested shoreline of Lake Michigamme (Mich-i-GAW-mee), with blue water and pristine islands visible from vistas and through the trees. Van Riper State Park is a 1,044-acre park. The headquarters, off U.S. 41 and M-28 at Lake Michigamme's eastern end, has a modern campground, excellent beach, picnic area and boat launch. A half-mile west on the Peshekee River is a rustic campground.

The quaint village of Michigamme, on the west end of the lake, offers diverse shopping with casual dining.

What's Next

About 5 miles (8 kilometers) east of the M-28/U.S. 41 junction at Tioga Creek at a fork in the road, Tioga Park is scenic, with a low waterfall, bridge, picnic tables and a pathway with signage explaining the logging history of this early town and sawmill site. By continuing east, you head for Ishpeming, Negaunee and Marquette.

West of Michigamme is the intersection of U.S. 41 and M-28. If you wish to enter the Keweenaw Peninsula, turn north on U.S. 41. This will take you to the lakeshore and an area of Lake Superior that is a playland unto itself, full of enticing history and year-round activities. This is also the easterly boundary of the Western Upper Peninsula Heritage Trails network to more than 70 historic sites, described in a guide available at Western Upper Peninsula infocenters.

By proceeding west on M-28, visitors can bypass the Keweenaw on a direct route into the Western Upper Peninsula and Big Snow Country through Bruce Crossing. This section of the Circle Tour takes you past farms and rolling hills that give way to forested lands. In Big Snow Country, any time of year is full of grandeur and excitement.

INFO & OPTIONS

Three Lakes Motel
27837 U.S. Hwy. 41
Michigamme, MI 49861
906-323-6101

L'Anse

Population 2,110

L'Anse (Lahnze) was named from the French word for "bay." It lies at the head of Keweenaw Bay on the lake. The Keweenaw Bay Band of Chippewa reservation is here, as is the Village by the Bay marina and park. A revitalization of the L'Anse waterfront with a new marina and park facilities, a pavilion and playground makes the city accessible to waterborne visitors. Tie-ups for eight to 10 boats. Another waterfront attraction is Steve Koski's Indian Country Sports store, with a 44-foot lighthouse that shines a beam to fishermen and boaters up to 5 miles away in the bay.

In L'Anse, Curwood Park has picnic tables and playgrounds and also historical displays, including L'Anse's first post office.

The Huron Mountains are to the northeast, remote and mysterious. Among the peaks are Mount Arvon and Mount Curwood. For many years, Curwood was recognized as the highest point in Michigan, but a 1982 U.S. Geological Survey found that Mt. Arvon measured 1,979.28 feet above sea level, while Curwood measured only 1,978.24, a bit more than a foot lower. The Visitor Information Center has information for those wishing to visit Mt. Arvon. It entails about a half-mile walk from a parking lot to the summit, from which there is only a limited view, but qualifies hikers for the Highpointers' Club for those reaching the highest peak in each state. Stop at the Baraga County Tourism & Recreation Association Visitor Information Center on U.S. 41 for directions to a viewpoint off Golf Course Road for a great vista of the area and the bay beyond. An interesting side trip is to Pequaming (see listing).

INFO & OPTIONS

Hilltop Restaurant
U.S. Hwy. 41
L'Anse, MI
906-524-7858
www.sweetroll.com

Hilltop Motel
18033 U.S. Hwy. 41
L'Anse, MI 49946
906-524-6321

L'Anse Motel and Suites
Rt. 2 Box 506, U.S. Hwy. 41
L'Anse, MI 49946
906-524-7820
www.lansemotel.com

Laurium

Population 2,125

Laurium was an active, booming copper capital when Copper Country produced the red ore. It was the home of George Gipp, the original "Gipper," football star of Notre Dame immortalized in a performance by Ronald Reagan in a movie with a coach's famous pleas to his team to "Win one for the Gipper." A memorial to the Gipper stands along the highway (M-26), and he is buried in the town cemetery. George Gipp Recreation Area commemorates him.

Maps are available for self-guided walking tours of the town of Laurium. Most homes on the tour were built in the early 1900s. Maps that cover the Calumet and Hecla Industrial Core and historic downtown Calumet have been updated by the Keweenaw National Historical Park and are sold at its headquarters on Red Jacket Road. Laurium is one of the Upper Peninsula's best Cornish pasty stops. Laurium Manor Inn, one of the largest mansions in the western U.P., reflects the wealth in Copper Country at the turn of the century. Self-guided tours available.

INFO & OPTIONS

Toni's Country Kitchen
79 Third St.
Laurium, MI 49913
906-337-0611

Laurium Manor Inn
320 Tamarack St.
Laurium, MI 49913
906-337-2549
www.laurium.info

Les Cheneaux Islands

From the very eastern tip of Michigan's U.P. at De Tour, M-134 takes us to Cedarville and Hessel in the Les Cheneaux Islands area in the southern U.P. There are 36 islands in the group, with marinas, beaches and waterfront walks to delight the visitor. Visit the Les Cheneaux Historical Museum for insight into the lake-oriented culture of the region. On the second Saturday in August, attend the Les Cheneaux Islands Antique Wooden Boat Show and the Festival of Arts in Hessel. Cedarville's annual Les Cheneaux Snowfest in February is also famed for its festive nature. Golfers will want to try out Hessel Ridge Golf Course.

What's Next

From here, we head for a junction with I-75 to visit St. Ignace, Mackinac Island (see separate listing) and the Mackinac Bridge, described in the St. Ignace listing. If you plan to continue your explorations along the south part of the Upper Peninsula, take U.S. Highway 2 from St. Ignace toward Wakefield in the western U.P. If this is your choice, you'll be traveling the northern leg of the Lake Michigan Circle Tour route, with many interesting places to poke around.

Mackinac Island

Population 469

A short ferry ride from St. Ignace in Michigan's southeastern Upper Peninsula takes you to world renowned Mackinac Island. Time all but stands still on this 3.5-mile-long (5.6-kilometer) island. Cars are banned; transportation is by bicycle or horsedrawn carriages, which clop past shops, hotels, museums and Victorian mansions. The island's main season is May through October, and highlights include a lilac festival in June and a fudge festival in August.

Eighty percent of the island is state park land, with Fort Mackinac offering exhibits, demonstrations of cooking, blacksmithing and spinning – a living-history museum with interpreters. Muskets and cannon are fired with regularity.

Golfers will want to challenge the 1898-era Wawashkamo Golf Club, with beautiful scenery punctuating the distinction of being Michigan's oldest continuously played 9-hole course. It is also listed as a state and national historic site.

Food is available in many gourmet restaurants and also in the Fort Tea Room overlooking the Straits of Mackinac. While on the island, you can take narrated carriage tours, visit fudge and souvenir shops and enjoy the finest of hotels – the Grand Hotel. The 286-room hotel has the world's longest porch (880 feet). Reservations are a must, and there's a fee to simply enter the grounds. Still, there are about 2,000 rooms on the island, ranging from economical to extravagant.

After your visit, ferry back to continue your Circle Tour. Return to the Lake Superior by traveling I-75 north from St. Ignace toward Sault Ste. Marie. For a trip along Lake Michigan's northern route, take Highway 2 west from St. Ignace. A number of highways travel north from Highway 2 rejoin the Lake Superior Circle Tour on M-28 wherever you choose.

INFO & OPTIONS

Mackinac Island Tourism Bureau
P.O. Box 451
Mackinac Island, MI 49757
906-847-3783
www.mackinacisland.org

Across the U.P., you don't have to look far to find fudge even on Mackinac Island.

Manistique

Population 3,580

Traveling Highway 2 in Michigan's southern Upper Peninsula, the shoreline city of Manistique offers a good selection of lodging facilities, including several state and private campgrounds, motels, resorts and bed-and-breakfast inns, and dining for whatever your taste may be. The city's commercial harbor is now mainly used by fishing boats but provides full amenities for recreational boaters.

What to See and Do

The historic "Siphon Bridge" on Old Highway 2 was once a subject of Ripley's "Believe it or Not" as the only road at the time 4 feet below water and partially supported by water under it. Today, the bridge is still in place and a 73-year-old water tower and museum are adjacent to it.

Near the downtown, the Lakeshore Boardwalk is a good place for a stroll.

Other sites to consider are Thompson Fish Hatchery, Wyman Forest Nursery, the iron furnace relics at the ghost town of Fayette on the Garden Peninsula and the southern entry to the Seney National Wildlife Refuge (see separate listing).

What's Next

To continue your Circle Tour of the southern U.P., continue on Highway 2. To the east, you head for St. Ignace and the Mackinac Bridge through a string of smallish towns. To the west, you'll also pass through several small towns to Rapid River, where U.S. 2/41 bends southward for Gladstone and Escanaba.

INFO & OPTIONS

Manistique Tourism Council
800-342-4282
visitmanistique.com

Anyone visiting Mackinac Island should see the enchanting Grand Hotel, with the world's longest porch (880 feet). The hotel played a major role in the movie "Somewhere in Time."

Schoolcraft County Chamber of Commerce
1000 West Lakeshore Dr.
Manistique, MI 49854
888-819-7420
www.schoolcraftcountychamber.com

Manistique Kewadin Inn
1908 East Lakeshore Dr.
Manistique, MI 49854
800-770-9336

Gogebic Lodge
N 9600 Hwy. M-64
Marenisco, MI 49947
www.gogebiclodge.com

Lake Gogebic State Park
N 9995 Hwy. M-64
Marenisco, MI 49947
906-842-3341

Marquette

Population: 19,661

A beautiful harbor city and cultural center on Lake Superior's south shore and the largest city in Michigan's Upper Peninsula, Marquette (Mar-KETT) serves as both a bustling commercial port for outbound shipments of iron ore from mines near Negaunee and Ishpeming and a destination for incoming coal cargoes for the large electric generating plant, and is also a comfortable setting for recreational boaters who dock there permanently or for transitory stays in pleasant surroundings.

Marquette's downtown offers nearly everything that visitors might be seeking. Art to convenience items can be found within walking distance of the harbor.

Depending on your direction of travel, Marquette is accessible on Michigan Highway 28 from either the east or west and northbound visitors can pick up U.S. 41 at Escanaba or M-35 at Gladstone in the southern U.P. to travel to the city. Airline service is provided at Sawyer International Airport at Gwinn, south on M-553. Area bus service is operated by the Marquette County Transportation Authority (Marq-Tran) on Commerce Drive. Taxi service is also available.

A Bit of History

Marquette is named for Father Jacques Marquette, the early French Jesuit missionary-explorer who ministered to the Ojibway and other native people in the area from 1669 until his death in 1675. A statue of Marquette stands on a boulder in a small rock garden adjacent to the Marquette Chamber of Commerce at 501 S. Front St.

Although Native American and French voyageurs used the sheltered waters of Marquette Harbor for rest, fishing and transport of furs and other cargo, no significant settlement existed at the site until the late 1840s. The 1844 discovery of iron ore at Teal Lake was the spur that led to development of the harbor and the city starting in 1849. The Marquette Iron Range took on the city's name, despite the fact that the iron mines exist closer to the cities of Negaunee and Ishpeming, about 10 miles inland from the harbor.

Following the discovery of iron, it was clear that a harbor was vital to the efficient transportation of the product to eastern steel making facilities. Early prospectors and mining people had landed at the Marquette site and picked it as the ideal location for such shipping facilities. With that in mind, clearing of the waterfront began, with a young Peter White credited for felling the first tree in that effort. Thus the foundation was laid for one of the area's legendary pioneer businessmen – one who wrote the bill of lading for the first iron ore shipment from Marquette and whose name years later would grace an ore freighter and remains etched today on the public library in Marquette.

Within two weeks of the start of clearing, a dock was built of the downed timber filled with sand and rocks from the area, but was immediately washed away by one of Lake Superior's legendary storms.

Undaunted, the founding fathers used manual labor to land everything necessary for sustenance, mining and construction of an iron forge on the beach until a second dock could be built. Ore was transported by teams of draft animals during winter freezeup from the Teal Lake mines to the Marquette forge for smelting into iron "blooms." The iron blooms were shipped the spring of 1851, but the endeavor did not prove economical, with the iron selling for much less than the cost of production and transportation. Thereafter, iron ore became the main commodity that the docks at Marquette handled, and that remains true to the present.

Through the years, other influences like commercial fishing and timber production would have an impact on the history of the city, but it remains a city dominated by waterfront activity and by the shipments of iron ore and, today, large coal cargoes to serve the Presque Isle Power Plant. Its waterfront is a haven for many recreational boaters using Lake Superior waters.

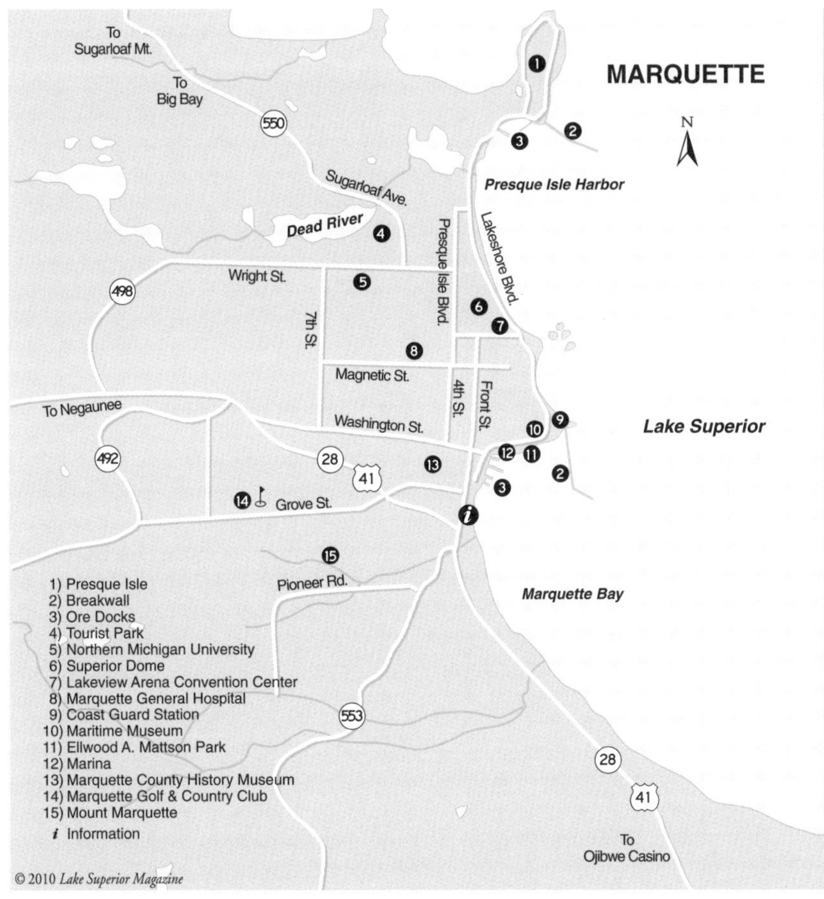

Marquette

Today

The largest city in the Upper Peninsula, Marquette is the regional shopping, medical, banking and service center of the U.P., as well as an important iron ore shipping port. The downtown remains vibrant and vital, preserving many historic aspects of its past.

Returning visitors to Marquette will notice that the old railroad trestle that once bisected downtown is gone. The abandoned property has been transformed into the Marquette Commons Building, a heritage and cultural complex. Events in this new public gathering space include the holiday tree lighting, a summer concert series and the farmers' market. There is an outdoor ice-skating surface.

The city's waterfront continues to undergo changes. Founder's Landing, a former railroad and industrial site, has been converted to beaches and biking and walking paths. It may be the site of residential and other development.

The 10,000-student Northern Michigan University (NMU) contributes to the quality of life with education, arts, sports, music, entertainment, lectures and other programs, such as exhibits at the DeVos Art Museum. Marquette and NMU are home to the U.S. Olympic Education Center. At NMU, training covers four of the Olympic sports. Tours are offered 3-5 p.m. Tuesday through Friday. The Superior Dome at NMU is an 8,000-seat domed stadium made of 781 Douglas fir beams and more than 100 miles of fir decking. It is second in size only to a dome in Japan that is 2 feet larger. It houses U.P. history, environmental displays and athletic memorabilia.

Marquette Regional Hospital is the regional center for medical and health care. A major employer in Marquette, it also affiliates with many associated health care providers, specialists and clinics that serve a wide range of needs in the area.

What to See and Do

A full calendar of artistic, cultural and

Marquette: Insider Tips

- **Park Cemetery**, 301 North Seventh Street, bordered east and west by Seventh and Lincoln streets, was developed as both a park and a cemetery. The Kauffman mausoleum, with its columns, marble and stained-glass, is a popular spot for wedding and prom pictures. Nice place for a relaxing, and intriguing, stroll.
- **Marquette County Courthouse**, 234 West Baraga Avenue, is constructed of a combination of local Marquette raindrop brownstone and Portage Entry redstone from the Keweenaw Peninsula. This beautiful building is where director Otto Preminger filmed the court scenes in the 1959 movie "Anatomy of a Murder" starring Jimmy Stewart and Lee Remick.
- **Wattsson & Wattsson Jewelers**, 118 West Washington Street, may be the most fun jewelry store you're likely to experience, with 8-foot-tall "Slim," a 40,000-year-old cave bear fossil, and an indoor "mine" to tour in which kids must wear a hardhat.
- **Peter White Public Library**, 217 North Front Street, like the courthouse, is not really a hidden gem but is a must-stop site for several reasons: Inside and out, it's an architectural treat that provides a great view of the city and Lake Superior (from the upstairs windows). There are rooms of displays, an art gallery and a cafe, Tu Kaluthia, Greek for "little cookie." The library was dedicated on the same day as the courthouse on September 17, 1904. This wonderful library has been updated and expanded.

other area activities is published in *Marquette Monthly*, a free tabloid found in many newsstands. The daily *Mining Journal* provides the latest news, and on Public Radio 90, WNMU-FM, you can hear news, music or great local shows.

One of our favorite pastimes is walking the breakwater to the lighthouse and watching arriving ships. Rockhounding is great! In the winter, there's ice watching, snowshoeing and cross-country ski trails. But guard against inclement weather.

Marquette County Courthouse on West Washington is a lovely building with first-floor marble and mahogany paneled walls. It also was the setting for *Anatomy of a Murder*, late author-attorney John Voelker's fictional account of an actual homicide case in nearby Big Bay. John Voelker (pen name Robert Traver) was from Ishpeming and served as county prosecutor here, as well as a period as a state Supreme Court justice. In 1959, the story was made into a popular movie by director Otto Preminger, who brought a cast that included Jimmy Stewart, Lee Remick, Ben Gazzara and George C. Scott to Marquette County for filming.

Voelker's original manuscripts and memorabilia are displayed at the Superior Dome at NMU.

The Marquette area is known for its creative bent, with many artists in residence, and it's one of several Upper Peninsula venues where the Pine Mountain Music Festival holds performances during the months of June into July.

Shiras Planetarium at the high school has been called one of the best in the country. Public shows are Monday evenings (unless Monday is a holiday, when it is closed).

Ojibwa Casino II is at Kawbawgam Road and M-28 East, providing Las Vegas-style action with progressive slots, craps, blackjack and other gaming.

The 97-slip, full-service Presque Isle Marina is on Lakeshore Boulevard, as is a quaint shopping area with arts and crafts. Rent bikes to pedal the 17 miles (27 kilometers) of paths from Presque Isle along the Lake Superior shoreline.

Uncle Ducky's Cruises offers guided fishing and sightseeing trips with charter boats, canoes and kayaks at Presque Isle Marina. Cinder Pond Marina, immediately east of Ellwood Mattson Lower Harbor Park, has 101 slips.

For golfers, there are three 18-hole public courses in the area: Chocolay Downs near Harvey, Red Fox Run in Gwinn and Wawonowin Country Club in Ishpeming. At Marquette Golf & Country Club, the recently added second course called Greywalls – whose 18 holes have drawn accolades – brings the club's total number of holes to 36. Homestead, offers a 9-hole challenge on County Road 480.

Moosewood Nature Center is a nice family stop at Presque Isle Park, offering a variety of nature programs for kids of all ages.

Marquette Fish Research Station (hatchery) in Harvey is a good family stop. Open daily, year-round on Cherry Creek Road, near routes 28 and 41.

Tour services in the Marquette area include Great Northern Adventures for outdoor adventure vacations; Marquette Country Tours, specializing in historic and cultural visits and outdoor treks; and Superior Adventures, with charter fishing and hunting guide services.

Notable Museums

On Front Street, the Peter White Public Library hosts the Marquette Arts and Culture Center for classes, exhibits, performances and other cultural events. Its gallery offers gifts by area artists.

Marquette Maritime Museum specializes in Great Lakes maritime history with emphasis on the Marquette area. (Did you know Evinrude tested the first outboard motor in Marquette?) Also displayed is a birch-bark canoe that Charles T. Harvey used while building the first lock at Sault Ste. Marie in the 1850s. The museum added the Second Order Fresnel lens from Stannard Rock Lighthouse to the other two lenses in its collection. It dedicated a memorial to World War II submariners by erecting a conning tower (bridge) honoring Marquette native Capt. David McClintock and the crew of the USS *Darter*'s heroic action in the Battle of Leyte, Philippines. Small fee. Gift shop. Open daily Memorial Day to October.

Marquette County History Museum on Front Street is a treasure that should not be missed. It tells a good overall story of the area's history. Look for interactive dioramas – one depicts a mid-19th century Ojibwe summer camp, with details about wild rice and maple syrup making – and displays about the prehistoric copper culture, the history of firearms and the fur-trade era. Recent special exhibits have included "Anatomy of a Yooper," exploring the cultural identity of Upper Peninsula residents. The museum has a fine research library (J.M. Longyear Research Library) and offers a special event series. The museum is scheduled to open in its newly renovated home in summer 2010 in the former Marq-Tran bus station on Spring Street. The state-of-the-art museum will be handicapped-accessible and have four times the exhibit space of the old museum, as well as on-site programs, classroom, research library, modern climate controls and more storage for artifacts. Exhibits will trace regional history and include development of natural resources, the role of Lake Superior, the first inhabitants and the fur trade. The "Arrivals and Departures" exhibit will examine the role of U.P. veterans on the front, and their families at home, from the Civil War through the Cold War. As part of this exhibit, an interactive computer station will have letters and audio clips from veterans and their families, and visitors will be encouraged to add their own family stories about wartime.

The museum is open Monday through Friday (also Saturdays from June through August). Small fee.

Upper Peninsula Children's Museum on West Baraga Avenue is a great stop for families and offers interactive education displays and outreach services throughout the U.P. Open daily 10 a.m.-6 p.m., except noon to 5 p.m. Sundays. Fee, although reduced with membership.

Parks and Public Areas

Presque Isle, an almost-island of 328 acres at the end of Lakeshore Boulevard, offers picnicking, hiking, biking, tennis, a swimming pool with 160-foot (49-meter) water slide, playground and Thursday night summer band concerts. Black Rocks and Sunset Point at the park are especially nice to view sunsets. Be careful near the cliff edges. Along Lakeshore Boulevard, visitors may still see the aftermath of a May 2003 flood that washed out a bridge, shut down the Presque Isle Power Plant, washed out the dam impounding the lake at Tourist Park and isolated businesses and residents

Beautiful old buildings like the courthouse are part of the charm of Marquette, which has retained much of its downtown as a hub of shopping, business and social activity.

from the rest of the town for several weeks.

Elwood Mattson Lower Harbor Park is just out of downtown, with beautiful grounds, a range of amenities and Cinder Pond Marina for boaters.

McCarty's Cove and Shiras parks occupy about a mile of lakeshore on Lake Shore Boulevard from Lighthouse Point going north toward Presque Isle Harbor.

Sugarloaf Mountain, a 600-foot-high granite peak overlooking Lake Superior, is 8 miles (13 kilometers) north on County Road 550 toward Big Bay. This is a good hike with a spectacular view from the top of the mountain.

Notable Events

• Noquemanon Ski Marathon occurs in mid- to late January and attracts thousands of competitors from the upper Midwest.

• U.P. 200 Sled Dog Race/Winterfest takes place in mid-February, stimulating sled dog teams with a challenging trail and a nighttime start. Winterfest is a fun family event featuring outdoor activities.

• Mid-February visitors to the Marquette/Munising area should consider taking in the races at the Trenary Outhouse Classic. In this fun competition, two people push "outhouses" 500 feet along a snowy road. It attracts more than 3,000 spectators to the downtown area of the city, at the junction of highways 41 and 67 southeast of Marquette.

• Superior Bike Fest is a chance to explore area trails in early June.

• International Food Festival in early July features scrumptious foods in a beautiful waterfront setting.

• Fourth of July Festival features a huge parade and other events for family fun.

• Blueberry Festival occurs in late July with many activities celebrating and eating food using the area's favorite wild fruit.

• Art on the Rocks in late July is a giant exhibit and sale of regional arts and crafts in the special Presque Isle Park.

• Seafood Fest serves sumptuous fish and other seafoods on the waterfront in late August.

• Ore to Shore Mountain Bike Epic in early August is a tough biking challenge for riders of all skill levels.

Where to Shop

The Studio Gallery on Lakeshore Boulevard features works by local artists Maggie Linn, Kathleen Conover, Vicki Allison Phillips and metalsmith artist Yvonne LeMire.

Historic Downtown Marquette is a vital, growing area offering many opportunities for the shopper. Michigan Fair features Michigan-made products. Art of Framing, Art UP Style and Screened Image and Graphic Design offer a variety of gift items. Town Folk Gallery has antiques, beading and handcrafted women's wear and the Hotplate is a paint-your-own pottery shop. Needleworks carries yarns, fabrics, quilting supplies and looms and spinning wheels. Mole Hole has charming service and quality gifts. Wattsson & Wattsson Jewelers carries a line of items made from 14 karat gold and features an underground mine experience right in the store. Photographer Jack Deo's Superior View Historic Photo & Art Gallery is at the corner. There are bookstores, restaurants and clothing stores. Down the hill on Front Street, Getz's offers three floors of clothing and footwear for men, women and children.

The shopping district around the university is known as The Village, full of restaurants and nifty gift shops. A stop at Scandinavian Gifts or Habitat will definitely fulfill your gift list.

Westwood Mall is a major shopping center. Marquette Mall also houses a number of businesses, including an indoor miniature golf course. Both are on U.S. 41 West, site of a number of restaurants. Along the way in that area, watch for the Touch of Finland for a wide variety of Finnish items, including an ample supply of sauna products.

What's Next

Sugarloaf Mountain, 8 miles (13 kilometers) north on County Road 550 toward Big Bay, is a good hike with a spectacular view from the top of the mountain.

Explore Little Presque Isle along Lake Superior in Escanaba River State Forest off County Road 550 on the way to Big Bay.

Take an interesting side trip to Gwinn to see the historic display in the terminal of Sawyer International Airport, which offers air service from the former K.I. Sawyer Air Force Base. Here, the Marquette County Aviation Wall of Fame honors both military and civilian local airmen who made significant contributions to flight. And as long as you're in the neighborhood, take a ride through the Gwinn townsite, an early model townsite designed and built for employees of Cleveland Cliffs Iron Co. The entire town is on the National Register of Historic Places.

Follow Highway M-28 east toward Munising or Highway U.S. 41/M-28 west from Marquette headed for Negaunee and Ishpeming.

INFO & OPTIONS

Marquette Area Chamber of Commerce
501 South Front St.
Marquette, MI 49855
888-578-6489
www.marquette.org

Marquette Country Convention & Visitors Bureau
337 West Washington St.
Marquette, MI 49855
800-544-4321
www.marquettecountry.org

Casa Calabria
1106 North Third St.
Marquette, MI 49855
906-228-5012
www.thecasa.us

Lagniappe Cajun & Creole Eatery
145 Jackson Cut
Marquette, MI 49855
906-226-8200
www.marquettecajun.com

Upfront & Company
102 East Main St.
Marquette, MI 49855
906-228-5200
www.upfrontandcompany.com

Vierling Restaurant
119 South Front St.
Marquette, MI 49855
906-228-3533
www.thevierling.com

Holiday Inn of Marquette
1951 U.S. Hwy. 41 West
Marquette, MI 49855
800-HOLIDAY

Landmark Inn
230 North Front St.
Marquette, MI 49855
888-752-6362
www.thelandmarkinn.com

Gitche Gumee RV Park
2048 M-28 East
Marquette, MI 49855
866-447-8727

Little Presque Isle State Forest Campground and Cabins
5 miles north of Marquette County Rd. 550
906-228-6561

Marquette Tourist Park
2145 Sugar Loaf Ave.
Marquette, MI 49855
906-228-0465/906-228-0460 (off season)

Mohawk

Population 200

Mohawk offers two shopping opportunities while traveling U.S. 41 and the Circle Route north on the Keweenaw Peninsula from Houghton/Hancock through several ghost mining towns. Here Superior Wood Works Inc. makes and sells rustic indoor and outdoor furniture. For a nice selection of specialty items crafted from bird's-eye maple, stop at Bird's-Eye Creations Inc. From here you can continue to follow Highway 41 toward Copper Harbor at the tip of the Keweenaw, but we recommend turning southeast on South Shore Drive from Fulton-Mohawk to Gay. This route hugs the eastern edge of the peninsula and travels several miles right on the shore of Keweenaw Bay. See listings for Gay and Lac La Belle for information.

INFO & OPTIONS

Mount Bohemia
100 Lac Labelle Rd.
Mohawk, MI 49950
231-420-5405, 906-289-4105
www.mtbohemia.com

Munising

Population 2,580

The century-old Munising (MEW-ni-sing) may be one of the best kept "secrets" on Lake Superior. From friendly dining and lodging to wonderful hiking and interesting tours, this is a stop that may tempt visitors to spend a day or two longer than they originally planned.

On a natural harbor, the town and

harbor are protected by Grand Island, the second largest of the lake's U.S. islands. The Ojibway name for the island was *Kitchi minising* (literally, great or grand island), which was altered and later transferred to the town on the mainland.

A concerted, collaborative effort between public and private groups in Alger County to promote "heritage tourism" has resulted in an emphasis on historical and cultural information and sites within Munising and the county. Information is available at the visitors centers or the Alger County Historical Society (906-387-4308).

What to See and Do

Ferry service to Grand Island, which is protected by the U.S. Forest Service, is at Grand Island Landing. Hiking, camping and biking are available, but private vehicles are not allowed. This is the site of an archaeological exploration of artifacts from an A.D. 1200-era village the Ojibway call *Geta Odena* (Kay-tay O-day-na).

Water is the attraction in Munising. A number of waterfalls are found within the city and Lake Superior is at its front door.

Alger County All Veterans Memorial stands at the head of Munising Harbor in Bayshore Park.

Pictured Rocks Cruises offers tours regularly from Munising dock mid-May to early October. The memorable cruises run 2½ to 3 hours and carry sightseers near Grand Island, Grand Island East Channel Light and formations such as Miners Castle, one of the most photographed landmarks on Lake Superior. Skylane Air Tours offers aerial views of the area.

Alger County Historical Society Museum includes a fur trader's cabin on the grounds overlooking Lake Superior. It is on Washington Street near the lakeshore's Munising Falls Visitor Center.

Stop in at Muldoon's Pasties on State Highway M-28 for homemade pasties and gifts. Open 9 a.m. to 9 p.m. Memorial Day to Labor Day. Fall and winter hours may vary.

Golfers can try the Pictured Rocks Golf and Country Club, an 18-hole par 72 course that's 4 miles (6.4 kilometers) east of Munising on Highway H-58.

The original iron blast furnace has been restored at Bay Furnace Recreation Area. The furnace produced pig iron in the 1870s when the town was known as Onota. The U.S. Forest Service campground and picnic area now occupies that spot on Lake Superior to the west of Christmas, where you'll find good agate hunting and sandy beaches. In Christmas check out Santa's Workshop, a shop where it's Christmas all year. Owner Sharon Tesch can cancel letters with a special "Christmas" stamp. Kewadin Casinos operates a casino in Christmas.

Parks and Public Areas

Headquarters for Pictured Rocks National Lakeshore is 4 miles northeast of downtown Munising at a former Coast Guard Station. On display is an old U.S. Coast Guard Lifesaving self-righting rescue boat. The park shares a visitor center with Hiawatha National Forest at the junction of Highway M-28 and County Highway H-58. Open year-round Monday through Saturday and Sundays from mid-May through mid-October.

Pictured Rocks National Lakeshore operates a visitor center at Munising Falls, 2 miles (3 kilometers) northeast of downtown. Open Memorial Day to Labor Day.

Boat tours out of Munising pass Miners Castle at Pictured Rocks National Lakeshore, among Lake Superior's most-photographed landmarks. (Gregg Bruff / National Park Service)

Alger Underwater Preserve includes 113 square miles (293 square kilometers) of Lake Superior shoreline at Munising. Scuba divers regularly descend to view major shipwrecks in the harbor.

Diving services are available. The public can view wrecks of the Alger Preserve on the Glass Bottom Boat shipwreck tour. Make reservations with Munising Bay Shipwreck Tours.

A large section of the 860,000-acre Hiawatha National Forest near Munising has hiking and mountain bike trails and campgrounds. Some of the best snowmobile trails in the Upper Peninsula are in this area, as well as some of the best cross-country skiing in the region. Lodging is available within the forest at a number of motels in Munising.

INFO & OPTIONS

Munising Visitors Bureau
P.O. Box 421
Munising, MI 49862
906-387-3536
www.munising.org

Pictured Rocks National Lakeshore/ Hiawatha National Forest Visitor Center
400 East Munising Ave.
Munising, MI 49862
906-387-3700
www.nps.gov/piro/

Dogpatch Restaurant
325 East Superior St.
Munising, MI 49862
906-387-9948
www.dogpatchrestaurant.com

Grand Island National Rec. Area
Ferry landing 1 mile west of Munising
Munising, MI 49862
906-387-2512

Otter Lake Campground
7609 Otter Lake Rd.
Munising, MI 49862
906-553-4921, 906-387-4648
www.playatotterlake.com

Wandering Wheels Campground
M-28 East
Munising, MI 49862
906-387-3315, 906-387-1580
www.wanderingwheelscampground.net

Bay Furnace Campground
5 miles west of Munising on M-28
Christmas, MI 49862
906-387-2512

Negaunee

Population 4,500

Negaunee (Na-GAW-nee) is an iron mining town on M-28 and U.S. 41 a short way west from Marquette. More than 150 years ago, the first iron on the Marquette Range was discovered in the roots of an upturned tree on the shores of Negaunee's Teal Lake, which offers the area's best walleye and trout fishing.

What to See and Do

An Iron Ore Monument is just east of Negaunee on U.S. 41.

Lucy Hill is the site of the first naturbahn luge (loozh) course in the United States to meet International Luge Federation standards. What is luge? Basically, it's hurtling down an icy course on a small sled while lying feet first on your back. For the winter visitor, national and international competitions are held each year between late December and early March. Open to spectators every weekend. The bottom one-sixth is open to the public for instruction and "trial sliding" on weekend afternoons when no competitive event is scheduled. Lucy Hill is just south of Negaunee on old M-35.

There are 17 miles (27 kilometers) of cross-country ski trails in the area that offer beautiful vistas. A snowshoe race and the Guts Triathlon, a rare combination of snowshoeing, cross-country skiing and running, are held here. The area celebrates winter with Heikki Lunta WinterFest in January, and hosts Pioneer Days in July.

Notable Museums

Follow the signs to the Michigan Iron Industry Museum at 73 Forge Road. It's a good stop for children. Open daily, May through October. Free. As part of an expansion, the museum added 4,000 square feet several years ago to house exhibits, a store and, after its restoration, the locomotive *Yankee* (circa 1868).

Negaunee Historical Museum is at Main Street and Brown Avenue and is open daily and Sunday afternoons Memorial Day through August.

Antiques enthusiasts will enjoy the Old Bank Building, an 1874 three-story triangular structure with 25 rooms of antiques and collectibles from Upper Peninsula settlers.

What's Next

To either the east or west, the Circle Tour route follows Highway M-28/U.S. 41. To the west lies the Keweenaw Peninsula and a world of interesting sights and experiences. About 10 miles east, Marquette beckons.

INFO & OPTIONS

Tall Pines and RV Park
349 U.S. Hwy. 41 East
Negaunee, MI 49866
906-475-9452

Newberry

Population 1,917

Newberry is on M-123 just off M-28 about halfway between Sault Ste. Marie and Marquette. Designated by the Legislature as "Michigan's Moose Capital" and the southern gateway to Tahquamenon Falls State Park, Newberry also opens the way to a number of attractions like the Manistique lakes and Seney National Wildlife Refuge to the south and west. This old lumbering town holds an aura of the past and contributes to the timber industry with several mills and logging operations. There are good lodging and eating establishments in the area. Find out what's happening in the area in the weekly *Newberry News*.

What to See and Do

Golfers can play the Newberry Country Club, an 18-hole par 71 course just south of the village.

You can take a ride on a narrow-gauge train and a riverboat cruise, with destination Tahquamenon Falls. Drop down through Newberry to M-28 and back east to catch the Toonerville Trolley at Soo Junction. The longest 24-inch narrow-gauge railroad now operating, the train takes you to the Tahquamenon River where you board a boat to the falls – one trip daily at 10:30 a.m., sharp!

Ask directions to Oswald's Bear Ranch, which has 30 black bears to view off H-37. The compound includes three walk-about bear habitats, with newborn and yearling cubs cavorting near a lake. Open Memorial Day weekend through September.

Luce County Park and Campground has 28 sites on 33 wooded acres on the south shore of Round (also known as North Manistique) Lake to the north of Curtis. An excellent place to plant yourself for full access to inland-lake swimming, fishing and hiking opportunities. Open Memorial Day to October.

Notable Museums

Luce County Historical Museum is in the old sheriff's residence on West Harrie Street.

Tahquamenon Logging Museum houses a collection of lumbering artifacts. The 29-acre camp is on the banks of the Tahquamenon River outside Newberry.

Notable Events

- Woodchoppers' Ball celebrates the logging heritage of the area in March.
- Lumberjack Days in August pulls out all the stops to remember the time when white pine was king.
- Michigan Fiddlers Jamboree in September attracts the state's best fiddlers.

What's Next

From Newberry, you can stay on Highway M-28 in either direction, with the Circle Tour eastern route toward Sault Ste. Marie and the western leg heading to Munising through Seney and Shingleton. A more scenic – though rustic – path westward is to turn north on M-77 at Seney to Grand Marais.

Another off-the-beaten path locale is Deer Park, a lumbering town of the late 1800s. Take County Highway 37 north of Newberry off M-123. You'll be in Big Two-Hearted River country which has excellent fishing, agates, driftwood and seascapes. This region was made famous by Ernest Hemingway's character Nick Adams, who fished and canoed here. Muskallonge Lake State Park and campgrounds are above the Lake Superior shoreline.

From Deer Park to Grand Marais on Forest Road H-58, you'll count 13 miles

The Upper Falls at Tahquamenon Falls State Park near Paradise is one of the largest waterfalls east of the Mississippi River. A nearby platform allows close-up views for visitors.

(21 kilometers) of washboard road, all hard sand, surrounded by sand lots, forest and Lake Superior beach. The going is slow (30 minutes of travel), but most interesting with beautiful views. This is a difficult route for motorcycles, especially in some conditions.

INFO & OPTIONS

Newberry Area Tourism Council
P.O. Box 308
Newberry, MI 49868
800-831-7292
www.newberrytourism.com

Pickleman's Pub & Pantry
14045 County Rd. 460
Newberry, MI 49868
906-293-3777

Tahquamenon Falls Brewery & Pub
Barrett Camp 33
P.O. Box 26
Newberry, MI
906-492-3300
www.superiorsights.com/tahqfallsbrew/

America's Best Value Inn
12956 M-28
Newberry, MI 49868
800-293-3297
www.abvitahquamenoncountry.com

Rainbow Lodge and Canoe Trips
32752 County Rd. 423
Newberry, MI 49868
906-658-3357

Clementz's Northcountry Campground & Cabins
13209 M-123
Newberry, MI 49868
906-293-8562
www.northcountrycampground.com

Luce County Park & Campground

546 County Rd. 479
McMillan, MI 49853
906-586-6460

Muskallonge Lake State Park

Rt. 1 Box 245
Newberry, MI 49868
906-341-2355

Newberry KOA

13724 M-28
Newberry, MI 49868
906-293-5762
www.koa.com

Pike Lake State Forest Campground

29 miles northeast of Newberry via M-123, County Road 500 and County Road 414
906-293-3293

Norway

Population 2,910

In the southwestern Upper Peninsula on Highway 2 at Norway, the Jake Menghini Historical Museum is housed in a historic log cabin that once served as a carriage stopping place. Displaying artifacts from Jake's personal collection, as well as exhibits that change yearly, the museum is open free of charge Memorial Day through the Saturday prior to Columbus Day in October, although donations are accepted.

Waterfalls aficionados can check out Piers Gorge, where white water tumbles over a 10-foot falls and roars wildly through canyon walls. Plan to stop at nearby Vulcan east of Norway for an underground tour by train of the Iron Mountain Iron Mine, where you'll travel 2,600 feet (792 meters) through the drifts and stopes (tunnels and roomlike areas) of the mine. On the western side of Norway, a roadside park with tables, water and toilets at Quinnesec gives a nice view of Fumee Falls.

Ontonagon

Population 1,770

Ontonagon (On-toe-NAH-gun) is a historic port that had early significance in the copper boom years. This is the terminus of historic U.S. 45, which extends from Lake Superior's shore to the Gulf of Mexico. The historical sign in the downtown explaining the highway's importance is a great place to take a memory picture. To find Ontonagon, follow U.S. 45 northward from M-28 at Bruce Crossing. The *Ontonagon Herald* will bring you up to date on the area and give you leads to meet your needs.

What to See and Do

The 5-acre Riverfront Park provides waterfront access with picnic facilities and a playground. The full-service Ontonagon Marina has slip space for visiting boats.

Notable Museums

Ontonagon County Historical Museum on River Street has mining, maritime and folk exhibits, the Fifth-Order Fresnel lens from the Ontonagon Lighthouse and a replica of the famous Ontonagon Boulder, a 3-ton mass of pure copper that was discovered nearby in the Ontonagon River. Daily tours of the lighthouse in summer start at the museum, which is open year-round Monday through Saturday. Small fee.

Notable Events

- On Labor Day weekend, Ontonagon has a dandy celebration with a parade.

What's Next

The Circle Tour passes westward along M-64, a soothing shoreline drive which offers easy Lake Superior beach access. To travel the route to the east, take

M-38 heading for Baraga, but watch for the intersection with M-26, where you'll want turn left if you plan to visit the Keweenaw Peninsula.

INFO & OPTIONS

Ontonagon Area Chamber of Commerce
P.O. Box 266
Ontonagon, MI 49953
906-884-4735
www.ontonagonmi.org

Porcupine Mountains Convention & Visitors Bureau
P.O. Box I
Ontonagon, MI 49953
906-8884-2047
www.porcupinemountains.com

Harbor Town Cafe
409 River St.
Ontonagon, MI 49953
906-884-6525

AmericInn Lodge & Suites - Silver City
120 Lincoln Ave.
Ontonagon, MI 49953
800-396-5007
www.americinn.com/hotels/MI/SilverCity

Sunshine Motel, Cabins & Campground
24077 M-64 West
Ontonagon, MI 49953
906-884-2187
www.ontonagonmi.com

Superior Shores Resort
26156 M-64 West
Ontonagon, MI 49953
800-344-5355
www.superior-shores-resort.com

Ontonagon Township Park
Two miles from downtown Ontonagon on Lakeshore Drive
906-884-2930

Porcupine Mountains State Park
412 South Boundary Rd.
Ontonagon, MI 49953
906-885-5275

River Pines RV Park & Campground
600 River Rd.
Ontonagon, MI 49953
906-884-4600

Paradise

Population 500

The aptly named village of Paradise along M-123 is a jumping-off point for divers exploring shipwrecks in Whitefish Point Underwater Preserve and is a destination for honeymooners. It's also the nearest town and the northeast entry to Tahquamenon Falls State Park (see separate listing), Michigan's second-largest state park. Paradise offers fishing, hiking, birding and extensive sandy beaches as well as rock-picking opportunities. It's a popular location for kayakers. It overlooks Whitefish Bay, infamous for its treacherous waters and many shipwrecks.

At the end of Tom Brown Sr. Memorial Highway, which winds past the ghost town of Shelldrake 10 miles (16 kilometers) north of Paradise, is Whitefish Point Harbor, offering safe refuge, a boat launch and parking next to the former Brown Fishery (not open to the public). About 5 miles farther on the road brings you to Whitefish Point Lighthouse, Bird Observatory and the Great Lakes Shipwreck Museum. (See separate listing for Whitefish Point.)

NOTABLE EVENTS

- Mardi Gras de Snow Festival in January celebrates winter activities.
- Annual Blueberry Festival in August continues the area's long reputation as a treasury of this favored fruit.

The vast sandy beaches found near Paradise attract many visitors to the area, despite its remote location. It's also a great area for birding activities.

• Halloween Fun: "The Haunted Trail" is a scary romp for kids of all ages at Halloween time in October.

INFO & OPTIONS

Paradise Area Tourism Council
P.O. Box 64
Paradise, MI 49768
906-492-3927
www.paradisemi.org

Tahquamenon Falls State Park
41382 West M-123
Paradise, MI 49768
906-492-3415
www.michigan.gov/dnr/

Best Western Lakefront Inn & Suites
8112 North M-123
Paradise, MI 49768
906-492-3770
www.bestwesternmichigan.com

Curley's Paradise Inn
M-123 at Whitefish Point Rd.
Paradise, MI 49768
800-236-7386

Tahquamenon Falls State Park
41382 West M-123
Paradise, MI 49768
800-44-PARKS

Paulding

Paulding is 9 miles south of Bruce Crossing on U.S. Highway 45. Here you can visit Bond Falls Park for a view of the falls. There are hiking trails, fishing and camping facilities in the area.

Paulding is famous for the Paulding Light, a mysterious reddish glow that appears almost every evening once darkness has fallen. Not an official attraction, the phenomenon draws hundreds to observe this bright light rising out of the forest to the north, hovering, changing hue and then disappearing. A real mystery light, many claim it is the ghost of a railroad brakeman, others the lights of distant cars. No one has the final explanation. South of Paulding, watch for signs to take the Robbins Pond Road (a Forest Service road) for about a mile. The cars parked along the way will tell you when to stop. Then you decide what creates the light.

There is no lodging in Paulding, but if your night encounter with the mysterious light detains you longer than planned, lodging can be found a few miles south in Watersmeet, where you can pick up Highway 2 as an alternate route to Wakefield, Bessemer and Ironwood. Farther east on Highway 2 at Iron River, AmericInn welcomes travelers.

What's Next

To return to the Circle Tour Route, catch Highway M-28 at Bruce Crossing. To the west is Wakefield, Bessemer and Ironwood. To the east, you're heading for Marquette, but will want to consider taking U.S. 45 north toward Ontonagon and the Porcupine Mountains country. This route also opens the Keweenaw Peninsula for a visit.

Pequaming

In the 1940s, the Huron Peninsula, northeast of L'Anse, was the center for Ford Motor Company Upper Peninsula enterprises, which produced millions of board-feet of lumber each year for use by the automaker. Henry and Clara Ford had a summer home in Pequaming called The Bungalow, which is listed on the National Register of Historic Places, but privately owned. Pequaming also has a marina and some residential cottages.

Continue to the northeast to visit Skanee (see separate listing), or backtrack to return to L'Anse. Point Abbaye, at the tip of the peninsula, offers an expansive view of Lake Superior. Huron Islands rise above the waves to the east, the Keweenaw Peninsula to the west. Limited camping at the mouth of the Huron River.

Pictured Rocks National Lakeshore

From either Grand Marais or Munising, a drive through Pictured Rocks National Lakeshore is highly recommended. Alger County Road H-58 links Munising and Grand Marais and soon will be paved the whole way.

There is no fee to enter the lakeshore, which is open 24 hours daily year-round (many roads are closed by snow in winter).

You can plan your visit through one of the visitor centers. The Pictured Rocks National Lakeshore/Hiawatha National Forest Interagency Visitor Center in Munising is open year-round but closed Sundays and holidays from October to mid-May. Grand Sable Visitor Center, Miners Castle Information Center and the Munising Falls Visitor Center are open Memorial Day through Labor Day.

For this listing, the route is described westerly from Grand Marais to Munising.

This is Hiawatha Country, made famous in Henry Wadsworth Longfellow's epic poem, "The Song of Hiawatha." Multicolored sandstone cliffs, beaches, sand dunes, waterfalls, inland lakes, wildlife and the forests of Lake Superior's shoreline beckon visitors to explore the 73,000-plus acre park, which is only 3 miles wide at its widest point but hugs the shore for 40 miles.

Sand dunes cover 5 square miles and tower 85 feet (26 meters) in height. The dunes sit atop 275-foot-high (84-meter) glacial deposits of Grand Sable Dunes, reaching inland to form Grand Sable Lake. A path with wooden steps and overlooks follows Sable Falls to the mouth of the river. Watch for signs to Log Slide parking lot and viewpoint, where the towering dunes meet Lake Superior. In heavy logging days, logs were shoved down the 500-foot (154-meter) chute and rafted to market. There's a scenic overlook and wayside exhibits, which make for a pleasant experience. If you decide to shoot-the-chute, keep in mind that it may take less than five minutes to go down the slope but more than an hour to climb back up.

Au Sable Light Station is visible from this overlook. The 87-foot-high Au Sable Lighthouse is being restored. The original 6-foot-high Fresnel lens that once warned mariners away from the rocky coast has been returned. The lighthouse, accessible by a hiking trail from Hurricane River Campground, has tours (fee) in the summer. The grounds are always open.

Pictured Rocks has three campgrounds accessible by vehicle (with fee): Hurricane River, Twelvemile Beach and Little Beaver Lake. Thirteen backcountry campgrounds and eight group sites are sprinkled along 42 miles of the North Country National Scenic Trail. Permit required for overnight camping. You should watch for the signs at Melstrand to Chapel Beach, which doesn't have camping sites.

For other lakeshore attractions, take Miners Castle Road north to Miners Castle, a sandstone formation and possibly the most-photographed natural feature on the lake. In 2006, one of Miners Castle's two familiar sandstone turrets collapsed.

Some of most spectacular fall color anywhere is in Pictured Rocks, one of five U.S. national park sites on the lake. Winter enthusiasts also enjoy the park. Two systems of cross-country ski trails offer spectacular views of Lake Superior, waterfalls and the Grand Sable Dunes.

See the Munising listing for information on boat cruises along the national lakeshore.

INFO & OPTIONS

Pictured Rocks National Lakeshore/Hiawatha National Forest Interagency Visitor Center

400 East Munising Ave.
Munising, MI 49862
906-387-3700
www.nps.gov/piro/

Rockland

Population 267

Rockland is just west of the junction of U.S. 45 and M-26. It is well worth a slow drive through the streets of this small town to view the interesting and well-decorated Victorian homes. At the Rockland Historical Museum, there are photographs, antiques and historic documents. A park and playground are in the center of town, a community-wide effort that is open to the public.

Incidentally, Rockland is the site of Michigan's first telephone system. The original switchboard is now housed in the Ontonagon County Historical Museum.

From Rockland, take a quick side trip southwest on Victoria Road to a restored ghost mining village, Victoria, about 5 miles (8 kilometers) off Highway 45.

Here, log homes constructed in the early 1900s as homes for the miners working at Victoria Mine have been restored and are open for guided tours from Memorial Day through mid-October. Daily tours of the homes or interesting surrounding sites are offered. Fee.

The famous three-ton pure-copper Ontonagon Boulder, now housed in the Smithsonian Institution in Washington, D.C., was discovered on the Ontonagon River at the site where Victoria Dam was built.

St. Ignace, Mackinac Area

Population 2,570

St. Ignace is a gateway to Mackinac Island. It is also considered the gateway to the Upper Peninsula from Lower Michigan, as well as being the junction where we join two other Great Lakes

Circle Tours: the Lake Huron and the Lake Michigan Circle Tours. A city full of good eating and lodging options, St. Ignace and its surroundings are good for several days of sightseeing, if you have the time.

What to See and Do

The massive, awe-inspiring Mackinac Bridge is a dominant feature of this area. At 8,614 feet (2,625 meters) with anchorages, it's the world's third-longest suspension bridge. Twin towers rise 552 feet (168 meters) above the Straits of Mackinac, which join Lake Huron with Lake Michigan. Maximum water depth at midspan is 295 feet (90 meters). The "Mighty Mac" is closed to pedestrian traffic except on Labor Day, when two lanes open to walkers. More than 45,000 people annually make the walk from St. Ignace to Mackinaw City on the Lower Peninsula, beginning at 7:30 a.m.

To the north of St. Ignace, you'll find Castle Rock, an interesting and accessible example of several similar rock formations in the area called "sea stacks." A stairway takes visitors to a viewing platform 195 feet (59 meters) above water level atop the rock which native people once used to scan the surrounding area. Other sea stacks are St. Anthony's Rock, also in St. Ignace, and Arch Rock on Mackinac Island.

Named for and honoring the life of French missionary Father Jacques Marquette, the Marquette National Memorial is located off U.S. Highway 2 in Straits State Park. It offers a magnificent view of the Mackinac Bridge. No charge. Open June to Labor Day.

Walk the waterfront on the Huron Boardwalk, with a view of the many bay activities and the island. Historic events are described on the signs along the way. For boaters, the city operates a 100-slip marina with full fuel, water, pumpout and dockside power service.

Mackinac Island (population 469) has three ferry lines regularly making the trip across the 7-mile (11-kilometer) span of Lake Huron from St. Ignace. See separate listing for Mackinac Island.

Notable Museums

Visit the Museum of Ojibwa Culture at Marquette Mission Park, which explores the culture and folkways of the Huron and Ojibway people who first inhabited this important route to the west. No charge to enter the park, but there is a fee for the museum.

Notable Events

• The annual Straits Area Auto Show and St. Ignace Car Show Weekend is at the end of June and includes a parade and cruising, concerts and Mackinac Bridge Rally.

INFO & OPTIONS

St. Ignace Visitors Bureau
6 Spring Street, Ste. 100
St. Ignace, MI 49781
800-338-6660
www.stignace.com

Days Inn of St. Ignace
1067 North State St.
I-75 & U.S. Hwy. 2
St. Ignace, MI 49781
800-329-7466
www.daysinn.com

Holiday Inn Express St. Ignace
965 North State St.
St. Ignace, MI 49781
888-465-4329
www.ichotelsgroup.com

The brilliance of nature's artwork is viewed from a trail at Pictured Rocks National Lakeshore. (Gregg Bruff / National Park Service)

Bay View Campground

West 1900 U.S. Hwy. 2
St. Ignace, MI 49781
906-292-5549

Carp River Campground

North 4664 Mackinac Tr.
St. Ignace, MI 49781
906-292-5549

Sault Ste. Marie

Population: 16,542

Sault Ste. Marie offers history, shopping, a variety of waterborne commerce to watch, nightlife, fine dining and all of the other amenities of an international metropolitan center.

A Bit of History

At Sault Ste. Marie, you're in

Soo Locks

No matter what else catches your attention in Sault Ste. Marie, it's a fact that you cannot ignore the waterfront and maritime activity on the St. Marys River. Central to that fact are the famed Soo Locks, four of which are on the Michigan side, with one on the Ontario side. A visitor center operated by the U.S. Army Corps of Engineers is a vital stop for Soo, Michigan, visitors, with detailed information about the operation of the Soo Locks, which raise and lower ships and recreational craft more than 20 feet to compensate for the different water levels of Lake Superior and Lake Huron. While the raising or lowering of up to 1,000-foot (308-meter) ships carrying as much as 60,000 tons of cargo seems awesome, the concept of the locks is relatively simple. Gates enclose the ship in the lock and water is admitted or discharged, depending on whether the ship is being raised or lowered. When the water level reaches the level of that beyond the gate, it is opened and the vessel glides away at the new elevation.

The Canadian Lock on the Ontario shore once handled commercial shipping traffic, but was damaged in 1987 and rebuilt to handle smaller boats and recreational traffic. The new Canadian Lock was constructed inside the original and is surrounded by beautiful grounds and buildings that give visitors walking access on the structure for close-up views.

In 2009, the Corps, as part of a long-planned lock replacement project, started building dams to hold back water and allow excavation and other work. The new Soo lock, to be built in the footprint of the outdated Sabin and Davis locks, will take eight to 10 years to finish. It will serve as a backup to the Poe Lock, the only one large enough to give 1,000-foot freighters access to Lake Superior.

Tour services are available on both sides of the river to get visitors close to the shipping and locking activity. In 2005, Michigan celebrated the 150th anniversary of the opening of the first lock in 1855.

Michigan's oldest city and the third-oldest U.S. city west of the Appalachians. The rapids of the St. Marys River had been, for regional Indian people, a spring meeting place for generations (and, yes, St. Marys without the apostrophe is the proper spelling in this case). They would come to talk and to spear and eat whitefish. This traditional fishing and gathering place of the Chippewa and other Great Lakes tribal people first saw Europeans when voyageur Etienne Brule passed this way in 1620. A Jesuit mission was established by fathers Jacques Marquette and Claude Dablon in 1668. After establishing the mission, Marquette and Dablon named the city to honor the Virgin Mary and the nearby rapids. It is home to the Sault Tribe of Chippewa, also known as Ojibway.

Before the white men came to the area, the Ojibway, who lived nearby, portaged their canoes around the bahweting (rapids) to reach Lake Superior. In the three centuries since, the two cities of Sault Ste. Marie (nicknamed Sault on the Ontario side and Soo on the Michigan side) have been divided by the St. Marys River and an international boundary, but gained worldwide shipping importance after the first Soo Lock was opened on the Michigan side in 1855. The 2-mile (3-kilometer) span of the International Bridge opened in October 1962, improving transportation between the two Sault Ste. Maries. Prior to the bridge, ferries taxied automobiles and passengers across the St. Marys River. There are now more than 3.5 million vehicular crossings of the bridge annually. Travel time from downtown to downtown is generally 15 minutes, but certain times of day (morning and evening commutes) can double the wait time. Today, together, this is the third-largest metropolitan area on Lake Superior, behind Thunder Bay and Duluth-Superior.

Today

The economy of Soo, Michigan, is closely tied to Great Lakes and international shipping via the St. Marys River. Much of the commercial activity on the river has historically depended on cargoes passing between Lake Huron and Lake Superior. In earlier times, when the rapids made marine passage impossible, that included unloading ships, warehousing cargo, moving the cargoes past the rapids that stopped interlake transportation, then reloading it on other ships to continue its journey. Much of that effort ended in 1855 when the first Soo Lock opened. Today, the Soo Locks remain important to local commerce by employing many skilled workers, and passing ships continue to contribute to the economy by contracting for some supplies from merchant firms in the city. In addition, the Soo Locks attract thousands of visitors to the city each year to watch the locks in operation, making tourism an important ingredient in the city's economy.

Soo is also a regional education center. Lake Superior State University occupies the site of old Fort Brady, with some historic buildings still intact. The 115-acre campus is a good spot to photograph the International Bridge to Ontario. The university offers many interesting programs like a robotics laboratory, criminal justice, nursing, fisheries and wildlife and many professional degrees. The LSSU hockey team is a consistent contender on the national collegiate hockey scene.

What to See and Do

Four American navigational locks make the Michigan Soo a major center of marine transportation, as well as a center of tourism and the most visited site on Lake Superior. With the opening of the St. Lawrence Seaway in 1959, foreign-flagged vessels, known on the Great Lakes as "salties," are now much in evidence, giving the Soo Locks a truly international flavor. Poe Lock is the largest lock in the St. Lawrence Seaway and is the only one that can handle superfreighters, which are more than 1,000 feet (305 meters) long and 105 feet (32 meters) wide. In about 45 minutes from entry into a gate, the locks raise and lower lakers and oceangoing vessels 21 feet (6 meters) between Lake Superior and Lake Huron. More than 95 million tons of cargo pass through the locks annually.

Parks parallel the locks, with three observation platforms (no charge to visit) and a U.S. Army Corps of Engineers Information Center. From the platforms, visitors are within feet of the vessels going through the locks. There are good exhibits at the info center, explaining exactly how the lock system works. Once a year in June the Corps allows visitors to walk out to the locks for a closer inspection. Portage Avenue runs parallel to the lock and has a row of souvenir and gift shops (ranging from touristy to artistic), restaurants and attractions.

Beginning at the information center in the upper Locks Park, take a stroll along the city's 1-mile (1.6 kilometer) Historic Waterfront Pathway, extending through Brady Park and the lower Locks Park, past four major historic buildings and to the SS *Valley Camp* museum ship. The pathway has been signed with information describing the history of the St. Marys River. Stop at the John Johnston House, the oldest house in Michigan, built in 1793. A plaque marks the site of the restored 19th century homes of Bishop Frederic Baraga and Henry Schoolcraft. Another historic spot is the Kemp Commercial Building, long influential in the city's affairs through shipping and commercial fishing.

The Museum Ship SS *Valley Camp* is a retired 550-foot (170-metre) Great Lakes freighter and maritime museum, one of only two such floating ore boat museums on Lake Superior, the other being in Duluth. See the gleaming stainless steel galley, dining rooms, the crew's quarters and bridge, authentically maintained. The two recovered lifeboats from the *Edmund Fitzgerald* are on display. There is also a large aquarium with Lake Superior fish. The Ship's Store has gifts and many nautical items for sale and is a must stop on your visit. Open daily from mid-May to mid-October. Operated by Le Sault de Ste. Marie Historic Sites.

Tower of History takes visitors up 21 floors for a 20-mile (32-kilometer) panoramic view of the city, locks, lakes and Sault Ste. Marie, Ontario. There's a video depicting the history of the Great Lakes and Sault Ste. Marie. Open mid-May to mid-October.

Although the city's oldest church, the majestic twin-towered United Presbyterian Church, was destroyed by fire in 2000, it was rebuilt and is again open. History buffs can walk past Sault Ste. Marie's four remaining historic churches and the new United Presbyterian edifice by following a pathway marked on the sidewalks. Visitors can get maps and information at the Tourist Information Center.

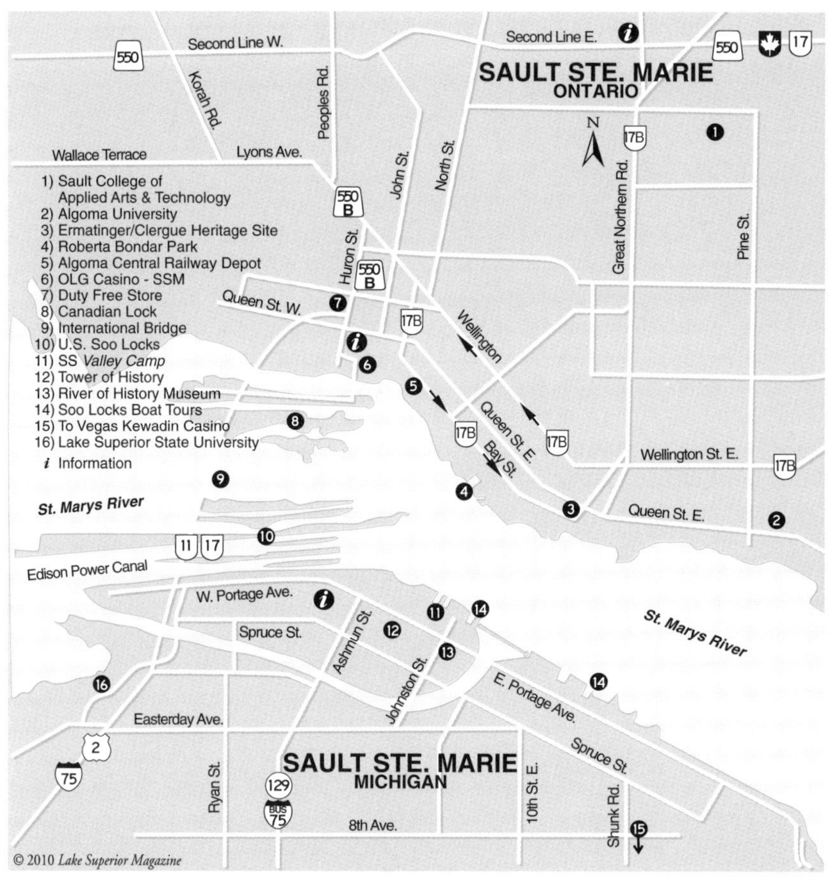

Sault Ste. Marie, Ontario & Michigan

Soo Locks Boat Tours leave from two docks for narrated two-hour cruises through the locks alongside huge ships, up river to Algoma Steel Mill and past the St. Marys Rapids. Docks are east on Portage Avenue. Tours run daily May 15 to October 15. Also 2½-hour dinner cruises include the locks tour. The company offers 4½-hour Saturday morning St. Marys River lighthouse cruises with water-level views of Point Iroquois, Gros Cap Reef and the remains of Round Island lighthouses, as well as other sites. Boarding at 7:45 a.m. with continental breakfast. Reservations recommended for dinner and lighthouse cruises. A nice added service is free kenneling for your pets during the tour.

Linksters will want to sample the pleasures of Sault Ste. Marie Country Club or Tanglewood Marsh, both with 18 holes.

Visitors to the city using boats can use the Charles T. Harvey Marina on Riverside Drive near the golf course. It has a rest station and provides fuel and other services. Adjacent to the *Valley Camp* in Mariners' Park, the city-owned George Kemp Downtown Marina features 62 slips for transient traffic. To camp next to the river, try Aune-Osborn Campground on Riverside Drive. It has 100 sites and is across from the Country Club golf course. Open mid-May to mid-October.

Kewadin Casinos (key-WAY-den) has Vegas-style gaming and entertainment. On Shunk Road within the city limits, the casino is operated by the Sault Band of Chippewa Indians. DreamMakers Theater, which seats 1,500, hosts entertainment headliners. Shuttle bus and limousine service from area hotels are available.

Notable Museums

Art lovers must visit Alberta House Arts Center and its Olive M. Craig Gallery and Gift Shop featuring U.P. arts and crafts and regularly changing exhibits and workshops. Open February through November, Tuesday through Saturday.

The River of History Museum at 531 Ashmun St. is owned by the Sault Foundation for Culture and History and managed by Sault Historic Sites. Its galleries, exhibits and audio presentation tell the story of Native Americans, French fur traders and others who helped tame the St. Marys River. Its store has local books, artwork and gifts. The Sault Ste. Marie Tribe of Chippewa Indians Cultural Division has exhibits by the entrance and its Cultural Interpretive Center is in the building.

The River of History Museum is open Monday to Saturday from noon to 5 p.m., with admission fees.

Archaeology fans will want to stop by the Federal Heritage Building to see artifacts from digs on the site of Old Fort Brady. Dating from 1822, the fort is the scene of an encampment of more than 100 re-enactors in July. It is the site of a history and culture camp for kids in summer.

Notable Events

- I-500 Snowmobile Race challenges

Sault Ste. Marie: Insider Tips

- The St. Marys River seems made for kayaks and canoes. And fishermen are drawn to it for an abundance of fish, ranging from native whitefish in the upper river above the rapids to the steelhead or Atlantic salmon found in the rapids.
- Rotary Park on the east end is a great place for boatwatching. Here, the ore boats pass so close to shore that you'll think it's possible to reach out and touch them. And the kids (16 and younger) can try their luck at catching rainbow trout in the Sault Kids Fishing Pond, which is free and run by the Soo Area Sportsmen's Club.
- Ashmun Street offers interesting shops, such as Superior Coast Winery and Brewery. Some shops feature a "two-for-one" experience, with one store in front and something else in the back, such as Northwoods Gifts & Backdoor BBQ. Or there's Austin's Oak, Fine Pipes & Tobacco, which has furniture in the front, a tobacco shop in the back and a basement full of antiques.
- West Pier Drive-In, on the Lake Superior side of the approach to the Soo Locks, and Clyde's Drive-In, on the downriver side of the Locks at the Sugar Island ferry dock, have spurred lively discussions about which has the best local burgers. You decide. Both are open seasonally only.
- Water Street has historic architecture starting with the home of John Johnston, one of the city's first European settlers. A block of homes includes that of Henry Rowe Schoolcraft, the area's first Indian agent.

snow sledders on an oval track in early February.

• Soo Locks Festival in June celebrates the impact of the U.S. locks on Great Lakes commerce.

• International Bridge Walk/Engineers Day is a June opportunity for visitors and residents to hike across the International Bridge as well as to walk out on the locks to examine them.

• Great Tugboat Race is an annual competition in July to determine the fastest boat in the twin Saults' tug fleets.

• Summer Arts Festival is an August celebration of the region's artistic skills on the Michigan waterfront.

What's Next

If your Circle Tour Route crosses into Canada from the Soo, you'll cross the International Bridge to Sault, Canada, where you'll want to explore a bit before picking up Trans Canada Highway 17 north. Note that non-residents older than 17 must have a Crown Land Camping Permit to overnight on Crown Land. Permits are found at most Ontario license issuers and Ministry of Natural Resources offices. You also should review the border crossing section earlier in this book.

If your itinerary is across Michigan's U.P., we suggest leaving the Soo area south on I-75/U.S. 2 toward St. Ignace. About 10 miles south you'll pick up Michigan Highway 28 and head west. If you intend to stop at Brimley, you can take either Business Interstate 75/County H-63 or Highway 129 south and turn west at Six Mile Road, which takes you closer to shore and cuts several miles. We urge a visit to eastern and southern U.P. by traveling south to St. Ignace to see the mighty Mackinac Bridge and other interesting sights.

INFO & OPTIONS

Sault Ste. Marie, Michigan, Chamber of Commerce
2581 I-75 Business Spur
Sault Ste. Marie, MI 49783
906-632-3301
www.saultstemarie.org

Sault Ste. Marie Convention & Visitors Bureau
536 Ashmun St.
Sault Ste. Marie, MI 49783
800-647-2858
www.saultstemarie.com

The Antlers Restaurant
804 East Portage Ave.
Sault Ste. Marie, MI 49783
906-632-3571

Freighters Restaurant
240 West Portage Ave.
Sault Ste. Marie, MI 49783
906-632-4100

Best Western
4335 I-75 Business Spur
Sault Ste. Marie, MI 49783-3621
906-632-2170
www.bestwesternmichigan.com

Kewadin Casino Hotel
2186 Shunk Rd.
Sault Ste. Marie, MI 49783
800-632-0530
www.kewadin.com

Lockview Motel
327 West Portage Ave.
Sault Ste. Marie, MI 49783
800-854-0745
www.lockview.com

Ramada Plaza Ojibway Hotel
240 West Portage Ave.
Sault Ste. Marie, MI 49783
800-654-2929
www.waterviewhotels.com

Super 8 Sault Ste. Marie

I-75 Exit 392
3826 I-75 Business Spur
Sault Ste. Marie, MI 49783
800-800-8000
www.super8.com

Kewadin Casino RV Park

2186 Shunk Rd.
Sault Ste. Marie, MI 49783
800-632-0530
www.kewadin.com/hotel/rv-park

Seney & Seney National Wildlife Refuge

Township Population 180

The Lake Superior Circle Tour follows M-28, shooting arrow straight eastward for more than 23 miles (37 kilometers) between Shingleton and Seney – known as the "Seney Stretch." If approaching on M-28 from the east, Seney is about 20 miles west of the junction with M-123 near Newberry. A quiet village of fewer than 200 residents and one saloon today, Seney was once "Sin City of the North" or "Hell Town in the Pine" during heavy white pine lumbering days of the late 1880s.

South of town on M-77, Seney National Wildlife Refuge is a magnet that draws visitors. The 96,000-acre refuge and visitor center on M-77, 5 miles (8 kilometers) south of Seney and 2 miles (3 kilometers) north of Germfask in the Great Manistique Swamp, is one of the larger U.S. wildlife refuges east of the Mississippi. Programs are offered in summer. The refuge has hiking and auto tours, many species of birds and other wildlife to see.

Silver City

Population 120

Silver City has a rich, traditional seaside feel and plenty of lodging options to make any vacation pleasurable. Silver City's main claim to fame is a primary entrance to Porcupine Mountains Wilderness State Park, Michigan's largest. The town is about 18 miles north of Bergland on M-64 from the M-28 Circle Tour Route or 13 miles southwest along Lake Superior from Ontonagon on M-64.

The interesting shops in Silver City include Great Lakes Trading Company, with art, antiques and woolens.

Parks and Public Areas

One of mid-America's highest mountain ranges (1,958 feet or 597 meters above sea level) contains the 58,332-acre Porcupine Mountains Wilderness State Park. Route 107 takes you to the visitors center, just off the main road on South Boundary Road. Oft-photographed Lake of the Clouds has an escarpment overlooking the incredibly blue lake and forest that guarantees vivid memories and pictures. A handicapped-accessible boardwalk and viewing platform offers easier access and another viewpoint.

The Porcupine Mountains Ski Area is 1 mile (1.6 kilometers) west of the park headquarters on Union Bay. A section of the North Country National Scenic Trail cuts through the park. Admission by park permit.

The Porcupine Mountains Chamber offers a brochure for people who want to experience the mountains, but aren't up to a deep wilderness backpack excursion.

What's Next

To travel toward Ontonagon and the Keweenaw Peninsula, take M-64 easterly from Silver City. To return to M-28, take

M-64 south from Silver City through White Pine to Bergland. About 2 miles from Silver City, Greenwood Falls (also called Bonanza Falls) on the Iron River is a local favorite. The adjacent lands were donated to the local government by Copper Range Company to preserve the site.

If your route is west to Wakefield, a scenic, interesting path is South Boundary Road from Silver City through the state park to County Road 519, then south. On the way, visit Summit Peak Observation Tower above Mirror Lake. Cut back to the lake to see the waterfalls on the Presque Isle River, where there are modern private campgrounds and access to backpacking trails that criss-cross the park.

Skanee

Township Population 480

Skanee is a dot of a town that offers the Joyce Witz Marina, which has good facilities for boats and anglers, but the area is tight for large vehicles. There is a free launch at Arvon Township Park. Skanee Town Hall dates to 1895. The Skanee Historical Museum has artifacts from the late 1800s to early 1900s. Twelve miles (19 kilometers) from L'Anse on the way to Skanee, stop at Silver River Falls, where the river cuts its way through slate rocks on the west end of the Huron Mountains. There are facilities in the parking area. You'll return to the Circle Tour route by backtracking.

INFO & OPTIONS

Big Eric's Bridge Campground
Twenty miles from L'Anse, Skanee Road to Big Erick's Road, Skanee, MI
906-353-6651

Tahquamenon Falls State Park

Michigan Highway 123 makes a northerly loop from and to Michigan Highway 28 in the eastern Upper Peninsula, giving access to Paradise (see separate listing) and Tahquamenon Falls (Ta-KWAH-meh-non), one of the largest U.S. waterfalls east of the Mississippi River. Tea-colored water approaches the 48-foot-deep (15-meter), 200-foot-wide (61-meter) sandstone cliff in low rapids, then plunges over the edge into a pool of boiling bubbles. More than 50,000 gallons of water per second flow over the edge. Handicapped-accessible paths lead from the parking area to overlooks. A 94-step stairway continues down to the overlook at the edge of the falls. Other steps wind down to the river's edge below the falls.

Four miles (6 kilometers) downstream, the river wraps around an island in a series of smaller falls and rapids. The island is accessible by rowboat from a Lower Falls riverside concession. Small fee. There are separate entrances for both falls, part of the nearly 40,000-acre Tahquamenon Falls State Park, second in size only to Michigan's largest state park, Porcupine Mountains Wilderness State Park in the Western U.P. Vehicle permit required.

WHAT'S NEXT

If your Circle Tour is west to east, M-123 heads south from Paradise, but if your route is east to west you can reconnect with M-28 at Newberry through Lake Superior State Forest. If that's your choice, watch for a turnoff on County 500 toward Little Lake and the old Two-Hearted River Life-Saving Station. Little Lake affords boaters a harbor of refuge from Lake Superior, although it is subject to shoaling activity. Little remains of the original station at Two-Hearted River, but a historical marker commemorates the exploits of the life-saving team that served so well in this remote locale, 17 miles from the main road.

Once isolated but now accessible on a seasonal extension of County Road 412 on the shore east of Little Lake is Crisp Point Lighthouse. Crisp Point Light Historical Society mounted a rescue effort that won the *Lake Superior Magazine* Achievement Award in 2000.

Wakefield

Population 1,875

At Wakefield, M-28 meets with U.S. Highway 2 from the lower part of the U.P.

Camp inside the city limits at Sunday Lake Campground with a boat launch, swimming and day facilities. Wakefield Historical Society Museum opens mid-June through mid-September every afternoon except Sundays. Wakefield July Fourth festivities have a nice parade.

INFO & OPTIONS

Wakefield Chamber of Commerce
673 M-28
Wakefield, MI 49968
906-224-2222
www.visitwakefield.com

Watersmeet

Township Population 1,441

Watersmeet is at the junction of U.S. Highways 2 and 45 in the southwest Upper Peninsula. Near the town are a number of recreation opportunities.

What's Next

The Ottawa National Forest Visitor Center is in Watersmeet, with information on the forest's 27 campgrounds, hiking, biking, canoeing, fishing, hunting or any other recreational activity within this wonderfully scenic area.

Southwest of town, the 19,000-acre Sylvania Wilderness Area and Sylvania Recreation Area, part of the National Wilderness Preservation System. Sylvania has it all: camping, fishing, canoeing, hiking and skiing amid 34 lakes and tall old trees. Besides a 48-unit drive-in campground, there are wilderness campsites accessible by canoe or on foot. Permits available at the main entrance.

Whitefish Point Lighthouse is next to the Great Lakes Shipwreck Museum.

Lac Vieux Desert, a large lake south of town, is nestled between Michigan's Ottawa and Wisconsin's Nicolet national forests. This headwaters of the Wisconsin River, home of a world record tiger musky, is great for walleye, bass, northern, and panfish, too. Options range from camping to deluxe American-plan resorts. Also here is the Cisco Chain of Lakes with 15 lakes interconnected for more than 270 miles (435 kilometers) of scenic shoreline. Many year-round resorts operate in the area.

Golfers will want to try Gateway Golf Club, a public 9-hole course with lounge and pro shop in the nearby border town of Land O' Lakes, Wisconsin.

West from Watersmeet on U.S. Highway 2, we're entering "Big Snow Country." To return to the Lake Superior Circle Tour route, take U.S. 45 north to Michigan Highway 28.

INFO & OPTIONS

Lac Vieux Desert Resort Casino
North 5384 U.S. Hwy. 45
Watersmeet, MI 49969
800-583-3599
www.lvdcasino.com

Whitefish Point

About 15 miles north of Paradise is the Great Lakes Shipwreck Museum at Whitefish Point. More than 350 known shipwrecks are in Lake Superior. This and Copper Harbor are the sites of the first lighthouses on Lake Superior. Now automated, its predecessor began operating in 1849. The museum has an excellent video on shipwrecks, a gift shop and a great beach for swimming and rock picking. Its exhibit about the famous 1975 *Edmund Fitzgerald* wreck features the bell recovered from the wreck in 1995. This is a stop well worth the travel.

The restored 1923 Crews Quarters are open for lodging with five modern rooms with private baths and continental breakfast. Reservations are a must.

Next door, Whitefish Point Bird Observatory, operated by the Michigan Audubon Society, documents bird migration. There is an exhibit building near the Great Lakes Shipwreck Museum, and a series of wooden walkways through the dunes lets visitors venture into the sanctuary without disturbing foliage. Admission is free.

INFO & OPTIONS

Great Lakes Shipwreck Museum
18335 North Whitefish Point Rd.
Paradise, MI 49768
888-492-3747
www.shipwreckmuseum.com

Whitefish Point Bird Observatory
16914 North Whitefish Point Rd.
Paradise, MI 49768
906-492-3596
wpbo.org

White Pine

Population 625

South of Silver City on M-64, White Pine was the last copper mining "boom town" in Michigan's fabled Copper Country, hosting the homes of company employees. Copper mining ended years ago with the closing of Copper Range Company facilities, but the town survives. At the shopping area, Konteka Resort and Restaurant offers gifts to lodging, fine dining, a lounge, bowling, snowmobile rental and wildlife viewing from indoor comfort behind large windows.

What's Next

M-64 continues south to a junction with M-28 at Bergland.

LAKE SUPERIOR Minnesota

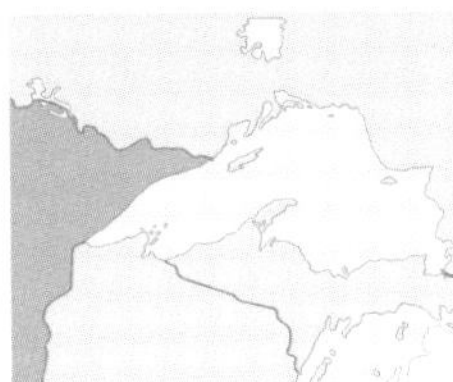

Since 1905, a bridge has spanned the canal between the mainland and Minnesota Point in Duluth. Today the Aerial Lift Bridge is a Duluth icon and major tourist draw.

Minnesota offers travelers more than 150 miles of Lake Superior shoreline from Duluth to the Ontario border. The North Shore of Minnesota on Highway 61 features rugged, often dramatic, cliffs and panoramic overlooks, as well as charming harbor towns like Grand Marais and Two Harbors. For hikers and other outdoor lovers, there are eight state parks and the famous Superior Hiking Trail. Split Rock Lighthouse and Gooseberry Falls should be on your itinerary even if you've seen them before. Or spend time in Duluth, second largest city on the lake and a regional cultural center with prime shipwatching spots.

Explore Minnesota Tourism
888-868-8476
www.exploreminnesota.com

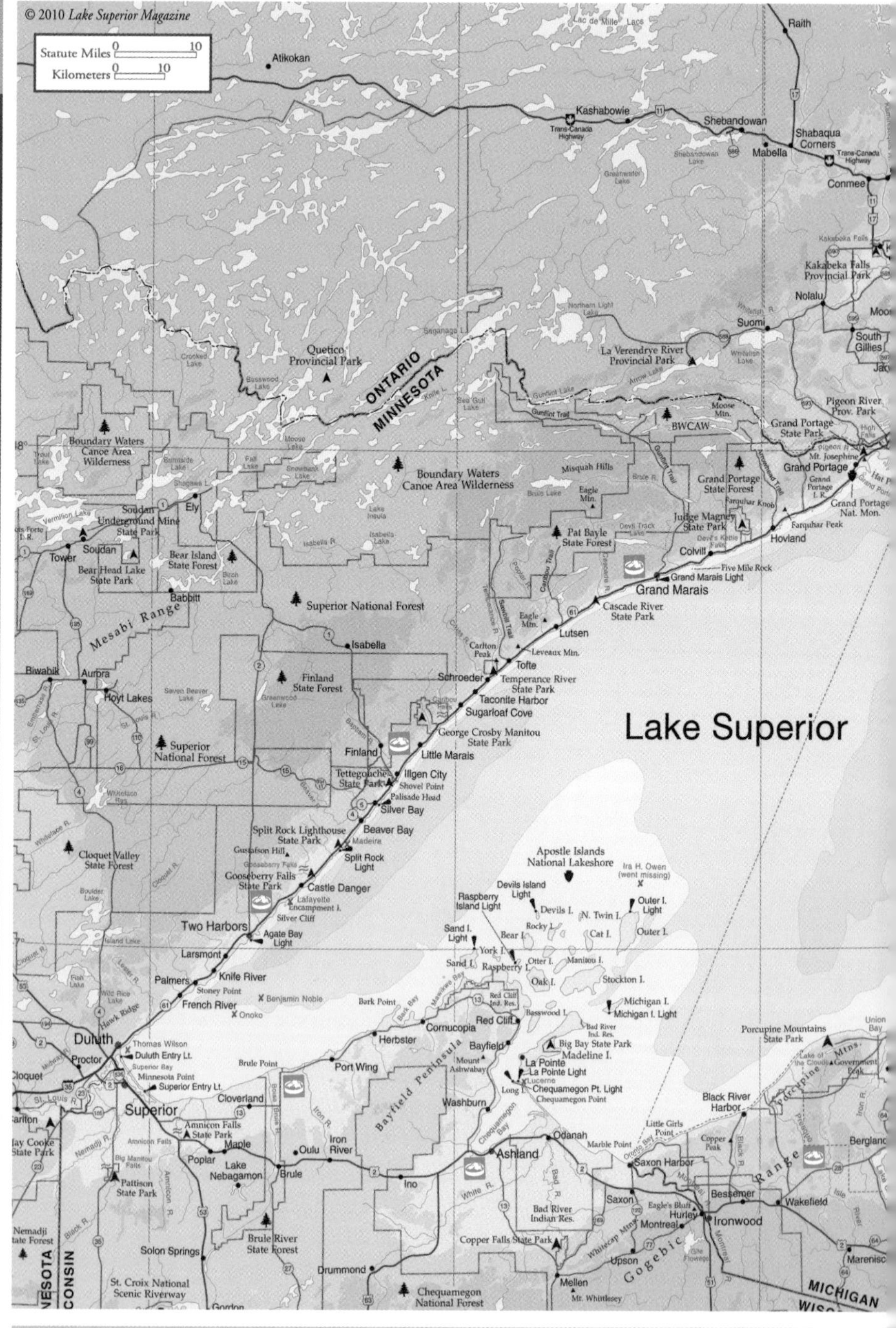

Minnesota's North Shore [Detailed Iron Range Map, Page 18]

Aurora

Population: 2,000

At the eastern tip of the Mesabi Iron Range are the towns of Aurora, Biwabik and Hoyt Lakes, each important in the history of Minnesota iron mining. Aurora and Biwabik were early mining locations when the rich Mesabi hematite ore was being mined. Hoyt Lakes was built as housing for employees concurrent with the construction of the giant Erie Mining Company taconite plant a few miles north of the townsite. The plant was shut down in 2000.

A Bit of History

Aurora was once the site of several important iron ore mines that have long since been shut down. An early taconite test plant was located at Aurora and developed many proven processes by which the abundant, flintlike low-grade taconite iron ore could be upgraded to a usable product. That pilot plant was the precursor of Erie Mining Company, which was built a few miles northeast of town in the mid-1950s. The plant produced up to 14 millions tons of iron ore a year until it was closed in 2000. Although it was already an active city when the taconite plant was built, Aurora was bypassed by the mining company for residential development and Hoyt Lakes was built a few miles east to house workers and their families.

Today

A resilient town that has seen many economic ups and downs through its more than 100-year history, Aurora retains much of the robust character that has sustained it through boom and bust. Its main street is dotted with several saloons. Some, like Rudy's Bar and Grill in the middle of downtown, have long histories of serving miners, construction workers, loggers and folks from the large rural area south of town.

Aurora can fill any need, from emergency health care to novelty gifts and good restaurants. A stop at Zup's Grocery meets every grocery need and is sure to reward the shopper with specialty meats for any occasion, from campfire cooking to holiday feasts. Ron's Bakery on Main Street has provided baked goodies to generations of residents and visitors. Cherro's Italian Market provides specialty items for the Mediterranean taste. A couple of times each summer the A&W Drive In on South Main sponsors Classic Car Cruise Nights that are a must for classic car buffs throughout northeastern Minnesota.

What's Next

To the east is Hoyt Lakes (population 2,200) and to the west is Biwabik (population about 1,000), each described in separate listings.

INFO & OPTIONS

Timber Wolf Lodge
9130 Escape Rd.
Babbitt, MN 55706
800-777-8457
www.timberwolflodge.com

Beaver Bay

Population 150

Beaver Bay is the oldest settlement with a continuous existence on Minnesota's Lake Superior shore. It was founded in 1856 by German immigrants, who opened the region's first successful sawmill. In addition to townspeople, they employed many Ojibway people in the area. Look for the chainsaw-carved beaver that welcomes visitors. For information, check the Visitors Center operated by Bay Area Historical Society.

An Indian cemetery sits beside County Road 4 on the east side of town and is considered a sacred space. John Beargrease, best known as one of the early mail carriers who made the weekly trip between Two Harbors and Grand Portage, is buried here. The annual John Beargrease Sled Dog Marathon held in February between Duluth and Grand Marais is named in honor of Beargrease, who became a north shore legend for his dependability, no matter what the weather.

Where to Shop

A small town, Beaver Bay is loaded with fun shops. Several are in the Beaver Bay Mini-Mall on Highway 61, including the Cedar Chest, offering a wide variety of gifts, souvenirs, collectables, books and a large array of Christmas items. Beaver Bay Agate Shop is one of the best rock shops on the shore. There is a terrific bakery, a Christmas store and the unique Shipwrecked Gift Shop, which has a wide selection of merchandise. Operated out of East Beaver Bay, Beaver Bay Sports Shop offers a wide array of outdoor and fishing equipment.

What's Next

To continue the Circle Tour route, take Highway 61 either southwest to Two Harbors and Duluth or northeast to Silver Bay heading for Grand Marais.

INFO & OPTIONS

Bay Area Information Center
1001 Main St.
Beaver Bay, MN 55601
218-226-3317

Cove Point Crossings Bar & Grill
4614 Hwy. 61
Beaver Bay, MN 55601
800-598-6221
covepointlodge.com

Lemon Wolf Cafe
Hwy. 61
Beaver Bay, MN 55601
218-226-7225
www.lemonwolfcafe.com

Cove Point Lodge
4614 Hwy. 61
Beaver Bay, MN 55601
218-226-3221
www.covepointlodge.com

Biwabik

Population 910

On the eastern side of Minnesota's Mesabi Iron Range, the alpine-styled town of Biwabik is on Highway 135 a few miles east of Virginia. Through a century, this area has been important in the history of iron mining activity and was the site where the second iron mine was developed on the Mesabi Range. Evidence of mining is almost everywhere, from gaping red-hued holes in the earth to huge mounds of waste rock and overburden stockpiled around the mines.

Today, Biwabik is home to Giants Ridge Golf and Ski Resort, which features "ski or golf from the door" lodging. The resort has 36 holes of championship golf on its well-touted Quarry and Legend courses. For about 50 years Giants Ridge has been a popular ski area that features all the amenities of a major resort.

In winter, Giants Ridge offers alpine and nordic skiing and an excellent terrain park. Biwabik has a lighted sliding hill and skating rink, adding a Norman Rockwell touch to snowy evenings. This is also the hometown of *Honk the Moose,* a popular children's book by Biwabik school teacher author Phil Stong. A life-sized statue of a moose stands in the park at the center of the city to commemorate the story's origin in Biwabik.

What's Next

Leaving Biwabik on Highway 135, you'll travel either west to Gilbert and Virginia-Eveleth or east to Aurora, with Hoyt Lakes a bit farther. A delightful way to return to Lake Superior's Minnesota North Shore is to follow the Superior National Forest Scenic Byway (Lake County 15/St. Louis County 16) south from Hoyt Lakes to Silver Bay on Lake Superior through scenic beauty, overlooks, lakes and forests.

INFO & OPTIONS

Giants Ridge Golf & Ski Resort
6325 Wynne Creek Dr.
Biwabik, MN 55708
800-688-7669
www.giantsridge.com

Calumet

Population 380

The village of Calumet is the unofficial gateway to the western Mesabi Iron Range and home to the last intact iron ore pit mine in Minnesota that can be toured. Listed on the National Register of Historic Places, the Hill Annex Mine outlines the development of mining from animal use through steam power to modern high-tech equipment. Miners' Day celebrations are held in July. Fossil hunting in the mine is encouraged and pontoon boat rides on the mine pit lake are a nice diversion.

Winter skiers will want to visit Mont Itasca nearby at Coleraine, which is now designated as a U.S. biathlon training center and also offers ski jumping, snowboarding, downhill and cross-country trails.

What's Next

Travelers will take U.S. 169 either northeast toward Hibbing or southwest through Bovey and Coleraine to Grand Rapids.

Cascade River State Park

About midway between Lutsen and Grand Marais, on U.S. Highway 61, Cascade River State Park has 10 streams flowing within its boundaries. Headwater swamps, swift midsections and roaring mouths can be easily explored from hiking trails. Most picturesque is the Cascade River itself, which falls 900 feet (274 meters) in a wispy 3-mile descent to Lake Superior within an easy walk of the highway. Wintertime draws a lot of fox to Deer Yard Lake.

Historic Cascade Lodge and Restaurant's dining room overlooks the lake and is well worth the stop, even if you can't stay over. The lodge caters to cross-country skiers in winter since it adjoins the 30-mile (48-kilometer) ski trail of the state park. There's always great food.

Traveling on Highway 61 toward Grand Marais, as you approach Good Harbor Bay, prepare to stop at the Thomsonite Beach Jewelry Shop, which features thomsonite, a gem unique to Lake Superior, set in gold. The gemstones come from a private mine on the Thomsonite Beach Inn and Suites property, 5 miles (8 kilometers) southwest of Grand Marais. The Good Harbor Scenic Overlook, which provides a nice lake vista, has been upgraded by the Minnesota Department of Transportation, part of the highway improvement going on over several years and in several areas along Minnesota's North Shore. Famed Duluth architect David Salmela designed the "facilities" at this stop. Nearby is Cut Face Falls.

About 15 miles inland, in the Boundary Waters Canoe Area Wilderness, Eagle Mountain is Minnesota's highest peak at 2,301 feet (701 meters). Ask for directions in either Lutsen or Grand Marais.

Traveling northeasterly leads to Grand Marais. Southward from the Cascade area, you're heading for Tofte.

Castle Danger

Castle Danger is 10 miles (16 kilometers) east on Highway 61 from Two Harbors, and the origin of the name is still cloaked in mystery. Once a fishing and logging area, some say it was named for the castlelike formation along the shore, a dangerous area for ships. Another story attributes the name to the ship *Castle,* reputed to have foundered here, although no evidence of that ship has been found.

Castle Danger is home to the year-round Rustic Inn, a historic log cabin restaurant with a gift shop, delectable dinners and homemade pies.

Across the highway, Grand Superior Lodge is the only log resort in the area and occupies the site of the oldest cabin resort on the north shore, Emil Edison's 1920s Campers' Home. A new log lodge opened in 2000 with suites, the Splashing Rock Restaurant and Lounge, meeting and banquet facilities and other amenities. The resort continues its cabin heritage, however, offering nice log guest homes with their own fireplaces (books months in advance). The same management operates Caribou Highlands Lodge at Lutsen.

Nearby, the coffee is always on at Northwoods Pioneer Gallery & Gifts, a shop where you will find many works from local artists and craftspeople. For a traditional North Shore stay, try Castle Haven Cabins, with its delightful Quilter's Cabin shop. Or stay at Gooseberry Park Motel & Cabins.

As you approach Gooseberry Falls from Castle Danger, watch on the left for The Lodge at Gooseberry Falls, a new development whose plans include shops, housing and amenities with the look of log construction.

Castle Danger is only a stone's throw from Gooseberry Falls State Park (see separate listing), one of the most visited spots on Minnesota's North Shore.

Chisholm

Population 4,960

Chisholm, located on U.S. Highway 169 north of Hibbing, is a good stop to experience the history of iron ore mining that was so crucial to the development of this region.

What to See and Do

The history of iron ore mining can be experienced at the Minnesota Museum of Mining, which allows visitors to actually climb up on the equipment used to mine the Mesabi Range's rich iron ore. Open Memorial Day through Labor Day. On the edge of the Glen Mine, the Minnesota Discovery Center (formerly Ironworld) museum, trolley line and historic mining settlement preserve the story of this region's rich history. The Discovery Center tells the story of how immigrants settled Minnesota's Iron

The Iron Man Monument in Chisholm is a tribute to those who worked on Minnesota's Iron Ranges. This area also has mines to tour and the Minnesota Discovery Center.

"Lakers," freighters as long as 1,000 feet, make their way through the ship canal in Duluth, much to the delight of residents and visitors. "Salties," or oceangoing vessels, also come to port.

Range in search of their dreams. A 1920s Mesabi Railway trolley takes riders along the edge of the mine for a panoramic view of what mining entailed. Enjoy heritage activities or visit the research library and archives to trace your family's roots. Discovery Center's museum, theater, Overlook Gallery with traveling exhibits, restaurant and research library are open year-round. Closed Mondays. Fees.

Across the road, the Iron Man Memorial is a statue dedicated to the thousands of miners who have worked on the Minnesota Iron Ranges and is the third-largest free-standing statue in the United States.

Notable Events

• Check for summer events, such as Iron Ranger Days, at Minnesota Discovery Center.

Cloquet

Population 11,352

The official Circle Tour route follows Highway 61 on Minnesota's North Shore, but travelers with a zest for the north woods might consider a side trip that meanders south from Duluth through towns in Carlton and Pine counties. You'll see Black Bear Casino Resort, which was recently rebuilt and expanded, and also has a golf course in Carlton. Moose Lake is home to the Blacklock Photography Galleries, which feature the work of well-known Lake Superior photographer Craig Blacklock.

The city of Cloquet, 20 minutes south of Duluth, is well worth the stop. Created as a paper mill company town, the paper plant, now owned by Sappi Limited, remains a major influence and employer. A long-time favorite for great hamburgers and onion rings, Gordy's Hi Hat drive-in is a local sign of spring when it opens in March. Also worth noting is the gas station designed by Frank Lloyd Wright in 1956 at the corner of Minnesota Highway 33 and Cloquet Avenue. And as you're driving into Cloquet on Highway 33, look for Bergquist Imports, which sells gifts from Scandinavia, including china, crystal, books, foods and items with Swedish, Finnish and Norwegian phrases.

Duluth

Population 86,920

At the Head of the Lakes, where the St. Louis River, the natural headwaters of the great Kitchi Gami (Gitche Gumee), is located, the cities of Duluth, Minnesota, and Superior, Wisconsin, though in different states, are the northern Twin Cities, or "Twin Ports."

The overall Duluth-Superior area, with a population of 243,815, is one of the three largest metro areas beside Lake Superior, each made up of dual cities. Thunder Bay, Ontario, with a metro population of 122,907 (or 109,141 within city limits), is an amalgamation of the former cities of Port Arthur and Fort William. Sault Ste. Marie, Ontario, and Sault Ste. Marie, Michigan, with a combined total of about 95,000 people, make up the third metro area. All heavily use the lake for commerce.

A Bit of History

Over the years, Duluth (second largest city on the lake) and Superior (population 27,370) have had a friendly – and in the distant past not so friendly – rivalry, yet it seems almost impossible to mention one city without the other because their history and commerce are

Even in September in Duluth, it's possible to catch lovely views of a serene Lake Superior as you stroll through the Rose Garden in Leif Erikson Park.

so intertwined.

Superior was developed earlier than Duluth by virtue of the fact that all of northeastern Minnesota remained Indian territory until the 1854 Treaty of La Pointe was ratified in early 1855, opening up Lake Superior's Minnesota North Shore to exploration and settlement. Prospectors immediately flooded to the area, expecting to find a continuation of the fabulous copper ore being mined to the east in Michigan's Copper Country. Traces of copper kept that hope alive, but never led to any substantial mining.

Meanwhile by the 1870s, railroads were being built to the Twin Ports. The promise of shipping huge tonnages of western grain, timber products, freight and passengers was the magnet that led to rapid boom and bust development during the next decade. Although Superior's flat terrain seemed a more logical choice for railroad development, Duluth prevailed in attracting the attention of the rail and shipping developers, becoming the larger city within a few years.

With discovery of iron ore in northern Minnesota, first on the Vermilion Range in the 1860s and later on the Mesabi Iron Range in the early 1890s, a flurry of construction and development kept pace with the explosion of iron ore shipping and a rapidly expanding timber industry that settled sawmill operations along the waterfronts of Duluth and Superior.

By the early years of the 20th century, the Twin Ports were a major force in the economy of Midwest and, indeed, the entire country. Despite the collapse of the timber boom by 1920, the importance of grain and iron ore shipping remained and other enterprises like shipbuilding, commercial fishing, tourism, health and education and, recently, shipping huge cargoes of western coal have each had an impact on the Head of the Lakes and on the lives of people who live here.

Today

Duluth's and Superior's primary products relate to their position on Lake Superior and the Great Lakes. Iron ore, grain, coal and other bulk cargoes are shipped throughout the world from the port, which also receives shipments from many foreign sources via the St. Lawrence Seaway.

But shipping, while important, is not the dominating local economic factor that it once was. Today, health care and the medical field constitute the largest source of employment in Duluth. In addition, three major educational institutions and several non-degree institutions provide professional and

Duluth, Minnesota & Superior, Wisconsin

vocational skills to thousands of students each year, making the Twin Ports the regional education center for a large area, as well as freshwater research and educational facilities that rank it as the freshwater capital of the region.

This is also the starting point for many people planning a Circle Tour of Lake Superior. The route northeast on Highway 61 along Lake Superior's Minnesota North Shore is one of the most popular and scenic routes in the country, designated as a National Scenic Highway from Canal Park in Duluth all the way to the international border. For those planning a counterclockwise Circle Tour, Highway 2 east from Duluth through Superior and on into Wisconsin to Michigan's Upper Peninsula is also a scenic and pleasant route to many of the big lake's most attractive destinations.

To find out what's happening in the Twin Ports, pick up a copy of the *Duluth News Tribune* or the *Superior Telegram* from the Superior side of St. Louis Bay. Several large shopping complexes and numerous tourist attractions from golf and museums to in-town fishing make these cities one of the most popular tourist destinations in the Midwest. Duluth and Superior each serves as the county seat for, respectively, St. Louis County, Minnesota, and Douglas County, Wisconsin. Each is also a regional center for other governmental agencies at both the state and federal levels.

Duluth stretches some 25 miles (40 kilometers) along an old mountain bordering the lake, with streams, hills and woodlands distributed throughout the city. The counterpoint of residential, commercial and industrial development sits well on the hillsides, providing an urban wilderness of beauty and comfortable living.

Duluth's neighborhoods all have personalities of their own. Each exhibits an individual style when it comes to shopping. Along East Superior Street from the downtown area, you'll pass through historic neighborhoods with block upon block of magnificent older homes, many qualifying as mansions. This leads to the Lakeside and Lester Park neighborhoods, which are the "newer" residential areas that offer their own hometown shopping experiences.

Gary/New Duluth and Morgan Park on the extreme western edge of the city have their company homes and shopping areas. Busy Spirit Valley in West Duluth has a rapidly expanding shopping mall, plus many Grand Avenue and Central Avenue establishments that can provide you with a full day of shopping. In Duluth's Lincoln Park (formerly West End) on Superior Street, the well-designed streetscape affords a pleasant opportunity to visit some of the city's big furniture stores and shops.

Canal Park area of Duluth strives to recapture the historical flavor of the city. The area is a popular attraction during the daytime and late into the night with entertainment and restaurants. It has really come alive with the addition of sculptures, other outdoor art and fountains. An Art Walk brochure is available in most information racks with a walking tour of Waterfront Art, listing sculptures and art objects located from Bayfront Festival Park to Lake Place Park and other sites around town.

Park Point, across the Aerial Lift Bridge from Canal Park, is formally called Minnesota Point, a 7-mile-long (11.3-kilometer) sand bar that separates

Lake Superior from the sheltered Superior Bay and the Duluth and Superior harbors. At its end, visitors find a 22-acre recreation area, sand beaches, a few with lifeguards (water temperatures near shore can range from 70 to 85 degrees Fahrenheit in the summer, honest), picnic tables, playgrounds, ball fields, a sheltered beach house and Sky Harbor Airport. Windsurfing is a popular pastime on the harbor side. Numerous marinas along the Point harbor private yachts and cruisers. The Duluth Rowing Club often practices and holds races on Superior Bay. A bird sanctuary is maintained beyond the airport at the end of Park Point.

Despite seemingly long distances in town, visitors without their own transportation will find easy access to transportation by contacting one of several cab companies or boarding Duluth Transit Authority buses that connect to virtually all areas of both Duluth and Superior. Duluth International Airport serves airline

Duluth: Insider Tips

• Brighton Beach in Kitchi-Gammi Park, at Congdon Boulevard and 63rd Avenue East near the northeastern edge of Duluth, is one of the city's best spots for stargazing. Here you can curl up on the shoreline's big rocks or on a blanket on the grass and stare into space pondering life's big questions and catching sight of the occasional meteorite or UFO.

• Marshall W. Alworth Planetarium, University of Minnesota Duluth, College Street and University Drive, hosts free one-hour presentations most Wednesday nights. UMD professors impart their wisdom and project the night sky on the 30-foot planetarium dome.

• Minnesota Point (in photo below) contains several wonderful public beaches, where you can stand with your feet in the waves and look out at the huge freighters and sailboats and nothing but blue water over the horizon. On the bay side you can look toward Superior and Barker's Island. And Park Point offers a nice park for picnics, gatherings and events.

• When shopping for beautiful imported gifts, try Coppola Artistica, 728 E. Superior Street, a small shop just beyond Fitger's Brewery Complex. You're surrounded by floor-to-ceiling examples of flamboyantly painted dishware. The bright colors will make you feel better just by walking in. Owner-artist Antonino Coppola sells hand-painted ceramics from Italy, but look also for pieces that represent Duluth and the region.

passengers or charter and general aircraft arriving in or departing the northland, also offering car rental service. Greyhound Bus Lines provides connections to the Twin Cities from both Duluth and Cloquet.

Duluth serves as the health center for the region and a focal point for educational services, shopping, cultural expression and recreational activities. St. Luke's Hospital operates a 24-hour walk-in emergency care facility on East First Street and also has facilities in the Denfeld neighborhood, Hermantown and Superior. Nearby, the St. Mary's/Duluth Clinic hospitals join St. Luke's in offering a wide range of general and specialized care that have made Duluth a major medical center in the Upper Midwest.

The University of Minnesota Duluth (UMD) offers both four-year and graduate programs in liberal arts, science and technology, human resources, fine arts and business and is becoming a major center for freshwater research. It has an excellent medical school. UMD is the home of the Tweed Museum of Art, Marshall Performing Arts Center, Natural Resources Research Institute, the Large Lakes Observatory, a new library that offers a spectacular lake view to the public, the copper-domed Weber Music Hall and KUMD Radio, offering an interesting variety of programming.

Just a country block away from UMD, the College of St. Scholastica is a startling wonder of majestic Norman Gothic architecture featuring intricately placed stonework. Reminiscent of Olde

Viewed from one of the downtown high-rise condominiums, it's easy to see why Canal Park in Duluth is popular, with a coming together of lake, beach, bridge, lodging and shopping.

England, the college offers four-year and graduate programs. Mitchell Auditorium is the home of its renowned Early Music Concert program, among other events scheduled. Lake Superior College offers students up to two years of academic or vocational education.

For information on the Superior, Wisconsin, side of the bay, see its separate listing.

What to See and Do

In the harbor area, activity never seems to stop. From gigantic ore carriers moving in and out of their berths, grain ships slipping next to grain elevators or tourist boats scuttling back and forth throughout the harbor, there is much to see and do.

Thompson Hill Travel Information Center and observation area off Interstate 35 near Spirit Mountain not only is loaded with information, it has a breathtaking view of the entire lower St. Louis River basin, the Duluth-Superior harbor and the lake beyond. Visitors and residents always comment on the impact of the vista as they drive over Thompson Hill, day or night.

The Duluth waterfront centers on the refurbished Canal Park at the very tip of Lake Superior. Lake carriers ("lakers") and saltwater vessels ("salties") enter and leave the Duluth harbor through the Duluth Ship Canal. Built in 1871, its piers extend 1,700 feet (518 meters) into Lake Superior. Sightseers can enjoy the plentiful gulls and stroll along the canal's walkways to its lighthouses. And there's a feeling that you can virtually reach out and touch the huge ships towering above you as they pass through the canal.

Next to the Aerial Lift Bridge (see side story), Lake Superior Maritime Visitor Center is one of the most visited sites in Minnesota, offering film shows, model ships and hands-on exhibits featuring commercial shipping on Lake Superior. Former visitors will want to check out this museum again, since many artifacts on display are changed at intervals. Kids love to try their hand at the large ship's wheel. Announcements about shipping activities are made from the museum as traffic moves through the Duluth Ship Canal. Open daily, with shortened hours in the cooler months. There is no fee for this service of the U.S. Army Corps of Engineers with exhibits from the Lake Superior Marine Museum Association, which also runs a small gift shop inside the center. Boatwatcher's Hotline at 218-722-6489 is a special phone service of the Lake Superior Maritime Visitor Center, U.S. Army Corps of Engineers and the Duluth Seaway Port Authority, providing up-to-the-minute information concerning the arrivals and departures of ships.

Great Lakes Aquarium is an international facility that focuses on freshwater issues. The aquarium's $38 million, 62,000-square-foot exhibition building houses huge aquarium tanks with a multitude of species of freshwater life above and below the surface, in addition to interactive exhibits of environmental significance to Lake Superior and its watershed. The aquarium focuses on Lake Superior as a means to examine freshwater lakes throughout the world. For the most enjoyment, be sure to be a "hands-on" visitor. The aquarium conducts regular presentations for the public and outreach programs for schools, as well as interesting and entertaining exhibits of lake-related subjects. Aquarium membership allows reduced or free admission.

The city's most popular attraction is the Lakewalk, which hugs the shoreline for more than a mile along the North Shore Scenic Railroad from Canal Park past the Fitger's Brewery Complex to Leif Erikson Park, home of Duluth's famed Viking Ship and the Duluth Rose Garden, and then continues on for several miles. The Lakewalk soon will be extended to 60th Avenue East. The large structure sitting in the water just off the Lakewalk in Canal Park is an old coal-unloading dock from years gone by and is known locally as Uncle Harvey's Mausoleum. It was named for Harvey Whitney of the Whitney Brothers Company from Superior, who had it built in 1919 originally to serve as a receiving facility for Apostle Islands sand and Grand Marais gravel. Within a few years, Lake Superior proved too powerful and Whitney abandoned it. Today, kids dive from it into the cool waters of Lake Superior during the summer. Above the Lakewalk at the "corner" of the lake is Lake Place Park, which covers the interstate highway. This landscaped area is also accessible from downtown. A storm pavilion allows visitors to watch tremendous waves crash into the shore from the protection of its shelter. Flowers and benches provide a pleasant atmosphere at this park in the heart of the city. The Viking Ship celebrates the Vikings' landing in Duluth. The restored Viking Ship sailed from Norway in the early part of the 20th century to celebrate the Nordic tradition. The Rose Garden was rebuilt and restored by the highway department after construction of the interstate highway. More than 3,000 rose bushes and flowering arrangements are maintained. There are many interesting annotated stops along the wide Lakewalk explaining sights and history of the area, including an amazing mosaic history Image Wall that overlooks the lake. The Vietnam Veterans Memorial and the Korean War Memorial honor area members of the armed forces who served in those wars. Access to the Lakewalk from East Superior Street is made by a wide stairway at Eighth Avenue East near Fitger's or through the historic brewery itself.

Skyline Parkway reveals the entire Duluth-Superior harbor and surrounding scenery. The dramatic 30-mile (48-kilometer) drive along the hilltop 600 feet (182 meters) above the shoreline of Duluth is designated as a State Scenic Byway. The route follows the shoreline of ancient Lake Superior when it was much deeper, extending from one end of the city to the other. It offers superb views of Lake Superior, the Duluth and Superior harbors, Hawk Ridge on Seven Bridges Road, rocky canyons and tumbling streams. Frequent observation points and markers help the driver and photographer. Hawk Ridge is a favorite vantage point in September for watching the annual migration of birds of prey. The city has marked the route with signs.

Pause at the Clayton Jackson McGhie Memorial at First Street and Second Avenue East, which honors the lives of three young black men lynched in 1920 by a mob angered by the alleged rape of a white woman. Remembered as one of the most painful events from Duluth's past, the unjust hangings of Elias Clayton, Elmer Jackson and Isaac McGhie from a lightpole in the downtown area remained virtually unacknowledged for six decades. A grassroots committee gained

The popular Lakewalk in Duluth attracts people of all ages to enjoy the waterfront.

momentum to help the city to face this dark event. Three bronze figures and quotes from a number of civil rights advocates are indelible reminders of brighter future possibilities.

The gigantic Duluth Entertainment Convention Center (DECC) complex offers complete facilities, including an arena, auditorium, curling rink, exhibition halls, meeting space and catering for significant conventions, entertainment and sporting events. Duluth Omnimax Theatre provides IMAX panoramic films on a regular schedule throughout the year. A 10-screen multiplex cinema is adjacent. The DECC's 72,000-square-foot Harborside Convention Center offers 10 meeting rooms and a ballroom with a spectacular view of the Aerial Lift Bridge and harbor. The whole facility is connected to a parking ramp and the downtown area via skywalks. A major expansion with a new arena, skywalk and parking ramp addition is scheduled to open December 31, 2010.

Bayfront Festival Park is another spectacular waterfront showcase. Located just west of the DECC and Aquarium on the Duluth harbor, the 14-acre park was upgraded with permanent structures, landscaping and special features. Equipped with a 400-foot (122-meter) boardwalk, it's a good spot for ship watching, fishing and frequent summer entertainment outdoors under the stars, including the annual Bayfront Blues Festival the second weekend each August. Departing ships make their final turn before the Aerial Lift Bridge right in front of the Bayfront area. In one corner of the area, Playfront Park, built entirely with volunteer help and donations, provides skating in winter and an outstanding place for children to enjoy themselves at all times of the year. Additional upgrading of the Bayfront area is planned in the near future so watch for new features.

In addition to regularly scheduled concerts, musical comedies and other entertainment offered at the DECC, Duluth and Superior have numerous other venues for the performing arts. Renegade Comedy Theatre at Teatro Zuccone on Superior Street offers its satiric look at the world and the Duluth Playhouse has regular dramatic and musical comedy performances at The Depot Performing Arts Center. Both offer the opportunity for kids to perform or to attend children's theater events. The Play Ground, an alternative performing arts venue, is in the Technology Village. The four colleges and universities in the metropolitan area also offer a rich blend of musical, dramatic, comedic and dance performances, and independent organizations like Duluth Superior Symphony Orchestra and Matinee Musicale add to your entertainment choices. Check for schedules of performances for the time you plan to visit.

Cinema enthusiasts will find about 22 screens of movie selections in Duluth, with seven more available across the bridge at Mariner Mall in Superior. The selection includes two downtown Duluth

Duluth's Aerial Lift Bridge

Once the Duluth Ship Canal opened in 1871, residents of Minnesota Point (Park Point) needed a connection to the rest of Duluth. For 34 years, ferries provided that connection, transporting people and freight back and forth across the canal, but that service ended after winter freeze-up. Planks were laid across the ice to accommodate traffic and an unsatisfactory suspension bridge was tried, but problems were apparent with those early efforts.

After the channel was widened to 300 feet and concrete piers installed, the city determined that a better solution had to be found. A contest was held and the winning entry was a lift bridge quite similar to the present structure. Officials, however, opted to build an aerial ferry system, with a suspended gondola car moving back and forth on wheels atop the bridge trestle.

It served well for 25 years, but increasing traffic after Henry Ford introduced his Model T in 1908 finally doomed the ferry to obsolescence and in1929-1930 the city rebuilt the superstructure as Duluth's world-famous Aerial Lift Bridge of today.

One of the most spectacular sites on Lake Superior, the Aerial Lift Bridge rises to a full height of 138 feet (42 meters) in 55 seconds to allow vessels to enter and leave the harbor. Visitors are within yards of foreign ships, giant Great Lakes carriers and spectacular pleasure craft. Well lighted after dark, the bridge is a favorite subject for photographers day or night. Patience is a virtue when the Lift Bridge slightly delays traffic flow.

options – Duluth 10 near the DECC and the city's newest cinema, the independent Zinema 2 on Superior Street.

Port Town Trolley is a motorized trolley that loops through the downtown business section and Canal Park past attractions along the harbor's edge every half-hour during the summer, enabling riders to explore various points of interest. If your Duluth visit is based in Canal Park, then old-fashioned horse-drawn carriages offer a leisurely, scenic trip through Duluth's downtown and along the city's magnificent waterfront Lakewalk. There are also rental motor scooters and four-wheeled passenger bicycles available.

Duluth-Superior Excursions offer two-hour narrated tours of the Duluth-Superior harbor from May through mid-October aboard the 255-passenger *Vista King*, which is moored across Harbor Drive from the ticket office in the Duluth Entertainment Convention Center. Access from Canal Park can be made via the Minnesota Slip Pedestrian Draw Bridge near Bellisio's Restaurant. Lunch and dinner cruises are available on the 300-passenger *Vista Star*. Excursions include close-up views of the ore docks, Aerial Lift Bridge, Great Lakes cargo carriers, visiting foreign vessels, grain elevators along Rice's Point and other points of interest, all in the comfort of the boat. Private charter cruises and group rates are available. A complete information counter is operated there by Visit Duluth.

Downtown, the Duluth Skywalk system connects businesses and City Hall to the DECC and the waterfront with a covered, climate-controlled walkway. On inclement days, the skywalk offers a pleasant stroll within the city and its major buildings, including dozens of interesting stores, restaurants and most of the city's downtown multilevel parking lots.

North Shore Scenic Railroad offers 52-mile (84-kilometer) round-trip excursions between Duluth and Two Harbors and shorter 14-mile (23-kilometer) rides between The Depot in downtown Duluth and the Lester River area of Duluth. The daily historic rail service provides 32-mile (51-kilometer), two-hour dinner and pizza trains from Duluth to Knife River and back. Charters are also available.

The *William A. Irvin* ore carrier moored in Canal Park was once the flagship of U.S. Steel's Great Lakes fleet. The ship is permanently berthed alongside the DECC as part of the convention facilities. It is one of two such floating ore boat museums on Lake Superior, the other being *Valley Camp* in Sault Ste. Marie, Michigan. The *Norgoma*, a passenger ship that is now a museum ship, is in Sault Ste. Marie, Ontario's Bondar Park. The *Irvin*'s rich staterooms were once used to entertain VIPs as "thanks" for past and future business. Launched in 1938, the "Pride of the Silver Stackers" has been brought back to life as a floating museum. It provides sightseers with a close-up view of a past era of Great Lakes shipping. Open daily during summer with expanded hours Fridays and Saturdays in July and August. The annual Halloween Ship of Ghouls is a ghostly tour that never fails to delight children and others who get a kick out of bumps in the night.

Lake Superior and Mississippi Railroad Company near the Lake Superior Zoo on Grand Avenue and Fremont Street behind the Little Store, offers a 90-minute journey from the Zoo area to Gary-New Duluth aboard a vintage train from a bygone era. Ride the rails as travelers did in the 1870s for a 12-mile (19-kilometer) round trip along the scenic St. Louis River. Operated on weekends by an all-volunteer group from mid-June to the Labor Day weekend, the train departs twice each Saturday and Sunday. During the autumn color season, special color trips are operated.

For those who prefer to walk or bike, the Western Waterfront Trail is a 5-mile (8-kilometer) path along the St. Louis River that connects with trails at Jay Cooke State Park. The hiking/biking trail includes picnic areas and boating access sites. It offers cross-country skiing and snowshoeing in the winter. Located at Grand Avenue and 71st Avenue West. Mission Creek Trail is a challenging 3.25-mile (5.2-kilometer) trail, beginning off Highway 23 at 131st Avenue West in Fond du Lac Park. Those seeking a longer route will want to challenge the 15-mile (24-kilometer) section of the Munger Trail between West Duluth (74th and Grand Avenue) and Carlton. Other hiking/biking opportunities abound, including: the Lakewalk, which begins at Canal Park; Kingsbury Creek Trail, above the picnic grounds at Lake Superior Zoo; Lincoln Park Trail, 25th Avenue West and Third Street; Park Point Trail, at Sky Harbor Airport, the farthest point reachable by car past Park Point Recreation Area; Chester Park Trail, 18th Avenue East and Skyline Parkway; Congdon Park Trail, at 32nd Avenue East and Superior Street; Lester Park Trail, 61st Avenue East and Superior Street.

The Superior Hiking Trail Association has completed a 39-mile section of the Superior Hiking Trail through Duluth, featuring Jay Cooke State Park, Ely's Peak, Bardon's Peak, Spirit Mountain, Enger Park, UMD's Bagley nature trails, the Lakewalk on Lake Superior and Hartley Nature Center. The trail currently remains uncompleted between Duluth and Two Harbors. Find details at www.shta.org.

Lake Superior Zoo in West Duluth features animals from the region and around the world: kangaroos, kookaburra, a polar bear, a cougar, a Kodiak and an Alaska brown bear, African lions and snow leopards. The Contact Corral allows hands-on contact with goats and gentle species. Picnic areas and campgrounds are nearby. Open daily year-round with reduced winter hours. 71st Avenue West and Grand Avenue, adjacent to Fairmont Park. Admission, but free with membership. Group rates.

At the airport, check out the display of more than 100 inductees into the Minnesota Aviation Hall of Fame. Nearby, the Commemorative Air Force Lake Superior Squadron 101 Museum displays World War II artifacts, including two PBY Catalina aircraft that are being restored.

Duluth's public golf courses have had major improvements made within the past few years, rating this area a top golf destination by *Golf Digest*. Enger Park Golf Course on Skyline Boulevard, Grandview Golf Course on the city's west end and Lester Park Golf Course on Lester River Road in the east provide outstanding public access. Private courses include the historic Northland Country Club on East Superior Street and Ridgeview Country Club on Red Wing in the Woodland area of Duluth.

Anglers have plenty of choices for

fishing in the Duluth area. A number of charter captains operate from Canal Park next to the SS *William A. Irvin*. River fishing is a popular sport in the spring and fall in a number of rivers along the State Scenic Byway North Shore Scenic Drive, particularly the Lake Superior waters off the Lester and French rivers. North Shore Charter Captains Association provides state-licensed guides for deep-sea sport fishing on Lake Superior. Anglers try for steelhead, chinook, coho, Atlantic salmon and lake trout. All necessary equipment is provided. Half- and full-day charters are available. For a list of charter boat options, contact Visit Duluth. Sailing enthusiasts can experience Lake Superior aboard one of the many boats available to rent. Training is offered. Call Lakehead Boat Basin, Duluth, for charter fishing and sailboat rental (experienced sailors only).

The Twin Ports are laced with bikeways, which vary in grade from flat to steep. In addition, the city's buses are equipped with bicycle racks during the bicycling season to help transport riders between locations. A bikeways map has been developed to aid in route selection. It is available in most information locations and at bicycle shops.

Winter sports fans will find many opportunities in Duluth. Cross-country ski trails include Spirit Mountain Ski Area, off Interstate 35 at Boundary Avenue; Magney, off Boundary Avenue near Spirit Mountain; Piedmont, at Adirondack Street and Hutchinson Road; Chester Park, off East Skyline Drive in

The Great Lakes Aquarium is the perfect hands-on place for children (and adults) to learn about the freshwater environments around Lake Superior and elsewhere in the world.

Chester Bowl; Hartley, at the end of Fairmont Street off Woodland Avenue and the end of Hartley Lane off Arrowhead Road, where Hartley Nature Center operates an interpretive center offering interesting environmental programs; and at Lester-Amity, at Lester River Road and Superior Street. Ski trails are lit for evening skiing at Chester Bowl and Lester Park.

Downhill and cross-country skiing are offered at Spirit Mountain and Mont du Lac at the western edge of Duluth on the Superior, Wisconsin, side and Chester Bowl at Chester Park. Spirit Mountain has several excellent chair lifts and 20 downhill runs. Mountain Villas at Spirit Mountain offers year-round contemporary-styled housekeeping units for extended stays. In the vicinity is AmericInn, which also has lodging south on I-35 at Moose Lake. A Country Inn and Suites is nearby. Snowflake Nordic Center on Rice Lake Road is a full-service cross-country skiing center with more than 15 kilometers of groomed trails.

For a pleasant stay near the zoo and the Willard Munger State Trail, try the Super 8 Motel just off the freeway at 40th Avenue West.

If you'd like a little more adventure, the Outdoor Program at the University of Minnesota Duluth offers beginning and advanced instruction in kayaking, canoeing and climbing. It sponsors a variety of trips for folks to test their skills

Glensheen The Historic Congdon Estate

A must-visit-more-than-once destination is Glensheen The Historic Congdon Estate, a stately home built by Chester and Clara Congdon between 1905 and 1908. Tours explore the 39-room, neo-Jacobean mansion, carriage house and formal gardens on Lake Superior. The estate reflects an elegant way of life that existed in Duluth in the early 1900s. The 22-acre historic site on London Road is owned and operated by the University of Minnesota. It has been featured on A&E's "America's Castles." Tours of the manor house last about an hour; grounds tours are self-guided. An additional tour of the home's third floor "arts and crafts decor" and attic is available, with costumed interpreters present during June through August. The mansion offers daily tours from May-October, with a reduced schedule in winter and spring. It is always best to call first. Tickets are on sale at the Museum Shop. This facility is specially decorated for the holidays, with brunches during December. Concerts are performed on the grounds at Glensheen on Wednesday evenings in July beginning at 6:30 p.m. (1-888-454-GLEN).

COURTESY GLENSHEEN THE HISTORIC CONGDON ESTATE

and the program's U.S. Kayak and Canoe Center challenges the skills of paddlers on a white-water stretch below Thomson Dam on the lower St. Louis River, which is operated by Minnesota Power, a major utility and corporate citizen of the area.

Notable Museums

Duluth abounds with museums.

Nine independent organizations make up The Historic Union Depot, a reclaimed 1892 vintage depot in downtown Duluth. Between 1910 and 1920, Historic Union Depot served seven railroads. The Depot was recognized by the U.S. Department of Transportation as one of the best re-uses of a historic railroad depot. The building was listed on the National Register of Historic Places in 1971. Within the Depot, the St. Louis County Heritage and Arts Center preserves the area's rich mining, railway and logging history. The most notable organization is the Lake Superior Railroad Museum, where visitors stroll the streets of a 1910 village, Depot Square, and explore the nationally acclaimed collection of antique locomotives, passenger cars, freight cars and snowplows. There are trolley rides available on a seasonal basis. One of the stars of the collection is Minnesota's first locomotive, *William Crooks*, built in 1860. Other Depot exhibits include four levels of dolls, fashions, furnishings, industry and art of a bygone era. The Depot also includes the Duluth Children's Museum and the St. Louis County Historical Society. The Depot Performing Arts Center houses the Arrowhead Chorale, Minnesota Ballet, which has its main office and studio at 301 West First Street, Duluth Playhouse, Matinee Musicale and the Duluth Art Institute. Open year-round. Gate fee, group rates. 506 West Michigan Street.

At University of Minnesota Duluth, the Tweed Museum of Art has five galleries with changing exhibitions drawn from all aspects of contemporary and historical art activity, including a sculpture wing. More than 5,000 objects make up the permanent collection. The 50-year-old museum is closed Mondays and holidays.

Karpeles Manuscript Library houses rare documents, including original handwritten drafts, letters and other historic relics, such as the U.S. Bill of Rights and the Emancipation Proclamation. One of seven such private libraries in the country, it is on the corner of Ninth Avenue East and First Street, across from St. Luke's Hospital. Open daily in the afternoon, except closed Mondays, September through May. Free.

Parks and Public Areas

Duluth is full of parks, picnic and wildlife areas, many of which have been improved and expanded. Chambers Grove in Fond du Lac is on U.S. Highway 23 at the western edge of the city. Fairmont Park is adjacent to Lake Superior Zoo. Chester Park houses one of Duluth's ski jumps. Lester Park, on the eastern end of the city, is next to the Lester River, a favorite fishing location. The restful Brighton Beach with its Kitchi-Gammi Park is nearby.

Notable Events

• Duluth's annual events include Grandma's Marathon, which features upwards of 9,500 world-class runners competing in a 26.2-mile (42-kilometer) run that follows Lake Superior's scenic North Shore from Two Harbors to Canal

Park in Duluth. It's been held annually in June since 1977. The Garry Bjorklund Half-Marathon and the *William A. Irvin* 5K Race are held for those folks not up to the full run. The same route is used the second weekend after Labor Day for the NorthShore Inline Marathon, the largest inline skating race in North America and third largest in the world.

• Park Point Art Fair is an invitational, juried fair held each June with artists displaying and selling paintings, pottery, jewelry, candle-making and glass-blowing artifacts.

• The annual Fourth Fest Celebration is centered at Bayfront Festival Park and its fireworks display over the Duluth Harbor is one of the largest in the region.

• Great Lakes Aquarium hosts an annual Scarium at the Aquarium family Halloween event, which is held in late October, and also offers an annual Valentine's Day event in February. As mentioned, the SS *William A. Irvin* becomes a "Ship of Ghouls" each October.

• Gales of November program, co-sponsored by the Lake Superior Marine Museum Association and *Lake Superior Magazine*, is held early in November in commemoration of shipwrecks, storms and maritime life.

• Christmas City of the North Parade brings Santa to downtown Duluth and starts off the Christmas season. Sponsored by KBJR Television, it's held each year the Friday before Thanksgiving. It also features the lighting of the city's Christmas tree in Lake Superior Plaza.

• The Bentleyville Tour of Lights has been added at Bayfront Festival Park from November through New Year's Day.

• On Thanksgiving weekend, Spirit Mountain is the site for the Duluth National Snocross Races, the largest on-snow (vs. grass) snowmobile race in the world.

• Lake Superior Zoo sponsors Zoo Year's Eve in the afternoon on December 31 at the zoo, a family-oriented event that culminates with a gigantic fireworks display in the early evening.

• The Duluth Winterfest presents more than 100 winter activities from January 1 through early March. Centered around the 375-mile (604-kilometer) John Beargrease Sled Dog Marathon that starts at Duluth's Ordean Field and makes a round trip to Grand Marais, ending back in Duluth at Lester Park, it's one of the highlights of the year all along Minnesota's North Shore.

Where to Shop

Duluth is visitor friendly and a mecca for shoppers, be they curio-seekers wanting a souvenir of their visit or serious antique buffs seeking authentic relics of the past.

In Canal Park, you'll find art galleries like Sivertson Gallery, which features a large selection of local, regional and Native art, or bookstores like Northern Lights Books and Gifts with regionally connected offerings on Canal Park Drive.

Just down the street, Toys for Keeps has toys from yesterday and today.

Nearby, the quaint Spirit of the Lake sells shirts, souvenirs, books and nautical-themed gifts on Canal Park Drive.

The Duluth Pack Store offers not only great backpacks but a wide range of other high-quality outdoor gear, much made locally.

After dining at the Canal Park Grandma's Saloon & Grill, peek in the gift shop, Rosa & Sons, for chocolates, books, gifts and Grandma's shirts and souvenirs.

Waterfront Plaza houses a hotel, restaurants, and a number of businesses. Behind the building, a number of charter captains book half- and full-day angling excursions on the big lake.

DeWitt-Seitz Marketplace in Canal Park features locally owned shops and restaurants, including the upscale Lake Avenue Cafe, Northern Waters Smokehaus, The Art Dock, Amazing Grace Bakery, Taste of Saigon, Hepzibah's Sweet Shoppe, Blue Heron Trading Company and J Skylark, a neat store that's full of toys for kids and adults. The DeWitt-Seitz building, a former warehouse and manufacturing site, is on the National Register of Historic Places.

Duluth's downtown waterfront offers more than 185 retail businesses, providing a full range of general and specialized merchandise. Along the bricks of Superior Street from Fifth Avenue West to the Fitger's Brewery Complex on Sixth Avenue East, you'll find the heart of downtown shopping. There's a cross section of small shops to be found along the enclosed skywalk system in downtown's concentrated retail area, which extends from Fifth Avenue West to Third Avenue East.

Downtown is home to some fine art galleries, all on Superior Street, such as the Frame Corner Gallery and Lizzard's Art Gallery and Framing. In the 300 block (west), you'll find unique shops like John Marxhausen Jewelry Designer

At the Lake Superior Zoo, Phoebe, a Kodiak brown bear, doesn't mind an audience while she snacks on fruits and vegetables. She's one of several types of bears represented in the zoo.

and Goldsmith, one of the most creative Lake Superior designers we've found. In the 200 block from Second to Third avenues west, the Holiday Center houses many shops and restaurants and is the center of the skywalk system. Also on West Superior Street, Explorations is a toy store that's fun and educational for both kids and adults, selling a variety of books, games and educational toys.

A couple of blocks east at the corner of Lake Avenue, the Duluth Technology Village houses a number of businesses and organizations involved in high-tech endeavors, as well as specialty shops and a restaurant, Pizza Lucé, on the street level with a variety of dining.

For information on Duluth downtown waterfront merchants, attractions and activities, contact the Greater Downtown Council at 118 East Superior Street, the Duluth Area Chamber of Commerce at 5 West First Street, or Visit Duluth in Lake Superior Place, Suite 100 at 21 West Superior Street.

On Superior Street, Sheraton Duluth Hotel has 147 rooms and suites, many with outstanding views. The hotel links by skywalk to SMDC. For dining, try the hotel's Restaurant 301. Luxury condos fill the upper floors.

On East Superior Street, Lake Superior Port Cities, publisher of *Lake Superior Magazine*, its annual *Lake Superior Travel Guide* and *Lake Superior The Ultimate Guide to the Region*, operates from offices at 310 E. Superior Street. A special display in the offices includes the metal spiral staircase recovered from the *America*, still underwater near Isle Royale.

Fitger's Brewery Complex is a renovated 1885 brewery on scenic Lake Superior that features service and specialty shops and year-round courtyard activities, as well as dining. At Christmastime, reindeer can be found in the courtyard. The Bookstore at Fitger's specializes in northeastern Minnesota regional books and also carries new releases, bestsellers and children's books and toys. The complex is on the National Register of Historic Places and has a free parking ramp for visitors who get their ticket stamped.

Farther east, merchants along London Road have an overview of Lake Superior while offering many shopping, lodging and dining opportunities. The Wedding Chapel on the Lake is a charmer, should you wish to be married or renew your vows near Lake Superior.

Miller Hill Mall, "over the hill," is the area's major shopping complex, housing more than 100 stores, including three major department stores, a bookstore, entertainment, services, restaurants and even a car dealership. It's at Highway 53 North and Trinity Road. The area also contains many additional smaller malls, stores and restaurants, including the Village Mall, Burning Tree Plaza, Stone Ridge Shopping Center, with a new development across Highway 53 that houses more shopping and dining opportunities.

Along Central Entrance and the Miller Trunk Highway corridor on the hilltop, many retail businesses have gathered, making the corridor one of the shopping meccas of the lake. Other retail and restaurant spaces continue to be developed in this area. In nearby Hermantown at Haines and Stebner roads, a multiplex theater features a range of cinema selections for movie buffs. Motorcyclists, of course, will want to check out Harley-Davidson Sport Center on Stebner Road.

What's Next

If your route is northeast, follow

Highway 61 heading for Two Harbors and the Scenic North Shore Drive (see Roadtrips section). If you plan to head east along the south shore, catch Highway 2 to cross the bridge into Superior or to visit Minnesota's Iron Range, catch Highway 53.

INFO & OPTIONS

Thompson Hill Information Center
8525 Skyline Dr. West
I-35 at Hwy. 2
Duluth, MN 55810
218-723-4938

Visit Duluth
21 West Superior St.
Duluth, MN 55802
800-438-5884
www.visitduluth.com
Waterfront Visitors Center
(at the Vista Fleet store in the DECC)

Amazing Grace Bakery & Cafe
394 South Lake Ave.
Duluth, MN 55802
218-723-0075
www.amazinggracebakery.com

Bellisio's Italian Restaurant & Wine Bar
405 South Lake Ave.
Duluth, MN 55802
218-727-4921
www.grandmasrestaurants.com

Fitger's Brewhouse
600 East Superior St.
Duluth, MN 55802
218-279-2739
www.brewhouse.net

Grandma's Saloon & Grill
522 Lake Ave. South
Duluth, MN 55802
218-727-4192
www.grandmasrestaurants.com

Lake Avenue Café
394 Lake Ave. South
Duluth, MN 55802
218-722-2355
www.lakeavenuecafe.com

Lakeview Castle
5135 North Shore Dr.
Duluth, MN 55804
218-525-1014
www.lakeviewcastleduluth.com

Lighthouse on Homestead Road
5730 Homestead Rd.
Duluth, MN 55804
218-525-4525
www.lighthouseonhomestead.com

Midi Restaurant & Wine Bar
600 East Superior St.
Duluth, MN 55802
218-727-4880
www.midirestaurant.net

New Scenic Cafe
5461 North Shore Dr.
Duluth, MN 55804
218-525-6274
www.sceniccafe.com

Nokomis Restaurant & Bar
5593 North Shore Dr.
Duluth, MN 55804
218-525-2286
www.nokomisonthelake.com

Pickwick Restaurant
508 East Superior St.
Duluth, MN 55802
218-727-8901
www.pickwickrestaurant.com

Pizza Lucé
11 East Superior St.
Duluth, MN 55802
218-727-7400
www.pizzaluce.com

At Sara's Table / Chester Creek Cafe
1902 East Eighth St.
Duluth, MN 55812
218-724-6811
www.astccc.net

Sir Benedict's Tavern on the Lake
805 East Superior St.
Duluth, MN 55802
218-728-1192

Top of the Harbor Restaurant
505 West Superior St.
Duluth, MN 55802
800-395-7046
www.radisson.com/duluthmn

Va Bene Caffe
734 East Superior St.
Duluth, MN 55802
218-722-1518
www.vabenecaffe.com

Best Western Downtown
131 West 2nd St.
Duluth, MN 55802
218-727-6851
www.bestwesternminnesota.com

Canal Park Lodge
250 Canal Park Dr.
Duluth, MN 55802
800-777-8560
canalparklodge.com

Comfort Inn West
3900 West Superior St.
Duluth, MN 55807
218-628-1464
www.comfortinn.com

Comfort Suites Canal Park
408 Canal Park Dr.
Duluth, MN 55802
218-727-1378
www.comfortsuites.com

Edgewater Resort & Waterpark
2400 London Rd.
Duluth, MN 55812
800-777-7925
www.duluthwaterpark.com

Fitger's Inn
600 East Superior St.
Duluth, MN 55802
888-348-4377
www.fitgers.com

Hampton Inn
310 Canal Park
Duluth, MN 55802
218-720-3000
hamptoninn.hilton.com

Holiday Inn Hotel & Suites Downtown Waterfront
200 West First St.
Duluth, MN 55802
800-477-7089
www.hiduluth.com

Inn on Lake Superior
350 Canal Park Dr.
Duluth, MN 55802
888-668-4352
www.theinnonlakesuperior.com

Radisson-Duluth-Harborview
505 West Superior St.
Duluth, MN 55802
218-727-8981
www.duluthhotelrestaurant.com

Sheraton Duluth Hotel
301 East Superior St.
Duluth, MN 55802
218-733-5660
www.starwoodhotels.com

South Pier Inn
701 Lake Ave. South
Duluth, MN 55802
800-430-7437
www.southpierinn.com

StayinDuluth.com
access to several lodgings

The Suites Hotel at Waterfront Plaza
325 Lake Ave. South
Duluth, MN 55802
800-794-1716
www.thesuiteduluth.com

Lakehead Boat Basin (RVs)

1000 Minnesota Ave.
Duluth, MN 55802
218-722-1757
www.lakeheadboatbasin.com

Buffalo Valley Camping

2586 Guss Rd.
Duluth, MN 55810
218-628-7019
www.buffalohouseduluth.com

Indian Point Campground

75th Ave. West and Grand Ave.
Duluth, MN 55807
800-982-2453
www.indianpointcampground.com

Spirit Mountain Campground

9500 Spirit Mountain Pl.
Duluth, MN 55810
800-642-6377
www.spiritmt.com/campground

Ely

Population 3,473

The Ely area is entry to the vast Boundary Waters Canoe Area Wilderness and boasts 500 fishing lakes within a 20-mile radius, as well as comfortable lodging and fine dining.

Ely is at the far end of Highway 169 from the Mesabi Iron Range or scenic Highway 1 from the North Shore Circle Route.

As a result of tourism, the city is home to many outfitters and outdoor equipment purveyors. Permits are required to enter the BWCAW and may be reserved in advance.

A Bit of History

Ely owes its existence to iron ore, which was discovered on the shore of Shagawa Lake in 1883 and proved to be so abundant that five mines were eventually developed nearby and a sixth, Section 30 Mine, would operate a few miles northeast in the vicinity of Winton. By 1886, the Pioneer Mine was opened, but did not prove profitable.

At that time, the Duluth & Iron Range Railroad connected Two Harbors and Tower and was shipping ore by the thousands of tons but did not extend beyond Tower-Soudan.

In 1887, when the Chandler Mine began production, the railroad rushed to extend its line to the area and by the 1890s the Ely mines were producing more ore than the original Vermilion Iron Range mine at Tower-Soudan.

Also by the 1890s, lumber companies were active in the area and nearby Winton became a hub for that industry, with two huge mill complexes located on Fall Lake and dozens of logging camps scattered throughout the surrounding forestlands.

The populations of both Ely and Winton mushroomed during this period.

While the mines would continue producing ore for nearly a century, the pine forests were logged off before 1920 and Winton's population, which may have reached 500 at its peak, nosedived as lumberjacks and millworkers moved on and the merchants that catered to their needs closed up shop.

After World War II, iron ore production began declining, as more and more mines scraped bottom and closed.

When the last of the Vermilion Range mines, the Pioneer, closed in 1967, the Ely area had already blossomed into a tourist and recreation destination city, with dozens of resorts on lakes surrounding the town. It was also known as a premier entry point to the Boundary Waters Canoe Area ("Wilderness" was added to the name in 1978), as thousands of paddlers passed through town on their way to the recreation area – which it remains to the present.

What to See and Do

The winter and summer cabins of Dorothy Molter, long-time BWCAW resident who died in 1986, were moved from her land on Knife Lake to the edge of town as a tribute. Known to thousands of paddlers as the "Root Beer Lady," she offered her homemade brew, wit and compassion to passing paddlers for decades. The cabins reflect her choice for living simply and in contact with nature. You can still get the root beer at the Dorothy Molter Museum, which is on the south side of Highway 169 on the east end of Ely. Guided tours available daily from Memorial Day weekend to Labor Day weekend and weekends in September. Fee.

International Wolf Center offers field trips and information on the timber wolves that live in northeast Minnesota. Fee. Learn about bears at the North American Bear Center, 1 mile west of Ely, featuring live bears, video footage and documentaries. Fee.

Ely-Winton History Museum at Vermilion Community College is a good place to learn more about the area, from prehistory to the expeditions of Ely-based polar explorers Will Steger and Paul Schurke. Open Monday through Saturday from Memorial Day to the week after Labor Day. Fee.

To the southwest on Highway 169, be sure to tour the Soudan Underground Mine in Soudan Underground Mine State Park. The only underground iron mine in the world open for tours, visitors are guided to a depth of 2,341 feet where the year-round temperature is a constant 50 degrees Fahrenheit.

In the nearby Embarrass area, tours of Finnish farms and homesteads explore the importance of this large ethnic group that pioneered settlement here. Fee.

Visit Lake Vermilion, one of the largest lakes in northeast Minnesota. It's also recommended that visitors plan to take the daylong scenic trip on the boat that delivers mail to waterbound residents.

For gaming fun, take Highway 77 from Tower to Fortune Bay Resort Casino on the Bois Forte Ojibway Reservation. The tribe also operates its "Legend House" or *Atisokanigamig* heritage museum and its championship 18-hole golf course, The Wilderness, that opened on tribal lands.

Where to Shop

This is a good place to stock up on outdoor and winter gear, with a number of local manufacturers like Steger Mukluks and Wintergreen Designs offering gear tested in the area and on polar expeditions headed by Will Steger and Paul Schurke.

A number of gift stores, galleries and specialty shops make interesting kibitzing and shopping, and Ely has a full range of other stores to meet any "necessity." Piragis Northwoods Company, a canoe trip outfitter, rents canoes and camping gear for trips in the BWCAW and Canada's Quetico Provincial Park; it handles trip planning and also offers guided wilderness trips. The company sells canoes and kayaks.

World renowned outdoor photographer Jim Brandenburg makes

his home near Ely and offers his artwork at Brandenburg Gallery in town.

Mostly Moose & More on Sheridan Street is a terrific stop for moose collectors of all sorts.

NOTABLE EVENTS

• The Blueberry Art Festival at the end of July attracts hundreds to see the art and food exhibitors.

WHAT'S NEXT

To exit Ely, take Highway 1 to the North Shore Circle Tour route or travel Highway 169 southwest through Tower and Soudan to continue to other Iron Range cities and sights described elsewhere.

INFO & OPTIONS

Ely Chamber of Commerce
1600 East Sheridan St.
Ely, MN 55731
800-777-7281
www.ely.org

Chocolate Moose
101 North Central Ave.
Ely, MN 55731
218-365-6343

Evergreen Restaurant (Grand Ely Lodge)
400 North Pioneer Rd.
Ely, MN 55731
800-365-5070
www.grandelylodge.com

Blue Heron Bed and Breakfast
827 Kawishiwi Trail
Ely, MN 55731
218-365-4720
www.blueheronbnb.com

Grand Ely Lodge Resort & Conference Center
400 North Pioneer Rd.
Ely, MN 55731
800-365-5070
www.grandelylodge.com

Eveleth

Population 3,582

The town of Eveleth was made famous by its iron mines and continues as an important source of iron ore in the form of taconite pellets. Here you can visit the United States Hockey Hall of Fame Museum on Highway 53, which features an extensive display of regional and national hockey artifacts. Open daily in summer and on weekends in the off-season. In saluting its status as the historic home of U.S. hockey, the city erected the World's Largest

Eveleth is home to the Hockey Hall of Fame.

Hockey Stick in the downtown. There is a challenging 9-hole golf course open to the public on nearby St. Mary's Lake. The Leonidas Mine overlook provides not only a panorama of several active and abandoned mines, but is the highest point on the Mesabi Iron Range. The Sax-Zim Bog southwest of town is exceptional for birders and is home to many rare and scarce species.

Businesses seeking economic development assistance or information should contact the Iron Range Resources near Eveleth. The agency's building also houses a nice sampling of area art by the Fine Arts North group. Works are rotated regularly to bring fresh pieces to the ongoing exhibit.

Depending on their itinerary, visitors can travel Highway 53 to the south to return to Duluth, take Highway 37 east to Gilbert, Biwabik and the far eastern Mesabi Range, or travel north a couple of miles on Highway 53 to Virginia.

Finland

Area Population 637

To find Finland, take Highway 1 at the intersection with Highway 61 at Illgen City. The village of Finland is perhaps the proudest little village in the Arrowhead. Settled in the early 1900s by many people of Finnish descent, the town took its name when a railroad went through in 1910. The town's designation as Finland predates that of the nation by about a decade.

For travelers heading to or from Ely on Highway 1, Finland is one of the only chances to get a bite to eat. Check at Our Place Restaurant for an all-day menu, or try the Four Seasons Restaurant or West Branch Bar and Grill, which open at noon. All have full bars. Groceries are available at Finland Cooperative Co.

Surrounded by forest and rugged country, this is a great place to begin snowmobile treks into the woods and there is good fishing in area lakes.

What to See and Do

Finnish Heritage Site, located on County Road 6, features the hand-hewn log home of pioneer John Pine (Petaja) with furnishings and other artifacts from the early 1900s.

Nearby Wolf Ridge Environmental Learning Center is an accredited residential school, with year-round fun and educational programs on the outdoors for school groups, families and adults. Stop for a brochure. There are lots of activities and events, including an Elderhostel summer program.

For a side trip of approximately 10 miles (16 kilometers), hikers and backpackers will appreciate the unspoiled beauty of the George Crosby-Manitou State Park east of Finland on Lake County Road 7. The Manitou River flows through the park before plunging into Lake Superior through a deep gorge on private land along Highway 61. It is the only falls in Minnesota with a straight drop into the lake, but there is no public access to the falls. The park features 24 miles (39 kilometers) of hiking trails and 21 backpack campsites. A beautiful boardwalk encircles Benson Lake for about three-quarters of a mile. The name derives from the Ojibway word manitou, which often means "spirit."

For another treat, continue along County 7 deeper into the hills to visit Crooked Lake Resort and the Trestle Inn for a dandy meal and a drink at a bar built from an old logging railroad trestle. It's an ideal year-round destination and is accessible directly by snowmobile trail during the winter.

Notable Events

• Each year, residents and hundreds of visitors celebrate St. Urho's Day with a fun parade and other antics on the weekend nearest to March 16. St. Urho is a tongue-in-cheek Finnish spoof of Ireland's St. Patrick. The story goes that St. Urho saved the Finnish grape crop by driving out a plague of grasshoppers.

What's Next

If you plan to visit Ely and the Vermilion Iron Range, Highway 1 is the only highway between Two Harbors and the international border that runs inland through Minnesota's Arrowhead. It's a hilly, sinuous track that runs 63 miles (101 kilometers) through the Superior National Forest to Ely. If you hit Highway 1 around sunrise, it's practically guaranteed you'll encounter moose. Be watchful, since vehicles can experience sudden dangerous encounters with these massive creatures. Some of the region's most spectacular colors are found along this route in the fall.

To return to the Highway 61 Circle Tour route on Lake Superior, you can backtrack on Highway 1 to Illgen City or take County Highway 6 and join the route at Little Marais (see separate listing) a bit east of the Highway 1 junction.

Gilbert

Population 1,847

At Gilbert, visitors find an international welcome at two entries to town and there are flags from many countries along the main street.

Like most Iron Range towns, Gilbert owes its existence to the early 1900s mining activity. An earlier townsite called Sparta was originally planned to hold the populace, but had to be abandoned when iron ore was discovered under the site. Gilbert grew nearby and was incorporated in 1909. Through its history, it has boomed at times and ebbed at others, but has maintained an active business district and residential area.

Gilbert is home to the Iron Range Off-Highway Vehicle Recreation Area, the state's first designated system of trails on abandoned mine land designed for ATVs, dirt bikes and 4x4 trucks.

With typical Iron Range tongue in cheek, local folks have dubbed the body of water in the abandoned mine as Lake Ore-Be-Gone.

What's Next

There are three routes to exit Gilbert. Take Highway 37 westerly toward Eveleth to Highway 53 to visit other Iron Range towns. Highway 135 heads eastward toward Biwabik, Aurora and Hoyt Lakes or west heading for Virginia.

Gooseberry Falls State Park

Gooseberry Falls State Park is a must stop between Two Harbors and Beaver Bay-Silver Bay on Minnesota's North Shore of Lake Superior and provides lessons in history, geology and beauty. Seven other state parks are located along this stretch of Minnesota's North Shore, offering natural beauty at every turn.

Gooseberry is Minnesota's most visited state park. The Gooseberry River is said to have been named for explorer/fur trader Sieur des Groseilliers, whose French name means "gooseberry bush." The river drops through a series of spectacular falls and rapids to the rocky shore of Lake Superior.

Visitors love exploring the series of waterfalls in Minnesota's Gooseberry Falls State Park.

A Bit of History

From the time the highway first passed through this area and a bridge across the river was built in 1924, efforts were undertaken to preserve the scenery around the falls on the Gooseberry River. In 1933, those efforts bore fruit and about 660 acres of land along the river were acquired by the state. In the 1930s, a Civilian Conservation Corps (CCC) camp at Gooseberry laid out the various areas and built the stone buildings.

Today the park encloses 1,675 acres of natural North Shore beauty and wildlife. Numerous trails through conifer, aspen and birch take the more adventurous to each of the cascading falls and the homes of the wildlife. Some trails are difficult. Allow one to five hours to see the park.

The new Gooseberry River Bridge over the gorge allows for safe pedestrian traffic to view the falls and surrounding scenery. This construction also opened most of the nearby walking paths for easier access.

What to See and Do

Among the highlights of the park are the upper and lower falls, the Gooseberry River, the mouth of the river and adjoining lakeshore, trail hikes up to the fifth falls, a segment of the paved Gitchi-Gami State Trail and the cliffs along Lake Superior.

A beautiful visitor center and highway information stop is on the lakeside of Highway 61 just before the bridge. The striking building contains an excellent interpretive center and gift shop.

The delightful Gooseberry Falls State Park Campground is located at the water's edge. It's always full, so book early. There's also wonderful cross-country skiing here.

What's Next

If your route takes you northeast,

about a mile from Gooseberry Falls State Park is a boat launch, paved parking space and nice trails to beach areas. The former site of Twin Points Resort, the site was acquired by Sugarloaf: The North Shore Stewardship Association and traded to the state for the site of that organization's property near Schroeder. The boat launch and parking areas are handicapped accessible, but some trails will prove difficult for the handicapped.

Grand Marais

Population 1,418

In describing the harbor village of Grand Marais (Mah-ray), overused adjectives like quaint, casual and charming are often offered. But here they are entirely appropriate and the city's cultural, recreational and comfortable facilities make it a year-round destination. Located on Highway 61 about 45 miles (72 kilometers) south of the international border or 52 miles (84 kilometers) northeast of Silver Bay on Minnesota's North Shore, you'll want to consider an overnight or longer stay to see the town at all times of the day. There are plenty of lodging choices in Grand Marais, although in the busy season even this multitude of rooms can fill up fast.

A circular harbor is the centerpiece of this tourist-oriented town with a reputation for hospitality. The harbor provides one of the few safe refuges for boaters along Minnesota's Lake Superior shoreline. Artists' Point, a point of rocks to the east, is perfect for sunrise watching. Access is behind the Coast Guard station.

To capture the local feel, pick up the *Cook County News Herald.*

Radio listeners will want to tune in WTIP-FM (90.7).

Much of this part of the North Shore is within the Superior National Forest, 3 million acres of original America. A U.S. Forest Service district ranger office is in Grand Marais and another is maintained in Tofte. Both provide walk-in information centers about the forest. Handicapped-accessible fishing piers are located throughout the forest.

What to See and Do

With its excellent harbor and breakwater, Grand Marais is often crowded with sailing yachts and the deep-sea fishing boats. To plan an adventure trip, check with Bear Track Outfitting.

Eco-tours aboard the North House Folk School's *Hjördis* leave the school's dock daily in summer.

Arrowhead Center for the Arts at Cook County Schools offers a variety of visual and performing arts productions. It's home to groups like the Grand Marais Playhouse, and North Shore Music Association, also serving as a site for workshops, exhibits, art classes and performances for the entire community. There are also facilities for conferences and meetings. Grand Marais Art Colony is the longest-lived art colony in Minnesota, established in 1947.

North House Folk School on the harbor provides classes in kayak and boat building and many traditional crafts.

Just east of Grand Marais is the small, but historic, village of Croftville. Visit the Indian cemetery site and the historic St. Francis Xavier Church, listed on the National Register of Historic Places.

Notable Museums

History buffs will be interested in the Cook County Historical Society Museum, housed in a former lighthouse keeper's home that's on the National Register of Historic Places. It features a replica of a working fish house on the harbor circa 1930. Visitors also see artifacts, photos and the historic tug *Neegee* as part of the exhibit. The museum, at 8 South Broadway (behind the World's Best Donuts store), is open from June to October.

The outstanding Johnson Heritage Post Art Gallery is devoted in part to paintings by Anna Johnson, but most of the space is used for special exhibits – about nine shows a year – of area artists. Located in the log building across from the harbor downtown. It's best to call for the schedule, as the hours are shortened during winter months. Donations welcome.

Notable Events

- An Arts Festival in early July adds to the appeal of summer in Grand Marais.
- The North Shore Dragon Boat Festival is in late July.
- Grand Marais Fisherman's Picnic has been held in Grand Marais since the 1920s. It's a complete package of festivities, held the first weekend of August.
- The Cook County Historical Society Fishcake Contest and Dinner is held in early October.

Where to Shop

In the downtown area, there are many gift and other shopping opportunities. A few special locations are:

Lake Superior Trading Post is loaded with clothing and gifts. This is one of the best shopping experiences around the lake. Linda Zenk has assembled a wonderfully eclectic collection, from snowshoes to crystal pitchers.

Drury Lane Book Store has a nice, varied selection of titles and authors. It's next door to World's Best Donuts.

Joynes Ben Franklin and Department Store offers everything from quality clothing (Woolrich, Merrell) to candy,

In lovely Grand Marais, the beach offers a nice respite for puppies as well as other tourists.

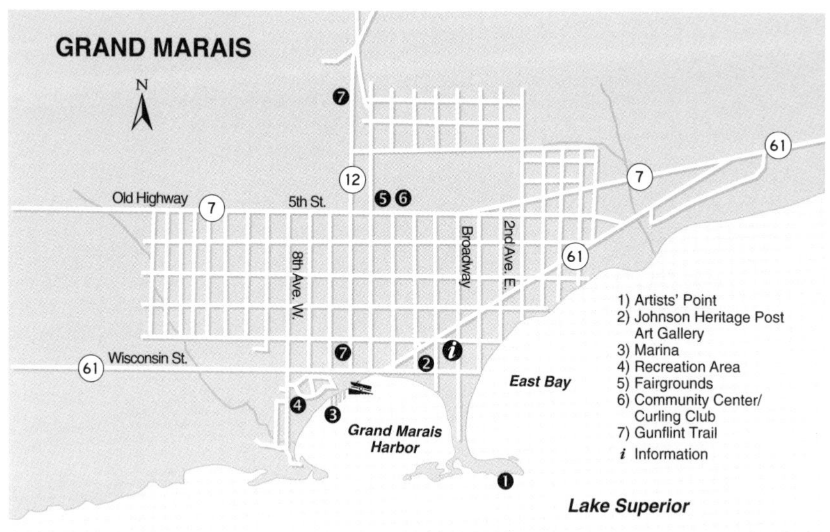

Grand Marais

wild rice, toys and games, hardware and souvenirs.

Sivertson Gallery houses one of the largest collections of Lake Superior paintings in the country. Sivertson also has a gallery in Duluth's Canal Park. Howard Sivertson, the late George Morrison, Liz Sivertson, Betsy Bowen and Hazel Belvo are some local artists of note whose works are featured.

Beth's Fudge & Gifts has a fun variety of T-shirts, gifts, toys and homemade fudge. Owner Beth Kennedy also operates Birchbark Books & Gifts, which offers a really nice selection of regional authors, including signed copies, as well as endearing stuffed animals and other toys.

White Pine North on Wisconsin Street offers distinctive north woods gifts, local items and collectables.

What's Next

Before leaving Grand Marais, we recommend a 58-mile side trip on the Gunflint Trail, which is described in its own listing.

If your route is south on Highway 61, you'll pass Lutsen, Tofte and Schroeder. If you head to Grand Portage and the international border, there are several sites of interest. The tiny settlement of Colvill has a Civil War tie. It was named after a colonel in the war, who took "R&R" here. A marker tells the tale. One of the quietest "towns" on the shore, you can match the colonel's quest to rest frazzled nerves with a stay at a local establishment. Nearby is the Kadunce River, which offers a wading trek of less than a mile past several low falls and through a spectacular narrow, high gorge. Here, hikers will be able to climb relatively easily to the Superior Hiking Trail bridge and return to the highway via the SHT. Rated: moderate to difficult.

Fourteen miles (23 kilometers) up from Grand Marais, at the mouth of the Brule

River, is another historic Minnesota resort, Naniboujou Lodge and Restaurant. It's a much-photographed attraction due to its brilliantly colored interior designs, in the Cree style, and its history as a private club during Prohibition. After June, schedule your arrival to savor afternoon high tea. Drop-ins are welcome for this event. Reservations for non-lodgers at dinner are recommended for groups of five or more.

Unusual lava flows make for unusual rapids in the Brule River as it seeks Lake Superior. Judge C.R. Magney State Park has a woodsy ridgeline trail to the strange and spectacular Devil's Kettle Falls, which mysteriously disappears into the bedrock. Named after Clarence Magney, once mayor of Duluth and a Minnesota Supreme Court justice, the preserve has fishing and 5 miles (8 kilometers) of cross-country ski trails.

The Arrowhead Trail starts at Hovland, another Scandinavian-immigrant fishing settlement. This most northeasterly of roads in Minnesota ends on McFarland Lake within sight of Canadian territory.

Shopping and dining are part of the fun in downtown Grand Marais.

INFO & OPTIONS

Grand Marais Area Tourism Association
13 North Broadway Ave.
Grand Marais, MN 55604
888-922-5000
www.grandmarais.com

Gunflint Trail Information Center
218 Wisconsin St.
Grand Marais, MN 44604
800-338-6932
www.gunflint-trail.com

Angry Trout Café
P.O. Box 973
Grand Marais, MN 55604
218-387-1265
www.angrytroutcafe.com

Birch Terrace Supper Club
601 West Hwy. 61
Grand Marais, MN 55604
218-387-2215

Gun Flint Tavern
111 Wisconsin St.
Grand Marais, MN 55604
218-387-1563
www.gunflinttavern.com

Harbor Light Supper Club
1615 West Hwy. 61
Grand Marais, MN 55604
218-387-1142

Sven and Ole's Pizza
9 West Wisconsin St.
Grand Marais, MN 55604
218-387-1713
www.svenandoles.com

Antler Inn Guesthouse
118 Third Ave. West
Grand Marais, MN 55604
218-387-3131

Best Western Superior Inn and Suites
104 First Ave. East
Grand Marais, MN 55604
800-842-VIEW
www.bestwestern.com

Dreamcatcher Bed and Breakfast
2614 County Rd. 7
Grand Marais, MN 55604
800-682-3119

East Bay Suites
21 Wisconsin St.
Grand Marais, MN 55604
800-414-2807
www.eastbaysuites.com

Gunflint Lodge
143 South Gunflint Lake
Grand Marais, MN 55604
800-328-3325
www.gunflint.com

Harbor Inn Motel & Restaurant
P.O. Box 669
Grand Marais, MN 55604
800-595-4566
www.bytheharbor.com

Naniboujou Lodge
20 Naniboujou
Grand Marais, MN 55604
218-387-2688
www.naniboujou.com

Skara Brae Scottish B&B
1708 East Hwy. 61
Grand Marais, MN 55604
866-467-5272
www.skarabraebb.com

Superior Overlook
1620 East Hwy. 61
Grand Marais, MN 55604
877-387-9335
www.superioroverlookbb.com

Thomsonite Beach Inn & Suites
2920 West Hwy. 61
Grand Marais, MN 55604
(888) 387-1532
www.thomsonite.com

Golden Eagle Lodge, Resort & Campground on the Gunflint Trail
468 Clearwater Rd.
Grand Marais, MN 55604
800-346-2203
www.golden-eagle.com

Grand Marais RV Park & Campground
Hwy. 61 & 8th Ave. West
Grand Marais, MN 55604
800-998-0959
www.grandmaraisrvparkandcampground.com

Judge C.R. Magney State Park
4051 East Hwy. 61
Grand Marais, MN 55604
218-387-3039

Grand Portage

Area Population 582

Named by the voyageurs, the "Grand Portage" consists of an 8.5-mile (13.6-kilometer) uphill trek rising 600 feet from the lake shore and intersecting Pigeon River's water routes to Lake of the Woods and fur-trading posts to the west.

On Ojibway reservation land, the town of Grand Portage lost its early importance after the land where the reconstructed fur outpost now sits was abandoned by the North West Company in 1803 under terms of the Treaty of Paris that ended the Revolutionary War. It was a mid-continent hub for voyageur activity. The Ojibway name *Kitchi Onigum* ("Great Carrying Place") reflects this heritage. At the foot of Mt. Josephine the modern village of Grand Portage sits snuggled on Grand Portage Bay, with Isle Royale floating miragelike on the horizon, 26 miles (42 kilometers) away.

You'll reach Grand Portage on Highway 61 either from the

International Border at Pigeon River or from the southwest via Grand Marais.

What to See and Do

The reconstructed Grand Portage National Monument is a replica of the first white settlement in Minnesota, originally constructed in 1731. The stockade, kitchen, the great hall, canoe warehouse and other re-creations of the early fur-trading settlement make for an interesting morning or afternoon. Interpretive and other events are scheduled during the months of operation, including historic cooking and baking, Native American craft demonstrations and walking tours. The Grand Portage Band of Lake Superior Chippewa maintains the monument, in the first such agreement between a tribe and National Park Service.

The new Grand Portage National Monument Heritage Center fulfills a 50-year-old promise by the U.S. government to the Grand Portage Band to create a center and museum. The promise was made when the band gave land in the heart of its reservation to create a national park. The 16,600-square-foot center, which opened in 2007, commemorates the fur-trading era as well as the history of the Ojibway people. Part of the center is used for archives, rare books and artifacts. It's also the monument's offices.

The national park is open mid-May to mid-October. Summer tours are available daily with a nominal admission. Average visit is one to two hours.

The 8.5-mile (13.6-kilometer) Grand Portage Trail can be hiked from the stockade to the site of Fort Charlotte on the Pigeon River, where the voyageurs began their marathon portaging/paddling trip to the far-flung wintering posts to the west.

Grand Portage Lodge and Casino is a good full-service resort for hiking, nature programs, snowmobiling or gaming. It

At Grand Portage National Monument Heritage Center, interactive displays help visitors learn about Ojibway history and the fur-trading era. (David Cooper / National Park Service)

features special gatherings all year. The tribe operates Grand Portage Marina and Campground nearby.

At the tip of Hat Point near Grand Portage, growing from an outcropping of rock hanging over the lake, the gnarled and tenacious Spirit Little Cedar Tree (Witch Tree) has watched Lake Superior for at least 300 years. Important spiritually to the Ojibway, the tree seems to create reverence within all who visit it. There is restricted land access to protect the tree and the old trails have been closed off. In the meantime, it is easily visible from the water to kayakers and boaters and on *Wenonah* cruises to Isle Royale.

Grand Portage is the closest access from the mainland to Isle Royale National Park, Michigan. See the listing for Isle Royale for more information. Providing passage from Minnesota are the *Voyageur II* for a two-day circumnavigation of Isle Royale, and the *Wenonah* for a day-trip to Isle Royale. Reservations required. Contact Grand Portage-Isle Royale Transportation Line.

A must stop is the Grand Portage Bay Rest Area just above Highway 61 and 5 miles (8 kilometers) from the border. There's an overlook of Lake Superior.

A get-your-camera-out view of the Susie Islands is from Mt. Josephine northeast of Grand Portage. A group of three large and several small islands, the Susies lie just south of the Canadian border near Pigeon Point. A pulloff for safe stopping has been provided on Mt. Josephine. This is the last easily accessible view of Lake Superior's shoreline before passing into Canada, where the highway moves inland several miles.

Ryden's Border Store on the U.S. side of the border features money exchange, customs information and a Duty Free Store.

Grand Portage State Park on the U.S.-Canadian border is the only park in the United States that's operated jointly by the state and a tribe. Acquired from private hands by the Minnesota Parks and Trails Council, the land is held in trust for the Grand Portage Band of Chippewa and dedicated for use as a state park. The park includes the site of an Indian trading post, as well as an old logging flume that was used in the late 1800s and early 1900s. Hiking and ski trails have been developed. Visitors of all abilities can take a one-half mile trail and boardwalk to the overlook area of the spectacular Pigeon Falls (or High Falls) on the Pigeon River, nearly 120 feet (36.5 meters) high and Minnesota's highest waterfall. A new visitor center, serving as a rest area with travel information and an exhibit hall, is expected to open in summer 2010. The park entrance is just before the U.S. Customs gate and there are plans for new road signage to direct travelers there. The turn is hard to catch if you're not watching carefully. Ontario's Pigeon River Provincial Park borders the park to the north.

Notable Events

• The Grand Portage Great Rendezvous is held each year the second weekend in August, a traditional powwow sponsored by the band. The Friends of Grand Portage have nationally known speakers as a Rendezvous event.

What's Next

You'll exit Grand Portage either southwesterly bound for Grand Marais or northward to the International Border with Canada.

INFO & OPTIONS

Grand Portage National Monument Visitor Center
P.O. Box 426
170 Mile Creek Rd.
Grand Portage, MN 55605
218-475-0123
www.nps.gov/grpo

Island View Dining Room (Grand Portage Lodge)
70 Casino Dr.
Grand Portage, MN 55605
218-475-2520
www.grandportage.com

Grand Portage Lodge & Casino
70 Casino Dr.
Grand Portage, MN 55605
218-475-2520
www.grandportage.com

Grand Portage Marina & RV Park
218-475-2476
www.grandportage.com

Grand Portage State Park
9393 East Hwy. 61
Grand Portage, MN 55605
218-475-2360

Grand Rapids

Population 8,743

On the western edge of the Mesabi Iron Range where Highway 2 from the east and west intersects Highway 169 from the south or north is Grand Rapids. Best known for its thriving wood products industry through its history, that heritage is carried on by Blandin Paper Company, which supplies coated paper for many magazines and catalogs. Grand Rapids has ample lodging, good dining and many activities throughout the year that will appeal to visitors.

What to See and Do

Old Central School is a prime example of Romanesque Revivalist architecture. It houses Itasca County Historical Society Museum and a children's museum.

For a golf outing, check out the "grand slam" that includes Sugarbrooke, Pokegama, Wendigo and Eagle Ridge golf courses in the area.

Tours of Blandin's paper mill are offered from June through Labor Day.

Minnesota Forest History Center also fosters the area's timber heritage and includes an interpretive building displaying themes of forest history, including a realistic 1900 lumber camp. Special events are scheduled throughout the summer. For winter opportunities, call ahead for information.

Notable Events

- The annual Judy Garland Festival is in June, celebrating the star's origins in this town.

What's Next

Visitors seeking a wider range can travel west on Highway 2 to Deer River, at the eastern edge of the Leech Lake Reservation. The Leech Lake Band of Ojibwe operates the White Oak Casino there, the Palace Hotel Casino farther west at Cass Lake and the Northern Lights Gaming Casino, Hotel and Events Center near Walker. Leech Lake is at the center of Minnesota's Heartland tourism area and offers great muskie and other fishing.

From Grand Rapids, travelers can return to Duluth and the Lake Superior Circle Tour via U.S. Highway 2 or travel northerly to other Mesabi Iron Range cities and sites.

INFO & OPTIONS

Grand Rapids Chamber of Commerce
1 Northwest Third St.
Grand Rapids, MN 55744
800-472-6366
www.grandmn.com

Visit Grand Rapids
501 South Pokegama Ave., Ste. 3
Grand Rapids, MN 55744
800-355-9740
www.visitgrandrapids.com

Sawmill Inn Dining Room
2301 South Pokegama Ave.
Grand Rapids, MN 55744
800-235-6455
www.sawmillinn.com

AmericInn Lodge & Suites
1812 South Pokegama Ave.
P.O. Box 435
Grand Rapids, MN 55744
888-950-8999 (reservations)
218-326-8999 (front desk)
www.americinn.com

The Lakes Inn
1300 East Hwy. 169
Grand Rapids, MN 55744
218-326-9655
www.thelakesinn.com

Gunflint Trail

The Gunflint Trail, which begins in Grand Marais, is a 58-mile long (93-kilometer) Minnesota Scenic Byway that runs almost to Canada.

The Trail is a major resort area, with accommodations varying from camping and rustic housekeeping cabins to bed-and-breakfast inns and elegant resorts. On a drive up the Trail, you'll see signs for Bearskin Lodge, Golden Eagle Lodge, Poplar Creek Guesthouse, Old Northwoods Lodge, Clearwater Canoe Outfitters and Lodge and perhaps the most well-known resort, the Gunflint Lodge. Founded by Justine Kerfoot and her family in the 1920s, the Gunflint Lodge has been operated by the family ever since.

The Gunflint is home to hundreds of miles of groomed cross-country ski and snowshoe trails, as well as extensive snowmobile routes. You'll find both the silent sport enthusiast and the snowmobiler here.

Most lodges offer packages of instruction, guided treks and equipment rental. Specialty trips such as those offered by Boundary Country Trekking (cross-country ski treks with overnight stops at Mongolian yurts) have been featured in national magazines. You may ski or hike lodge-to-lodge, with your bags and car transported for you.

The Gunflint Trail is a major entry point to the Boundary Waters Canoe Area Wilderness (BWCAW) and fishing rarely gets much better. In summer, hikers may explore hundreds of miles of trails, many of which offer spectacular views. The Trail is home to several outfitters who will supply everything you need for a weeklong trek into the BWCAW or an afternoon paddle on one of the many surrounding lakes. Most resorts also provide canoes and kayaks for guests' use.

Because it's the wilderness, visitors might be surprised to find fine gourmet dining here. The Gunflint Lodge has long been known for its fine dining. Old Northwoods Lodge, with its enormous stone fireplace, offers superb dining as well as an excellent wine and beer list. For more casual dining, try the Trail Center for a burger. The Trail Center is also one of the only spots to pick up provisions and gasoline on the Trail.

Paulucci Space Theater offers night sky shows, planetarium multimedia programs and large-format films.

At the end of the Gunflint Trail, you'll find Way of the Wilderness Canoe Outfitters' Trail's End Café in the middle of the wilderness where you can get a burger or a cup of good homemade chili. It's definitely worth the trip.

Hibbing

Population 16,209

Hibbing, located almost exactly in the heart of the Mesabi Iron Range on U.S. Highway 169, boasts a number of attractions of interest to travelers of the Iron Trail. Here are manmade canyons and hills of waste reflecting the city's history as "the iron ore capitol of the world." Here, too, are beautiful lakes in the surrounding area, perfect for recreation and relaxation. The city is a retail center for the area, offering virtually anything a shopper needs. There are good lodgings, fine dining and other amenities.

A Bit of History

Hibbing takes its name from Frank Hibbing, a timber cruiser and prospector who first discovered iron ore in the region in the mid-1890s. A village was platted and grew almost overnight as miners and others moved in to look for their bonanza. Unfortunately for the town, iron ore lay directly under it and the original townsite had to be abandoned in 1918, with all of its buildings being either demolished or moved to the present site. That move was completed by 1921 and mining progressed into the former city site, which came to be known as North Hibbing. Vestiges of that townsite still exist and are described below.

What to See and Do

Hull Rust Mahoning Mine is the world's largest open pit iron mine and a historic landmark. At the edge of the mine and townsite, a viewpoint provides a full view of the mine. Exhibits of massive equipment used in iron mining are located nearby and allow close-up examination of the machinery that keeps mines working.

A few blocks from the mine viewpoint, markers denote all that remains from the original village, which was moved to allow mining of iron ore under parts of the location.

Also near the mine viewpoint, the Greyhound Bus Origin Center commemorates the start of this company important to the growth of the country.

Paulucci Space Theater, on the Hibbing Community College campus, offers night sky shows, planetarium multimedia programs and large-format films.

Hibbing is the hometown of Bob Dylan (raised here as Bob Zimmerman), and the Hibbing Public Library has an interesting collection of memorabilia, photos and Dylan material. In late May, the city takes note of its famous son with a Bob Dylan Days celebration.

Hibbing High School auditorium was designed after New York's old Capitol Theatre and has long been a showplace of the area.

Take some time for browsing at Howard Street Booksellers on East Howard Street, an independent bookseller that stocks local authors and hosts events and signings.

Golfers find bargains at the 9-hole Hibbing Municipal Golf Course or may want to check out the 18-hole Mesaba Country Club.

Notable Museums

Hibbing Historical Society Museum in the Memorial Building at 23rd Street and Fifth Avenue East, is open all year. Fee.

What's Next

Dependent on your route of travel, you can take U.S. 169 northeasterly to the eastern Mesabi Range or west through several smaller cities to visit Grand Rapids. Another choice is to catch Highway 37 east to U.S. 53, which will take you to Duluth.

INFO & OPTIONS

Hibbing Chamber of Commerce
211 East Howard St.
Hibbing, MN 55746
800-4-HIBBING
www.hibbing.org

Hoyt Lakes

Population 2,280

Hoyt Lakes is the site of mining pioneer E.J. Longyear's first use of a diamond drill to test for iron ore. The Longyear Drill Site is commemorated a few miles beyond Hoyt Lakes on Highway 110.

Built in the mid-1950s as a self-contained town to house Erie Mining Company employees, Hoyt Lakes is adjacent to Colby and Whitewater lakes. Hoyt Lakes is home to the municipal Fisherman's Point Campground (reservations strongly recommended), a paved hiking, biking and skating trail and the Hoyt Lakes Country Club.

Travelers enter Hoyt Lakes at the western end of the Superior National Forest Scenic Byway (on St. Louis County Highway 110 to St. Louis County 16, then Lake County 15 and Lake County 5), which takes them toward Lake Superior, making an easy connection between the Iron Range cities and Minnesota's North Shore.

The byway's eastern end is at Silver Bay.

Hoyt Lakes hosts a Water Carnival each summer in late July.

INFO & OPTIONS

Hoyt Lakes Chamber of Commerce
P.O. Box 429
Hoyt Lakes, MN 55750
800-244-4802

City of Hoyt Lakes
Municipal Building
206 Kennedy Memorial Dr.
Hoyt Lakes, MN 55760
877-955-2344
www.hoytlakes.com

Country Inn of Hoyt Lakes
99 Kennedy Memorial Dr.
Hoyt Lakes, MN 55750
866-444-3555
www.hoytlakes.com

Fisherman's Point Campground
Campground Rd.
Hoyt Lakes, MN 55750
218-225-3337, 218-225-3444 (off-season)
www.hoytlakes.com

Iron Ranges

No exploration of northern Minnesota's wonders would be complete without a visit to to the Mesabi and Vermilion iron ranges. We recommend that visitors venture about an hour north from Duluth on Highway 53, or take the Superior National Forest Scenic Byway that runs from Silver Bay on Minnesota's North Shore to the range town of Aurora (from Silver Bay, take Lake County Highway 5 to Lake County 15, then St. Louis County 16 to St. Louis County 110). Other route options: catch Highway 1 at Illgen City or Highway 6 at Little Marais to visit the iron ranges. Here you can find museums, overlooks of active and inactive iron mines, interpretation of the area, entertainment, recreation, great accommodations, melt-in-the-mouth ethnic foods and the opportunity to descend into an underground iron mine for a one-of-a-kind tour.

If traveling on Highway 53 directly from Duluth or you choose the Superior National Forest Scenic Highway from Silver Bay to the Mesabi Iron Range, be sure to stop at the Mineview in the Sky at the edge of Virginia from May through September for an outstanding view over an abandoned iron mine and for help in planning a visit.

Once you're on the Iron Range, there are several directions of travel on what has come to be called the Iron Trail, which opens the way to many experiences and is home to 35 sites listed on the National Register of Historic Places.

While the Iron Range is world famous for its huge iron ore mines, it is an area with more than 2,000 miles of scenic groomed snowmobile trails, is surrounded by the beautiful Superior National Forest and offers wildlife watching, silent and motorized sports adventure and a range of fishing – some in depleted mine pits that have filled with water and been stocked with game fish.

The paved Mesabi Trail eventually will extend 132 miles (212 kilometers) from Grand Rapids to Ely and connect more than 25 communities. (About 102 miles were complete in early 2010.) The trail, partially built on old railroad beds, is there for hikers, bikers and inline skaters. Users of all ages are welcome; those over 18 must purchase a Wheel Pass. For the adventurous, there are lodge-to-lodge biking packages and a shuttle. The trail offers access to swimming, canoeing, camping and fishing. Winter activities may include cross-country skiing, snowshoeing and winter hiking.

For information on individual Iron Range sites, see descriptions in the listing for the city where they are located.

Knife River

Population 260

You can easily identify the county line between St. Louis and Lake counties on Scenic North Shore Drive; it is at the North Shore Scenic Railroad bridge that you pass under before Knife River. The town's name comes from the Ojibway *makomaani ziibing,* literally "Knife River," after sharp rocks in the river.

A Bit of History

Settled in the 1880s by commercial fishermen, the town survived a few years on fish and farming, but from 1898 to

1919, a logging operation was active here and Knife River boomed. Alger Smith Lumber Company also operated a 100-mile logging railroad nearly to Grand Marais. Until 1929 the area was the scene of attempts to mine copper. None of the veins proved commercially viable.

Today only a few fishermen continue the long tradition of catching and peddling fish from this rural community. It is still one of the North Shore's most active sport-fishing areas. Knife River Marina is home to several dozen Lake Superior pleasure vessels and charter fishing operations. Many boats work full time out of the Knife River Marina to take fishing enthusiasts approximately 1 mile from shore in several different directions to try their luck at hooking onto a large lake trout, coho or chinook salmon and to view the shoreline from a waterborne perspective. Lake Superior deepens to more than 500 feet (152 meters) within a mile of shore, so it is no more than 15 minutes from the time the boat leaves the marina until customers can be fishing. The charter boats work from the Knife west to the French River and east as far as Two Harbors.

Fresh and smoked fish are available locally. Try the legendary Russ Kendall's Smoke House. Don't miss the seasonally open Great! Lakes Candy Kitchen, featuring yummy fudge and other delightful homemade treats.

Larsmont

Population 280

A few miles between Two Harbors and Knife River on the North Shore Scenic Drive is Larsmont, once important in the fishing and timber industries. Larsmont's Little Red Schoolhouse, which is on the Register of Historic Places, is used as a community building. The Larsmont area is now popular for its cabin resorts and private campgrounds right on the lake. These include Larsmont Cottages, operated by Odyssey Development, and resorts like Stonegate, Bob's Cabins on Lake Superior and Breezy Point on Lake Superior. Mocha Moose Coffee and Gift Shoppe is a great coffee break and hosts an August picnic.

Just before you get to Two Harbors, you pass the traditional starting line for Grandma's Marathon. More than 9,000 runners cue up each June to make the 26.2-mile (42-kilometer) run that follows the Scenic North Shore to Canal Park in Duluth. Among the top running events in the nation, the race also features several related shorter races on the same weekend. Nearby is the starting line for the NorthShore Inline Marathon, the largest inline skating race in North America and third largest worldwide, the second weekend after Labor Day.

Little Marais / Taconite Harbor

On the Minnesota Circle Route along Highway 61, the county line between Lake and Cook counties intersects the Lake Superior shore at Morris Point near the Caribou River, where prehistoric lake beaches can be seen near the highway.

This section of Highway 61 is one of spectacular scenery. The area was settled by Scandinavian fishermen drawn by the craggy beauty so like their homeland fjords. The communities along the way – Schroeder, Tofte, Lutsen, Grand Marais and Hovland – all retain some of their fishing village charm. Net-drying reels, double-ended dories and fish sheds with their front doors opening into the lake can still be seen in many rocky inlets.

One such inlet, Sugarloaf Cove, once served as an important timber rafting site and has subsequently been acquired by Sugarloaf: The North Shore Stewardship Association, which has worked to restore natural features and has also built an interpretive center. There's an easy 1-mile interpretive hiking trail. Watch for the sign just past milepost 73 on the lake side of Highway 61.

Where to Shop

Eagle's Nest Gifts offers a nice stop to pick out a memorable gift item. Spirit of Gitche Gumee features a gourmet coffee bar, a bed-and-breakfast inn and a seasonal gift store that carries a wide variety of locally produced gifts, art and craftwork, specializing in north shore cedar and other wood items.

Minnesota's North Shore Tunnels

Silver Creek Cliff rises a sheer 300 feet (92 meters) out of Lake Superior's waters. The old highway, built in 1923, used to hug the face of the rock at 125 feet (39 meters) above the waves, providing a breathtaking view of the lake. A privately owned gazebo on the point is often photographed in winter with its intricate icy covering formed by water thrown upward by high, pounding waves just before a freeze.

The Minnesota Department of Transportation opened the tunnel through Silver Creek Cliff in 1994 to improve the safety of the Highway 61 drive. In 2004, work by the Department of Transportation began on a paved bike path, automobile pulloff and viewpoint on the old highway to take in that famous Lake Superior view. A similar tunnel was completed earlier at Lafayette Bluff, a few miles farther east on Highway 61.

Fish Out of Water spotlights wood-crafted Scandinavian items, but also has many other lines of arts and crafts available. There's bound to be something that appeals to you. With flags and a large area for parking, you can't miss it.

What's Next

The former LTV Steel Mining Company dock and power plant at Taconite Harbor remain a visible part of this stretch of lakeshore, and Minnesota Power now operates the electric generating plant. A state harbor of refuge for boaters is here.

Traveling southwest on Highway 61 from Little Marais, you'll soon come to Silver Bay on the way to Duluth.

INFO & OPTIONS

Fenstad's Resort
6572 Hwy. 61
Little Marais, MN 55614
218-226-4724

Lutsen

Area Population 250

At Lutsen stands a year-round recreational complex built in the 1890s by C.A.A. Nelson, a commercial fisherman who became Minnesota's "Pioneer in Pleasure." Lutsen Resort on Lake Superior was the North Shore's first resort. After fires destroyed earlier lodge buildings, a new lodge was built by 1952 using mostly white pine logs and following the Scandinavian design of Edwin Lundie. It's the classic building that you see today featuring a great restaurant and rustic atmosphere. The range of accommodations includes the lodge, townhomes, condominiums, log homes and sea villas. The health spa was added in 2008.

At Silver Creek Cliff, a tunnel makes safe passage through an area once known for rockslides.

What to See and Do

The area's predominant claim to fame is winter activities, including excellent downhill and cross-country skiing. Once the home of former Olympic skier Cindy Nelson, the area is a part of the extensive North Shore Trail System. Lutsen is the perfect point to start your winter trail exploration. All-season trail maps, with information on cross-country skiing and snowmobiling, canoeing, camping, hiking, mountain biking and fall color touring, are available along the shore.

In addition to the 90 downhill runs for which Lutsen Mountains ski area is famous, a summer attraction at Lutsen Mountains is the Alpine Slide, an iceless sled track that winds down Eagle Mountain (this one a mere 1,660 feet/506 meters high). Gondola rides from mountain to mountain are a must for fall color seekers. If you like mountain biking, Lutsen Mountains offers nearly 50 miles (80 kilometers) of marked bike trails in its Mountain Bike Park. The scenic Caribou Trail runs north inland from Lutsen to Brule Lake. The road is 20 miles (32 kilometers) long. Also in this area is the North Shore Mountain Ski Trail, a 130-mile (209-kilometer) groomed cross-country system from Temperance River to Bally Creek north of Cascade River State Park near Grand Marais, much of which is right on the Lake Superior shore. Information is available at resorts and at the Visitor Information Center in Tofte's North Shore Commercial Fishing Museum.

After a day of skiing or alpine sliding, visit the Mountain Shop at Lutsen for ski wear and accessories, T-shirts and gifts.

Highly rated 27-hole Superior National at Lutsen overlooks Lake Superior and the Poplar River. The clubhouse serves as a winter recreation and information center.

The area includes many modern and classic lodging spots with fabulous views.

On the way to Grand Marais, watch for the flag on the highway at Kah-Nee-Tah Gallery and Cottages, which has fine art, gift items and lakeshore cabin rentals.

Approaching Good Harbor Bay, stop at Thomsonite Beach Jewelry Shop to see thomsonite, unique to Lake Superior and from a mine on the Thomsonite Beach Inn and Suites property.

What's Next

Traveling northeast on Highway 61 takes you to Grand Marais. Southwesterly points the visitor toward Silver Bay, Two Harbors and Duluth.

INFO & OPTIONS

Caribou Highlands
371 Ski Hill Rd.
Lutsen, MN 55612
800-642-6036
www.caribouhighlands.com

Cascade Lodge
3719 West Hwy. 61
Lutsen, MN 55612-9534
218-387-2911
www.cascadelodgemn.com

Eagle Ridge Resort at Lutsen Mts.
565 Ski Hill Rd.
Lutsen, MN 55612
800-360-7666
www.eagleridgeatlutsen.com

Hidden Cove
5640 County Road 35
Lutsen, MN 55612
218-663-7379

Lutsen Resort on Lake Superior
5700 West Hwy. 61
Lutsen, MN 55612
800-258-2736
www.lutsenresort.com

Solbakken Resort
4874 West Hwy. 61
Lutsen, MN 55612
800-435-3950
www.solbakkenresort.com

Cascade River State Park
3481 West Hwy. 61
Lutsen, MN 55612
218-387-3053

Mountain Iron

Population 2,999

Mountain Iron is where iron ore was discovered on the Mesabi Range by the famous "Seven Iron Men" of Duluth's Merritt family in 1890. This is home to the world's largest taconite plant. Wacootah Overlook Viewpoint overlooks the mine. The plant atop its mountainous site is visible for miles as you travel toward Mountain Iron/Virginia. If you seek lodging, an AmericInn is located in the Virginia/Mountain Iron area.

To visit the western Mesabi Iron Range area, take U.S. 169 west from Mountain Iron toward Chisholm and Hibbing. To return to the Circle Tour, take Highway 53 south toward Duluth or Highway 135 east from Virginia through Biwabik, Aurora and Hoyt Lakes to catch Superior National Forest Scenic Byway (Lake County 15/St. Louis County 16) to Silver Bay on Minnesota's North Shore of Lake Superior.

Schroeder

Population 187

Schroeder, Tofte and Lutsen on Lake Superior's Minnesota North Shore are rapidly growing in popularity as year-round tourist destinations. They are villages with populations of several hundred each a few miles apart, with parallel histories as Scandinavians came in the late 1800s and settled. These immigrants lumbered, mostly in Schroeder, and fished, more so at Tofte and Lutsen, to feed their families.

Near Schroeder, Taconite Harbor is a large industrial complex housing a coal-fired power plant operated by Minnesota Power and iron ore docks that formerly served the needs of LTV Steel Mining Company. A state harbor of refuge for boaters is at the west side of the complex on the lake, with parking and a boat ramp that give a great view of the docks, which are occasionally visited by large freighters delivering coal for the power plant.

What to See and Do

In the spring, the Cross River, normally a quiet stream falling through the rocks, becomes a raging torrent of water on its way to the lake. The spectacular falls pass directly under Highway 61 at "downtown" Schroeder, well worth a 20-minute stop. Highway upgrading in this area has made it much more visitor-friendly, so pull over, park and grab the wide-angle lens for the camera. Visit at different times of the year for varying flows over the falls.

It was in Schroeder that Father Frederic Baraga (BEAR-a-ga), the legendary Snowshoe Priest from Michigan's Upper Peninsula, landed after struggling through a terrific storm on the lake in 1846. As a tribute, he erected a wooden cross at dawn the next day. A symbolic granite cross now stands at the site on the mouth of the Cross River, named after the event. Follow the road to the boat ramp and park in the little paved lot. A well-worn but ill-marked path toward the river across private land will take you to the cross and a wonderful beach with direct access to the lake. Not easily accessible for the handicapped. There are facilities at the boat launch. During summer, there is a Lutheran Church service at 7:30 a.m. Sunday mornings on the rocks near the cross.

Cross River Heritage Center is on the south side of the highway and serves as a museum/interpretive center with many displays and exhibits. Handicapped accessible, this facility is headquarters of the Schroeder Area Historical Society (and maybe a ghost).

A bit east of Schroeder on Highway 61 is Temperance River State Park. Legend has it that the Temperance River was playfully named because it has no "bar" at its mouth. In a steep gorge, the water drunkenly falls 160 feet (49 meters). Along the rim in Temperance River State Park are potholes and cauldrons visible from hiking trails. The park offers campers two campgrounds on Lake Superior and is the only state park on the North Shore to have electrical hookups. Carlton Peak is popular with rock climbers and offers even more recreational opportunities to park visitors.

Nearby, on the upper side of the highway, Temperance Traders features gifts and modern one- and two-bedroom cabins.

What's Next

Continue the Circle Tour on Highway 61 heading northeast toward Tofte, Lutsen and Grand Marais or southwest to Silver Bay, Two Harbors and Duluth.

INFO & OPTIONS

Lamb's Resort on Lake Superior
4 Lamb's Way/Hwy.61
Schroeder, MN 55613
218-663-7292
www.lambsresort.com

Palisade Head, off Highway 61 about 3 miles outside of Silver Bay, draws sightseers and rock climbers. In the distance is another shoreline landmark, Shovel Point at Tettegouche State Park.

Satellite's Country Inn
9436 West Hwy. 61
Schroeder, MN 55613
218-663-7574

Temperance Landing
Hwy.61
Schroeder, MN 55613
218-663-7220

Temperance River State Park
7620 West Hwy. 61
Schroeder, MN 55613
218-663-7476

Silver Bay

Population 2,068

Silver Bay is nestled in the Sawtooth Mountains northeast of Two Harbors and Duluth and just a short distance off Highway 61. Growth of the town primarily provided homes and other amenities for employees of the former Reserve Mining Company, Minnesota's first large-scale iron-ore pellet operation.

Sitting in a natural, scenic amphitheater, Silver Bay is a "company town" that has many recreational facilities, including tennis courts and the scenic 9-hole public Silver Bay Country Club with adjoining driving range. The city also operates a municipal business park for businesses seeking space.

Silver Bay's amenities include a municipal airport, business park and great snowmobile, hiking and ski trails, including the Red Dot Trail, a 27-mile ATV and snowmobile route through Tettegouche State Park connecting Silver Bay and Beaver Bay.

This is also the beginning of Superior National Forest Scenic Byway (west from Silver Bay, take Lake County 5 to Lake County 15, then St. Louis County 16 to St. Louis County 110). The byway connects the lakeshore with the Iron Range.

Many of the town's businesses are in the shopping mall at the center of the townsite, including two banks, a well-stocked grocery store and restaurant. Other shopping opportunities are along Outer Drive that leads from the highway.

A Bit of History

Originally homesteaded by fisherman Oscar Pederson in 1920, the town gained its name when Pederson asked the captain of the steamship *America* what he should call his place. The captain suggested "Silver Bay" because he thought the rocks along the shoreline of the bay had the appearance of silver. When the town was incorporated in 1956, it kept the name.

Today

Northshore Mining currently operates the large iron-ore pellet ("taconite") plant, which can produce more than 7 million tons of pellets per year at full capacity. The ore is moved down the Great Lakes by giant ore ships, which call regularly in Silver Bay. Visitors can view a mining equipment display at the plant. Cleveland Cliffs Company, which owns and operates the facility, has created a series of three scenic overlooks along a mile-long loop of hiking trail on a hillside offering vistas over the big lake, the plant site and the city. A different theme is presented and interpreted at each site, identifying landmarks and explaining what is seen. Paved parking areas are available for cars and RVs. Tours of the plant are offered Tuesdays, Thursdays and Saturdays. Check with the Information Center, operated along Outer Drive by the Bay Area Historical Society. It also has a nice display of artifacts from the society's collection.

In 2003, a pilot plant on Northshore's property successfully produced the first run of a special process called "direct-reduced iron" nuggets. With more than 96 percent pure iron content, compared with 65 percent in taconite pellets, the iron nuggets are worth about six times the value of taconite pellets. Subsequent trials proved the process and generated so much interest that the Minnesota Legislature passed legislation to speed construction of a commercial plant at the former Erie Mining Company in Hoyt Lakes, which is likely to be important to the Minnesota's Iron Range and the American iron industry.

What to See and Do

Silver Bay Marina, west of Northshore Mining's plant, offers a harbor of refuge and a 61-slip, full-service facility for North Shore boaters. Adjacent is Bayside Park, with picnic facilities, a nice beach and a scenic overlook of the lake and the iron-ore processing facilities.

On the way along Outer Drive, be sure to notice the statue of Rocky Taconite, as well as the award-winning landscaping that blossoms from spring into fall.

What's Next

Depending on your travel plans, you'll take Highway 61 either northeasterly toward Grand Marais or southwesterly toward Two Harbors and Duluth. About 3 miles to the southwest, Beaver Bay makes an interesting stop.

A few miles east of town on Highway 61, a narrow lakeside road at milepost 57 takes tourists to the top of a high coastal bluff known as Palisade Head, much like those extending easterly for 40 miles (64 kilometers). Watch closely for the right turn, which is on a slight downgrade of Highway 61. The road to the top is steep but safe.

The face of the 350-foot (107-meter) cliff is sheer rock and can be viewed safely from a stone wall at the top. This is a popular spot for blueberry picking and is also especially popular with rock climbing enthusiasts, who have adopted several such locations on Minnesota's North Shore. White-tailed deer are often seen quietly eyeing visitors from protective foliage, and dedicated birders may catch a glimpse of peregrine falcons that nest in the area. You'll want to bring your camera for the excellent views of Shovel Point to the northeast and other vistas. Open daily.

Indian archers are said to have tried to shoot their arrows to the top of the cliff from their canoes on the surface of the lake, with few achieving such a feat. The rugged coastline along Palisade is often likened to that of Maine and Oregon. The site has been used by Hollywood filmmakers for such movies as "The Good Son" with Macaulay Culkin.

INFO & OPTIONS

Bay Area Historical Society
80 Outer Dr.
Silver Bay, MN 55614
218-226-3143

Northwoods Cafe
6 Shopping Center
Silver Bay, MN 55614
218-226-3699

AmericInn Lodge & Suites – Silver Bay
150 Mensing Dr.
Silver Bay, MN 55614
877-254-1827
www.americinnsilverbay.com

Tettegouche State Park
5702 Hwy. 61
Silver Bay, MN 55614
218-226-6365
www.dnr.state.mn.us

Split Rock Lighthouse State Park

One of the most photographed lighthouses on the Great Lakes, Split Rock Lighthouse was built in 1910 in response to six shipwrecks within a dozen miles of the Split Rock River. Some were ore carriers whose compasses were rendered useless by the nature of their cargo and masses of iron under the lake, but the main diasters came during a horrific storm in November 28, 1905, when 29 ships wrecked on the lake. One vessel lost during that storm, the *Madeira*, remains under the waters near the cliffs. Fog and dangerous reefs made travel unusually treacherous under such conditions.

The construction of the lighthouse was a heroic feat, since there were no roads in the region at that time. All of the materials down to the last brick had to be shipped in and hoisted up the 130-foot (40-meter) cliff by a derrick, which itself had to be lifted by rope and pulley to the top of the cliff. Split Rock Lighthouse State Park and the Split Rock Lighthouse Historic Site give tourists triple their money in historical detail, entertainment and nostalgia. A sizable recent addition to the visitor center adds much more space for interesting displays about the lighthouse and the area (including a wall-sized replica of *Lake Superior Magazine*'s travel map).

Visitors to the site of the historic Split Rock Lighthouse can walk the winding stairs for an unparalleled view. (Lee Radzak / Split Rock Lighthouse)

Visitors to the 25-acre Historic Site are guided by staff through the lighthouse and invited to climb the winding stairs to the top where they can get a close-up view of the multicrystal-lensed beacon that was made in France. They will hear stories about problems that threatened the lighthouse keeper and nearly caused the beacon to fail from time to time. The view from the lamproom is unparalleled. Picnic facilities are available.

Each November 10, the light shines across Lake Superior in commemoration of the 1975 wreck of the *Edmund Fitzgerald*.

The operation of the 2,200-acre park and the interpretive center are the result of a joint venture of the Minnesota Historical Society and the state park system. Open normal hours mid-May to mid-October daily; in the winter the lighthouse and historic buildings are closed, but the Visitor Center and Museum Store are open Thursdays through Mondays. Split Rock Museum Store carries nautical, north woods and Split Rock merchandise, including puzzles, books and clothing. State park sticker required for park use, but not when visiting the lighthouse during the regular season. There is a small fee for touring the lighthouse and grounds. Hiking and picnicking in the park are included in the lighthouse admission fee. During the off-season, visitors at the lighthouse will need a state park vehicle permit.

The popular Split Rock Lighthouse State Park Campground offers an excellent opportunity for camping with families. Cart-in camping is available for those with young children.

Just beyond Split Rock is Gold Rock, another jut of land into Lake Superior. This 80-acre property was acquired in 1998 and was incorporated into Split Rock Lighthouse State Park.

Superior Hiking Trail

The Superior Hiking Trail runs along the ridgeline overlooking Lake Superior and parallels Scenic Highway 61 from Two Harbors to the Canadian border for 205 miles (330 kilometers). Plans are to eventually connect the trail between Two Harbors and Duluth. A recently completed portion through Duluth has a 39-mile (63-kilometer) trail that features Jay Cooke State Park, Ely's Peak, Bardon's Peak, the Magney-Snively old growth forest, Spirit Mountain, Enger Park, the Lakewalk on Lake Superior, the University of Minnesota Duluth's Bagley Nature Trails and Hartley Nature Center.

Earning high praise from hikers and hiking organizations, additional sections of the trail are being completed by volunteers, allowing free and easy access from many places of lodging along the way. The trail's 244 miles (393 kilometers) are well-signed and maintained by volunteers to provide hikers with challenges at whatever level they desire. The Superior Hiking Trail also has become a part of a lodge-to-lodge hiking system on the shore. Superior Shuttle service is available on Fridays, Saturdays and Sundays at many of the participating lodges, as well as numerous pickup and drop-off points along the trail from May to late October.

Tettegouche State Park

A few miles northeast of Silver Bay on Highway 61 is Tettegouche (Teh-Teh-Gooch) State Park. Tettegouche offers extensive hiking covering more than 23 miles (38 kilometers). Rugged, mountainous terrain, 2.5 miles of Lake Superior shoreline, six inland lakes, cascading rivers and undisturbed hardwood forest highlight this pristine area.

Access to the park is by roadway or foot trail from the Baptism River highway rest area, where park headquarters, an information center and small gift shop are located. Campers have the choice of two campgrounds. In the cart-in campground, they can load their gear onto two-wheeled pull-carts and move it to their site. The other semimodern campground features 28 drive-in sites and six walk-in sites. Lodging in the park includes the historic Tettegouche Camp, unique in architecture with log buildings from the late 1800s. The park also offers the Illgen Falls Cabin, a drive-to cabin that is handicapped-accessible. Inquire at the main office.

Inland, four waterfalls on the Baptism River include Minnesota's highest waterfall fully inside the borders, which drops 70 feet (21 meters). The hike to the high falls is 1.5 miles (2.4 kilometers) from the park office, or three-quarters of a mile (1.2 kilometers) from the trailhead, and takes about 45 minutes, or 15 minutes, respectively, one way. The waters of the Baptism River were used to anoint new converts to the Christian faith. In the park you'll find Conservancy Pines, a stand of Norway pines growing since the early 20th century, as well as other small old-growth stands of white pine and yellow birch. From the park's wayside parking lot, the three-quarter-mile Shovel Point Trail is a perfect viewing platform to see the palisade shoreline. Many of the park's trails are open in winter for cross-country skiing and snowshoeing.

Just to the east a bit, Whispering Pines Motel in Illgen City is on land originally owned by 3M Company. Over the years the highway passed through the property, another inn burned down and buildings were moved. Today, it's a quiet resort at the intersection with Highway 1 heading inland and is close to the lake and state park.

What's Next

You can continue your Circle Tour either northeast or southwest by following Highway 61. To the east, you're heading for Grand Marais through Schroeder, Tofte and Lutsen. Westerly takes you to Silver Bay, Beaver Bay and Two Harbors.

INFO & OPTIONS

Tettegouche State Park
5702 Hwy. 61
Silver Bay, MN 55614
218-226-6365

Tofte

Population 256

Tofte is a small town sitting between Lutsen on the north and Schroeder on the south. Highway 61 bisects the town and gives virtually a complete view of town.

The Tofte area has blossomed with visitor comforts. A half-mile southwest of Tofte, Sugar Beach Resort offers lakeside cabins. Other lodging facilities include an AmericInn and the popular Bluefin Bay on Lake Superior. The old dock for the steamer *America* still stands at Bluefin as testament to the old boat that was once a major cargo and passenger link along the lakeshore. The new Surfside on Lake Superior has luxury townhomes and features that include a recreation center with heated pool and Superior Waters Spa at Surfside, a full-service destination spa. Superior Waters offers massage, manicures, pedicures, facials and other services; it also includes an indoor pool, hot tub, sauna, state-of-the-art fitness center and Superior Waters Cafe, a coffee bar with sandwiches and salads.

Although Highway 61 is the only major east/west road through Cook County, much of the north/south traffic moves on four trails: the Sawbill Trail at Tofte, Caribou Trail at Lutsen, Gunflint Trail at Grand Marais and the Arrowhead Trail at the Brule River. These trails are closely connected with the fur trade, logging and mineral exploration. After the 1854 Treaty of La Pointe, Wisconsin, released all of northeastern Minnesota from the control of the Ojibway, white settlers moved in and began cutting these trails into the backcountry.

Today these are main arteries for vacation travel in the county. These roads head to good fishing, canoe country, resorts, outfitters and private cabins of those who have found their dreams where the lordly moose roam and loons fill the wilderness nights with their winsome laughter. It has become a popular area for winter enthusiasts who snowmobile, snowshoe and cross-country ski.

What to See and Do

Fall color arrives along Minnesota's North Shore in two waves, the first peak occurring between mid-September to early October inland from the lake. Drive the trails and back roads to see the brilliant reds and oranges. The second season of color runs right along the shore, following Highway 61. It usually peaks between the first and third weeks of October.

Sawbill Trail (County Road 2) runs 25 miles (40 kilometers) from Tofte to Sawbill Lake and the Boundary Waters Canoe Area Wilderness. The highest

Tofte's Lake Walk affords nice views of Lake Superior, and it gets a lot of traffic from people staying at Bluefin Bay on Lake Superior, a popular North Shore getaway.

point directly on Minnesota's shore, Carlton Peak, towers 927 feet (283 meters) above the lake, a total of 1,529 feet (466 meters) above sea level. Trails wind to the top for an impressive view of the Sawtooth Mountains and Lake Superior. In the autumn, the peak offers an outstanding view of the colorful valley. Access to the trail is from the Sawbill Trail. Visitors planning to travel inland on Sawbill Trail for a day or longer visit may want to check Sawtooth Outfitters for information and canoe, kayak, bike, ski or snowshoe rentals to expand their pleasure potential. They are also a full-service sales and service shop for pedalers.

Two other area hiking experiences are Oberg Mountain (2.25 miles/3.6 kilometers) and Leveaux (3.4 miles/5.5 kilometers) hiking trails. Both are round trips from the parking lot 5 miles (8 kilometers) east of Tofte on Forest Road 336. They offer breathtaking views of Lake Superior and are spectacular in fall.

If you prefer to shop instead of hike, stop at WatersEdge Trading Company. The store, next to Coho Cafe on the lakeside of the highway, sells quality clothing and outerwear as well as an eclectic mix of books, toys, cards and jewelry. And if you need to stock up on groceries, liquor and other items, try North Shore Market on Highway 61.

Notable Museums

Learn about past life on the lake with a stroll on Tofte's Lake Walk. Start at the North Shore Commercial Fishing Museum, the red museum that preserves the area's heritage with stories, boats and tools from fishing families. Three outside plazas have imaginative, interactive displays on the way to Tofte Town Park with charming stone walkways and bridges.

What's Next

The Circle Tour continues on Highway 61 either to the northeast to Lutsen and Grand Marais or southwest to Silver Bay, Two Harbors and Duluth.

INFO & OPTIONS

Lutsen-Tofte Tourism Association
7136 West Hwy. 61
Tofte, MN 55615
888-61NORTH
www.americasnorthcoast.org

Bluefin Restaurant
7192 West Hwy. 61
Tofte, MN 55615
800-BLUEFIN (258-3346)

Bluefin Bay on Lake Superior
7192 West Hwy. 61
Tofte, MN 55615
800-BLUEFIN (258-3346)
www.bluefinbay.com

AmericInn Lodge & Suites – Tofte
Hwy.61 at Mile Marker 82
Tofte, MN 55615
800-625-7042
www.americinntofte.com

The Mountain Inn at Lutsen
360 Ski Hill Rd.
Tofte, MN 55615
218-663-7244
www.lutsenlodgingcompany.com

Sugar Beach Resort
P.O. Box 2236
Tofte, MN 55615
218-663-7595ko
Www.toftesugarbeach.com

Surfside on Lake Superior
Hwy.61
Tofte, MN
877-361-7873
www.surfsideonsuperior.com

Tower-Soudan

Population: Tower 477, Soudan 200-300

The twin towns of Tower and Soudan on Highway 169 between Ely and Virginia offer some intriguing visits. Tour the Soudan Underground Mine in Soudan Underground Mine State Park between the towns. The only underground iron mine open for tours, visitors are guided to a depth of 2,341 feet where the year-round temperature is a constant 50 degrees Fahrenheit. In the nearby Embarrass area, tours of Finnish farms and homesteads explore the importance of this large ethnic group that pioneered settlement here.

Also at Tower/Soudan, visit Lake Vermilion, one of the largest lakes in northeast Minnesota. Visitors may want to reserve a daylong scenic trip on the boat that delivers mail to waterbound residents. Take Highway 77 to find Fortune Bay Resort Casino on the Bois Forte Ojibway Reservation. The tribe also operates its "Legend House" or *Atisokanigamig* heritage museum and its championship 18-hole golf course, The Wilderness.

Two Harbors

Population 3,356

North Shore Scenic Drive from Duluth meets the Highway 61 expressway at the approach to Two Harbors, incorporated in 1888. At that time, the area around Agate and Burlington bays (the two harbors) was a well-known Ojibway hunting and fishing ground. Two Harbors owes its growth to the railroad and shipping of iron ore, although it was also a significant logging center.

Highway 61 becomes Seventh Avenue and runs straight through Two Harbors. But many of the attractions in town, like the lighthouse and harbor, are downtown and closer to the lake. Don't miss the directional signs to take you there.

What to See and Do

Two Harbors is fast becoming a destination town with many attractions. You have not seen Two Harbors unless you head to the downtown and waterfront. Watch for the signs at Seventh Street or Waterfront Drive (Sixth Street) that take you just a few blocks toward the lake, where viewing areas at Lighthouse Point allow you to watch huge lakers, some as long as 1,000 feet (308 meters), loading iron ore.

Paul VanHoven Park includes a gazebo on a grassy knoll opposite the historic iron ore docks and within sight of the retired *Edna G.*, the last coal-fed, steam-powered tugboat to operate on the Great Lakes. Retired from service in 1981, the *Edna G.* was renovated at Fraser Shipyards in Superior, to be preserved as a historical interpretive display. Tours of the tug, owned by the city and managed by the Lake County Historical Society, can be arranged at the Depot Museum.

Dock #1, once the largest iron ore loading dock in the world, is closest to shore. Two Harbors became the state's first iron ore port in 1884 with the completion of the railway from the town of Tower on Minnesota's Vermilion Iron Range. Iron ore is now mined as taconite, a low-grade iron-bearing rock that must first be processed and concentrated before it can be used by the steel mills. Two Harbors is still one of the busiest ore harbors on Lake Superior, visited by the giant ore boats.

Two Harbors Area Chamber of Commerce manages the R.J. Houle Information Center on the east side of town, providing information about area businesses and attractions. It is open year-round. The center was constructed as a ranger fire station and was relocated to Two Harbors in 1977. Another attraction at the site is a hand-hewn totem pole, a sculpture given to the American people by nationally renowned artist Peter Toth as a tribute to Native Americans. The artist returned recently to restore the sculpture.

A 30- to 45-minute walking tour of historic Two Harbors will take you past many of the significant locations in town. Organized by the historical society, brochures with the route are available in many places in addition to the depot.

Walkers will want to check out Sonju Trail, a portion of which is paved and handicapped-accessible. It follows the shore from downtown through Lighthouse Point and takes a beautifully natural route all the way to the Municipal Campground and the 18-hole municipal Lakeview National Golf Course, which offers wonderful lake vistas from its grounds.

Thursday evening concerts in Thomas Owens Park by the Two Harbors City Band are informal affairs, 7:30 p.m., in July. The City Band is the oldest continuous operating volunteer band in the state.

In mid-June and mid-December, the summer and winter solstices are celebrated at the lighthouse grounds.

Along the harbor is a public boat launch, free parking and a view of the harbor. A walk along the east Agate Bay breakwater takes visitors safely out onto the lake about one-quarter mile and provides an opportunity for stretching the legs or

Picturesque Two Harbors Lighthouse, home of a bed-and-breakfast inn.

fishing for trout and salmon. Off the west breakwater, accessible only by boat, lie the remains of the *Samuel P. Ely*, a sunken three-masted schooner. The *Ely* went down in 1896 and is one of the oldest recorded shipwrecks on western Lake Superior, as well as a popular dive for scuba enthusiasts.

On Highway 61, Lakeview National Golf Course is a par-72 course. Players can see Lake Superior from 14 of the 18 holes. It has a full pro shop and lighted cross-country ski trails have been added for winter recreation. It is across the highway from the Burlington Bay Campground.

Flood Bay, 1 mile east of Two Harbors, is a natural harbor with yet another breathtaking view of the lake. The pebble beach is one of the finest agate beaches on the North Shore. It's a great way for kids to let off a little energy. The Minnesota Department of Transportation has provided an excellent wayside for those who wish to dip toes in the lake.

Notable Museums

Lake County Historical Society has several museums, including the Depot Museum in the old Duluth and Iron Range Railroad Depot. Here you can see two locomotives, the 1943 Mallet *#229* and the historic *3 Spot* from 1883. The "*Malley*" is a Mallet-type steam locomotive, one of the most powerful ever built. This forerunner of the diesel hauled iron ore to Two Harbors until 1961. The *3 Spot* is a steam engine that arrived during a storm in 1883 on a scow pulled by a tugboat from Duluth. It was used to build the tracks to Tower on the Iron Range and was a workhorse on the logging railroad of the Alger Smith Lumber Company for two decades as the white pine was logged along Minnesota's North Shore.

The depot was extremely active between 1907, when it was built, and the late 1950s. The last freight trains used the depot in 1967. Inside, the exhibits help bring local history to life. The museum stresses the three basic industries that "made" Two Harbors: shipping iron ore, logging and fishing.

The Depot Museum is open weekends beginning in May; it's open seven days a week after Memorial Day. Hours are limited in the fall, so it's best to contact the museum.

The historical society also operates the 3M Museum, which features interactive displays and information on the development and history of the company's many products. The museum is a two-minute walk from the Depot Museum. 3M Company had its star-crossed beginnings in 1902 on the northwest corner of Waterfront Drive and Second Avenue in a modest building owned by attorney John Dwan, an original investor. The 3M/Dwan Museum building has been restored to commemorate the company's important place in the history of the North Shore.

One can still catch a ride on the North Shore Scenic Railroad from the Depot. Visitors who arrive in Two Harbors by train will find inexpensive in-town transportation aboard an Arrowhead Transit bus that meets the train. A public transportation service, Arrowhead serves Lake County and Duluth communities with a regular schedule of routes.

Parks and Public Areas

There is no doubt that Lighthouse Point is the focus of most visitors. Here is ample parking, nice green spaces, benches for sitting to watch ore boats being loaded across Agate Bay and a great boat launch.

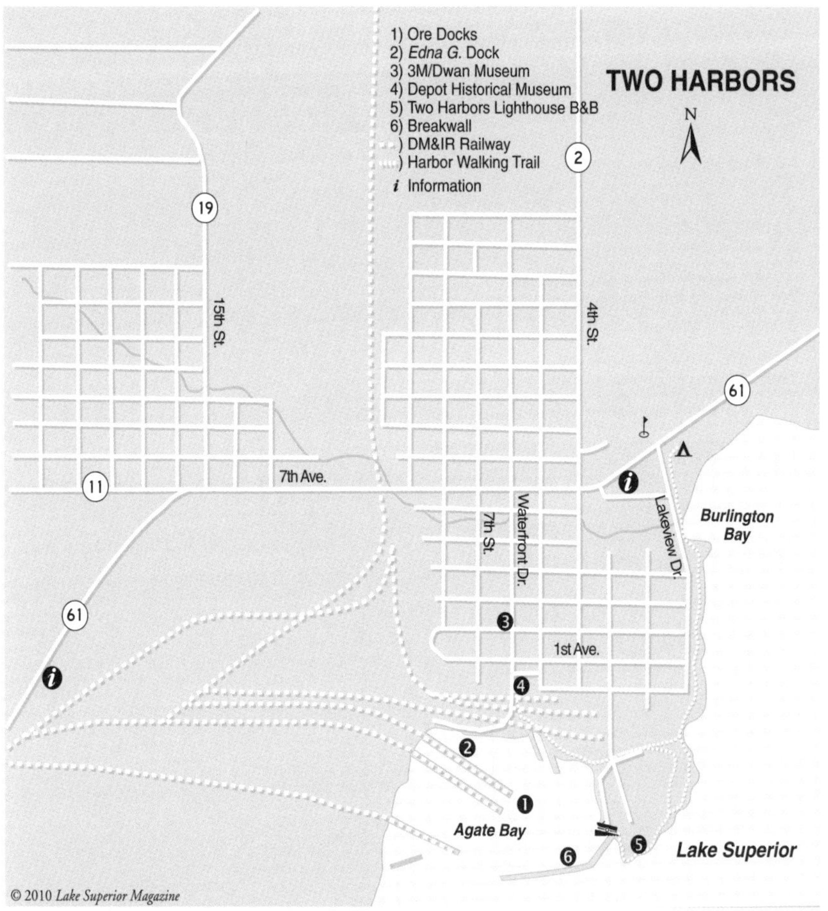

Two Harbors

The Two Harbors Lighthouse, built on Agate Bay in 1892, was acquired by the Lake County Historical Society from the U.S. Coast Guard in 1999 and is now operated as the delightful and popular Lighthouse Bed-and-Breakfast Inn. The nearby Fog Building has been converted into a museum, with a gift shop selling a nice assortment of items. The lighthouse was decommissioned by the Coast Guard in 1969, although it remains a navigational aid to commercial shipping and pleasure boaters. More than 200,000 people a year visit the attractive displays related to commercial shipping and fishing on the Great Lakes. The restored pilothouse from the *Frontenac* iron ore freighter is on the grounds and other exhibits are nearby. Also nearby, an authentic commercial fishing vessel, *Crusader*, built locally and christened by Norwegian Crown Prince Olaf, has been refurbished and is on display.

For parks, look for Thomas Owens Park, which has a bandshell downtown, and Lakeview Park at the eastern edge has a pavilion, washrooms, picnic tables and is traversed at lakeside by the Sonju Trail.

The historic Betty's Pies is about 2 miles northeast of town on Highway 61. Stop for pie or a meal. Open year-round.

Notable Events

• Summer Solstice at the Lighthouse is celebrated in mid-June.

• Heritage Days features a big parade and other activities in mid-July.

• Two Harbors Kayak Festival in early August includes kayak races, exhibitors, equipment demos, clinics, and a weekend of water-based activities.

• Annual Commemoration of *Edmund Fitzgerald* is held at Split Rock Lighthouse each November 10.

• Winter Solstice at the Two Harbors Lighthouse is celebrated in mid-December.

Where to Shop

On the southwest edge of Two Harbors on Highway 61, look for the 8-foot-tall rooster in front of Weldon's Gifts, which sells a range of souvenirs, T-shirts, jackets, sweatshirts, moccasins and jewelry.

In the 700 block, on Highway 61, the Superior Hiking Trail Association gift shop and headquarters are in the historic Anderson House (see separate listing for Superior Hiking Trail).

A stop at the nearby Agate City Rocks and Gifts, a marvelous rock shop and informal museum, will be time well spent. Sweet Peas in the 600 block has a charming selection of northwoods style

The *Edna G.* participated in many rescues during its more than one century of service.

gifts along with some whimsical figurines and cards and the Sawtooth Mountain Trading Post also has fun gifts.

Moosellaneous Gifts on Highway 61 sells an assortment of Northwoods-themed and whimsical pottery and china, stuffed animals, games, books, soaps and lotions.

The Oldest Sister is a gift shop with a little of everything and a lot of personality.

Silver Creek Gifts, just south of Silver Creek Cliff tunnel on Highway 61, sells a delightful mix of pottery, artwork, jewelry, books, bear and moose collectables, candles and T-shirts and sweatshirts among other items in its log cabin shop and gallery.

In Two Harbors' downtown, visitors also will find a jam-packed hardware store, the town's two banks, a cafe and an American Legion club that serves lunches and welcomes the public.

What's Next

The Circle Tour continues on Highway 61. To the east is Silver Creek Cliff and one of two tunnels carved from lakeside cliffs to realign Highway 61 for safer traffic. See description under the North Shore Tunnels listing. West from Two Harbors lies the Scenic North Shore Drive and Duluth.

INFO & OPTIONS

Two Harbors Area Chamber of Commerce
1313 Fairgrounds Rd.
Two Harbors, MN 55616
800-777-7384
www.twoharborschamber.com

R.J. Houle Information Center
1330 Hwy. 61
Two Harbors, MN 55616
800-777-7384

Gooseberry Falls State Park Information Center
3206 Hwy. 61 East
Two Harbors, MN 55616
218-834-3855

Split Rock Lighthouse Historical Site
3713 Split Rock Lighthouse Rd.
Two Harbors, MN 55616
218-226-6372
www.mnhs.org/places/sites/srl/index.htm

Superior Hiking Trail Association
P.O. Box 4
731 Seventh Ave.
Two Harbors, MN 55616
218-834-2700
www.shta.org

Betty's Pies
1633 Hwy. 61
Two Harbors, MN 55616
877-269-7494
www.bettyspies.com

Rustic Inn Café and Gift Shop
2773 Hwy. 61
Two Harbors, MN 55616
218-834-2488

Splashing Rock Restaurant
2826 Hwy. 61
Two Harbors, MN 55616
800-627-9565
www.grandsuperior.com

Vanilla Bean Cafe
812 Seventh Ave.
Two Harbors, MN 55616
218-834-3714
www.thevanillabean.com

AmericInn Lodge & Suites Two Harbors
1088 Hwy. 61 North
Two Harbors, MN 55616
800-634-3444
www.americinn.com

B&B Whistlestop
505 Eighth Ave.
Two Harbors, MN 55616
218-834-5571
www.bnbwhistlestop.com
www.dnr.state.mn.us

Castle Haven Cabins
3067 East Castle Danger Rd.
Two Harbors, MN 55616
218-834-4303
www.castlehaven.net

Country Inn
1204 Seventh Ave.
Two Harbors, MN 55616
218-834-5557
www.countryinntwoharbors.com

Gooseberry Trail Side Suites
3317 Hwy. 61 East
Two Harbors, MN 55616
800-715-1110
www.gooseberry.com

Grand Superior Lodge
2826 Hwy. 61
Two Harbors, MN 55616
800-627-9565
www.grandsuperior.com

Superior Shores Resort & Conference Center
1521 Superior Shores Dr.
Two Harbors, MN 55616
800-242-1988
www.superiorshores.com

Penmarallter Campsite
725 Scenic Dr.
Two Harbors, MN 55616
218-834-4603
www.penmaralltercampsite.com

Split Rock Lighthouse State Park
3755 Split Rock Lighthouse Rd.
Two Harbors, MN 55616
218-226-6377
www.dnr.state.mn.us

Two Harbors Burlington Bay Campground
626 Park Rd.
Two Harbors, MN 55616
218-834-2021

Virginia

Population 8,509

Virginia is a crossroads city where Highway 53 from Duluth meets Highway 169 from Hibbing on the west and Ely to the north.

Virginia has long served as a center point of the East Range. Called the Queen City of the Iron Range, it was named after the immense amount of virgin timber that surrounded the city in the late 1800s, but was already firmly established as a mining town by the time lumber barons began harvesting that timber.

What to See and Do

Mineview in the Sky features displays of giant mining equipment and a spectacular viewpoint over the abandoned Rouchleau Mine, and is also an excellent source of area information during the summer.

North of Virginia, the Laurentian Divide cuts across the territory and sends water flowing to three ultimate destinations: Lake Superior, the Mississippi River or northward toward Hudson Bay.

To do some shopping and browsing, Woodwards Books & Yarn in the Thunderbird Mall hits the mark with a selection of yarn and books.

Notable Museums

A Heritage Museum gives a nice peek into the city and region's past.

The world's largest floating loon (20 feet), on Silver Lake in Virginia, migrates indoors for winter.

Parks and Public Areas

Olcott Park is always populated by many species of wild birds. The Land of the Loon Ethnic Arts and Crafts Festival is held at Olcott Park in June.

What's Next

Leaving Virginia northward, stay on Highway 169 to visit the town of Ely (see separate listing), perhaps the best known and busiest entry point for the Boundary Waters Canoe Area Wilderness (BWCAW), which *National Geographic* magazine named one of 50 places in the world that everyone should visit in their lifetime. To return to the Circle Tour route on the north shore take Highway 1 out of Ely to Illgen City east of Silver Bay. Sights and points of interest can be found under the Finland, Ely and BWCAW listings.

For an interesting side trip, at the junction of highways 53 and 169 (which continues on to Tower-Soudan, Lake Vermilion and Ely), take Highway 53 north to visit Cook, Orr and Voyageurs National Park on the U.S.-Canadian border to the east of International Falls. Orr is home to the Vince Shute Wildlife Sanctuary, where people can see and learn about black bears in their natural habitat. It is also home to a uniquely styled AmericInn lodging, which features a waterslide in the pool area.

INFO & OPTIONS

Iron Range Tourism Bureau

403 North First St.
Virginia, MN 55792
800-777-8497
www.ironrange.org

Laurentian Chamber of Commerce

403 North First St.
Virginia, MN 55792
218-741-2717
www.laurentianchamber.org

Lake Superior **Ontario**

At Kama Bay, east of Nipigon, you are seeing the northernmost waters of Lake Superior from a spectacular wayside overlook.

Ontario is the less developed part of our Lake Superior region (compared with the states). Visitors will find astonishing beauty in the many wilderness provincial parks, or simply by driving the Trans Canada Highway. From the culture of Thunder Bay and Sault Ste. Marie, to the charm of small towns and villages in between, there is much to see and experience for newcomers and those making return trips.

Ontario Tourism Information
800-668-2746
www.ontariotravel.net

Ontario Parks
1-888-668-7275
www.ontarioparks.com

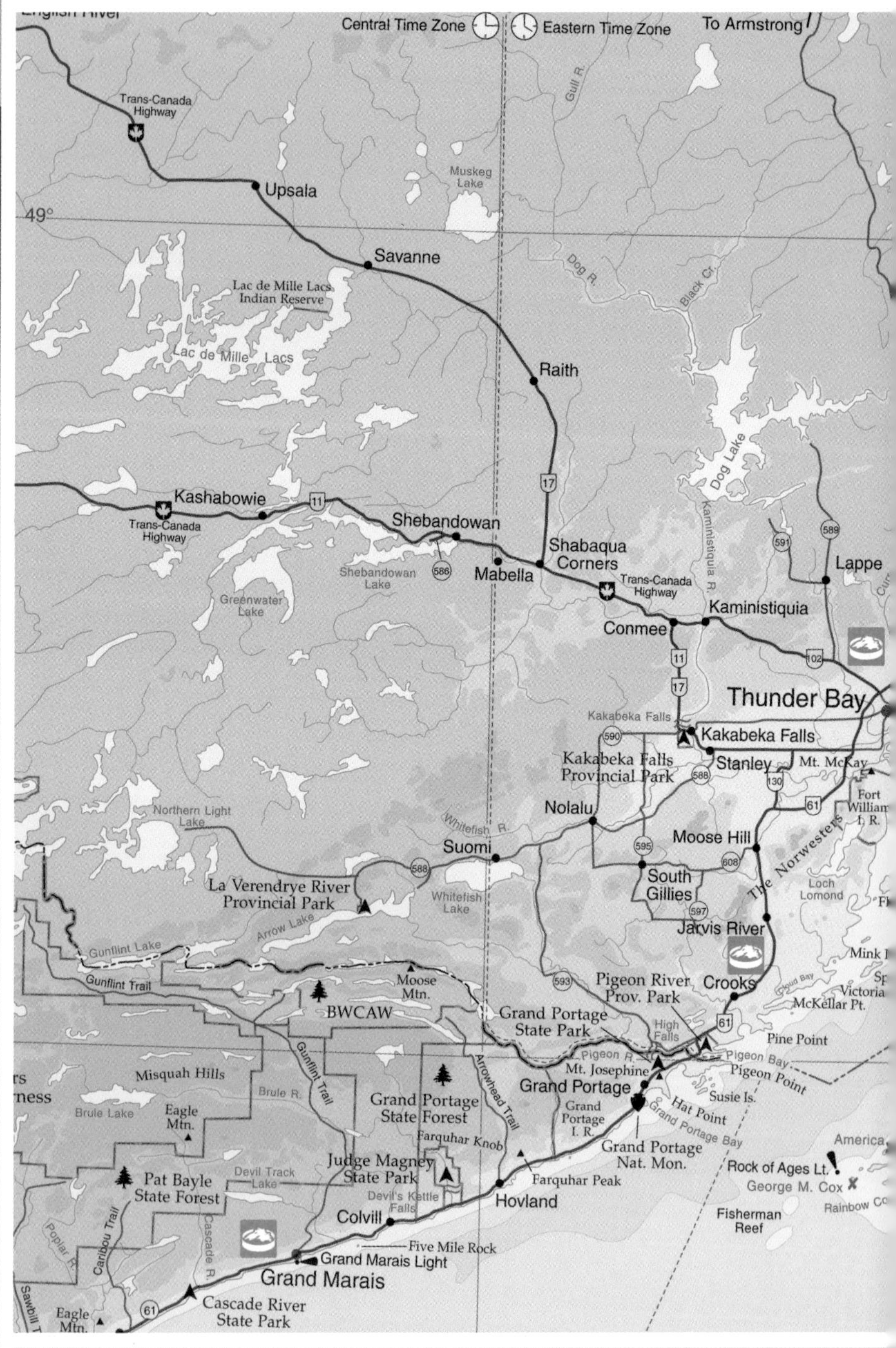

Ontario Western & Northern Lakeshore

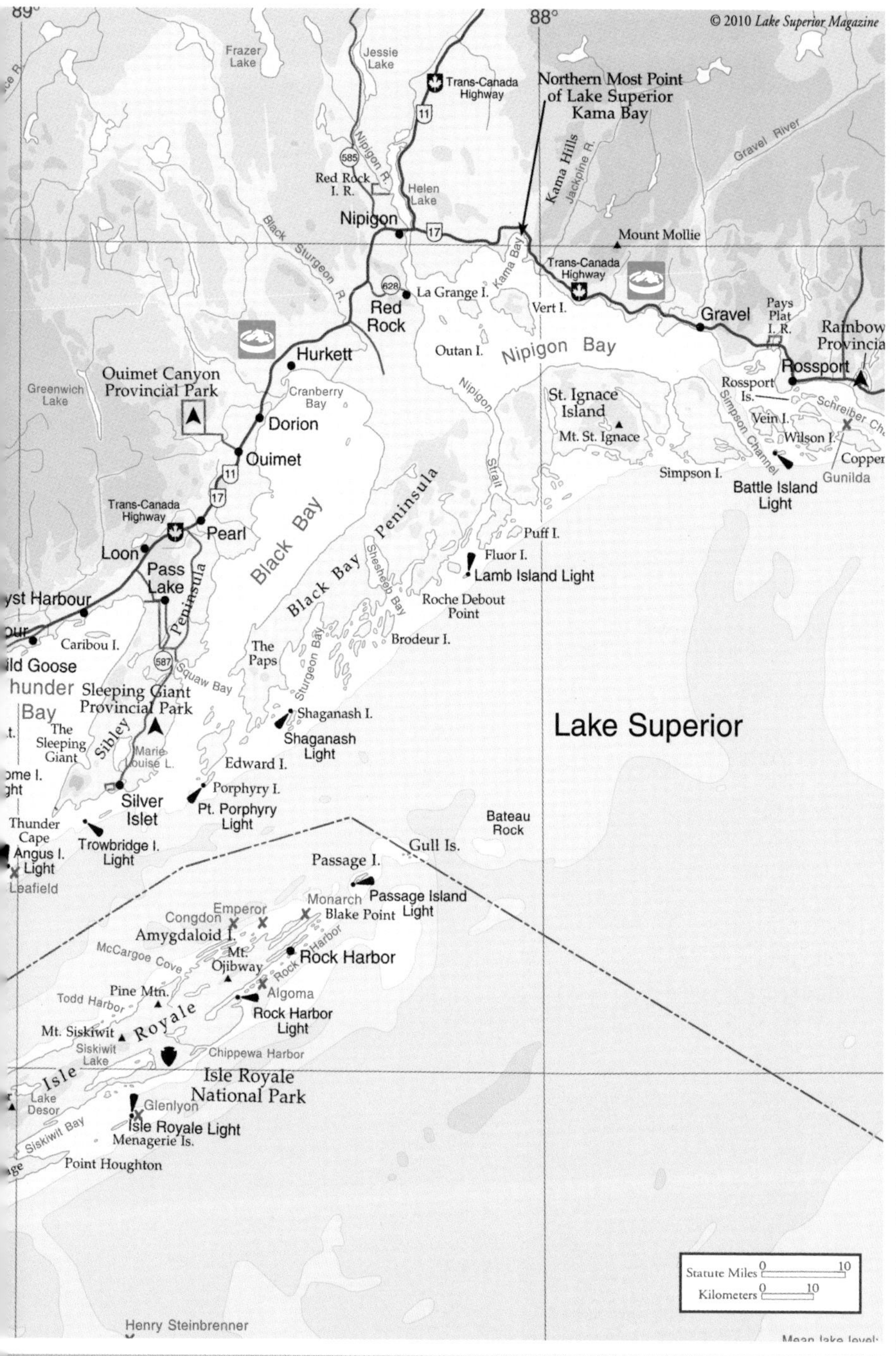
© 2010 Lake Superior Magazine
88°
Frazer Lake
Jessie Lake
Trans-Canada Highway
Northern Most Point of Lake Superior Kama Bay
Kama Hills
Jackpine R.
Gravel River
Nipigon R.
Red Rock I. R.
Helen Lake
Nipigon
Black Sturgeon R.
Mount Mollie
Kama Bay
Trans-Canada Highway
La Grange I.
Red Rock
Vert I.
Gravel
Pays Plat I. R.
Rainbow Provincia
Hurkett
Outan I.
Nipigon Bay
Rossport
Ouimet Canyon Provincial Park
Greenwich Lake
Cranberry Bay
Nipigon Strait
St. Ignace Island
Mt. St. Ignace
Rossport Is.
Vein I.
Wilson I.
Simpson Channel
Schreiber Ch
Copper
Gunilda
Dorion
Ouimet
Simpson I.
Battle Island Light
Black Bay
Black Bay Peninsula
Trans-Canada Highway
Pearl
Loon
Pass Lake
Peninsula
Puff I.
Fluor I.
Lamb Island Light
Sheshegb Bay
Roche Debout Point
Caribou I.
Brodeur I.
The Paps
Sturgeon Bay
Squaw Bay
Thunder Bay
Sleeping Giant Provincial Park
The Sleeping Giant
Sibley
Marie Louise L.
Shaganash I.
Shaganash Light
Lake Superior
Edward I.
Porphyry I.
Silver Islet
Pt. Porphyry Light
Thunder Cape
Trowbridge I. Light
Angus I. Light
Leafield
Bateau Rock
Gull Is.
Passage I.
Passage Island Light
Monarch
Blake Point
Emperor
Congdon
Amygdaloid I.
McCargoe Cove
Mt. Ojibway
Rock Harbor
Rock Harbor
Algoma
Pine Mtn.
Todd Harbor
Rock Harbor Light
Mt. Siskiwit
Isle Royale
Siskiwit Lake
Chippewa Harbor
Isle Royale National Park
Lake Desor
Glenlyon
Siskiwit Bay
Isle Royale Light
Menagerie Is.
Point Houghton
Statute Miles 0 10
Kilometers 0 10
Henry Steinbrenner

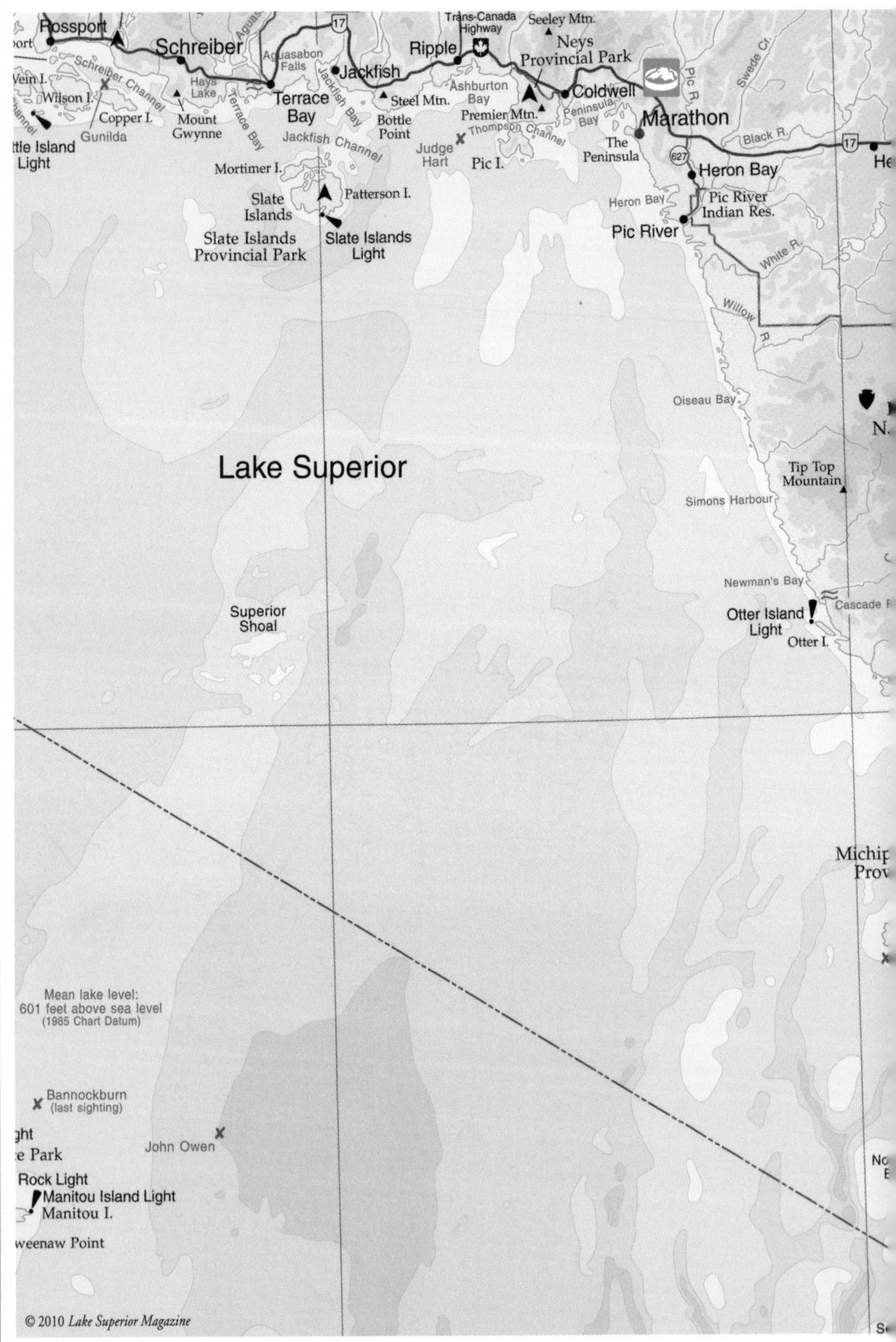

Ontario Northeastern Lakeshore

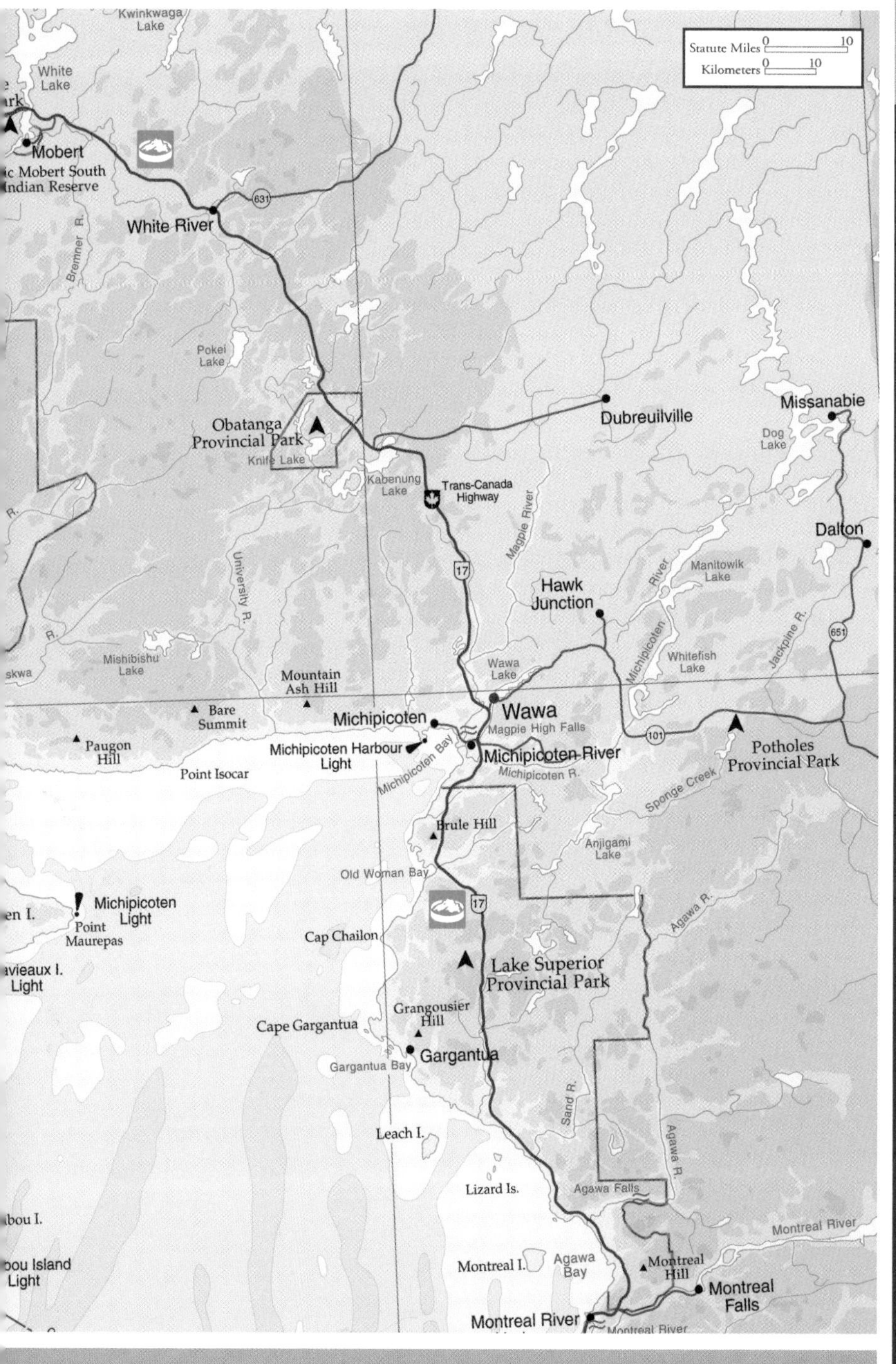
Statute Miles 0 10
Kilometers 0 10
Kwinkwaga Lake
White Lake
Mobert
Mobert South Indian Reserve
White River
Bremner R.
Pokei Lake
Obatanga Provincial Park
Knife Lake
Kabenung Lake
Trans-Canada Highway
Dubreuilville
Missanabie
Dog Lake
Dalton
Magpie River
Manitowik Lake
University R.
Hawk Junction
Michipicoten River
Whitefish Lake
Jackpine R.
Mishibishu Lake
Mountain Ash Hill
Wawa Lake
Bare Summit
Michipicoten
Wawa
Magpie High Falls
Paugon Hill
Michipicoten Harbour Light
Michipicoten River
Potholes Provincial Park
Point Isocar
Michipicoten Bay
Michipicoten R.
Sponge Creek
Brule Hill
Anjigami Lake
Old Woman Bay
Michipicoten Light
Point Maurepas
Agawa R.
Cap Chailon
Lake Superior Provincial Park
Grangousier Hill
Cape Gargantua
Gargantua
Gargantua Bay
Sand R.
Leach I.
Agawa R.
Lizard Is.
Agawa Falls
Montreal River
Montreal I.
Agawa Bay
Montreal Hill
Montreal Falls
Montreal River

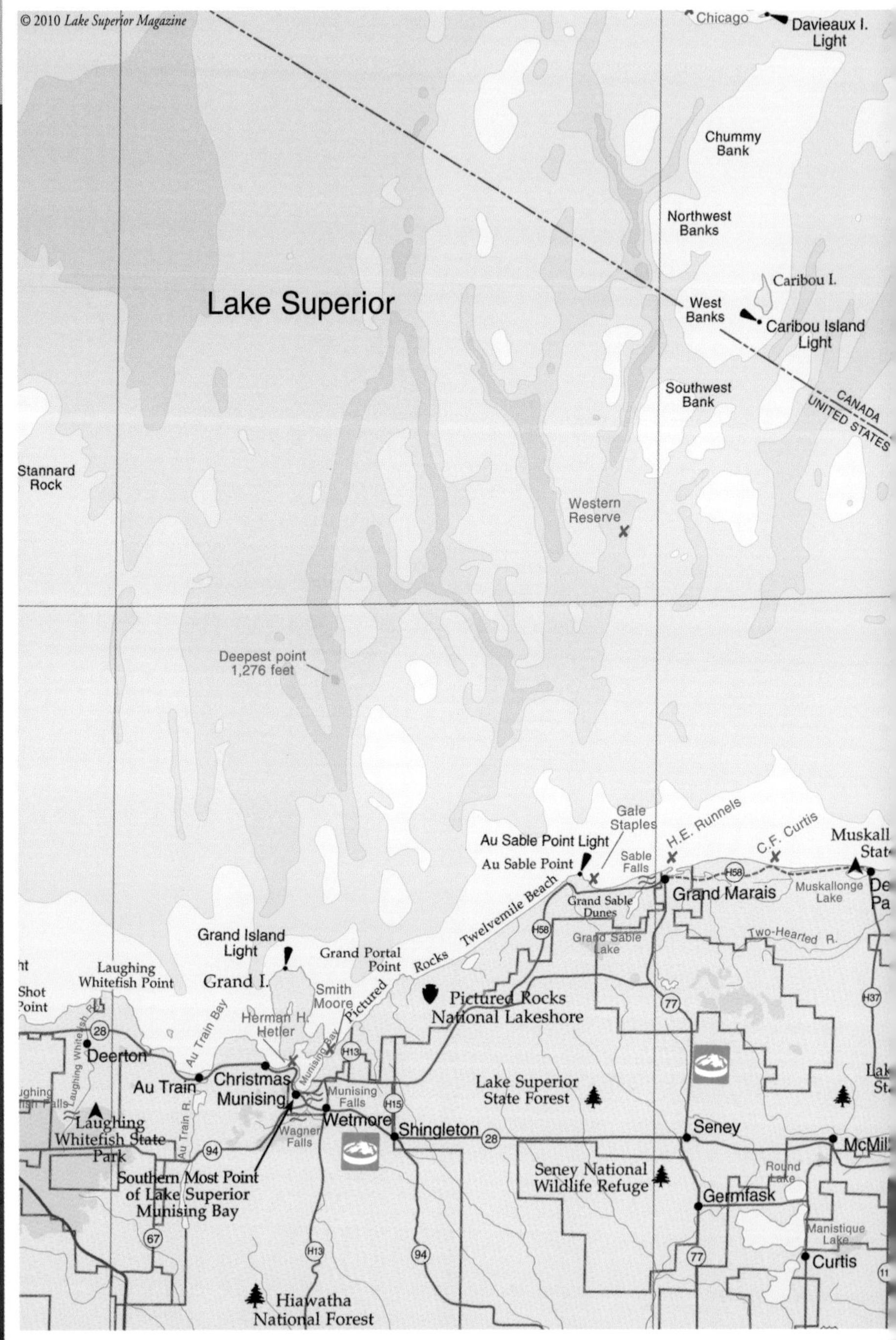
© 2010 Lake Superior Magazine
Chicago
Davieaux I. Light
Chummy Bank
Northwest Banks
Caribou I.
West Banks
Caribou Island Light
Southwest Bank
CANADA
UNITED STATES
Lake Superior
Stannard Rock
Western Reserve
Deepest point 1,276 feet
Gale Staples
H.E. Runnels
C.F. Curtis
Au Sable Point Light
Au Sable Point
Sable Falls
Grand Marais
Muskallonge Lake
Grand Sable Dunes
Grand Sable Lake
Twelvemile Beach
Two-Hearted R.
Grand Island Light
Grand Portal Point
Rocks
Laughing Whitefish Point
Grand I.
Shot Point
Smith Moore
Pictured
Pictured Rocks National Lakeshore
Herman H. Hetler
Au Train Bay
Munising Bay
Deerton
Au Train
Christmas
Munising
Munising Falls
Wetmore
Shingleton
Lake Superior State Forest
Seney
Laughing Whitefish State Park
Wagner Falls
Au Train R.
Southern Most Point of Lake Superior Munising Bay
Seney National Wildlife Refuge
Round Lake
Germfask
Manistique Lake
Curtis
Hiawatha National Forest

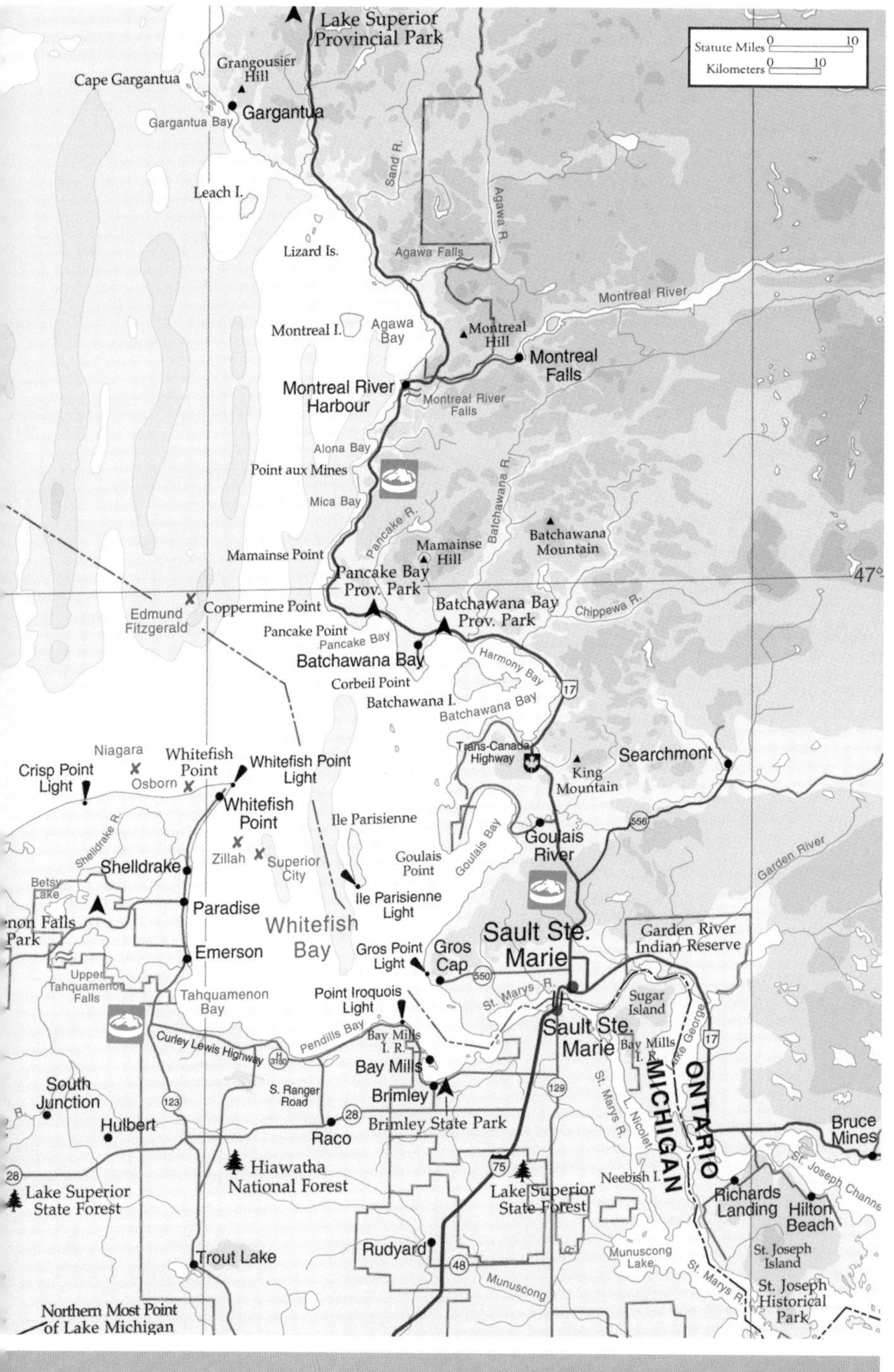
Lake Superior Provincial Park
Statute Miles 0 10
Kilometers 0 10
Cape Gargantua
Grangousier Hill
Gargantua
Gargantua Bay
Leach I.
Lizard Is.
Sand R.
Agawa R.
Agawa Falls
Montreal River
Montreal I.
Agawa Bay
Montreal Hill
Montreal Falls
Montreal River Harbour
Montreal River Falls
Alona Bay
Point aux Mines
Mica Bay
Pancake R.
Batchawana R.
Batchawana Mountain
Mamainse Point
Mamainse Hill
Pancake Bay Prov. Park
47°
Edmund Fitzgerald
Coppermine Point
Batchawana Bay Prov. Park
Chippewa R.
Pancake Point
Pancake Bay
Batchawana Bay
Harmony Bay
Corbeil Point
Batchawana I.
Batchawana Bay
17
Niagara
Whitefish Point
Whitefish Point Light
Trans-Canada Highway
Searchmont
Crisp Point Light
Osborn
King Mountain
Whitefish Point
Ile Parisienne
556
Shelldrake R.
Zillah
Superior City
Goulais Point
Goulais Bay
Goulais River
Garden River
Shelldrake
Betsy Lake
Ile Parisienne Light
Paradise
Whitefish Bay
Sault Ste. Marie
Garden River Indian Reserve
Emerson
Gros Point Light
Gros Cap
550
Upper Tahquamenon Falls
Tahquamenon Bay
Point Iroquois Light
St. Marys R.
Sugar Island
Curley Lewis Highway
Pendills Bay
Bay Mills I. R.
Sault Ste. Marie
Bay Mills I. R.
Lake George
17
Bay Mills
MICHIGAN
ONTARIO
South Junction
S. Ranger Road
Brimley
129
St. Marys R.
L. Nicolet
123
28
Hulbert
Raco
Brimley State Park
Bruce Mines
St. Joseph Channel
28
Hiawatha National Forest
75
Neebish I.
Lake Superior State Forest
Lake Superior State Forest
Richards Landing
Hilton Beach
Rudyard
Munuscong Lake
St. Joseph Island
Trout Lake
48
Munuscong
St. Marys R.
St. Joseph Historical Park
Northern Most Point of Lake Michigan

Batchawana Bay

Population 100

The village of Batchawana Bay is just off Trans Canada Highway 17 on the eastern Lake Superior shore and starts where Highway 563 meets the Carp River. At the end of H-563 is the Ontario Government Dock, which serves as a safe port for commercial and pleasure craft. The bay stretches to Batchawana Island, with a backdrop of Batchawana Mountain, which at 665 meters (2,181 feet) is the undisputed highest peak on the Ontario shores of Lake Superior.

What to See and Do

Batchawana Bay is a large inland bay 56 kilometers (35 miles) of shoreline in circumference, featuring the warmest swimming waters on Lake Superior at Batchawana Bay Provincial Park. It offers exceptional sailing, boating, windsurfing, exploring and sightseeing. Lodging, a post office and the picturesque St. Isaac Catholic Church are located in the village.

Visitors can rent canoes, participate in outdoor adventures or winter recreation at Voyageurs' Lodge and Cookhouse. Groups can relive the voyageur experience in a 26-foot Montreal canoe.

South on Highway 17, watch for Chippewa River Falls. This spectacular Circle Tour landmark is the halfway point of the Trans Canada Highway and features a foot trail to great camera shots, a cut stone monument, clean outhouses and plenty of parking.

Parks and Public Areas

The day-use Batchawana Bay

Agawa Indian Crafts and the Canadian Carver, at Pancake Bay, northwest of Batchawana Bay, has unique woodcarvings and other gifts, souvenirs and native collectibles.

Provincial Park has 5 kilometers (3 miles) of sandy beaches for swimming, picnicking and walking. A modern Tourist Information Centre houses the Batchawana Bay Tourist Association. Open early June to early September.

What's Next

Your Circle Tour route leaving Batchawana Bay either to the north or south follows Highway 17, with the northward route heading for Montreal River Harbour and Wawa. The southern route passes Heyden and Searchmont on the way to Sault Ste. Marie.

INFO & OPTIONS

Ontario Road Information
800-268-4686
www.mto.gov.on.ca

Lake Shore Salzburger Hof Resort
P.O. Box 118
Batchawana Bay, ON P0S 1A0
705-882-2323
www.salzburgerhofresort.com

Voyageurs' Lodge & Cookhouse
P.O. Box 129
Hwy. 17 North
Batchawana Bay, ON P0S 1A0
705-882-2504
www.voyageurslodge.com

Batchawana Bay Provincial Park
Box 61
Batchawana Bay, ON P0S 1A0
705-882-2209
www.ontarioparks.com/english/batc.htm

Pancake Bay Provincial Park
Box 61
Batchawana Bay, ON P0S 1A0
705-882-2209
www.ontarioparks.com/english/panc.html

Goulais River

The village of Goulais River is situated on Lake Superior's eastern shore about 25 kilometers (15 miles) north of Sault Ste. Marie or 40 kilometers (25 miles) south of Batchawana Bay, just off Trans Canada Highway 17.

What to See and Do

Shop at one of the area antique, flea markets or gift stores. There are also several Canadian craft stores.

In 1862, Bishop Frederic Baraga, the "Snowshoe Priest," built a church here that's still in use.

Buttermilk Mountain Resort, off Highway 552, has a 90-meter (295-foot) vertical drop and a double chairlift. A number of chalet rental units are available. Try the Austrian and German specialties at their Schnitzel Haus Dining Lounge, which is listed in"Where to Eat in Canada."

Cross-country skiers and snowshoers should check Stokely Creek Lodge for day skiing or a longer stay with all the comforts of a first-class resort. Its many miles of groomed trails are friendly to skiers of various skill levels and the center sponsors several special ski events during the winter. Hikers also will enjoy Stokely Creek, which has more than 8,000 acres of wilderness.

What's Next

Traveling south, the Goulais River Valley is the entry point into the Sault Ste. Marie area. Here, the granite hills of the Canadian Shield rise from the lowlands. It's a zone of lakes, waterfalls and streams, many stocked with trout. Due to the swamps, marshes, fens and bogs, a wide variety of waterfowl and shorebirds, as well as moose and beaver, inhabit the area. On the high ground stand maple forests, while white birch and pine dominate the remaining landscape.

The Lake Superior Circle Tour cuts through the heart of the valley via Highway 17, crossing the Goulais River about 24 kilometers (15 miles) north of Sault Ste. Marie. The Queen lady's slipper, an orchid with a large three-inch blossom, grows wild in the nearby swamp. It is found only in the Lake Superior region in midsummer.

North on Trans Canada Highway 17 and at the extreme southern end of Batchawana Bay is Havilland Bay and the small Gitchee Gumee Marina, which serves as one of the few refueling stops for boats between Michipicoten Harbour and Sault Ste. Marie. The trip through the bay is somewhat shallow, but good services are provided and there's a boat ramp. For a lake cruise or charter fishing, try Swan Charters at the marina.

INFO & OPTIONS

Blueberry Hill Motel & Campground
Hwy. 17 North, R.R. 2
Goulais River, ON P0S 1E0
705-649-5631
www.onblueberryhill.com

Old Mill Bay Campground
Hwy. 17 North
Goulais River, ON P0S 1E0
705-649-2318

Gros Cap & Prince Township

Combined Population 1,325

Translated as "Big Cape" from the French, Gros Cap is where Lake Superior is said to end or begin, depending on your orientation, and is where the St. Marys River begins. Along the 26-kilometer-long (16-mile) Highway 550 to the village of Gros Cap, take Marshall Drive to find several lookouts rising as much as 200 meters (656 feet) above the lake. All ships entering and leaving the locks at Sault Ste. Marie must pass this huge rock ridge, the base of the Canadian Shield rising to the north. Down at the hamlet of Gros Cap (population 350), rock hounds will want to search the bayfront for agates.

On the way to and from Gros Cap, Prince Township (population 973) offers a community center and a museum in the form of Prince United Church, built in 1885. The yard outside the church holds well-preserved farming artifacts. The township fathers and mothers have reconstructed a pioneer home on the premises. It's worth a brief stop even if you can't get into the buildings.

These two worthwhile stops off Trans Canada Highway 17 north of Sault Ste. Marie, Ontario, and westward on Highway 550 about 20 minutes take you to the point that the earliest voyageurs recognized as the beginning of Lake Superior's uncertainties, after their relatively peaceful passage through the St. Marys River. It's a sight that visitors have long relished.

The Sault Ste. Marie Airport is located off Highway 550, turning at Prince Township. Located at the airport is the Provincial Fire Centre, one of the largest centers of forest fire information and research in the world.

Heyden & Searchmont

Combined Population 600

In the winter, ski hills around the communities of Heyden and Searchmont, northeast of Sault Ste. Marie, come to life as excellent winter havens. The Heyden Adventure Base Camp sports a 65-meter (213-foot) vertical drop with five runs and 5 kilometers of cross-country trail. Its private hill rental is popular. Searchmont Resort on Highway 556 has a drop of 230 meters (755 feet), making it the largest of the region's ski hills. The town has a tourist association, several bed-and-breakfast inns, a groomed snowmobile trail to Wawa and a dog sled business that gives rides. Mountain Ash Inn offers a nice lodging choice in the area.

Buttermilk Mountain Resort is just north of Heyden at Goulais River off Highway 552, with an 85-meter (279-foot) vertical drop and a double chairlift. A number of chalet rental units are available. Try the Austrian and German specialties at their Schnitzel Haus Dining Lounge, which is listed in "Where to Eat in Canada."

At this point, you have reached the easternmost part of Lake Superior, where its waters empty into the downstream currents of the St. Marys River rapids and flow south to Lake Huron and the rest of the Great Lakes.

Kakabeka Falls

Township Population 600

Kakabeka Falls Provincial Park, 32 kilometers (20 miles) west of Thunder Bay on Highway 11/17, contains one of the more spectacular waterfalls on the Circle Tour route, attracting vast numbers of falls fanciers each year. Though small, the town of Kakabeka Falls has lodging, dining and businesses able to meet most needs.

Remember your camera when visiting Kakabeka Falls, about a half-hour drive west of Thunder Bay. This is one of the truly spectacular falls in the Lake Superior region.

Amethyst lovers in the area will want to check the Kakabeka Falls Gift and Amethyst Shoppe, which features "blueberry amethyst" from a vein of the mineral bearing the deep purple coloring of the fruit. Try tubing on the Kaministiquia River at Stanley between Kakabeka Falls and Thunder Bay. River Rat Rentals will provide the tubes for a three-hour relaxing trip down the river.

At 39 meters (128 feet), Kakabeka Falls is called the "Niagara of the North." Within Kakabeka Falls Provincial Park, numerous viewing platforms surround the falls. The site is friendly to the physically challenged. Some of the world's oldest fossils, known as stromatolites, are found in the 2-billion-year-old rocks within the park. The site offers some barrier-free facilities with a number of viewing platforms around the falls. Interpretive programs are offered at the park's visitor center in summer. Camping is available mid-May to mid-October. Winter activities include 15 kilometers (9 miles) of groomed cross-country ski trails.

INFO & OPTIONS

Kakabeka Falls Provincial Park
P.O. Box 252
Kakabeka Falls, ON P0T 1W0
807-473-9231
www.ontarioparks.com/english/kaka.html

Lake Nipigon

From the city of Nipigon on Lake Helen, Trans Canada Highway 11 heads

Lake Superior Provincial Park south of Wawa is full of wild country and lovely shoreline views. At Katherine Cove, seen here, there's a picnic area and easy hiking around the cove.

northeastward toward Lake Nipigon, which at 100-by-70 kilometers (62-by-43 miles) is the largest inland lake entirely within Ontario. This northeast route is called the Frontier Trail.

The trip opens the north to thousands of anglers, hunters and other outdoor enthusiasts who seek vast wild areas in wonderful scenery to pursue their adventures. This area is also the watershed that provides the greatest source of flow into the big lake via the Longlac Water Diversion and the Nipigon River. For beachcombers, many of the Lake Nipigon beaches consist of black sand that has been eroded from Lake Nipigon's basaltic cliffs and gathered by wave action on the shorelines. Some contain good rockhounding possibilities.

The southeast corner of Lake Nipigon at Orient Bay has many waterfalls that freeze in the winter and attract hardy visitors interested in climbing the icy precipices. It's a sport practiced in few other areas of the world and involves using mountaineering equipment to scale the icy surfaces.

Lake Superior Provincial Park

South of Wawa, Ontario, Trans Canada Highway 17 passes through Lake Superior Provincial Park, getting travelers to a number of points of adventure and interest. Established on the same day in 1944 that Sibley Provincial Park (now Sleeping Giant Provincial Park near Thunder Bay) was set aside, the park preserves 1,608 square kilometers (620 square miles) of wild country and a large section of the eastern Lake Superior shoreline.

The sights and activities in this park are worth a full day or more. The park's flora and fauna are mixes of southern and northern species. Moose with big racks are common. Other animals such as wolves, bears and woodland caribou have been reintroduced. There is a good variety of birds, too.

What to See and Do

This extensive park offers 11 hiking trails, walking trails to waterfalls and scenic lookouts and eight canoe routes ranging from several hours to several days in length, which access secluded places made even more beautiful by the extra effort required to reach them. The most rugged hiking trail is the Lake Superior Coastal Trail that follows 65 kilometers (34 miles) of shoreline and takes almost a week to hike. Rated: difficult.

The park offers interpretive programs in July and August and camping, fishing, hunting, boating and picnicking on the shore of Lake Superior. Canoe rentals are available at all campgrounds during peak summer months. There also are canoe rentals at Montreal River Harbour, and canoe and kayak rentals in Wawa.

Passing through the park, be sure to stop and put your feet in Lake Superior at the various bays along the way. Old Woman Bay on the north end of the park offers excellent photo opportunities at an interesting picnic area. Nokomis Hiking Trail is adjacent. There are 244 campsites at three campgrounds and 200 backcountry campsites along trails and canoe routes. Rabbit Blanket Lake Campground at the park's north end has flush toilets, showers, laundry; open early May to late October.

Once Highway 17 returns to the shore of Lake Superior, a stop at Katherine Cove is an absolute must. Some of the most unusual rock striations extend from the land into the clear waters of the lake, a guaranteed breathtaker for any photo album. The clean sand beach will captivate you. There's a picnic area and easy hiking around the cove. Small wildlife abound.

If you're a camera enthusiast or just like a nice hike, Pinquisibi Trail passes several waterfalls on the Sand River.

The pictographs at Agawa Rock are the park's high point, but due to the natural formation they are not handicapped accessible or, for many visitors, easily accessible. You descend to the water's edge via a rugged 400-meter (one-quarter-mile) trail, spectacular in its own right. On a cliff face directly on Lake Superior's shore, the extensive native paintings include canoes, caribou, horse and rider, and *Mishipeshu*, the Great Lynx spirit of the lake. These pictographs can be viewed when the lake is calm. *Extreme* caution (we can't stress it enough) is necessary when visiting the site. The rocks and ledge are slippery and waves are unpredictable and dangerous. Native people may have painted at this site for as long as 2,000 years, yet the paintings that remain visible today are likely only 150 to 400 years old. Allow plenty of time for the return hike.

There's a beautiful visitor center at the entrance to Agawa Bay Campground about midway between Wawa and Sault Ste. Marie. A must stop for families, it offers themed multimedia exhibits featuring "The Power of the Lake" and a wealth of information on all aspects of the park. The audio-visual displays include models that capture the logging era, local shipwrecks and disasters, bushplane history, commercial fishing, works of the Group of Seven artists, stories of early settlers, fur traders and voyageurs of North West Company and its rival, Hudson's Bay Company, sculptures, art of pictographs and a special version of the Lake Superior map that was developed by *Lake Superior Magazine*. Lake Effects Gift Shop, managed and staffed by Niijkiwenhwag – Friends of Lake Superior Park, is in the visitor center and offers clothing, books, local artwork and music, postcards, park publications and other souvenirs. Open May to mid-October.

Agawa Bay Campground, the largest of three campgrounds, has showers, flush toilets, laundry and is open from early May to early October. On the south end, Crescent Lake Campground, with few amenities, is open late June to early September.

Those seeking guided adventure can contact Naturally Superior Adventures south of Wawa for sea kayak and canoe trips, instruction and family and group activities (see Wawa listings, page 236).

INFO & OPTIONS

Lake Superior Provincial Park
P.O. Box 267
Wawa, ON POS IKO
705-856-2284
Agawa Bay Visitor Centre
705-882-2026
www.lakesuperiorpark.ca

Marathon & Hemlo

Population 4,000

Marathon is a dual-industry town on the lakeshore at the end of Peninsula Road (Highway 626), 5 kilometers (3 miles) from Trans Canada Highway 17 and the Marathon Airport. An Information Centre and Scenic Lookout are on Highway 17 another 2 kilometers (1 mile) beyond the intersection to

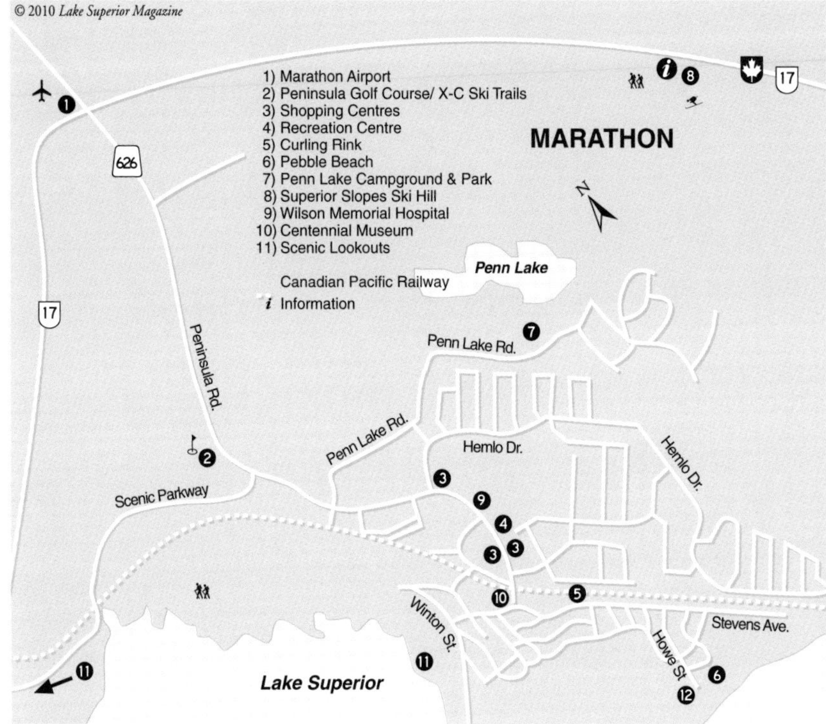

Marathon

Marathon. The facility is used in the winter as the Superior Slopes Ski Hill, operated by the township. Wintertime attracts snowmobile enthusiasts by the thousands, since the hills around Marathon are ideal for the sport.

A Bit of History

Rail building and lumbering fueled a city of 12,000 people in the last decades of the 1800s, when it was called Peninsula. The town was renamed for the Marathon Paper Mill, constructed in 1944, and more recently was Marathon Pulp Inc. Tales of gold have always circulated in the region. Prospecting started as early as 1869, but the first huge ore body was discovered in 1981. Rich veins of gold are mined in the Hemlo area. Two active mines are 2 kilometers (1 mile) beyond the intersection of highways 17 and 614. These are some of the largest gold mines in the country. Williams Mine and David Bell Mine make Marathon their headquarters.

As a result of new investment in gold, Marathon has seen the addition of houses, apartments, businesses, recreation facilities and several shopping malls like Marathon Centre Mall along Peninsula Road.

Golfers will want to try the scenic 9-hole Peninsula Golf Course, designed by Stanley Thompson, C.G.A.

In Ontario, an inukshuk, or "little man," can often be seen by the roadway guiding travelers.

Notable Events

• A Figure Skating Show in early April showcases the skills of area skating students.

• The Chamber of Commerce Trade Show in late-April/early May lets merchants display the latest goods and merchandise.

• A Fishing Festival in June celebrates the excellent angling in the area.

• Marathon Music Festival in early June is a chance to catch up on musical entertainment.

• The Children's Festival in July gives kids a chance to have a great time.

• Nostalgia Days at Neys Provincial Park celebrates the heritage and history of the area in August.

• The Pic Mobert and Pic Heron Bay Powwow in August is a celebration of First Nations people and culture.

What's Next

Traveling southward from Marathon, Highway 17 bends inland away from Lake Superior for a considerable distance, providing views of new and exciting scenery, wildlife and possible new adventures. The wild land and lakeshore that the highway skirts is occupied by Pukaskwa National Park. Westward from Marathon, the highway heads for Terrace Bay, Schreiber, Rossport and Nipigon.

INFO & OPTIONS

Marathon Community Services Department (Town of Marathon)
4 Hemlo Dr.
Marathon, ON P0T 2E0
807-229-1340
www.marathon.ca

Marathon Harbour Inn
67 Peninsula Rd.
Marathon, ON P0T 2E3
888-729-3404

Travelodge
Hwy. 17 and Peninsula Rd.
P.O. Box 700
Marathon, ON P0T 2E0
888-235-5555
www.travelodgemarathon.com

Neys Lunch and Campground
P.O. Box 1467
Marathon, ON P0T 2E0
800-939-0997
www.neyslunch.com

Penn Lake Park and Campground
4 Hemlo Dr.
Marathon, ON P0T 2E0
807-229-1340
www.marathon.ca

Michipicoten Island Provincial Park

The Ojibway name of Michipicoten refers to high bluffs. Michipicoten Island Provincial Park, 60 kilometers (37 miles) out in Lake Superior from Wawa, is one of the most mysterious and remote of Ontario's provincial parks. Michipicoten Island is the third largest island in the lake, sparking myths of mirages for generations because, viewed from the mainland, it seems to float above the water and is often obscured by fog, which is frequent in this area of the lake. On the island's south shore, Quebec Harbour is the site of a row of fishing huts and summer cottages. Accessible only by float plane or large boats, Michipicoten Island has no park facilities or campgrounds, but visits are permitted. Inquire at Lake Superior Provincial Park.

Montreal River Harbour

Population 21

As the southern gateway to Lake Superior Provincial Park, the tiny townsite of Montreal River Harbour is about midway between Wawa and Sault Ste. Marie on Trans Canada Highway 17. Here is a breathtaking gorge. If you park on one of the side roads on either end of the highway bridge over the Montreal River, you can walk back to the bridge to look down into the gorge. This is an unprotected view, so watch out for traffic.

The road to the north across from Twilight Resort will take you closer to the river. The view at the mouth of the river is spectacular. In various seasons, large runs of salmon, trout and smelt spawn at the mouth. Rock collectors will be more than sorely tempted by the treasure trove of washed pebbles. In mid-summer, look for blueberries and raspberries. Montreal River Harbour is also home to Mad Moose Lodge, a premier destination for hikers, rock and ice climbers, boaters, nature lovers and other outdoor adventure types.

South from Montreal River, watch for the scenic pullout at Alona Bay, location of important exploration for copper and silver since the late 1700s. This site offers a unique sunset experience. In the late 1940s, pitchblende, an indication of the presence of uranium, was rediscovered at Theano Point and an abandoned uranium mine is nearby.

Farther south on Highway 17, Pancake Bay Provincial Park and Pancake Bay take their names from the voyageurs, who would stop their canoes here on their way east to Montreal. Only one day from Sault Ste. Marie and fresh provisions, they would make pancakes with their remaining flour. The modern Pancake Bay offers a 3.2-kilometer (2-mile) stretch of sand beach, swimming, hiking and camping. *Edmund Fitzgerald* Lookout Trail offers spectacular views of Pancake Bay and Batchawana Bay. It provides a view out toward the location of the wreck of the *Edmund Fitzgerald*, which sank November 10, 1975. Interpretive panels tell the story of Lake Superior and the *Fitz* and point to the wreck site west of the lookout. Open early May to early October.

For gift buyers of souvenirs and native collectibles, visit Agawa Indian Crafts and the Canadian Carver at Pancake Bay for unique woodcarvings and other treasures. This popular stop offers a campers' grocery, packaged goods, fishing/hunting licenses and great service at the filling station. Attractions include handcarved wooden statues of bear, moose, wolf and other bush animals. Be sure to shoot a picture of their famous Weather Rock, guaranteed to accurately tell you what the weather is at any moment.

If your route is north from Montreal River, you soon enter Lake Superior Provincial Park and are on your way to Wawa at the north end of the park. See listings for information on both the park and Wawa.

Neys Provincial Park

Neys Provincial Park occupies the Coldwell Peninsula about midway between Marathon and Terrace Bay on Lake Superior's Canadian north shore. Neys is naturally significant as a habitat for woodland caribou and historically significant as a World War II prisoner-of-war camp. German officers captured in

A new town park in Nipigon reflects parts of the famed children's book by Holling C. Holling, *Paddle-to-the-Sea*, which begins in Lake Nipigon. (Art Laframboise / Art by Art Photography)

Europe were impounded at what is now the site of the park's campground. Remains of the camp and old logging booms are everywhere.

Activities in the park include hiking, boating, picnicking, swimming and interpretive programs. Neys is the site of an interesting shipwreck, old ore-carrying Whaleback *#115*, with artifacts exhibited in the park's interpretive center, where programs are provided during summer. There is ample camping, access to Lake Superior via the Little Pic River, boat docks and a launch area. Neys Nostalgia Days are the second weekend in August. The campground is open mid-May to mid-September.

This striking landscape has served as the subject of many paintings by A.Y. Jackson, Lawren Harris and other members of Canada's early 20th century Group of Seven artists fraternity from Toronto. They visited a vibrant Coldwell in the early 1920s. Now it is nearly a ghost village.

A must stop in the area is the pulloff at the Little Pic River above the gorge to the east on the south side of Highway 17. A spectacular view of the highway bridge over the river offers an excellent and famous photo opportunity. You can see the Canadian Pacific Railway bridge and the tracks as they round the Coldwell Peninsula. The pulloff is quick, however, so keep a careful watch for it.

On the small stream of Angler Creek between Coldwell and Marathon, not far from the Highway 17 bridge, was another World War II prisoner-of-war camp.

Nipigon

Population 2,500

A town of junctions, Nipigon, called the "Crossroads of Canada," is where highways 11 from the north and 17 from the east connect, and the Canadian National and Canadian Pacific rail lines cross. This is where the waters from Lake Nipigon tumble into Lake Helen and then the most northerly waters of Lake Superior.

A Paddle-to-the-Sea carving is part of Nipigon's theme park. (Art Laframboise)

Nipigon is known as a sportfishing haven and holds the world record for the largest speckled trout, caught in the Nipigon River below Rabbit Falls in 1916.

What to See and Do

Nipigon turned 100 in 2009. Its downtown has undergone a $4.6 million revitalization project that includes Paddle to the Sea Park, a family theme park based on the popular 1941 children's book by Holling C. Holling. The book tells the story of a native boy who carves a canoe and puts it on the banks of the Nipigon River; when the snow melts, the canoe travels through the entire Great Lakes and out to sea.

Nipigon was chosen as the location for Parks Canada's administrative offices for the new Lake Superior National Marine Conservation Area, bringing several full-time jobs to town. The conservation area is the largest freshwater protected area in the world, covering more than 10,000 square kilometers (3,861 square miles) and extending from Thunder Cape at the tip of Sleeping Giant Provincial Park on the west to Bottle Point just east of Terrace Bay on the east and then out to the U.S.-Canadian boundary in Lake Superior.

Nipigon Marina is in the downtown area on the Nipigon River. A well-marked channel leads to a beautiful harbor and the marina can accommodate vessels of all sizes. The marina sports 30 slips, full facilities, and is the only port on the Great Lakes where you can reach the 49th parallel by water (and earn a certificate from the town).

The Nipigon River Recreation Trail extends from the marina along the west bank of the Nipigon River for 8.2 kilometers (5 miles) to Red Rock. Average hiking time is 2½ to 3½ hours. The middle section of the trail is rated difficult but the stretch from Nipigon Marina to Stillwater Creek is quite easy and provides good access to the shoreline habitat. From the Red Rock end, the first kilometer to Lloyd's Lookout is uphill but can be rated moderate. The reward: panoramic views of Nipigon Bay and Red Rock from the bench at the lookout – and a handful of wild blueberries, in season.

A highlight of a visit to Nipigon are the three building-sized murals that grace the downtown streets. Painted by Dave Sawatzky, they represent the historic heritage of Nipigon.

The 9-hole North Shore Golf Club lies nestled among the cliffs surrounding the towns of Nipigon and Red Rock, offering plenty of challenge on a championship course.

Winter visitors will find cross-country skiing nearby at the privately owned Karhu Ski Trails on Maata Road, where the longest loop is 7.1 kilometers (4.4 miles).

The Lake Helen Indian Reserve houses St. Sylvester's Historical Church, built in 1870, and the Lake Helen Powwow Grounds that is home to an annual traditional powwow each July.

Campers will enjoy the Stillwater Tent and Trailer Park, which includes an amethyst gift shop and mineral museum.

Notable Events

- Blueberry Blast in late July is an opportunity to sample the delectables possible from the popular fruit.
- Nipigon Fall Fishing Festival in early September gives everyone some favorite activity to indulge in.
- Hike for Health in late September is a nice hike and benefit between Red Rock and Nipigon.

What's Next

The Circle Tour route heads either east on Trans Canada Highway 17 toward Rossport, Schreiber and Terrace Bay or southward on Highway 11/17 bound for Thunder Bay. If time allows, an interesting side trip following Highway 11 northward is described in the listing for Lake Nipigon, Frontier Trail.

INFO & OPTIONS

Royal Windsor Lodge

R.R. 1 (Orient Bay)
Nipigon, ON P0T 2J0
807-885-5291

Ouimet Canyon, northeast of Thunder Bay, presents a unique environment along the northern shores of Lake Superior. Tundra plants grow near the chilly floor of the canyon.

Stillwater Tent and Trailer Park
Hwy. 11/17
Nipigon, ON P0T 2J0
877-887-3701 or 807-887-3701
www.stillwaterpark.ca

Nolalu

Township Population 700

Nolalu, west and south of Thunder Bay on Highway 588, is where Artesian Wells Resort has housekeeping cabins close to fishing and winter activities. This is also where you'll find Nolalu Eco Centre, a home and learning center that offers an ecology centered learning environment and organizes house tours, workshops and special events. Farmers' Mercantile Gift Gallery is a neat stop, with a cafe and bakery and six retail outlets offering gifts and specialty products. It's one of 40 studios and galleries on a self-guided, mapped tour called "Handmade in Thunder Bay." Ask for a brochure at information centers.

If you're after a little leisure summer sport, try tubing on the Kaministiquia River. Backtrack a bit from Nolalu and take Highway 588 to Stanley between Kakabeka Falls and Thunder Bay. River Rat Rentals has tubes for a three-hour relaxing trip down the river.

Ouimet Canyon Provincial Park

A huge rift in the diabase caused by erosion or faulting, the canyon walls of Ouimet Canyon Provincial Park stand 150 meters (492 feet) apart and 100 meters (328 feet) high and face each other for 3 kilometers (1.8 miles). On the floor of the canyon, plants native to the Arctic tundra grow where lower temperatures and shadows are untenable for indigenous regional plants. To protect this fragile plant community, access to the canyon floor is not allowed.

Ouimet is a day-use only park, with hiking trails along the canyon rim. A barrier-free boardwalk to viewing platforms makes this area more accessible for visitors. Two spectacular viewing pods overlook the canyon's edge and feature interpretive signs. An impressive standing rock formation is nearby. Visitors should remain on designated trails. A visit here is well worth the trip. Rated: easy. Facilities include a small souvenir shop, privies, barrier-free boardwalk and packed trails, and use of an all-terrain wheelchair. The parking area is 11 kilometers (6.8 miles) off Highway 11/17. Open mid-May to mid-October. Visitor donations to Friends of Ouimet Canyon Provincial Park provide this volunteer group with funds for operations and maintenance.

Nearby on Valley Road, Eagle Canyon Adventures features a campground with 30 full-service RV sites, shaded tenting and picnic sites and Ontario's longest suspension bridge high above the canyon. A shop has food items, supplies, souvenirs and crafts.

INFO & OPTIONS

i ***Ouimet Canyon Provincial Park***
c/o Sleeping Giant Provincial Park
Pass Lake, ON P0T 2M0
807-977-2526
www.ontarioparks.com/english/ouim.html

Λ ***Wolf River Park***
251 Wolf River Rd.
Dorion, ON P0T 1K0
807-857-2521
www.wolfriverpark.ca

Pukaskwa National Park

If any stretch of coast on Ontario's shore could be deemed the wildest and most undeveloped, it would be in Pukaskwa National Park. Pukaskwa (PUK-a-saw) opened in 1983. It is Ontario's largest national park and the only Canadian national park on Lake Superior. The park offers vistas of Lake Superior, with a rugged landscape carved out of the Canadian Shield and northern forests. The wilderness is one of the reasons visitors choose Pukaskwa as their destination.

Only one road penetrates the boundaries. Highway 627 passes through the small community of Heron Bay and leads 12 kilometers (7.5 miles) to Hattie Cove, which is 25 kilometers (16 miles) from Marathon yet is in the extreme northern tip of the 1,887-square-kilometer (726-square-mile) preserve. The vast interior is accessible only by trail, river or lake. Rated: difficult. A campground with 67 sites, some with electricity, is near the visitor center. Short walking trails and access to three sand beaches on Lake Superior, plus a picnic area, are at Hattie Cove. Handicapped accessible. Fees. Reservations for the backcountry are recommended.

Although the park is open year-round, the road into Hattie Cove is not maintained in winter. However, visitors may walk, ski or snowshoe in.

The Canadian Shield, Lake Superior shore and boreal forest are combined in the park. Nowhere else is the resulting environment so striking. Here are jagged mountain crests (some rising 460 meters or 1,500 feet above the lake's surface), moose, wolf, caribou and bear and subarctic flora. Within Pukaskwa is a small herd of woodland caribou, the farthest south that these animals are found naturally in Ontario.

Visitors with adventurous desire, along with extensive wilderness experience, can backpack the trails deep into the park. From the trailhead at Hattie Cove, the trail follows the coast 60 kilometers (37 miles) to the North Swallow River. The Coastal Trail, with its marvelous suspension bridge over

White River Gorge, suits hikers' needs well. It is the route most often traveled if you have limited time. Canoes on interior rivers, as well as powerboats and sailboats on Lake Superior, are common means of seeing such sites as Otter Island Light and Cascade Falls, where the Cascade River ends its trek to Lake Superior in the grand flourish of a 15-meter (49-foot) plummet.

Backcountry visitors must register in and out with the park office, either in person or by phone. Group size limit is eight people. Kayak and canoe rental is available in Marathon.

INFO & OPTIONS

Pukaskwa National Park Headquarters
P.O. Box 212
Heron Bay, ON P0T 1R0
807-229-0801
www.pc.gc.ca

Red Rock

Population 1,260

No traveler can fail to notice the rusty red layers of stone that give this region and the town of Red Rock its name. A ruddy hematite-bearing stratum of rock called Red Rock Cuesta is sandwiched between a granite base and younger diabase that flowed into the red layer and was exposed by erosion. The picturesque cuesta is evidence of the direction of glacial movement and is at the end of Highway 628 on Nipigon Bay.

Red Rock offers the lakeside Pull-a-Log Park on the bay. A 50-slip Red Rock Marina combines a breakwall with fishing, wildlife habitat, boat docks, full fuel and pumpout facilities, fishing ramps and a park with a boardwalk along the beach within this most northerly town on the big lake. Hiking and cross-country ski trails extend to Nipigon.

For lodging with scenic surroundings, the Red Rock Inn is a historic inn that can offer couples a romantic getaway, but also caters to business travelers and handles weddings, banquets, corporate retreats or meetings.

Red Rock annually holds a June fishing derby, a Canada Day celebration with fireworks over the marina on July 1, the Paju Mountain Run and the "Live from the Rock" Folk Festival in August.

WHAT'S NEXT

As we leave Red Rock and turn north on Highway 11/17 for Nipigon or south toward Thunder Bay, we're now truly north of Lake Superior.

INFO & OPTIONS

Red Rock Inn
145 White Blvd.
P.O. Box 476
Red Rock, ON P0T 2P0
807-886-2111
www.redrockinn.ca

Rossport

Population 113

Founded as a stop on the Canadian Pacific, Rossport first developed into a fishing village known as McKay's Harbour. It was a port instrumental in delivery of supplies for the building of the railroad in the mid-1880s and trains still pass day and night. A stop in Rossport, which sits slightly off Highway 17, is well worth the time.

WHAT TO SEE AND DO

The many islands of Schreiber Channel dot Lake Superior's face, and you may well find beautiful yachts anchored in the harbor.

If you want to sightsee from water level, kayaks and canoes can be rented from Superior Outfitters, which sponsors a Sea Kayaking Festival the last weekend in June each year.

Walk quiet Church Street and visit the Rossport Cemetery, where many a historic figure lies in peace. The Catholic and Protestant cemeteries lie side-by-side.

Rossport continues to be an important starting point for lake divers, although no charter boats are available for either divers or anglers without their own craft. The marina improvements include permanent fuel and pumpout facilities.

Casque Isles Trail runs 53 kilometers (32 miles) along the rugged Lake Superior shoreline from Rossport to Terrace Bay. The trail, part of the Voyageur Trail in Ontario, is divided into five segments that can be hiked in either direction, each with access off Highway 17 and each varies in difficulty. The trail is maintained by the Casque Isles Hiking Club, which worked with the townships of Terrace Bay and Schreiber on putting up new trail signs on Highway 17 and at trailheads.

Notable Museums

Rossport Caboose Museum is loaded with historic artifacts, including a plethora of railroad photos.

Parks and Public Areas

Rainbow Falls Provincial Park has two campgrounds in the Rossport area. The lakeshore Rossport Campground has 36 sites, with showers, laundry facilities, a picnic shelter and a cobblestone beach on Lake Superior.

Rossport Inn occupies the original Oriental Hotel and pay station built by the Canadian Pacific Railway. It's one of the oldest hotels on Ontario's shore and perhaps its most-famed stopover.

Rainbow Falls' Whitesand Lake Campground, farther above the highway, encompasses the hills around Whitesand Lake and Whitesand River as it tumbles over Rainbow Falls. From a wooden hiking bridge over the river, sunlight can be seen refracted in rainbows by the mist from the cascades. An additional 97 tent and trailer sites are at the Rainbow Falls campground. Hiking trails – including the Casque Isles part of the Voyageur Hiking Trail – run through the park. Rated: difficult. Rossport Campground opens mid-May to mid-October. Whitesand Lake Campground opens mid-May to early September.

What's Next

From Rossport, follow Highway 17 either to the east toward Schreiber or west bound for Nipigon.

INFO & OPTIONS

Rossport Inn
6 Bowman St.
P.O. Box 3
Rossport, ON P0T 2R0
877-824-4032
www.rossportinn.on.ca

Serendipity Gardens Cafe and Guest House
8 Main St.
Box 1
Rossport, ON P0T 2R0
807-824-2890
www.serendipitygardens.ca

The Willows Bed and Breakfast
116 Main St., Box 21
Rossport, ON P0T 2R0
807-824-3389
www.bbontario.com/thewillowsinn.cfm

St. Joseph Island

On the Ontario side of the St. Marys River is St. Joseph Island, about 45 kilometers (28 miles) southeast of Sault, Ontario. Accessed by bridge on Highway 548 off Highway 17 (Trans Canada Highway), the towns of Richards Landing and Hilton Beach welcome visitors.

At the southeastern end of the island (51 kilometers or 32 miles), Fort St. Joseph National Historic Site contains the remains of an important outpost of the fur trade from the late 1700s to early 1800s, with walking trails, a bird sanctuary, a reception center and displays of artifacts from this historic era. Open daily mid-May to mid-October.

Boaters will find three marinas (Richards Landing Municipal, Hilton Beach and Whiskey Bay) along with other areas amenable to anchoring.

At Echo Lake, about midway to St. Joseph Island on Highway 17, a handicapped-accessible 340-meter (1,115-foot) boardwalk and viewing platform is in the Lake George Marsh. The 647-acre wetland is used by migrating waterfowl for feeding and rest. It is a Living Legacy Heritage site designated by the Ontario government.

INFO & OPTIONS

Hilton Beach, St. Joseph Island
705-246-2242
www.hiltonbeach.com

Sault Ste. Marie

Population: 78,000

Whether entering the city from Soo, Michigan, or via Highway 17 from the north, the Ontario Sault has a wealth of sites, shopping, dining and cosmopolitan charm deserving a generous period of exploring and poking around by visitors. Sault, Ontario, managed to become the larger of the twin cities by mixing an interesting blend of early fur trade wealth with later industrial production, importance as a shipping center and as the regional center for a wide range of other activities.

An enticing array of ethnic dining will tempt you to indulge in all your favorite foods, then walk away the calories by hiking along the riverfront or shopping for a nice assortment of Canadian and international goods. There is also a great assortment of lodging options that allow you to relax in whatever atmosphere you desire after a day of exploring.

A Bit of History

Despite being on a marshy flood plain, the Canadian Sault Ste. Marie became the larger of the two cities after 1783, when a treaty made the river the boundary between Canada and the new United States. The fur companies were headquartered in Montreal, so business needed to be conducted on Canadian soil.

The early history of this Sault is firmly tied to the fur trade and the exploits of the voyageurs. From the mid-1600s until the mid-1800s, huge volumes of beaver and other pelts were trapped and shipped from the northern United States and Canada to England via both the Great Lakes waterways and Hudson's Bay in the northern territory.

A canal for canoes was dug on Canadian soil in 1799. It included an 11.7-meter (38-foot) lock, used to raise and lower boat traffic between Lake Huron and Lake Superior. It was destroyed by U.S. troops during the War of 1812.

By the mid-1800s, development in the Lake Superior region and the need to carry resources to the populous down-lake markets on larger ships pressed for a new canal. Before the American canal and lock in 1855, a few ships, some weighing up to 400 tons, were laboriously portaged around the rapids with lots of mules, logs, men and grease.

The Canadian canal and lock began operating in 1895, and soon after it opened, Francis H. Clergue, a Maine entrepreneur, implemented a grand plan to reap the benefits of the river's hydroelectric power, regional lumber and iron ore from Michipicoten. Although he went bankrupt, his Algoma Steel Corporation has been successfully producing steel ever since, now as Essar Steel Algoma, and remains a significant Sault employer despite recent economic difficulty. Besides shipping and steel, the Sault boasts chemical, paper, lumber and veneer plants.

In the latter 20th century, the Sault waterfront was beginning to show deterioration, and a plan was put in place to reclaim and rejuvenate areas where tank farms and tired industrial buildings dominated. That effort, years in the implementation, has resulted in one of the most attractive, vibrant waterfronts on Lake Superior, attracting thousands of shoppers, tourists, strollers, anglers and others seeking an up-close lake experience. This helps to make a strong tourism economy in the Sault.

Today

In addition to producing a wide range of industrial products, the Sault serves as the regional shopping mecca for a large surrounding area. It also supports a strong cultural heritage that includes museums, performing arts, music and drama.

An educational center for the region, Sault Ste. Marie is home to Algoma

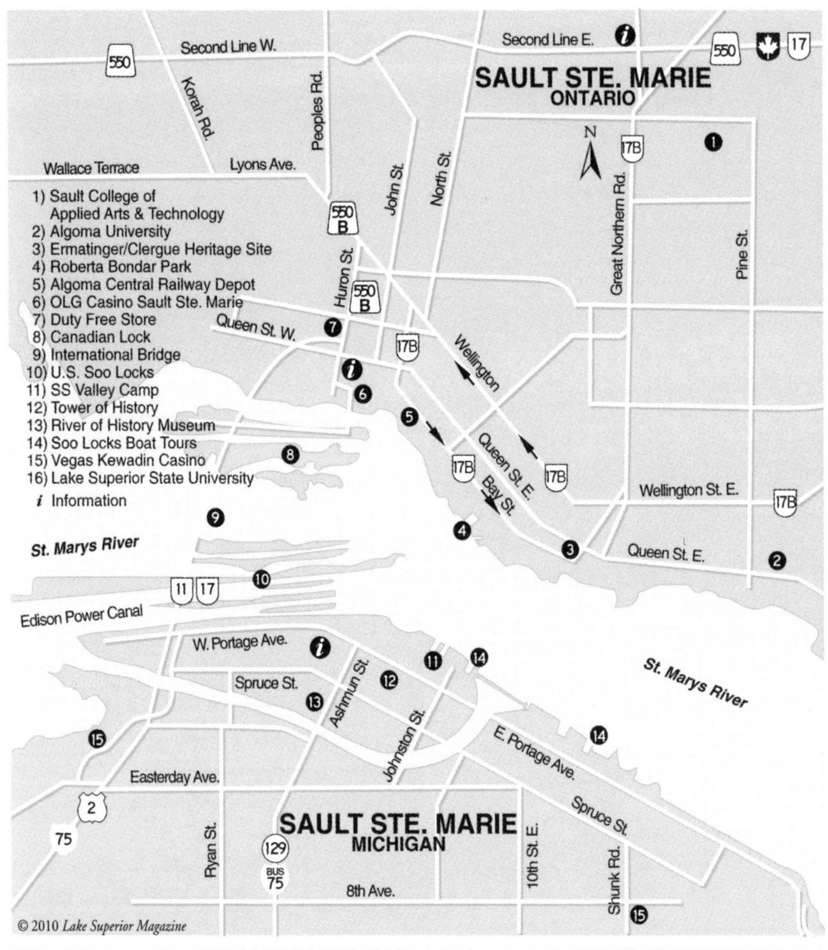

Sault Ste. Marie, Ontario & Michigan

University, strong in undergraduate arts and music courses, with a historically interesting campus, architecturally blending the old with the new and Aboriginal Canadian culture with European. The Old Shingwauk School, an early boarding school for First Nations students, is the base for the university's library/resource center. A 150-year-old cemetery on the grounds is regularly maintained. The campus overlooks the St. Marys River. Tours are available.

The Sault College of Applied Arts and Technology on Northern Avenue operates the Northern Ontario School of Hospitality, along with many other technical and vocational programs.

Sault serves as the medical and health care center of the Ontario Algoma area, with smaller outlying practices and facilities referring patients to medical personnel and facilities in Sault Ste. Marie, where Sault Area Hospitals and physicians in a wide range of specialties provide services to clients. The hospitals are a major employer in the city. The two main hospital sites are on the St. Marys River waterfront adjacent to each other. A new state-of-the-art hospital is being built in Sault Ste. Marie to replace the existing two hospitals, and is scheduled to be ready for patients in spring 2011.

WHAT TO SEE AND DO

The primary areas of interest to the visitor in the Sault, Ontario, are along the waterfront. The most visible and romantic thing about the Sault is the movement of lakers, salties, cruisers and pleasure boats along St. Marys River, but there is much else to see and do in this third-largest Lake Superior city.

After being damaged in 1987, the new Canadian Lock reopened in 1998 to serve small craft. Built inside the walls of the original commercial lock, which was 277 meters (909 feet) long, the new lock is 77 meters (253 feet) long, 15.4 meters (51 feet) wide and 13.5 meters (44 feet) deep, with a below-water draft of 3 meters (9.8 feet) and is surrounded by park land. Visit the interpretive center or walk across the gates and view the rapids.

The lock serves recreational navigation from May through October. Parks Canada runs the adjacent area as Sault Ste. Marie Canal National Historic Site of Canada. The heritage buildings in the lock area are constructed of red sandstone, excavated during construction of the canal.

Perhaps the Sault's most popular attraction is the St. Marys River Boardwalk, which extends from the Art Gallery of Algoma to the Canal. In addition to paths for biking and running, the pathway has viewing stations and a fishing platform that's guaranteed to produce a "big one." Interpretive signs and statuary are situated along the path.

The provincial OLG Casino Sault Ste. Marie offers more than 450 slot machines ranging from nickel to $5, as well as a range of table games, including blackjack and roulette. It's adjacent to the Boardwalk next to Station Mall.

On Foster Drive, the Civic Centre houses the municipal government. Fine art and sculpture are evident within the building and on the grounds. Tours of

St. Marys River Boardwalk

First-time visitors to Sault, Ontario, may find it hard to believe, but the waterfront area was once the scene of deteriorating industrial sites, large tank farms and other eyesores. Decades of planning and construction have resulted in renovation of that area into what can arguably be called the city's centerpiece.

A vital part of that waterfront rejuvenation is the St. Marys River Boardwalk, which stretches along the waterfront from the Civic Centre to Canadian Canal and Lock, offering a chance to stretch the legs and see many interesting sights along the way. There are fishing platforms, cute statues of wildlife, the Roberta Bondar Tent Pavilion, which often has interesting events scheduled, and the Roberta Bondar Marine Park and Marina, where visiting boaters can tie up. Named for the Sault native, the Bondar sites honor Canada's first female astronaut.

If you have time, be sure to visit the Penthouse Observation Gallery atop the Civic Centre for a grand panorama of the entire St. Marys waterfront area, as well as the interactive exhibits and artwork in the lobby of Roberta Bondar Place where the Ontario Lottery and Gaming Corporation is headquartered.

The Canadian Bushplane Heritage Centre in Sault Ste. Marie preserves the heritage of bush flying and aerial forest firefighting, which was first pioneered in this area.

the facility are available. The Penthouse Observation Gallery at the top gives a panorama of the St. Marys River region.

The Ontario Lottery and Gaming Corporation headquartered in Roberta Bondar Place overlooks the waterfront. The building houses some of the equipment that maintains the lottery operations. There are a number of exhibits in the main lobby that include interactive displays and works of art. The building also contains other governmental offices.

Kiwanis Community Theatre Centre is the major venue for concerts, theater productions, touring performances and other entertainment in Sault, Ontario. Other sites where performances may be scheduled include Verdi Hall and various churches.

The Arts Council of Sault Ste. Marie oversees many community events associated with the fine and performing arts. The Sault Symphony Orchestra, Algoma Conservatory of Music and local dance schools give regular performances in many locations. Theater groups present staged productions, including the Sault Opera. College and university groups schedule numerous performing groups that contribute to a rich cultural atmosphere on both sides of the St. Marys River.

The 85-meter (279-foot) museum ship *Norgoma* was the last passenger ship built to cruise the Great Lakes. The 1950 vessel, which is in the Bondar Marina area, has been undergoing renovation and is being restored to its original condition by the St. Mary's River Marine Heritage Centre. Open for tours during the summer.

No visit to the Sault area would be complete without devoting a day to the Agawa Canyon Train Tours of the Algoma Central Railway. The rails that connect Sault Ste. Marie with the French language town of Hearst pass through strikingly beautiful country. A daylong excursion through the Agawa Canyon area is offered seven days a week from late June through mid-October. Most popular is the 174-meter-deep (571-foot) Agawa Canyon tour, traveling about four hours to the canyon area just east of Lake Superior Provincial Park. After a two-hour exploratory layover, the train returns to the station on Bay Street in the late afternoon. A second, longer trip leads to Hearst for an overnight six days a week (not on Monday), returning the next day or later if you choose. No reservations on the Hearst train are required, although reservations at one of three Hearst motels (Companion, Northern Seasons or Queens) or two bed-and-breakfast inns are necessary. During winter months, the Snow Train plows north through the canyon on another daylong excursion. This is the only transportation for sleds and snowmobilers seeking the best wilderness trails and accommodations. Reservations should be made before traveling.

Spruce Haven Zoo features miniature horses, African pygmy goats, Vietnamese pot-bellied pigs, bunnies and many other animals friendly to kids. On Highway 550 and Carpin Beach Road, then follow the signs.

Both federal and provincial forestry centers are in Sault Ste. Marie. The Great Lakes Forestry Centre on Queen Street is one of the most advanced forestry research institutes in the world. Operated by the Canadian Forestry Service, weekday self-guided tours are available July and August. Tours feature greenhouses, laboratories and live insect displays. Next door is the Ontario Forestry Research Institute, a state-of-the-art, high-tech research facility that studies climactic effects on tree species. Complete with cold rooms and greenhouses, the Institute can "cheat the tree" by creating summer in winter and vice versa.

St. Mary's Ukrainian Church on St. George's Avenue East has no tours but is open for viewing.

The world's tallest free-standing cross stands regally at St. Basil's High School, off St. George's Avenue.

For golf, try one of the area courses: Maplewood Golf Course, Queensgate Greens, Root River Golf Club, Sault Ste. Marie Golf Club, Superior View Golf Course and the city's newest championship golf course, Crimson Ridge.

In-town fishing is available at various locations and the St. Marys River Boardwalk features a fishing platform that allows anglers to wet a line right downtown.

Winter visitors and hockey enthusiasts will want to check the schedule of the Sault Greyhounds, a Junior A class amateur squad that showcases top talent heading for Olympic and National Hockey League action. Playing a 34-game home schedule, the Greyhounds compete with 20 other league teams.

Boat visitors can use the Bondar Marina, a full-service facility with 38 transient slips for boats up to 100 feet (30 meters) long, which greets boaters at the Captain "Skipper" Manzutti Welcome Centre, named for a longtime prominent local businessman. The marina is a registered Canadian Customs check-in point and is the local outlet for Canadian and U.S. navigational charts. The marina is part of the Roberta Bondar Marine Park, named for Canada's first woman astronaut, who was born and grew up in Sault Ste. Marie. Downtown near the Civic Centre and adjacent to the boardwalk, the park features the 14,500-square-foot Roberta Bondar Park Tent Pavilion for concerts and special events. The tent-like structure dominates the waterfront.

Notable Museums

Sault Ste. Marie Museum, housed in the old post office in downtown, interprets Algoma District's history. Prehistoric and pioneer artifacts, a re-creation of Queen Street in 1912 and relics of industrial development let the visitor investigate lifelike history. Open daily year-round but closed Sundays. A few blocks away in front of the courthouse, a 22-foot-tall (7-meter) World War I "cenotaph" sculpture dedicated in 1922 by the Governor General of Canada honors those who gave their lives in World War I.

Built in 1814 by a wealthy fur trader, the Ermatinger Clergue National Historic Site is home to the oldest stone house in Canada west of Toronto. The house on Queen Street East was the early social and business focal point of the Sault, and is restored and decorated with artifacts. You'll meet interpreters in costume during self-guided tours. Also on the site is the Clergue Blockhouse, where industrialist F.H. Clergue, who established the rail, pulp and paper and

No visit to sault Ste. Marie is complete without a ride on one of the Agawa Canyon Train Tours of the Algoma Central Railway. The train also runs to Hearst.

steel industries in the area, once lived. Open June through mid-October.

On Pim Street, the Canadian Bushplane Heritage Centre is the only museum of its type in North America – it preserves the heritage of bush flying and aerial forest firefighting. The building is where water bombing of forest fires was developed. It's been named Canada's best indoor attraction by Attractions Canada. "Wings over the North" film in the Object Theatre brings the action to you ... *really*. Open daily year-round in the historic hangar at the end of Bay Street.

Art Gallery of Algoma has a permanent collection and regularly hosts exhibits from across the continent. It sits on the waterfront at East Street. Open Monday through Saturday.

Stop in at the Sault Ste. Marie Public Library and check out the Indian Pictograph mosaic by Jean Burke in the lobby, donated in 1967 by the Canadian Federation of University Women. Open daily.

Parks and Public Areas

Fort Creek Conservation Area is a getaway reserve for hiking and picnicking at Second Line West and People's Road. Bellevue Park, on the eastern waterfront at Queen Street East and Lake Street, has a greenhouse, plenty of green lawn and extensive flower gardens.

Kinsmen Park on Landslide Road contains great hiking and biking trails, and in the winter some of the best cross-country trails in the district. Pointe Des Chenes Park has hiking, picnicking and camping. The Forest Ecology Trail offers self-guided hikes.

Across the Canadian lock from the Canal Historic Site and on South St. Marys Island, is the Attikamek Wilderness Trail, which offers recreational activities like hiking and cross-country

Sault Ste. Marie: Insider Tips

• Whitefish Island is one of the few places in the Great Lakes where anglers can snare Atlantic salmon. Get here by crossing the Canadian Lock (this is not possible on the Michigan side). Walk over the lock and follow the trail to a boardwalk over beaver ponds and to the head of the rapids on the St. Marys River, and look for salmon to spawn at your feet on parts of the trail.

• Mockingbird Hill Farm, a turn-of-the-century farm on the edge of the city limits, offers a slice of the past. Here you can get Halloween pumpkins and Christmas trees, or challenge yourself in the area's only corn maze in the fall or take a sleigh ride in winter.

• The 1883 Shingwauk Fauquier Chapel, operated by the Anglican Church of Canada, is at the site of a former residential school for First Nations people and what is now Algoma University College campus. It's popular for weddings or wedding photos.

• The renovated Lock City Grand Theatre, built in 1948 as a movie theater, now hosts live performances from dinner theater to concerts.

• Biking enthusiasts will want to visit Velorution ("velo" is French for "bicycle") on Old Garden River Road. It's a bike shop, a repair shop and a campground for bikers. Anyone peddling through the Sault area (like those doing the Circle Tour by bike) will find a hot shower and a place to sleep. Shop owner Andre Roepel says "owning a bike shop is not a good way to make money, but it's a good way to have fun."

skiing. Whitefish Island, the third island in this area, located south of South St. Marys Island, is owned by the Batchawana First Nations and is designated a national historic site.

Notable Events

• Ontario Winter Festival Bon Soo in February offers winter fun that includes fireworks, outdoor recreation and family activities at the Bondar Pavilion.

• Great Outdoor Show and Sale is an April opportunity for outdoor recreationists to put together or to satisfy their wish lists.

• Rotaryfest in mid-July is a big celebration with food, Wheels on the Water car show, the annual Rotary Community Day Parade, music and other activities.

• Dragon Boat Races is a charitable June competition in which teams of paddlers vie in brightly colored boats on the waterfront.

• International Bridge Walk and Great Tugboat Race in late June is a chance to hike the 2-mile bridge spanning the St. Marys River and catch the excitement of tugs vying to be the fleetest of the fleets.

• Canada Day Celebrations marks the July 1 establishment of the nation.

• Arts at the Dock in July features 40 of Algoma District's talented artists and many works for sale, from painting, photography and stained glass to pottery.

• Can/Am Salmon Derby in mid-August pits top anglers and would-be anglers for nice prizes.

• Algoma Fall Festival, from September into November and includes a variety of entertainment and events nearly daily.

• Santa Parade in November gives kids of all ages a chance to celebrate jolly old St. Nick's arrival.

Where to Shop

The downtown area of Sault Ste. Marie has more than 60 shops in a five-block area that are sure to meet virtually any need, from souvenirs to toiletries.

In addition, the Station Mall on Bay Street has 120 outlets and the Cambrian Mall on Great Northern Road has more than 70 stores.

What's Next

If you're leaving the Sault to continue your Circle Tour, you'll cross into Michigan over the International Bridge. Check the "Crossing the Border" section in front of this book for information on customs and other requirements. If your journey is destined to go deeper north into Ontario, you'll take Trans Canada Highway 17, which is also designated in town as Great Northern Road. Either way, the Circle Tour has much more of interest along your route of travel.

INFO & OPTIONS

Algoma Kinniwabi Travel Association

485 Queen St. East, Ste. 204
Sault Ste. Marie, ON P6A 1Z9
800-263-2546
www.algomacountry.com

Sault Ste. Marie Chamber of Commerce

334 Bay St.
Sault Ste. Marie, ON P6A 1X1
705-949-7152
www.ssmcoc.com

Tourism Sault Ste. Marie

99 Foster Dr.
Sault Ste. Marie, ON P6A 5X6
800-461-6020
www.saulttourism.com

New Marconi Restaurant
480 Albert St. West
Sault Ste. Marie, ON P6A 1C3
705-759-8250

Quality Inn Bay Front
180 Bay St.
Sault Ste. Marie, ON P6A 6S2
www.qualityinnssm.com

Delta Sault Ste. Marie Waterfront Hotel & Conference Center
208 St. Mary's River Dr.
Sault Ste. Marie, ON P6A 5V4
888-713-8482

Glenview Cottages & Campgrounds
2611 Great Northern Rd.
Sault Ste. Marie, ON P6A 5K7
705-759-3436
www.glenviewcottages.com

KOA Tent & Trailer Park
501 Fifth Line East
Sault Ste. Marie, ON P6A 5K8
705-759-2344
www.koakampgrounds.com

Bell's Point Beach & Campsites
174 Hwy. 17 East
Garden River First Nation, ON P6A 6Z3
705-759-1561
www.bellspointbeach.com

Pointe Des Chenes Campground & Trailer Park
57 Pointe Des Chenes Dr.
Sault Ste. Marie, ON P6A 5K6
705-779-2696

Schreiber

Population 1,447

Nestled in a valley surrounded by rugged hills, Schreiber is one of the oldest communities on the north shore of Lake Superior, traditionally serving as a railroad center with some of the most vibrant railway history in Canada.

The town is known as "Little Italy" for its sizable Italian population. Shoppers will find a number of craft and gift shops to explore.

What to See and Do

Visitors will want to see two plaques in the downtown area that commemorate Sir Collingwood Schreiber, one of the builders of the Canadian Pacific Railway, and the Japanese Canadians who were relocated to the town in 1942. Also, view the rail yard, the historic Canadian Pacific Depot, a restored 1955 yard engine and an authentic railway motor car, the rail and heritage museum and a festival site.

At Winnipeg and Scotia streets, across from Schreiber Information Centre, Schreiber is working on a display of Canadian Pacific Railway exhibits, including the city's rail, cultural and natural heritage. Just after the underpass on Highway 17, turn immediately right to descend to adventure. Hike, bike or drive down Isbester's Drive, the rail heritage route, to a handicapped-accessible gazebo featuring exhibits and amenities at Schreiber Beach, Lake Superior's northernmost beach opening directly onto the big water from the mouth of Schreiber Channel. Examine the gazebo's interesting display panels, bring a picnic lunch, lounge on sand, pebbles or rocks and listen to the sound of the surf. Nearly $1 million was invested to improve the access road to the lakeshore, and visitors are likely to appreciate this investment in access to the beach and its amenities.

If you're up to it, explore the Casque Isles Hiking Trail, part of the Trans Canada Trail System and accessed at several points. To the east, follow the creek trail past a one-person suspension bridge to ascend to spectacular views, rugged terrain and, eventually, Mt. Gwynne. Beachside to the west are flowing formations of ancient, surf-smoothed rocks that lead immediately to a route to more distant conservation reserves.

Another point of interest is Worthington Bay Beach, accessible on the rugged Casque Isles Trail east past Mt. Gwynne or by following long and aging trails from town or off the highway. This lovely spot has remnants of the generating and milling site for the old Northshore Mines, including an engine block said to be from a captured submarine. If you're lucky, you may find the location of pictographs on Lake Superior's rugged shores. Trans Ontario Provincial Snowmobile Trail (TOPS) is immediately accessible and excellent fishing and hunting are found in the surrounding wilderness.

NOTABLE EVENTS

• Heritage Days, a townwide celebration in mid-July, features special meals, games and a townwide yard sale.

• The cooler season "Peel Off Winter" Carnival toward the end of February is a chance to celebrate winter.

WHAT'S NEXT

To continue on the Circle Tour, take Trans Canada Highway 17 either west toward Rossport and Nipigon, or east heading for Terrace Bay and Marathon.

INFO & OPTIONS

Township of Schreiber
608 Winnipeg St.
P.O. Box 40
Schreiber, ON P0T 2S0
807-824-2711
www.schreiber.ca

Circle Route Motel
28 Kingsway
Schreiber, ON P0T 2S0
www.voyageuresso.ca

Travel Rest Tent & Trailer Park
Hwy. 17
P.O. Box 697
Schreiber, ON P0T 2S0
807-824-2485

Schreiber Channel

The trip between Nipigon and Rossport offers many pullouts for rest, picnicking and sightseeing. Cast your eyes upon the multitude of islands in Nipigon Bay and the Schreiber Channel. You're looking at a group of 59 islands, designated as "Nirivia" by some locals, covering 583 square kilometers (225 square miles), the largest of which is St. Ignace, blessed with inland lakes, waterfalls and Mount St. Ignace with an elevation of 568 meters (1,863 feet) and one of the tallest peaks within Great Lakes waters. St. Ignace is the second largest island on Lake Superior after Isle Royale. More than 120 kilometers (75 miles) of hiking trails cut through island forests literally crawling with wildlife. Boaters who visit these islands find many with black sand similar to that found on Lake Nipigon. It is loaded with geodes and collectible rocks like agates and other semiprecious stones. Wilderness excursions into Nirivia are conducted by Nirivian Island Expeditions of Thunder Bay with biking, kayaking, camping, fishing and cruises.

Stop at the pullout overlooking Kama Bay. Here you are seeing the northernmost waters of Lake Superior. In the distance, you can see the town of Red Rock.

East of Kama Bay, you'll see a road (a quick turn) toward the lake to a picnic area. This area overlooks the lake from high atop the cliffs with the tracks of the Canadian Pacific running below. A wonderful spot for overview pictures, but don't get too close to the edge of the cliffs!

The Pays Plat Indian Reserve about midway between Rossport and Schreiber usually offers charter fishing, with access to some of the best trout fishing on the lake.

Sibley Peninsula & Sleeping Giant Provincial Park

Traveling either north from Thunder Bay or south from Nipigon and Red Rock on Trans Canada Highway 11/17, keep an eye out for signs pointing the way to Pass Lake, the gateway to Sibley Peninsula and Sleeping Giant Provincial Park.

Sleeping Giant Provincial Park offers more than 80 kilometers (50 miles) of hiking and backpacking trails taking you to the park's interior and to vistas atop the Sleeping Giant 300 meters (984 feet) above Lake Superior. The park's campground is on Marie Louise Lake via Highway 587 and is open mid-May to mid-October. Popular activities include coastal kayaking and biking.

The Visitor Centre is in the Marie Louise Lake Campground and features displays, slide shows and lectures, with a family activity area and gift shop. Open mid-May to early October. Cross-country skiing (both classic and skate styles) is available on more than 50 kilometers (31 miles) of groomed trails during winter, and is the site of the Annual Sleeping Giant Loppet (formerly the Sibley Ski Tour), the largest such event in Northwest Ontario.

Sibley's historic Sea Lion rock formation and the Top of the Giant Trail can be accessed from the Kabeyun trailhead, where parking is available. Park fees apply.

Return to the Circle Tour by backtracking to Pass Lake. and Trans Canada Highway 11/17.

INFO & OPTIONS

Karen's Kountry Kitchen
RR I
Pass Lake, ON P0T 2M0
807-977-2882
karenskountrykitchen.com

Silver Islet

Thirty kilometers (19 miles) beyond Pass Lake is the tip of the Sibley Peninsula where a mere rock sticks above Lake Superior's waters. It's called Silver Islet. From 1869 until 1884 this tiny island was blanketed with buildings and docks so it covered 10 times its natural area. The men on the island were silver miners. In total, they extracted $3 million worth of the precious metal. If you can get out on the water around the still privately held islet (namesake of the village), you can see pilings and deep shafts just below the surface which descend to the remaining treasure below. On the mainland, a few original cottages from the miners' village of the same name remain, although they're now private summer homes.

This is a favorite vacation destination, especially for residents of Thunder Bay. All have to generate their own power, and generally get their water directly from the lake. The historic Silver Islet General Store opens for summer business on Victoria Day weekend in late May and offers tea, pizza, soups, desserts and a pool table in the back. Moonlight teas on Saturday nights are a reservation must. A store has been in this location since 1871. Mountain bike rentals are available. Sometimes open after Labour Day, but rarely. Gift items are available nearby in the former assay office, now a gift store. Sibley's historic Sea Lion rock formation (in Sleeping Giant Provincial Park) can be accessed from the Kabeyun trailhead, where parking is available. Park fees apply.

On the government dock, transient tie-ups are allowed at moderate fees. To make arrangements, stop at the store.

What's Next

The return from Silver Islet to Highway 11/17 is along the same route followed on the way in, although there are occasional short side roads to allow exploration. Once on Highway 11/17, you've headed either southward for Thunder Bay or the northwest corner of Lake Superior to the north, with many kilometers of scenic beauty to lure us and a wealth to see and do along the way.

Slate Islands Provincial Park

The Slate Islands are an archipelago of eight isles, which together form a circle of land that rises sharply out of Lake Superior about 13 kilometers (8 miles) off Terrace and Jackfish bays. It has been designated Slate Islands Provincial Park. Geological studies indicate that the islands were formed by a meteor or asteroid impact more than a billion years ago. Scientists estimate the "rock" was as much as 30 kilometers (19 miles) wide when it struck the earth, burying itself 3 kilometers (2 miles) under the surface. The islands were logged in the 1930s, but have regained natural splendor and are now a favorite for pleasure boaters, kayakers and anglers. They even support a herd of woodland caribou, the densest population of caribou in North America.

Boaters will want to photograph the lighthouse sitting on the southern tip of Patterson Island. Landlocked visitors can check at the Terrace Bay Information Centre for a list of charter boat operators.

Twelve miles or so east of Terrace Bay on Highway 17 is the ghost town of Jackfish. Nothing remains of the town. Jackfish is thought to be the site of the first gold mine in Northwestern Ontario, dating from about 1871. Jackfish Lake, set in nearly ideal fishing and hunting habitat, is in fact a beautiful bay off Lake Superior. In this area, lodging is available at Jackfish Lake Motel Efficiency Cottages (807-825-9293), with two- and three-bedroom units, meals and gift shop.

South Gillies

Township Population 590

If you have the time, make a reservation and stop at Rose Valley Lodge and Restaurant in South Gillies, 16 kilometers (10 miles) to Rose Valley Road, then turn right for a half-mile. The lodge, a remodeled Finnish farmhouse on 440 acres, is an ideal place to sample gourmet meals and country living. Owners refurbished the dining room and offer lodging in two bed-and-breakfast rooms and two cottages. A sauna was added. Reservations are a must.

A short jaunt on Highway 590 leads to the Kakabeka Falls area (see listing).

Several other small towns can be explored in the immediate area, offering goods and services for visitors who take this trip inland.

What's Next

The direct route to Thunder Bay is to backtrack to Highway 61, but can also go a few kilometers north to catch Highway 588 and enter the southwestern edge of the city.

Terrace Bay

Population 1,900

Made famous by Louis Agassiz in an 1850 lithograph, Terrace Bay is named for three levels of glacial sand and gravel deposits that step up from the lake. They rise more than 100 meters (328 feet). The town, inland and to the east, was built more than 50 years ago for employees of the paper mill, an industry that's been part of the local history.

The Ogoki and Longlac rivers to the north were dammed by Ontario Hydro for a power-generating plant. The diversions direct water into Lake Superior rather than Hudson Bay. The flow from the diversions almost equals the flow of either the St. Louis or the Nipigon river, the two major natural tributaries to Lake Superior.

What to See and Do

Just west of town, a half-mile off the highway, an accessible boardwalk can be followed to an observation deck at the 30-meter-tall (98-foot) Aguasabon Falls and Gorge. The view is spectacular, and additional unprotected footpaths are nearby if you wish to hike down to the lakeshore. The river follows deep fractures in the bedrock, which is about 2.6 billion years old. The exposed rock is called granodiorite.

The Trestle Ridge Ski Area is just above the town, offering five ski runs from beginning to advanced, plus a snowboarding area and instruction.

If you are interested in snowmobiling, there are about 210 kilometers (130

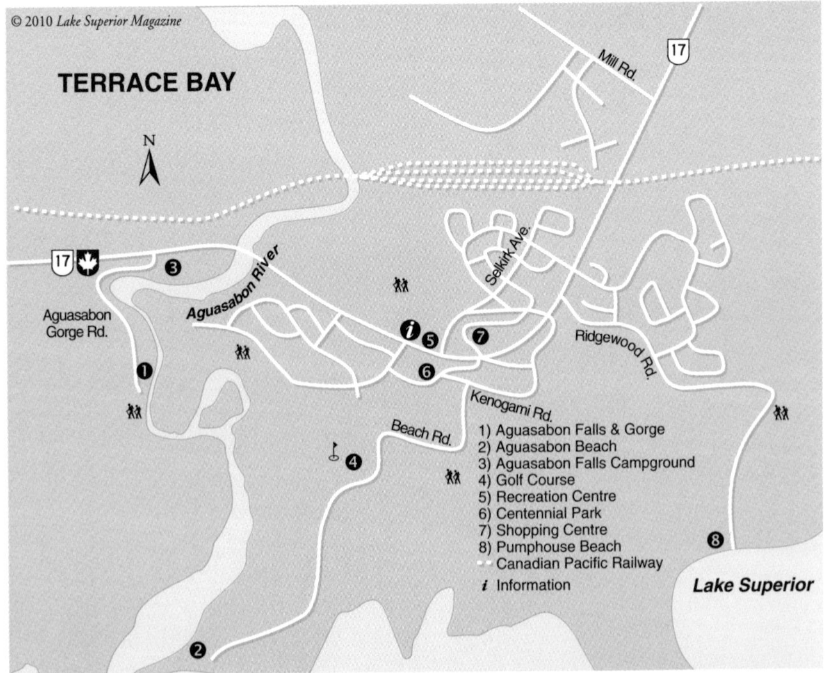

Terrace Bay

miles) of snowmobile trails going west, east and north from town. They're part of the TOPS (Trans Ontario Provincial Snowmobile) trail system running throughout Ontario.

Terrace Bay is a favorite of golfers and waterfall lovers. The 9-hole Aguasabon Golf Course scenically overlooks Lake Superior.

Stop and chat with the staff at the Terrace Bay Tourist Information Centre. Behind the center is a path to the top of the hill for a breathtaking panoramic view of the area. Or follow the caribou tracks to the downtown shopping center. The Information Centre is open mid-May to mid-October.

The Casque Isles Hiking Trail, a 53-kilometer (32-mile) stretch, begins in Terrace Bay, passes through Schreiber and ends in Rossport. The trail, part of the Voyageur Trail, is divided into five segments that can be hiked in either direction, each with access points off Highway 17 and varying in difficulty. The trail is maintained by the Casque Isles Hiking Club. For information and maps, contact the Information Centre.

Notable Events

• Terrace Bay hosts a well-attended Fish Derby in June.

• Canada Day Celebrations on July 1 are held in most Canadian towns.

• Terrace Bay's Annual Dragfest is the first weekend of August.

• The Annual Fall Fair is celebrated in September.

What's Next

To the west, Trans Canada Highway 17 heads for Nipigon, but watch for signs pointing you to Rossport. To the east, Highway 17 leads to Schreiber and the northeast corner of Lake Superior near Marathon.

INFO & OPTIONS

Terrace Bay Tourist Information Centre
1008 Hwy. 17
P.O. Box 1207
Terrace Bay, ON P0T 2W0
800-968-8616
www.terracebay.ca

Imperial Motel and Drifters Roadhouse
P.O. Box 338, Hwy. 17
Terrace Bay, ON P0T 2W0
877-825-1625

Red Dog Inn
Hwy. 17
Terrace Bay, ON P0T 2W0
807-825-3285
www.reddoginn.ca

Neys Provincial Park Headquarters
P.O. Box 280
Terrace Bay, ON P0T 2W0
807-229-1624
www.ontarioparks.com

Thunder Bay

Population: 109,141

Thunder Bay presents a multitude of sights, sounds and scents to greet the traveler. It ranks as the 14th most populous city in Ontario and the largest city on the 2,080-kilometer (1,292-mile) Lake Superior Circle Route. The 156-square-mile metropolitan area is almost in the center of Canada, 2,980 kilometers (1,852 miles) by water from the Atlantic Ocean and 2,530 kilometers (1,572 miles) by land from the Pacific. It is 280 kilometers (174 miles) from Duluth, Minnesota, and 690 kilometers (429 miles) from Sault Ste. Marie, Ontario.

The city is situated on a magnificent

natural harbour (spelled "harbor" in the United States) and is a worthy destination that adds to the delight of driving one of the most beautiful routes on the continent. If you arrive by air, the Thunder Bay Airport Terminal affords you panoramic views of the Sleeping Giant and Thunder Bay (the body of water to the east) and the Nor'wester Mountains to the west. A metropolitan transit system provides service throughout the city and about a dozen taxi companies also offer transportation.

Thunder Bay has many attractions. If you need any questions answered or want hints about Thunder Bay, stop by any of the Visitor Information Centres. In the downtown, the Pagoda is the oldest tourist bureau in Canada. On the corner of Water Street and Red River Road, the center is open June through early September, five days a week. For information on the wider area contact the Terry Fox Information Centre (open year-round) east on Highway 11/17, where you find a great info center along with the Terry Fox Memorial that's well worth a visit.

For travelers entering the area from the north and east, Trans Canada Highways 11 and 17 join at Nipigon and give an easy drive southward to Thunder Bay. (See the listing for Nipigon for detail.) This Canadian Lakehead section of the trip through Northwestern Ontario extends from the international border at Pigeon River to the Sibley Peninsula-Sleeping Giant east of Thunder Bay. The entire Circle Tour route in Ontario is in the Eastern Time Zone.

Visitors traveling southwest of the city on Highway 61 toward the international border may be surprised to find a fertile valley that sustains a variety of agricultural endeavors in these northern latitudes. Tidy farms dot the roadside and herds of livestock can be seen grazing in summer pastures against the rugged backdrop of stone mountains that hem in this farming area both to the east and west.

Sleeping Giant & Ouimet Canyon

Near Thunder Bay are two of the most intriguing Lake Superior regional parks noted for beautiful scenery and geologic formations.

Sleeping Giant (see Sibley Peninsula listing) is immediately noticeable from almost any hillside in the city, but requires about a 45-minute drive northeast on Trans Canada Highway 11/17 to Pass Lake to take Highway 587 into the park. The townsite of Silver Islet is at the end of the road and nearly the end of the park. The only route is to backtrack on H-587.

Ouimet Canyon Provincial Park (see separate listing) is about 65 kilometers (40 miles) northeast of Thunder Bay. The canyon walls stand 150 meters (492 feet) apart and 100 meters (328 feet) high and face each other for 3 kilometers (2 miles). On the canyon floor, plants native to the arctic tundra grow where the lower temperature and shadows are untenable for indigenous regional plants. Access to the floor is not allowed, but look for two viewing pods overlooking the canyon's edge.

A Bit of History

A fort was erected by the French in 1717 at the mouth of the Kaministiquia River (locally called "the Kam"). When the North West Company moved its

Across the bay from the city of Thunder Bay is the famed Sleeping Giant, part of the Sibley Peninsula and a great opportunity for hiking. (Lori Fox-Rossi / Tourism Thunder Bay)

mid-continent operations from Grand Portage, Minnesota, to Fort William in 1803, the fort became the site of the annual rendezvous, where goods from Montreal and furs from the wilderness traded hands. The trading remained steady until the mid-1800s and made this the world's largest fur trading post.

The importance of the area to lake and rail shipping made it prime for development. When the railroad arrived from the east in the 1870s and continued pushing westward, Port Arthur grew a bit to the north of Fort William, but the twin cities, which came to be called the Lakehead, became a crucial link in commerce between the agricultural west and ports to the east. Until relatively recent times, Thunder Bay ruled supreme as the largest grain handling port in the world.

For a century, the two cities vied in all aspects of business before Port Arthur and Fort William consolidated in 1970

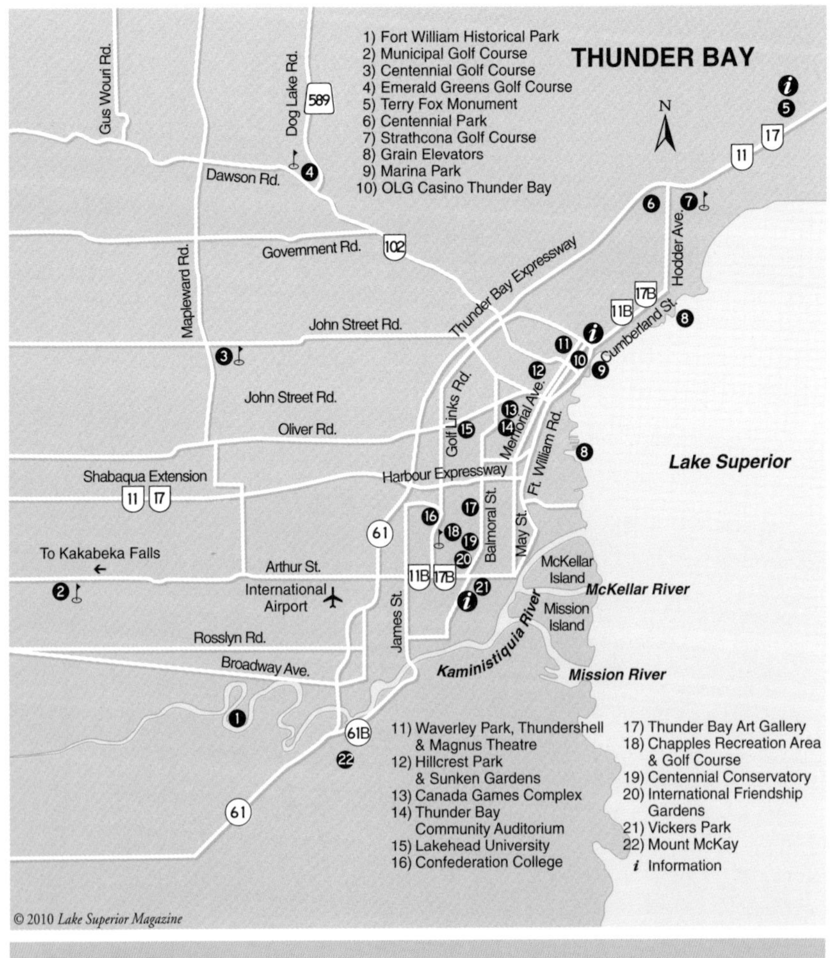

Thunder Bay

into a modern industrial center with paper and lumber mills, grain elevators and port facilities. The grand result is the city of Thunder Bay, which took its name from the body of water to its east.

Today

Thunder Bay is a working city, teeming with activity. It's a port city lying in the shadow of the legendary Sleeping Giant Provincial Park on the Sibley Peninsula, which protects the harbor to the east. Today, its shipping economy is bolstered by paper and forest products, major industrial and manufacturing facilities, education and tourism. With the Thunder Bay Regional Health Sciences Centre, the city serves the health needs of a broad area of northwestern Ontario.

Thunder Bay is the home of two institutions of higher education: Lakehead University, with a beautiful campus in the heart of the city, and, a few blocks away, Confederation College, site of Thunder Bay Art Gallery and a diverse range of technical, academic and Native courses.

As with other Lake Superior cities, tourism is an important part of the economic mix in Thunder Bay. With many must-see sights from the busy waterfront to its many attractive and interesting parks and public spaces, this is a city that most visitors will want to take time to explore.

What to See and Do

A must stop in the western part of Thunder Bay and close to excellent cross-country skiing is Fort William Historical Park (formerly Old Fort William), which has been reconstructed on an oxbow, 14 kilometers (9 miles) upstream on the Kam and has been named one of Canada's Top 10 Attractions. Inside the stockade, life returns to 1815. Craftsmen, voyageurs, company officials and native people interact as they might have on any business day two centuries ago. The summer is filled with daily demonstrations and events at Fort William, with a few festivals in winter. Among the notable celebrations are the Great Rendezvous in July and Anishnawbe Keeshigun celebrating First Nations culture in August. There are various programs that allow guests to dress as voyageurs and camp. One attraction is the Learning Wigwam. Open mid-May to mid-October.

The Sleeping Giant is clearly evident from any east-facing bluff in Thunder Bay. Some say Ojibway legend tells how Naniboujou, both spirit and human, watched over his people as they explored Lake Superior's waters, warning them that he would turn to stone if they revealed the presence of a fabulous island of silver. The legend is that he laid down in Thunder Bay and turned to stone after white men discovered the silver lode at Silver Islet, becoming the southern tip of the Sibley Peninsula, which juts into Lake Superior and displays his crossed-armed silhouette as a reminder. The majority of the peninsula is protected by Sleeping Giant Provincial Park.

Thunder Bay Art Gallery has a fine collection of Aboriginal art and is northwest Ontario's largest public gallery. A bit difficult to locate at the edge of the Confederation College campus, the gallery is well worth the effort. Open afternoons Tuesday through Sunday. Nominal fee, but free on Wednesdays.

The Terry Fox Monument, on a bluff above the highway at the eastern outskirts of Thunder Bay, commemorates Terry Fox who lost his leg to cancer. Running on an artificial leg across Canada in 1980 to raise funds for research, his disease recurred and forced him to stop when he reached Thunder Bay. He died less than a year later. His last stretch of highway is now named in his memory: Terry Fox Memorial Highway. Co-located with the Fox Memorial is an outstanding Travel Information Centre. From the Terry Fox Monument, enjoy a wonderful vista of the Sleeping Giant.

OLG Casino Thunder Bay on Cumberland Street provides gaming fun for a variety of good causes.The $30 million, 48,000-square-foot uniquely designed casino was the fourth provincial gaming operation to open (Sault Ste. Marie was first in 1999). A stunning mural by the late Roy Thomas alone makes the place worth a visit.

Thunder Bay Community Auditorium, an addition at the Canada Games Complex, is booked nearly every night with cultural events, Broadway shows and major performers. Home of the Thunder Bay Symphony Orchestra, the 1,500-seat auditorium hosts international personalities. The street in front of it was renamed to honor Thunder Bay native Paul Shaffer, musical director for the Late Show with David Letterman.

Magnus Theatre was home to professional community and touring performances on McLaughlin Street for more than 30 years. In 2001, the new "Magnus in the Park" Theatre opened in the Waverley Park area of town. It hosts a variety of locally produced dramatic and comedic performances each season.

Musical and performing arts productions are also offered by schools, colleges and independent arts organizations. Check the Info Centres for current programs.

Marina Park is at the end of Highway 102 (Red River Road in town). It has a large full-service marina called Prince Arthur's Landing, which is undergoing major changes as part of the waterfront development plan. Construction has begun on the waterfront, which will see a new hotel and condominiums in place by 2011. Thunder Bay's new Waterfront Skateboard/BMX Plaza at Prince Arthur's Landing had its grand opening in summer 2009. The skateboard area, unsupervised, is open 6 a.m. to 11 p.m. daily. It features local stonework on ledges and walls, and has modern skateboarding terrain with a California-style bowl.

Sailing cruises – from harbour tours to custom excursions – are available through Gregory Heroux's Sail Superior.com Yacht Charters & Sleeping Giant Sailing School, with departures from Pier 3 in Marina Park. Gregory offers a range of services, plus a dockside B&B on a 38-foot sailboat.

The venerable, refurbished tugboat *James Whalen* is at Kaministiquia River Heritage Park. Long critical to icebreaking and salvage operations, the *Whalen* was returned to Lake Superior in 1992 after its last duty on the lower lakes.

Three touring routes have been established for travelers trying to navigate Thunder Bay's multinamed streets. They are the Friendship, Memorial and Bayview routes, each offering something of interest to visitors.

Pick up an Architectural Walking Tour Map showing more than two dozen historical buildings at any of the information stops, which also distribute "Hand Made in Thunder Bay" guides to more than 40 arts and crafts studios and galleries in the area.

The Thunder Bay Blues Fest in early July brings music fans to Marina Park to hear a variety of international artists; past concerts have included Robert Cray, Dr. John and Rita Chiarelli.

If you'd prefer a guided tour or plan to arrive with a group, check with Lake Superior Visits, which offers an array of services for visitors in the area, including "Great Getaway" packages in winter/spring and summer/fall.

Mount McKay Scenic Overlook on Missions Road offers a 4-kilometer (2.5-mile) hiking trail from the base, with scenic views on the way to a commanding view from the top, which towers 300 meters (984 feet) over both the water body and city of Thunder Bay. It is steep and often slippery when wet. Rated: intermediate. About halfway up, at the 167-meter (500-foot) level, is a memorial chapel honoring First Nations military personnel killed in World War II. An authentic native village was added in 1995. The parkway, operated by Fort William First Nation, has a toll.

For golfers, Thunder Bay has 13 city or privately owned courses, including the new, 27-hole Whitewater Golf Course accessible from Highway 130 or Boundary Avenue off Highway 61 South. Thunder Bay Golf Dome provides an indoor, two-tiered 300-foot driving range and 18-hole miniature golf course for year-round enjoyment. The nine-hole Bayview and Giant Golf Course is on Highway 587 near Pass Lake on Sibley Peninsula.

Canada Games Complex, built for the 1981 Canada Summer Games, is a multisports training facility for world-class athletes. Numerous sports from swimming to squash are available for public enjoyment, along with programs for health and wellness, fitness and lifesaving.

Winter visitors will find plenty of action in the area. On the nearby

Nor'Wester peaks to the west of Thunder Bay, Loch Lomond offers prime ski slopes and aprés-ski facilities in winter and is open daily, except Tuesdays. Night skiing is available. On the other side of the city, Mount Baldy has the best view of Thunder Bay Harbour and is great for afternoon skiing. Or rent a snowmobile and ride the trails. There are also tubing and horseback-riding options, off Highway 11/17 some 6 kilometers (4 miles) north on Highway 527. Open Tuesday to Sunday, also Friday and Saturday evenings.

Recreational hiking trails and cross-country skiing are available throughout the region. Kamview is operated by the Thunder Bay Nordic Trails Association. Other challenging ski trails are at Centennial Park, Lappe and the Kakabeka Falls and Sleeping Giant provincial parks cross-country ski areas. Trail guidebooks are available from tourist information centers.

Nor'West Outdoor Centre is a short jaunt off Highway 61 down Mountain Road. Its 55-acre grounds are available for winter and summer recreation that can be arranged by calling ahead.

On Jarvis Bay Road off Highway 61 south of town, Norwest Sled Dog Adventures gives you a chance for a

Thunder Bay Insider Tips

• Thunder Bay has three Finnish bakeries that make great traditional fare. Kivela Bakery celebrates 100 years in 2010 at 111 Secord Street. Or try Harri Bakery, 223 Algoma Street South, known for its cheesecake, which sells out fast. And there's Current River Bakery at 301 Grenville Avenue.

• If stargazing through a powerful telescope appeals to you, Thunder Bay Observatory should be on your list. It was created and built by self-taught astronomer Randy McAllister. Every year, many students, scientists and tourists visit the dome-shaped building near the Nor'Wester Mountain Range to peer into the heavens. 807-577-3617.

• Whether you have already thought of it or not, here's a reminder: Do visit downtown's Marina Park to find a wonderful waterfront area with a boardwalk and the majestic Sleeping Giant in the distance.

• Consider visiting the labyrinth at St. Paul's Anglican Church, where anyone is welcome to stroll for meditation, contemplation and spiritual renewal. Labyrinth walking is a practice that actually goes back thousands of years. To celebrate its 100th anniversary in 2008, St. Paul's Anglican Church constructed a classic 11-circuit labyrinth, to replicate the world's most famous labyrinth in France's Chartres Cathedral.

• At Ahnisnabae Art Gallery you'll find a celebration of First Nations art and culture. It is owned by Louise Thomas, wife of the late Roy Thomas, the internationally known Ahnisnabae artist whose works are prominent at the gallery. Roy's murals grace the walls of OLG Casino downtown. The gallery is on the corner of James Street South and Frederica Street West in Mount McKay Place, at 7-1500 James Street South (807-577-2656).

• For some local fare, try the well-known "Stanley Burger" at the century-old Stanley Hotel, Highway 588. The historic hotel by the banks of the Kaministiquia River serves the humongous burger – juicy special-recipe meat patty with king-sized toppings – alongside a big plate of homemade fries.

wintertime wilderness trip or up to two-day overnight camping trips into the Ontario back country. There's nothing like it to enjoy the winter. They also offer a unique summer sled dog experience on wilderness trails for families.

Mink Mountain Properties near the international border is a four-season area with hiking and ski trails, biking and winter recreation, access to Lake Superior for water sports, a lodge, dining room and a bar. Turn east toward the lake on Sturgeon Bay Road to Mink Mountain Drive. The view of the islands from the bluff is fantastic.

Notable Museums

There is no admission fee to the Thunder Bay Military Museum, which showcases regional heritage. In the Armory on Park Avenue, it is open Monday through Friday and Tuesday evenings.

Thunder Bay Historical Museum houses an extensive collection of artifacts from northwestern Ontario that includes prehistoric Indian, fur trade, mining and shipping relics, with the largest collection of Aboriginal beadwork in Canada. Open daily from June 15 through Labour Day. In winter, it is open Tuesday through Sunday. On Donald Street East.

Founders Museum and Pioneer Village at Gillespie Road and Highway 61 south of town has a large, detailed collection of antiques displayed in realistic indoor and outdoor settings, creating an early 1900 pioneer village unique to northwestern Ontario. The village has a pioneer home, carpenter, cobbler and blacksmith shops, an original one-room schoolhouse, church and heritage community hall, along with a replica of a 1908 train station. Visit the general store, village shops and library, and see the vintage cars and farm equipment. Well worth a couple of hours. Open daily mid-May to Labour Day.

Paipoonge Museum reflects the pioneer's life of the late 1800s. Homesteading was complete by 1905. A bit out of town, this museum preserves the memory of those who faced the frontier hardships. Open 1-5 p.m. early May through August, but closed Mondays and holidays. Take Highway 130 west from Highway 61 to the Rosslyn Road corner.

Northwestern Ontario Sports Hall of Fame and Museum is located on South May Street, with photographs, trophies and some equipment and memorabilia from popular regional sports.

Parks and Public Areas

Thunder Bay offers many wonderful parks, public areas and provincial parklands which preserve incredible landscapes. Many also offer camping and other amenities.

While the Chippewa Park and Wildlife Exhibit has a beach, playground and amusement park, a prime attraction is a 400-meter (1,312-foot) elevated boardwalk overlooking a natural exhibit of timber wolves, bear, deer, foxes and coyotes.

Another spot for an overview of the port of Thunder Bay is from Hillcrest Park, with colorful sunken gardens and a memorial. Head down the hill to see the port up close. At the bottom of the hill, turn south on Water Street then watch on the right for the ore docks, the elevators and Keefer Complex, the multi-million dollar general cargo facility.

Boulevard Lake Park in the city has a beach, boating, playgrounds, tennis courts, picnicking and lots of room for simply strolling. Boat rentals are available.

At International Friendship Gardens on Victoria Avenue, the city's ethnic diversity is celebrated in flowering plants and monuments. More than a dozen of Thunder Bay's ethnic groups have contributed unique gardens. Watch for signs to Centennial Botanical Conservatory, on Dease Street off Balmoral Avenue, where you'll stroll through tasteful landscapes of hundreds of plant species, and everything from tropical plants to desert plants. The conservatory is full of exotic flowers, trees, shrubs and plants from around the world. Open afternoons every day.

Centennial Park and Bushcamp Museum is an 847-acre area on Centennial Park Road, a circa-1910 northwoods camp with logging museum, blacksmith shop, bunkhouse, sauna and cookery. There is a barnyard with farm animals to pet. A narrow-gauge railroad circles the park. The lumber camp is open June through September, although the park is open year-round. Winter sleigh rides and ski trails are available.

Several Lakehead Conservation Areas in and around Thunder Bay area offer wide recreational options, from boating and fishing to hiking by cascading waters. A number access the Lake Superior shoreline. South of town near the international border on Cloud Bay Road off Highway 61 is Little Trout Bay. Silver Harbour is on Thunder Bay, 10 minutes east of the city, and has a boat launch and picnic area.

Within the city, Mission Island Marsh, in the south end, is one of the more popular sites. The area boasts a panoramic view of the Sleeping Giant, Lake Superior and Thunder Bay Harbour, as well as the extensive shoreline marsh that gives the area its name. Paths for walking and biking are found from the waterfront through other parts of the city, including the Neebing-McIntyre Floodway and Mackenzie Point conservation areas. The Cascades in the city has extensive hiking trails that lead along a set of long rapids. Wishart Falls' large jackpine boreal forest is about 11 kilometers (7 miles) north of the city and is ideal for skiing in the winter.

Hazelwood Lake, about 25 minutes north of the city, is the largest of the conservation areas, providing an excellent opportunity for outdoor family activities such as swimming or canoe and kayak rentals.

A complete map of the conservation areas is available from Lakehead Region Conservation Authority.

Ontario Parks offers ample opportunity to get close to nature in this area of Lake Superior. Non-residents of Ontario older than 18 must have a Crown Land Camping Permit to stay overnight on Crown land in northern Ontario, available from most Ontario license issuers and Ministry of Natural Resources offices. A CANPASS Remote Area Border Crossing permit allows the bearer to cross into Canada at certain remote areas without reporting to a port of entry as long as imported goods are declared. The service is available on border waters from Pigeon River to and including Lake of the Woods on the west and on the shore of Lake Superior. Applications are available at the international border crossing at Pigeon River in Ontario or the Thunder Bay Immigration Centre.

At the border and just north of the Ontario Travel Information Centre at Pigeon River is Pigeon River Provincial

Park where the focal point is the Pigeon River and its waterfalls. This park has the first Ontario views of Lake Superior.

Near the Information Centre take the trail to the Lake Superior shoreline viewing pod or explore the coastal hiking trail to Finger Point Lookout (2.4 kilometers/1.5 miles). These trails and recent improvements to the High Falls Trail are part of the Great Lakes Heritage Coast project, a national undertaking to accent and protect vast areas of habitat of Great Lakes shoreline.

The park's High Falls Trail is accessible from the Information Centre and climbs to a viewpoint above the High Falls of the Pigeon River (known as Pigeon Falls to some in the United States). Steep sections have wooden steps. Rated: intermediate. Additional park trails can be accessed from the Middle Falls Parking Area a couple of kilometers (a little more than a mile) up Highway 593.

Other nearby provincial parks are Quetico; La Verendrye, a deep wilderness park for the hardiest of adventurers located inland on the way to Sunset Country; Kakabeka Falls; Sleeping Giant; and, at the extreme eastern edge of the Thunder Bay area, Ouimet Canyon.

Notable Events

Thunder Bay calls itself the "city of festivals" and hosts major celebrations ranging from the July 1 Canada Day Celebration to events focusing on a wide range of culture and heritage. A sampling follows:

- Fort William Historical Park offers a

Marina Park is part of the beautiful scenery along Thunder Bay's renovated waterfront, which is still undergoing updates to make it a great spot for visitors and residents.

full summer-into-fall schedule of celebrations, heritage festivals and other significant events commemorating area fur-trade history.

• The Thunder Bay Blues Festival in early July brings a host of international blues acts to Marina Park.

• Great Rendezvous at Fort William Historical Park in July commemorates the summer gathering of voyageurs, Aboriginals and traders at the world's largest fur trade post on the Kam River.

• Canada Day Celebrations are observed in most cities on July 1.

• Thunder Bay Dragon Boat Race Festival in mid-July is a fundraiser for charities annually on Boulevard Lake.

• Anishnawbe Keeshigun at Fort William Historical Park in August celebrates the rich heritage of First Nations people who contributed to the history and heritage of the area.

Where to Shop

For a great variety of Canadian goods, check out Intercity Shopping Centre on Fort William Road, Victoriaville Village Centre on Victoria Avenue, County Fair Plaza on Dawson Road, the Arthur Street Marketplace just off Highway 11/17 Expressway and the Grandview Mall off River Street.

Thunder Bay is full of ethnic neighborhoods, especially strong in Finnish and Italian heritage. On East Bay Street, stop by the Finnish Book Store or Fireweed, where author Bill MacDonald of Porphry Press displays his books and works of local artists. Antiquers will want to check out Northern Light Antiques on Cumberland Avenue across from the Prince Arthur Waterfront Hotel.

Stop and browse at Chaltrek & Ostrom Outdoors on Balmoral Street for outdoor gear for activities from camping to climbing and snowshoeing (and products for your dog). A great hiking store downtown is Take A Hike on East Victoria Avenue, selling quality outdoor clothing, footwear (Merrell, Vasque and Sorel), all manner of gear – and even advice about places to hike if you should need it.

If you're seeking Ontario's official mineral, check the Precious Purple Gemstone amethyst store on East Victoria.

Highway 61 south of town is an area where visitors can discover surprising and interesting stops and shopping possibilities. Thunder Oak Cheese Farm, Ontario's only Gouda cheese-producing farm, is on Boundary Drive, west off of Highway 61 in the scenic Slate River Valley. Jacob and Margaret Schep make the natural cheese in eight flavors using milk from their own Holstein cows and Dutch family recipes that have won international awards. Take time to watch the entire cheese-making process

Amethyst Mines of Ontario

Near Pearl on Trans Canada Highway 11/17 north of Thunder Bay, keep an eye out for signs offering the chance to mine amethyst. It's Ontario's official gemstone, as well as the February birthstone. Ontario's amethyst industry began in the mid-1950s with the discovery of large deposits of the rock near Thunder Bay. The semiprecious gem can be found at the Blue Points Amethyst Mine, Ontario Gem Mining Company, which has a gift shop, and Amethyst Mine Panorama, the largest amethyst mine on the continent. Watch closely for signage along the road.

in operation and sample selections. The shop is open Monday through Saturday. On the way, you'll pass landscape photographer Susan Dykstra's Window Light Photo Gallery on Boundary Drive. Stop and see her wonderful work.

A bit farther south of town, Early Snows Bed-and-Breakfast Inn and Pottery offers a nice selection of ceramic goods and other artworks along with a pleasant overnighting possibility. On 3rd Side Road is Camellia's Fine Flowers and Gifts, a quaint shop with quilting and decorating ideas and supplies. In somewhat the same vicinity, Gammondale Farm on McCluskey Drive offers fun events such as the Haunted Cornfield and the annual Pumpkinfest on weekends leading up to Halloween. Another nearby farm on Candy Mountain Drive, Belluz Farms-Valley Berry Patch has seasonal crops for the picking and offers kids a half-hour or more of fun finding their way through the cornfield "maze in the maize that's amazing."

Near the outstanding Kakabeka Falls west on Highway 11/17, Kakabeka Falls Gift and Amethyst Shoppe gives amethyst fanciers the chance to check out "blueberry amethyst" that is mined from a local vein of the deep purple mineral.

What's Next

The Lake Superior Circle Tour route departs Thunder Bay either south on Highway 61 to the international border or northeast on Highway 11/17 toward Sleeping Giant Provincial Park, Silver Islet, Red Rock and Nipigon – depending on your direction. When traveling north of town, watch for signs to amethyst mines where you can pick your own or purchase Ontario's official gemstone. You'll also want to watch for Pass Lake to enter the road to the Sibley Peninsula, Sleeping Giant and Silver Islet. (See listings for Sibley Peninsula and Silver Islet.)

INFO & OPTIONS

North of Superior Tourism Association
920 Tungsten St., Ste. 206A
Thunder Bay, ON P7B 5Z6
800-265-3951
www.nosta.on.ca

Thunder Bay Tourism
P.O. Box 800, Station F
Thunder Bay, ON P7C 5K4
807-625-3972
www.thunderbay.ca

Terry Fox Information Centre
1000 Hwy. 11/17
Thunder Bay, ON P7A 0A1
800-667-8386
www.visitthunderbay.com

Armando Fine Italian Cuisine
28 North Cumberland St.
Thunder Bay, ON P7A 4K9
807-344-5833

Caribou Restaurant & Wine Bar
727 Hewitson St.
Thunder Bay, ON P7B 6B5
807-628-8588
www.caribourestaurant.com

Hoito Restaurant
314 Bay St.
Thunder Bay, ON P7B 1S1
807-345-6323

The Keg Steakhouse & Bar
735 Hewitson St.
Thunder Bay, ON
807-623-1960
http://en.kegsteakhouse.com

River Rock Bar and Grill
698 West Arthur St.
Thunder Bay, ON P7E R8
807-473-1600
www.travelodge-airlane.com

Timbers Restaurant, Nordic Dining Room
Valhalla Inn
1 Valhalla Inn Rd.
Thunder Bay, ON P7E 6J1
800-964-1121
www.valhallainn.com/dining

Best Western Crossroads Motor Inn
655 West Arthur St.
Thunder Bay, ON P7E 5R6
807-577-4241
www.bestwesternontario.com

Best Western Nor'Wester
2080 Hwy. 61
Thunder Bay, ON P7J 1B8
8007-473-9123
www.bestwestern.com

Prince Arthur Waterfront Hotel
17 North Cumberland St.
Thunder Bay, ON P7A 4K8
800-267-2675
www.princearthur.on.ca

Travelodge Hotel Airlane
698 West Arthur St.
Thunder Bay, ON P7E 5R8
800-465-5003
www.travelodge-airlane.com

Valhalla Inn
1 Valhalla Inn Rd.
Thunder Bay, ON P7E 6J1
800-964-1121
www.valhallainn.com

White Fox Inn
1345 Mountain Rd.
Thunder Bay, ON P7J 1C3
800-603-3699
www.whitefoxinn.com

Chippewa Park
1735 City Rd.
Thunder Bay, ON
888-711-5094
www.chippewapark.ca

Kakabeka Falls Provincial Park
P.O. Box 252
Kakabeka Falls, ON P0T 1W0
807-473-9231

KOA Kampgrounds & Resort
162 Spruce River Rd.
Thunder Bay, ON P7B 6B3
807-683-6221

Thunder Bay International Hostel/Campground
R.R. 13
1594 Lakeshore Dr.
Thunder Bay, ON P7B 5E4
807-983-2042

Trowbridge Falls Campground
Hwy. 11/17 to Copenhagen Rd.
Thunder Bay, ON
807-683-6661
www.thunderbay.ca/parks

Wawa

Population 3,300

Wawa is near the northern boundary of Lake Superior Provincial Park on Trans Canada Highway 17 on the eastern shore of Lake Superior. The name is derived from the Ojibway language, traditionally thought to translate as "goose." Wawa salutes its namesake with an 8.5-meter-high (28-foot), 4,400-pound steel Canada goose statue and log-constructed, red-roofed Wawa Tourist Information Centre at highways 17 and 101. The Big Goose commemorates completion of the last link of the Lake Superior portion of the Trans Canada Highway (and Circle Tour).

Travel beyond the Big Goose up Highway 101 a couple of kilometers to a downtown fitted with nearly any service needed by travelers. Wawa has shops, restaurants and motels, a hospital, a licensed spirits store, golf course, airport and charter planes.

While in Wawa, pick up a copy of the *Algoma News Review*, one of our favorite hometown papers around Lake Superior. Little in town escapes the eye of owner Tammy Landry.

A few miles from Lake Superior's shoreline, Wawa's economy has relied less on forest products than it has on mining. Gold mining has occurred in the area for more than 100 years and Wawa was the site of the first mining office in Ontario. As the gold rush fizzled, iron ore to stoke the mills at Sault Ste. Marie began to be mined. The Algoma Central Railway was created, and the town of Wawa was born along its line. The discovery of diamonds in the area is the latest buzz on the mineralogical hotline. The information center has a self-guided geology field tour of the area.

The Wawa Airport is a key fly-in entry point to the 12,000 inland wilderness lakes. In addition to outstanding fishing, hunters find an abundance of game in the Canadian bush country.

What to See and Do

Mr. Vallee Park in Wawa was started in 1984 by a local citizen. Here you find walkways, a great view of the town and a picnic area on the shore of Anderson Lake. Wawa Lake beachfront facilities include

Wawa's Canada goose statue, at highways 17 and 101, commemorates completion of the last link of the Lake Superior portion of the Trans Canada Highway, and thus the Circle Tour.

beach houses, washrooms, playgrounds and designated swimming areas. The nice sandy beach is a popular spot on a hot day. At Lion's Beach on Wawa Lake, look for the Gem Panning Station where one can enjoy panning for gemstones and diamonds in an authentic sluice.

Nearby is the Rotary Blasthole Drill, used in the construction of the St. Lawrence Seaway and in local mining. It's a part of the Wawa Heritage Walk's pathway along the shoreline of Wawa Lake.

Golfers can try their skills at the Michipicoten Golf Club near the airport.

It's worth taking a gander (goose pun intended) at several other sites around Wawa. There's the new Grandma Door display: more than 200 colorful doors lining the road into town. The doors, created by local residents, tell the stories of grandmothers from Wawa and around the world.

Young's General Store, about a kilometer from the airport as you enter town, lives up to its name and seems to make time stand still. Try a pickle straight out of the barrel and sample fresh vegetables right from the crate on the front porch. Kids will love the fresh fudge. Bring your camera. Anita Young and her friendly assistants are all local authorities and will be more than happy to assist you with knowledge of the area.

Young's also obtained and restored the smaller original Wawa goose to its full grandeur, and it now stands beside the store on a special perch. There is also a larger-than-life display of the mysterious inukshuk monuments found along the highway. These Inuit "little

South of Wawa, the Magpie Scenic High Falls roar toward Lake Superior. Visitors should prepare to get a little wet.

men" icons guide travelers on their way.

For winter activity, Wawa's network of groomed snowmobile trails exceeds 560 kilometers (350 miles). With more than adequate snowfall, the season runs from December to April. Snowmobilers visit from throughout the Midwest. Wawa hosts an Ice Fishing Derby each March.

The area where the Magpie River enters Lake Superior is a sandy delight. Moving a short way south on the Circle Tour route again, turn west on an unpaved road off Highway 17 about 3 kilometers (2 miles) to see the Magpie Scenic High Falls roar toward Lake Superior. Prepare to get a little wet from the mist. The road and parking lot accommodate buses. A picnic area and washroom facilities are available.

Take the Michipicoten River Village Road 5 kilometers (3 miles) south of Wawa toward Lake Superior to visit the townsite at the mouth of the Michipicoten River. As a result of the early Jesuit church, it's still called "The Mission."

The sign on the highway is hard to spot, so watch carefully for Buck's Marina, a 97-slip full-service marina with showers and lockers at the junction of the Michipicoten and Magpie rivers. Turn left in the Mission for Buck's, which has had an operation on this site for decades. Charter fishing, boat rentals and launch facilities are available. Since Buck's is inland on the river, the marina will guide deeper draft boats if contacted on VHF Channel 68. The channel is dredged to maintain good depth, but Buck's will offer boaters a ferry service if the draft is too shallow. The annual Wawa Salmon Derby, one of the largest on Lake Superior, is in August. Inquire at Buck's.

You'll also want to see Silver Falls, so turn right at the townsite intersection and go to the bridge over the Magpie River. Park just before the bridge, which overlooks the confluence of the Magpie and Michipicoten rivers above Buck's Marina.

If you cross the bridge and proceed another kilometer (about a mile) past the hydro dam, you'll find a lookout we discovered that offers a panoramic view of Lake Superior, including the Michipicoten Harbour to the north and Michipicoten Island on the horizon. This area is unprotected, but there is room to pull the vehicle to the side of the dirt road. Signs mark the way.

Outdoor adventurers will want to check with Naturally Superior Adventures for either camping or accommodations at Rock Island Lodge at the mouth of the Michipicoten River and for sea kayaking, hiking or other outdoor pleasures in spectacular settings.

Notable Events

- Wawa hosts a Winter Carnival in February.
- Wawa Ice Fishing Derby is in late February/early March.
- Canada Day Celebration is held July 1.
- Wawa Salmon Derby is in late August.

What's Next

Gas up before leaving Wawa, since you're entering a leg of the Circle Tour route with fewer service stations. You'll travel Highway 17 to proceed either north or south. To the north is White River and Marathon. To the south you'll pass through Lake Superior Provincial Park and smallish towns on the way to Sault Ste. Marie, some 225 kilometers (140 miles) away.

INFO & OPTIONS

Wawa Tourist Information Centre
40 Broadway Ave.
P.O. Box 500
Wawa, ON P0S 1K0
800-367-9292
www.wawa.cc

Wawa Ministry of Natural Resources District Office
Hwy. 101
P.O. Box 1160
Wawa, ON P0S 1K0
705-856-2396

Young's General Store
111 Mission Rd.
P.O. Box 1459
Wawa, ON P0S 1K0
705-856-2626
www.youngsgeneralstore.com

Kinniwabi International Cuisine
136 Hwy. 17 South
Wawa, ON P0S 1K0
705-856-7226

Best Northern Motel
Hwy. 17
P.O. Box 1429
Wawa, ON PoS 1K0
800-434-8240
www.bestnorthern.ca

Mystic Isle Motel
P.O. Box 1490
Wawa, ON P0S 1K0
800-667-5895
www.mysticisle.com

Rock Island Lodge/Naturally Superior Adventures
R.R. 1 Lake Superior
Wawa, ON P0S
705-856-2939
www.naturallysuperior.com

Wawa Motor Inn
118 Mission Rd.
Box 1190
Wawa, ON P0S 1K0
800-561-2278
www.wawamotorinn.com

Lake Superior Provincial Park
P.O. Box 267
Wawa, ON P0S 1K0
705-856-2284
Agawa Bay Visitor Centre
705-882-2026
www.lakesuperiorpark.ca

Wawa RV Resort & Campground
Hwy. 17
Magpie Rd. 634A
Wawa, ON P0S 1K0
877-256-4368
www.wawarv.com

White Lake Provincial Park

White Lake Provincial Park, 60 kilometers (36 miles) east of Marathon on Trans Canada Highway 17, is an ideal family getaway with its sheltered basin, sandy beaches and swimming. Visitors can enjoy camping, hiking, fishing, boating, canoeing and interpretive programs. Look for natural treasures, such as orchids and bogs with insect-eating plants, along the trails. The park has 187 campsites (60 electrical); reservations are recommended. Embark for a five-day canoe trip along White River through Pukaskwa National Park into Lake Superior. Open mid-May to late September. Across the lake, Mobert Indian Reserve (population 232) was the site of an early Hudson's Bay Trading Post.

White River

Population 1,000

More than 75 kilometers (47 miles) from Lake Superior on the Inland Plateau (the rising topography to the northeast of Lake Superior), White River doesn't receive any climactic benefit from warm lake waters in winter. It gets cold here. In 1935, the mercury is reported to have bottomed out at minus 58 degrees Celsius (minus 72 degrees Fahrenheit). For the record, Environment Canada shows the lowest reading to be minus 52 C (minus 61 F). Some think the thermometer broke that day. Whatever the details, the sign reading "Coldest spot in Canada" still stands unchallenged.

White River is known as the birthplace of Winnie-the-Pooh, A.A. Milne's famous storybook character. Actually, Christopher Robin (Milne's son) really existed, and so did Winnie, a bear cub that Lieutenant Harry Colebourn, a veterinarian in the Canadian Army, bought in White River en route overseas. The officer named the female cub after his hometown of Winnipeg, Manitoba. When Harry went off to serve in France in 1914, Winnie was left with the London Zoo. Five years later, he gave Winnie to the zoo, where she was loved by many, including A.A. Milne and son, Christopher Robin. She sparked the idea for the author's fictional Winnie-the-pooh character. A statue of the bear cub reminds visitors of the town's place in history. Winnie's Hometown Festival is the third weekend in August.

There are several motels and gift stores in White River. Beyond White River on Highway 17, Obatanga Provincial Park is a vast area of northern wilderness laced with 32 lakes, rivers and streams. Visitors can enjoy canoeing, hiking, bird-watching and camping – the park has 130 campsites, 20 with electrical service – within a mature jack pine forest on the shores of Burnfield Lake. The interior, where anglers catch the best walleye, perch and pike, is often accessible only by canoe. Visitors have been known to observe great blue herons, bald eagles, osprey and songbirds of the boreal forest. Open mid-May to early September.

A Winnie-the-Pooh statue at White River, home of the real cub that inspired the tales.

What's Next

If there's a "corner" in this leg of the Circle Route, it occurs at White River. The Lake Superior Circle Tour follows Highway 17 either northwesterly to Marathon or south along the inland boundary of Pukaskwa National Park heading for Wawa. The route to Nipigon is about 272 kilometers (169 miles) and Sault Ste. Marie is a 319-kilometer (198-mile) drive.

INFO & OPTIONS

White River Visitor Information Centre

Hwy. 17 & Elgin St.
White River, ON
888-517-1673
www.whiteriver.ca

Lake Superior Wisconsin

Raspberry Island Lighthouse, recently restored, is one of many treasures to see as part of an Apostle Islands cruise excursion.

Wisconsin's Lake Superior shoreline includes the south shore's sandy beaches and the wondrous Apostle Islands National Lakeshore, a paradise for kayakers and sightseers, with its sea caves and historic lighthouses. Wisconsin is also small fishing villages and Bayfield Peninsula's fertile farms and fragrant apple orchards. It's a place of sailing and lighthouse tour boats, great concerts under the Big Top and a place of famous shipwrecks and cool museums waiting to be explored.

Wisconsin Tourism Information

Travel Wisconsin/Wisconsin Department of Tourism
800-432-8747
www.tourism.state.wi.us

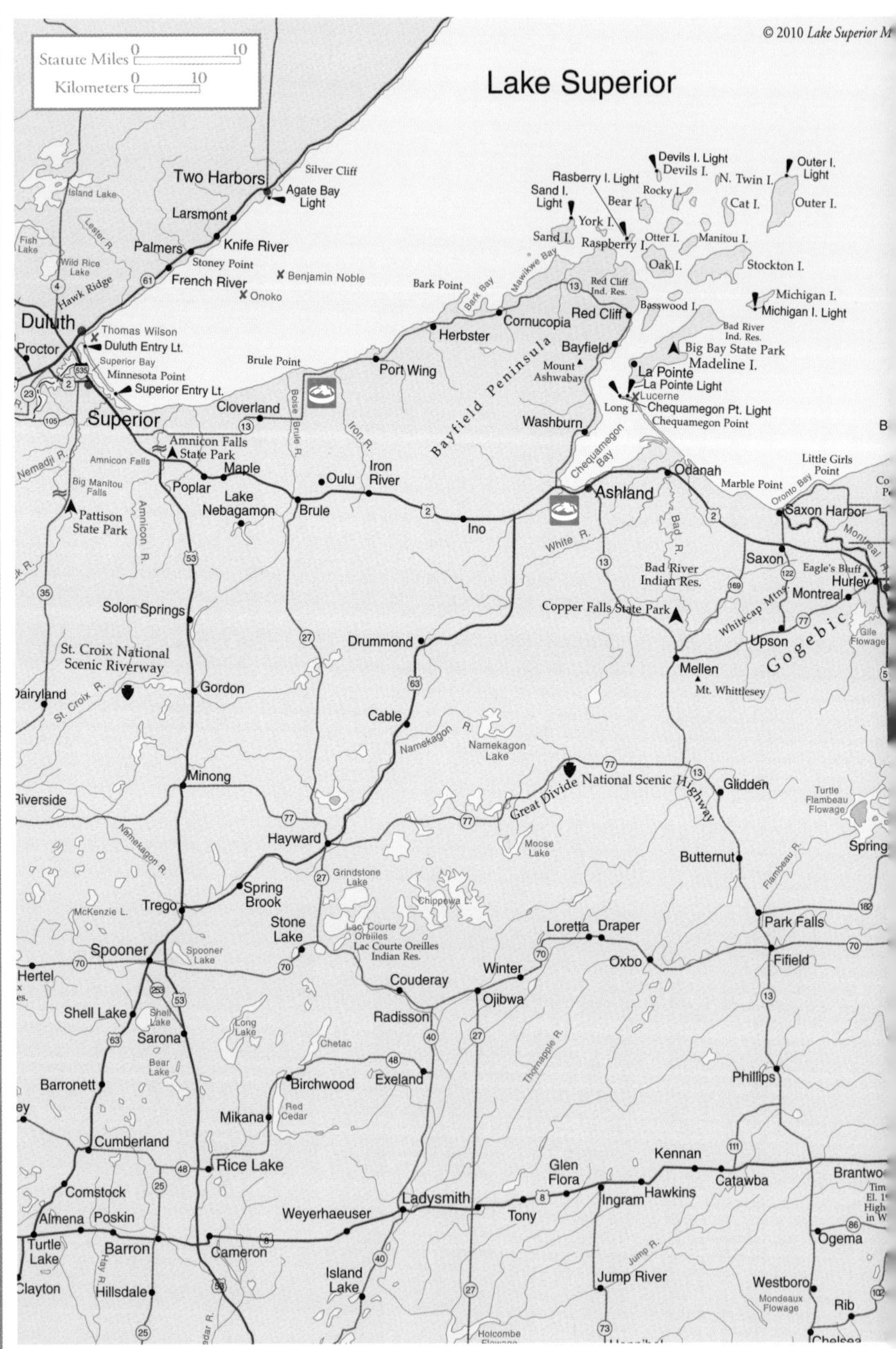
© 2010 Lake Superior M
Statute Miles 0 10
Kilometers 0 10
Lake Superior
Two Harbors
Silver Cliff
Agate Bay Light
Larsmont
Knife River
Palmers
Stoney Point
French River
Benjamin Noble
Onoko
Duluth
Thomas Wilson
Duluth Entry Lt.
Proctor
Superior Bay
Minnesota Point
Superior Entry Lt.
Superior
Cloverland
Brule Point
Port Wing
Bark Point
Herbster
Cornucopia
Bayfield Peninsula
Red Cliff
Red Cliff Ind. Res.
Bayfield
Mount Ashwabay
Washburn
Chequamegon Bay
Ashland
Odanah
Devils I. Light
Devils I.
Rasberry I. Light
Sand I. Light
Rocky I.
Bear I.
York I.
Sand I.
Raspberry I.
Otter I.
Manitou I.
Oak I.
N. Twin I.
Cat I.
Outer I. Light
Outer I.
Stockton I.
Michigan I.
Michigan I. Light
Basswood I.
Bad River Ind. Res.
Big Bay State Park
Madeline I.
La Pointe
La Pointe Light
Lucerne
Long I.
Chequamegon Pt. Light
Chequamegon Point
Little Girls Point
Marble Point
Oronto Bay
Saxon Harbor
Montreal
Saxon
Eagle's Bluff
Hurley
Montreal
Whitecap Mtn.
Gile Flowage
Upson
Gogebic
Bad R.
Bad River Indian Res.
Copper Falls State Park
Mellen
Mt. Whittlesey
White R.
Amnicon Falls State Park
Amnicon Falls
Maple
Poplar
Lake Nebagamon
Brule
Oulu
Iron River
Iron R.
Bois Brule R.
Ino
Nemadji R.
Big Manitou Falls
Pattison State Park
Amnicon R.
Island Lake
Lester R.
Fish Lake
Wild Rice Lake
Hawk Ridge
Solon Springs
St. Croix National Scenic Riverway
St. Croix R.
Dairyland
Gordon
Drummond
Cable
Namekagon R.
Namekagon Lake
Great Divide National Scenic Highway
Glidden
Turtle Flambeau Flowage
Minong
Riverside
Namekagon R.
Hayward
Moose Lake
Butternut
Flambeau R.
Spring
Grindstone Lake
Spring Brook
Chippewa L.
McKenzie L.
Trego
Stone Lake
Lac Courte Oreilles
Lac Courte Oreilles Indian Res.
Loretta
Draper
Park Falls
Spooner
Spooner Lake
Oxbo
Fifield
Hertel
Couderay
Winter
Ojibwa
Shell Lake
Shell Lake
Radisson
Sarona
Long Lake
Chetac
Thornapple R.
Bear Lake
Birchwood
Exeland
Phillips
Barronett
Red Cedar
Mikana
Cumberland
Rice Lake
Kennan
Glen Flora
Catawba
Brantwo
Comstock
Hawkins
Ingram
Ladysmith
Tony
Almena
Poskin
Weyerhaeuser
Ogema
Turtle Lake
Barron
Cameron
Hay R.
Jump R.
Island Lake
Jump River
Westboro
Mondeaux Flowage
Clayton
Hillsdale
Rib
Holcombe Flowage
Chelsea
Tim El. 1 High in W
Red Cedar R.

Apostle Islands National Lakeshore

Twenty-one of the 22 islands (Madeline Island excluded, see separate entry) and 2,500 acres of the Bayfield Peninsula mainland make up the Apostle Islands National Lakeshore area, one of only four national lakeshores in the country (two of which are on Lake Superior). It is operated out of Bayfield by the National Park Service and is available for visitors to enjoy. The park includes historic fish camps, lighthouses, beaches, sandstone cliffs, "sea caves" and remnant virgin timber. The lakeshore covers 69,372 acres (27.9 hectares), of which 42,140 (17 hectares) are above the waterline.

Stop at the lakeshore's Visitor Center in the Old County Courthouse in Bayfield, where you'll see the Fresnel lens from the Michigan Island Lighthouse exhibited. Turn north off Wisconsin 13, one block to Washington Avenue.

Other visitor or contact centers are at Little Sand Bay and Stockton Island. The Park Service maintains the Manitou Island Fish Camp, Hokenson Historic Site at Little Sand Bay and Raspberry Island Lighthouse and gardens. National Park Service volunteers usually occupy the light stations at Sand, Devils, Michigan and Outer islands. Tours are available daily when personnel are present.

From the west, we suggest approaching the Apostles via the western Bayfield Peninsula by taking Wisconsin Highway 13 from U.S. Highway 2 through the small villages of Port Wing, Herbster, Cornucopia and Red Cliff to Bayfield. From the east, catch Highway 13 north to Washburn and Bayfield just west of Ashland.

A Bit of History

Long known to Native Americans and voyageurs, the Apostle Islands, and more particularly Madeline Island, were important in the fur trade from about 1700 until about 1850. Commercial fishing commenced for a few years in the 1830s by the American Fur Company, but it would be the late 1800s before it became a major source of income to local fishermen. Logging was also important in the economy for a period in the late 1800s and early 1900s before the timber was depleted. Fishing remained a primary economic factor until the late 1900s, when the industry was devastated by the invasion of the lamprey eel. Meanwhile, the islands, again particularly Madeline, began attracting visitors. Some built summer homes, while others came back year after year to relish the fabulous scenery and the mild, healthful air. By 1970, enough support had been generated that the U.S. Park Service designated 21 islands and a sizable acreage of mainland as Apostle Islands National Lakeshore to protect and preserve the natural and historic qualities found there.

Today

Today, a few fishermen still eke out income by setting nets, but recreation and tourism have become the mainstay of the local economy. The national lakeshore attracts thousands of visitors each year and the communities of the Bayfield Peninsula have done much to accent their amenities for visitors.

What to See and Do

More than 50 miles (80 kilometers) of trails are maintained in the national lakeshore. Camping is permitted on 18 of

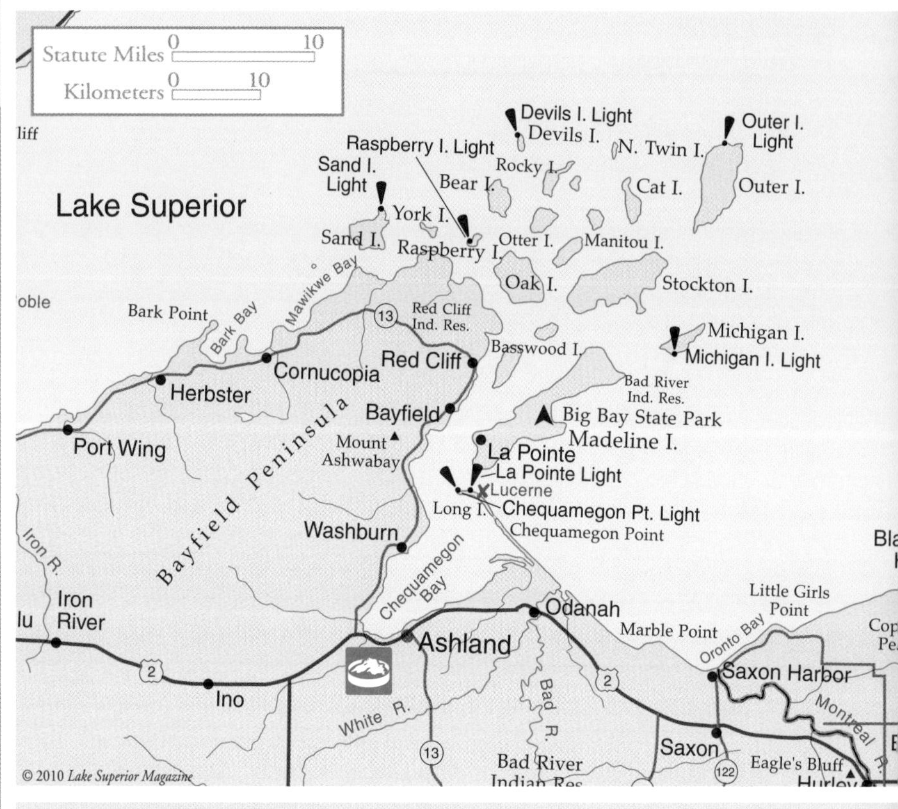

Apostle Islands

the 21 islands. A fee is charged for camping permits. The Apostle Islands Cruise Service is one way to get to the Apostle Islands aboard the *Island Princess* or *Ashland Bay Express*. The tours offer three-hour narrated boat excursions around 19 of the 22 Apostle Islands mid-May through mid-October. From mid-June through Labor Day, choose from a variety of cruises, including sunset cruises and island shuttles for camping, day hiking or touring a lighthouse.

The Apostles are the site of numerous shipwrecks. Divers will appreciate the installation of mooring buoys at two of the more popular wrecks. A number of wrecks are visible from the surface in good weather. Contact Apostle Islands National Lakeshore for free diving permits and a brochure describing dive sites.

Notable Events

• Round the Islands Race Week celebrates the marine heritage of the area with exciting sailing action each year in June.

• Apostle Islands Lighthouse Celebration through most of September is an annual celebration of the historic lights that shone the way through the island for early mariners.

• Chequamegon Chef's Exhibition in

June gives visitors and residents to Madeline Island a chance to sample the best of the area's cookery.

• Annual Star Bar Softball Tournament is a fun competition on Madeline Island challenging top teams from the area.

INFO & OPTIONS

Apostle Islands National Lakeshore Visitor Center
415 Washington Ave.
Bayfield, WI 54814
715-779-3397
www.nps.gov/apis

Ashland

Population 8,695

Ashland is situated on the southern shore of Chequamegon (Shu-kwa-ma-gon) Bay of Lake Superior right on U.S. Highway 2 from either the east or west. The city is home to Northland College and the Sigurd Olson Environmental Institute. The college specializes in environmental and Native American studies in a liberal arts setting. The Ashland campus of Wisconsin Indianhead Technical College offers training in many vocational and specialty areas and offers classes in other locations of the region.

Visitors will receive a warm welcome at the Ashland Area Chamber of Commerce on U.S. Highway 2, a good place to start. It's equipped with brochures, books and maps of the city, Ashland County, the entire Chequamegon Bay area and neighboring counties in northeastern Wisconsin. The Chequamegon Bay area offers a wealth of delightful birding opportunities for those seeking to add species to their list of sightings. A "Birding by the Bay" brochure guides birders to the best sites and is available at area information centers and other outlets.

Shopping, lodging and dining are terrific in this historic city. Ashland has public bus service between 6 a.m. and 4:30 p.m. through the Bay Area Rural Transit system, which serves the entire Chequamegon Bay area from Odanah and Ashland to Red Cliff on the Bayfield Peninsula. Ashland's JFK Airport is home to the only full-service "log" terminal in the state, constructed of red pine logs from Bayfield County.

Check Ashland's *Daily Press* for the latest news and events. Visitors are reminded that smoking is banned in most public places, so it's best to check before lighting up.

A Bit of History

The historical record of Ashland traces back to 1658 when the French explorers and fur traders Radisson and Groseilliers built a cabin on the waterfront of Chequamegon Bay and spent the winter there before going on to collect furs at other stops on Lake Superior. The cabin is the first residence known to have been built on Lake Superior by non-native people. In the intervening period to the present, Ashland has been successively important in the fur trade (circa 1700-1840), logging and lumbering (1880-1900), the quarrying of brownstone (1880-1900), transportation, manufacturing and tourism (1860s-present). Founded by Asaph Whittlesey in 1854, the town was almost immediately abandoned by all but one family in 1857 until the Civil War ended. The announcement that a railroad was planned through the city revived the hopes of pioneers and the 1877 arrival of that railroad assured the future of the settlement.

By the 1880s, Ashland became an important producer of lumber products, and Frederick Prentice started quarrying brownstone along Chequamegon Bay and the Apostle Islands for use in building construction. A significant number of buildings in the city reflect the importance of that enterprise.

Commercial fishing became significant in the 1890s and remained active until the lamprey eel invasion all but killed off the native fish species. A few fishermen still set nets, but their market is largely the area's eateries.

With mid-1880s development of the Gogebic Iron Range to the east, Ashland's harbor became a focal point of shipping interests, which had previously been devoted to handling lumber cargoes. With depletion of the iron ore in the 1950s, the harbor's importance waned, but the waterfront was rejuvenated by building a large marina and other attractions in the latter 20th century. Today, it's a vital player in the promotion of tourism, which increased significantly through the 1900s as visitors discovered the beauty and magic of the Lake Superior region.

Today

As the county seat of Ashland County, the city retains its role as the vibrant hub of government, business and retail for the sizable surrounding area to the present. Several manufacturing firms are located in and around the city, providing employment for a sizable number of skilled workers. In addition, Ashland's Memorial Medical Center is a regional facility for the area and a significant employer, as is Northland College and Wisconsin Indianhead Technical College. Timber remains a viable product in the area, with a number of successful logging firms and manufacturers of logging equipment in the area. And, as the area's tourism industry has grown, the number of facilities geared to visitors has grown apace. Northern Great Lakes Visitor Center is just one example of impressive amenities added in the area during the past decade or two.

What to See and Do

Downtown Ashland is home to a number of wall-sized murals that depict the heritage and early life of the area. In fact, Ashland has been named Historic Mural Capital of Wisconsin. Guides to the murals are available at the chamber office, or download a podcast of the mural walk from the chamber website's interactive page.

The historic Soo Line Depot near Central Railyard Park has been renovated. Baldwin Locomotive *#950*, the largest in the world when it was built, is exhibited at the Depot. An important workhorse in Ashland ore dock operations from 1942 to 1954, it was dedicated as a historical display by the city in 1957. A playground for children in nearby Central Railyard Park offers a welcome chance for travel-weary kids to burn energy.

Ashland Historical Society Museum holds the history of the first century and a half of the city in the 500 block of West Main Street. Open daily.

Behind Hotel Chequamegon, the 140-slip, full-service Ashland Harbor and Marina reflects the beauty of Chequamegon Bay. It has annual dockage, moorings, transient slips and full fuel and pumpout facilities. Seaplane dockage is available.

The Band Shell on the waterfront at Memorial Park has open-air concerts Thursday evenings during the summer and offers pleasant surroundings for a picnic. The park is the focal point for the annual Ashland Bay Days Festival in July. Ashland's Lakewalk is a delightful way to stretch your legs.

Each October, the city celebrates its heritage as a rail and shipping center with the Ashland WhistleStop Festival, which is marked with many fun activities centering in a huge heated tent in the downtown area.

Northern Great Lakes Visitor Center, 2.5 miles (4 kilometers) west of Ashland on Highway 2, provides information about the northern tri-state region and offers services every day, year-round with free admission. The 36,000-square-foot center gives visitors an over-the-trees panoramic view of Lake Superior from a 70-foot (21-meter) observation tower. Interactive exhibits help make regional stories come alive, and the 2,500-square-foot main exhibition hall shows how human cultures interact with the land and natural resources of the northern Great Lakes region. A 100-seat theater is used to further the interpretive and educational goals of the center. Look also for the nature discovery area, a place for kids to discover the great outdoors. Trails allow visitors access to the wetland area near the center, which is abundant with wildlife; and snowshoers and cross-

Northern Great Lakes Visitor Center, just west of Ashland, has interactive exhibits that make regional history come alive. Outside, look for the boardwalk and interpretive trails.

Yes, this is a mural. Ashland is home to a number of wall-sized murals that depict the heritage of the area. Guides to the murals are available from the Ashland Chamber of Commerce.

country skiers are welcomed in winter. The center houses the Wisconsin Historical Society's History Center and Archives, part of the area research center.

The city sports the Chequamegon Bay Golf Course, an 18-hole, par 72 course. Although owned by the Ashland Elks Lodge, which makes its home there, the course is open to the public.

During winter, Ashland gets a good share of snow, which makes snowmobiling and winter sports most attractive. An annual ice fishing event is held on the bay, along with the Ashland Snowcross and Terrain X Race. Auto racing on the ice is also popular. Cross-country skiing is available nearby.

Parks and Public Areas

Prentice Park, largest of Ashland's 12 parks, is a secluded area perfect for picnics. It offers the pure cold water of artesian wells and there are hiking trails, viewing platforms, a playground and tent camping. Other parks you may want to check out are Bayview on the east end, Kreher in the center of town, and Maslowski in the western side of town. Swimming beaches are available along Highway 2 at Bayview Park on Ashland's east end, Kreher Park and RV Campground in the center of town and Maslowski Beach on the west end of Ashland.

Notable Events

• Winter Lake Fest/Book Across the Bay Ski/Snowshoe Tour and Race in February attracts hundreds of winter enthusiasts for outdoor fun and a chance to race or tour across the bay by candlelight.

• Top of North Farm and Garden Show in February celebrates the upcoming growing season with the latest products for farmers and gardeners.

• Home & Sport Show in April showcases everything from appliances to outdoor gear.

• Wisconsin's Largest House-to-House Garage Sale in May is a citywide "housecleaning" where you may find just about anything for sale.

• Chequamegon Woods to Water Relay in late May is a race by teams from Cable in Chequamegon National Forest to the waterfront in Ashland.

• Big Granite Inline Marathon/Half Marathon in mid-June challenges skaters to post the fastest time from Marengo to Ashland.

• Ice Cream Social on the Courthouse lawn is held in conjunction with the city's July Fourth celebration, parade and fireworks.

• Bay Days in mid-July pulls out all the stops to celebrate life along Lake Superior and Chequamegon Bay.

• Red Clay Classic Stock Car Races and Racers' Ball in early October is the final auto racing challenge of the season at ABC Raceway.

• WhistleStop Festival in early October celebrates the city's heritage as an important railroading center.

• Garland City of the North Parade in early December anticipates the holidays with fun family events and a giant parade.

Where to Shop

A plenitude of shops offer a wide variety of regional gifts. Many of the city's businesses are located in historic buildings constructed of locally quarried brownstone. The city of Ashland offers many shopping opportunities both on Lakeshore Drive (U.S. 2) and one block south on historic Main Street. The designs of old Ashland have been preserved in a historic district, including the courthouse, City Hall and Post Office.

Find gifts, collectibles and fine area products at Superior Framing and Gallery, New England Store, Spirit of the North Gift Shop and Home Expressions.

What's Next

From Ashland, take Highway 2 east toward Hurley and Ironwood, Michigan. To the west lie several small towns on the way to Superior, Wisconsin, and Duluth, Minnesota. Highway 13 just west of Ashland leads to Washburn, Bayfield and the Bayfield Peninsula.

INFO & OPTIONS

Ashland Chamber of Commerce
800-284-9484
P.O. Box 746
Ashland, WI 54806
www.visitashland.com

L.C. Wilmarth's Deep Water Grille & South Shore Brewery
808 West Main St.
Ashland, WI 54806
715-682-4200
www.southshorebrewery.com

AmericInn of Ashland
3009 Lakeshore Dr. East
Ashland, WI 54806
800-396-5007
www.ashlandsplashland.com

Hotel Chequamegon
101 Lake Shore Dr. West
Ashland, WI 54806
800-946-5555
www.hotelc.com

The Inn at Timber Cove
1319 Sanborn Ave.
Ashland, WI 54806
715-682-9600
www.innattimbercove.com

Kreher Park & RV Campground

2020 Sixth St. East
Ashland, WI 54806
715-682-7061

Prentice Park

Turner Road off U.S. 2, Ashland
800-284-9484

Bad River Reservation

Population: 1,500

Traveling U.S. Highway 2 in northern Wisconsin, you'll go through the Bad River Indian Reservation, home of the Bad River Band of Lake Superior Chippewa. With the Red Cliff Chippewa tribal reservation, this is one of two reservations in Apostle Islands Country and the largest in Wisconsin. In Odanah, you can enjoy gaming at the Bad River Lodge and Casino. It's one of the log buildings beside the highway. The tribe also operates a grocery/convenience store near the casino, and construction has expanded convention and restaurant space at the lodge. The restaurant offers a variety of dining.

The band is known for its operation of a fish hatchery and wild rice gathering at the nearby Kakagon Sloughs.

Boaters will find a refurbished harbor of refuge, short-term dockage, parking, boat launch and restroom facilities at the western edge of the Bad River Reservation. Second Landing is at the foot of Reykdahl Road about 2 miles (3 kilometers) east of Ashland.

What's Next

Traveling east on Highway 2 from Bad River takes you to Hurley and Ironwood, Michigan. Westerly, you're heading for Ashland.

Bayfield

Population 611

Bayfield is a New England-style town, nestled into a Lake Superior hillside and sporting a sparkling bayfront on the eastern shoreline of Wisconsin's Bayfield Peninsula. One of the favorite destinations on Lake Superior, the population swells during summer.

Steeped in water heritage, Bayfield, closest town to the Apostle Islands, holds its annual Apple Festival the first weekend in October and presents original arts and crafts in all forms.

Called the Gateway to the Apostles, Bayfield was named the Best Little Town in the Midwest by the *Chicago Tribune*. Bayfield's waterborne commerce includes fishing, tour boating, sailing and ferryboats. Its bent for the arts has it boasting a variety of galleries displaying a wide choice of items. This is also right in the heart of some of the best birding opportunities around Lake Superior. A "Birding by the Bay" brochure guides birders to the best sites and is available at area information centers and other outlets.

The Circle Tour route follows Highway 13 from Bayfield, with westbound travelers heading northward to Red Cliff and the western Bayfield Peninsula villages of Cornucopia, Herbster and Port Wing. Eastbound travelers will head south out of Bayfield toward Washburn and Ashland to continue on their trip.

A Bit of History

Although nearby La Pointe on Madeline Island (see separate listings) is one of Lake Superior's oldest settlements, the area around Bayfield is the traditional homeland of the Ojibway people and was

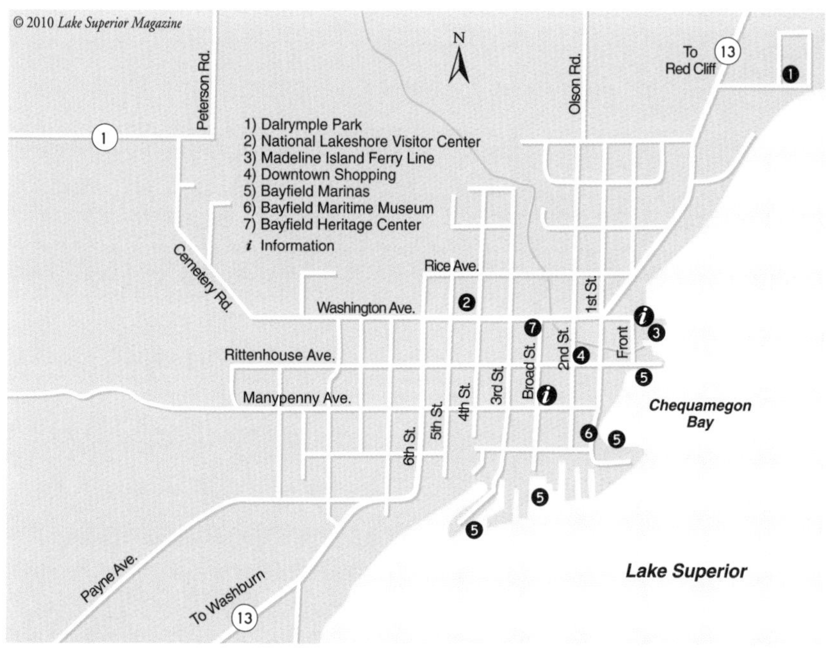

Bayfield

important during the voyageur and fur trade eras. By the latter 1800s, Bayfield had also become important in both the lumber industry (briefly) and commercial fishing, which is still taking place today. Many of the large homes in town date from that period. In the second half of the 20th century, tourism became a dominant economic factor, as visitors discovered the romantic charm and terrific scenic beauty of the Bayfield Peninsula.

Today

Visitors will find dozens of shops, bayfront lodgings, eateries and other amenities in the downtown area. Museums, nearly every service a visitor might desire, and friendly, attentive people make this a favorite destination. The turn-of-the-century mansions, churches and commercial buildings house the shops, galleries and bed-and-breakfast inns for which the town is known.

What to See and Do

A 50-block area of this charming hillside community has been designated as a historic district on the National Register of Historic Places. The Bayfield Chamber of Commerce & Visitor Bureau has information on a self-guided walking tour that will give you an afternoon of history as well as some exercise. There also are 90-minute Bayfield Heritage Tours that offer guided, narrated walking treks, including a Mansion & Gardens stroll that visits 24 historic Bayfield structures listed on the National Register, and a ghost walk lighted by lanterns.

During the summer, a farmers' market is open near Maggie's Restaurant on Manypenny Avenue each Saturday.

Do take a tour of apple orchards and fruit farms along the hilltop above town. Stop at Erickson Orchard & Country Store for good treats (like the apple cider doughnuts and pies), gourmet foods, gifts such as handmade glassware, and classic antiques. You can pick your own apples. Hauser's Superior View Farm takes its name from the view, 600 feet (183 meters) above lake level. A variety of plants, flowers and trees is available here, ready to be transplanted into your own garden. The farm has a large variety of apples and apple products, as well as homemade jams and jellies and dried flowers. It is home to the Bayfield Winery, which produces hard ciders and wines from local fruits and berries. Check out the miniature tractor collection and farm antiques in the historic Sears-Roebuck mail-order barn. Blue Vista Farm provides beautiful views of the area and features a picturesque 100-year-old barn – built with fieldstone, mortar and big timbers – that serves as the retail shop. Blue Vista sells apples, blueberries, raspberries, vegetables, gourds and pumpkins. Bayfield Apple Company has several interesting combinations of fruits and you can watch them concoct their juices, jellies, jams and apple mustard (absolutely delicious). Other orchards and farms to check for specialty produce include Highland Valley, Apple Hill, Rabideaux,Weber, Hillcrest and Sunset Valley.

On Bayfield's waterfront, sailboats may be heading out to explore the beautiful Apostle Islands National Lakeshore, while ferry boats handle visitors to nearby Madeline Island.

Three miles (4.8 kilometers) south of Bayfield on Wisconsin 13, wax your skis and enjoy 40 miles (64 kilometers) of groomed cross-country trails at Mount Ashwabay, a ski area with an acronym name made from the first syllables of Ashland, Washburn and Bayfield. Turn west on Ski Hill Road off Wisconsin Highway 13. Trails vary from old logging roads to hilly slopes. Mt. Ashwabay has 14 downhill runs for all skill levels, snowmaking capability, ski rental, instruction, food and a chalet. Open Wednesday through Saturday for downhill and daily for cross-country skiing.

Also at Mt. Ashwabay, signs will direct you to where Lake Superior Big Top Chautauqua offers unique professional summer entertainment – culture under canvas. The Big Top features the popular historical musicals of Bayfield, Washburn and the Chequamegon region and well-known national performers. The season runs from early June through Labor Day. Bay Area Rural Transit buses provide pickup from various locations in the area.

A series of hiking and biking trails begins near the Chamber visitor center at Manypenny and Broad. Of particular interest are the Brownstone and Iron Bridge walking trails. Visitors with kids will appreciate the playground near the Coast Guard station or the new playground at Manypenny Avenue and Seventh Street.

Apostle Islands Cruise Service offers water-level views among the Apostle Islands on its *Island Princess* or *Ashland Bay Express*. The three-hour narrated excursions around 19 of the 22 islands are offered mid-May through mid-October. From mid-June through Labor Day, a variety of cruises include sunset and island shuttles.

Madeline Island Ferry Line provides a regular schedule of vehicle and passenger service between Bayfield and La Pointe on Madeline Island on one of four boats. In winter, a windsled provides service until the ice freezes hard enough to support traffic, when an ice road is maintained between the towns. The ferry is a great way to see both towns, as well as the countryside around them. It's especially grand during the fall color season.

For boaters, Apostle Islands Marina offers services including seasonal and transient dockage, winter storage, a 35-ton Travelift, service department and ships store.

Golfers will enjoy Apostle Highlands Golf Course. It has golfers teeing off over a miniature Lake Superior on the first hole and offers a great panoramic view of the Apostle Islands and the entire bay area from 500 feet above the lake.

Outdoor enthusiasts can check out the services of Living Adventures, which offers a variety of kayaking adventures, including sea kayaking in the Apostle Islands. Apostle Islands Kayaks also provides kayaking opportunities on Madeline Island. Scuba enthusiasts will want to visit Superior Adventures.

Visitors wanting to stay fit or to get into shape can check out the Bayfield Recreation Center, offering a fitness center, swimming pool, whirlpool and racquetball court.

Anglers looking for Lake Superior fishing action should contact Hudson's on the Spot Guide Service.

Notable Museums

Bayfield Heritage Center on North

Broad Street is open during the summer with interpretive exhibits, tours, educational programming and seminars. Look for special events in the off-season. Fee.

Bayfield Maritime Museum at Wilson Avenue and First Street is an interesting stop, featuring exhibits of a wide range of nautical paraphernalia, items from Bayfield's commercial fishing industry and Great Lakes artifacts. Summers only. Fee.

Parks and Public Areas

Apostle Islands National Lakeshore is the predominant parkland of the area, encompassing nearly 70,000 acres of which 42,140 are above the water. With 21 of the 22 Apostle Islands and a sizable chunk of mainland within its boundary, this is one of two areas on Lake Superior to carry the national lakeshore designation (the other is Pictured Rocks in Michigan's Upper Peninsula). Stop at the lakeshore's Visitor Center in the Old County Courthouse for information and to check out the Fresnel lens from the Michigan Island Lighthouse. For additional information, see the Apostle Islands National Lakeshore listing.

Notable Events

- Bayfield in Bloom from mid-May to mid-June is a celebration of all things horticultural, featuring gardening tips and other activities for gardeners. The area's many orchards and wildflower farms are spotlighted.
- Apostle Islands Lighthouse Celebration is scheduled generally from late August to mid-September, with cruises offering views or guided tours of the lighthouses and other related events. Contact the Keeper of the Light (715-779-5619) gift shop for information.
- The first full weekend (Friday-Sunday) of October each year, the Bayfield Apple Festival transforms the town into a bustling festival city, loaded to the gills with people honoring King Apple. There are parades, contests, fish boils, a carnival, food booths, arts and crafts and waterfront regalia. Book lodging early; thousands pack this festival. Weekend highlights include the 400-member Wisconsin Mass Band.
- Old-Fashioned Christmas lasts from Thanksgiving until New Year's, complete with Santa arriving by boat and a tour of decorated historic and new homes.
- Apostle Islands Sled Dog Race is a mushing competition set in and around the islands in February.
- Blessing of the Fleet is a mid-June rite that features a lineup of many boaters seeking the blessing of their various vessels.
- Festival of Arts gives local artists the opportunity to exhibit their works on the waterfront in late July.

Where to Shop

The downtown waterfront area is loaded with shops, galleries and showrooms for the artistic creations of many talented artists and artisans. Fine art with a Native American emphasis is available from some studios.

Keeper of the Light on the waterfront has a fine collection of Apostle Islands and general lighthouse memorabilia and is full of interesting books and nautical stuff.

Kerr Studio & Gallery has jewelry and sculpture.

Stop at Donalee Designs for unique jewelry designs made with gemstones. Stone's Throw, in a turn-of-the-century building, is a gallery featuring a variety of items from handmade porcelain pottery

This lovely view of Bayfield from Lake Superior helps explain why this New England-style town is one of the favorite destinations on the lake and why its population swells in summer.

to jewelry, sculptures, prints and glass. At the south edge of Bayfield, Eckels Pottery and Fine Craft Gallery offers excellent stoneware and porcelain and encourages shoppers to watch the potters at work.

What's Next

Leaving Bayfield, you will take Highway 13 north to Red Cliff and then southwesterly through the small towns of Cornucopia, Herbster and Port Wing on the way to Superior. To the south, Highway 13 passes through Washburn on the road to Ashland to rejoin Highway 2.

INFO & OPTIONS

Apostle Islands National Lakeshore Visitor Center
415 Washington Ave.
Bayfield, WI 54814
715-779-3397
www.nps.gov.apis

Bayfield Chamber of Commerce & Visitor Bureau
42 South Broad St.
Bayfield, WI 54814
800-447-4094
www.bayfield.org

Greunke's First Street Inn
17 Rittenhouse Ave.
Bayfield, WI 54814
715-779-0153
greunkesinn.com

Maggie's Restaurant
257 Manypenny Ave.
Bayfield, WI 54814
715-779-5641
www.maggies-bayfield.com

Portside Bar & Restaurant
34475 Port Superior Rd.
Bayfield, WI 54814
715-779-5380

Wild Rice Restaurant
84860 Old San Rd.
Bayfield, WI 54814
715-779-9882
www.wildricerestaurant.com

Bay Front Inn and Gifts
15 Front St.
Bayfield, WI 54814
715-779-3330
www.bayfrontinnbayfield.net

Old Rittenhouse Inn
301 Rittenhouse Ave.
Bayfield, WI 54814
888-611-4667
www.rittenhouseinn.com

Seagull Bay Motel
325 S. 7th St.
Bayfield, WI 54814
715-779-5558
www.seagullbay.com

Winfield Inn & Gardens
225 East Lynde Ave.
Bayfield, WI 54814
715-779-3252
www.winfieldinn.com

Apostle Islands Area Campground
85150 Trailer Court Rd.
Bayfield, WI 54814
715-779-5524

Buffalo Bay Campground & Marina
14669 Hwy. 13
Bayfield, WI 54814
715-779-3743

Dalrymple Bayfield City Park
North of Bayfield on Hwy. 13
715-779-5712

Little Sand Bay Campground
32665 Little Sand Bay Rd.
Bayfield, WI 54814
715-779-5524
715-372-4866

Brule

Area Population 860

Brule is about midway between Superior and Ashland on Highway 2 and is an entry point to water adventure. Experience the beautiful Bois Brule River, world famous for trout fishing, scenery and exciting rapids. Canoe or kayak rentals are available in Brule.

Visit the Brule River Fish Hatchery to see how Lake Superior fish are reared. Self-guided tours. Open weekdays year-round and on weekends, June through September. No charge. Handicapped accessible.

The banks of the river from its source at Upper St. Croix to Lake Superior are protected by the Brule River State Forest, 600 acres of which have been designated as the Mott's Ravine Natural Area to foster pine barrens found there. Four different options for canoe or kayak trips available. Local outfitters will drop off and pick up paddlers. Below Highway 2 is another day's trip, recommended only for experts. For information and maps, contact the Brule River Forest Station in Brule.

Brule is one entry point of a side trip south via Highway 27. If you have time, turn east on County Road N to visit Barnes and Drummond, which has an neat museum of local history. Continuing on Highway 27 leads to Hayward.

What's Next

If traveling west, continue on Highway 2 toward Superior. To the east, you'll pass through several small towns on the way to Ashland.

INFO & OPTIONS

Brule River Motel & Campground
13844 East U.S. Hwy. 2
Brule, WI 54820
715-372-4815

Copper Range Campground and Bois Brule Campground
6250 South Range Rd.
Brule, WI 54820
715-372-5678

Chequamegon National Forest

If you're traveling across northern Wisconsin on U.S. 2 between Superior and Ashland, you'll find that the Chequamegon National Forest contains some of the loveliest forested lands in the northland. Hundreds of small lakes deep in the north woods are filled with fishing opportunities.

The forest preserves 850,000 acres of gently rolling terrain and timber, including some pine stands that have been in existence more than 100 years. In autumn, the color along this route is absolutely spectacular. There are numerous hiking and ATV riding trails and more than 500 miles (805 kilometers) of nicely groomed snowmobile trails through the woods, as well as the Chequamegon Area Mountain Bike Association trail system, which received an award for grassroots development from the U.S. Forest Service. Wintertime activities include cross-country skiing, snowmobiling and snowshoeing.

The highway is full of recreational opportunities, including the sighting of wildlife around almost every curve. You'll pass through the blink of a crossroad hamlet, Ino (see separate listing), where you can jog south through the scenic Delta Lakes area. The Moquah Barrens Wildlife Area lies about 5 miles (8 kilometers) north of Ino on Forest Road 236. Follow the Moquah Barrens Auto Tour route, using a guide prepared by Chequamegon National Forest personnel.

Cornucopia

Population 220

The village of Cornucopia on Lake Superior's south shore offers both a harbor of refuge for lake boaters and marina services. The old fishing village of "Corny" presents travelers with beautiful sandy beaches and wonderful sunsets over Lake Superior's westerly waters 18 miles (29 kilometers) beyond Red Cliff or 15 miles north of Port Wing on Highway 13 at the junction with County Trunk Highway C.

Cornucopia is the northern-most community in Wisconsin and boasts of having Wisconsin's northernmost post office.

What to See and Do

There are three churches in town, including Lutheran and Roman Catholic, but the early Eastern architecture at the Russian Orthodox St. Mary's Church, topped with its three-armed Russian Orthodox cross, is most likely to surprise and charm visitors.

Nearby, the sea caves, a popular kayaking and winter snowshoeing or skiing destination in Apostle Islands Country, are accessed via Meyers Beach Road about 4 miles (6.4 kilometers) east of Cornucopia. The road is also the entry point for a delightful 2-mile (3.2-kilometer) summer hike to a grove of ancient pines above the sea caves. Call Apostle Islands National Lakeshore headquarters (715-779-3397) for information on where to put in.

The old fishing village of Cornucopia offers visitors beautiful south shore sandy beaches.

There are two marinas, the town of Bell Marina and the Siskiwit Bay Marina.

The former home of an Ehlers family herring processing operation, the "Green Shed," as locals call it, was renovated and developed into a social center and home of the Cornucopia Historic Museum, where a continuous arts, crafts and community flea market operates amidst exhibits of area history. Open Thursday through Sunday during warm weather months only.

Where to Shop

Ehlers General Store in "downtown Corny," is full of fresh fruits, vegetables and country charm. An institution in the area since its establishment in 1915, its current owners have expanded the store to include hardware, a deli, organic foods, wine and fresh-made pizzas.

Just down the street is the Siskiwit Bay Coffee and Curiosities shop, with baked treats, some antiques and other gift items. The town is also home to Spinoza Bear Co., makers of the talking teddy bear.

Notable Events

• The Community Club Fish Fry in July brings the community and many visitors together for delicious food as a benefit for civic projects.

• Cornucopia Day in August is a celebration of more than a century of Corny's history and culture, featuring many fun events.

• Community Turkey Feed in November looks toward the holiday season with tasty food and community camaraderie.

INFO & OPTIONS

Cornucopia Business Association
P.O. Box 316
Cornucopia, WI 54827
715-742-3941 (Village Inn)
or 715-742-3232 (Ehlers Store)
www.cornucopiawisconsin.net

Fish Lipps Bar & Restaurant
88540 Superior Ave.
P.O. Box 219
Cornucopia, WI 54827
715-742-3378

The Village Inn
22270 County Hwy. C
Box 328
Cornucopia, WI 54827
715-742-3941
www.villageinncornucopia.com

Siskiwit Bay Lodge
89405 Jack Pine Rd.
Cornucopia, WI 54827
866-882-6939
www.siskiwitbaylodge.com

Fo'c'sle Bed & Breakfast
P.O. Box 116
Cornucopia, WI 54827
715-742-3337
www.siskiwitbay.com

South Shore Campground
23650 State Highway 13
Cornucopia, WI 54827
715-682-7722 or 715-790-4676
www.southshorecampground.com

Hayward

Population 2,130

Traveling south from Brule on Wisconsin Highway 27 from U.S. Highway 2 leads to Hayward, the home of the National Fresh Water Fishing Hall of Fame and Museum, documenting the exploits of noteworthy anglers and their prize-winning catches. Here you can take a walk right through the granddaddy of muskies, a $4^{1}/_{2}$-story fish complete with an observation deck in its open mouth. This is also home to the World Lumberjack Championships. Just east of Hayward is the Lac Courte Oreilles Casino and Convention Center, operated by the Lac Courte Oreilles Band of Lake Superior Ojibway. If your route is easterly, you can reconnect to the Circle Tour route by taking U.S. Highway 63 northeasterly toward Ashland. If traveling to the west from Hayward, catch Highway 77 through areas dotted by inland lakes and interesting towns to reconnect to the Circle Tour via Highway 35.

In Cable, also on U.S. 63, check out the Cable Museum of Natural History, which moved into its new building in 2008. The museum is on County Road M in Cable, just a couple of blocks east of U.S. 63. Besides wildlife displays and changing exhibits, the museum offers a summer lecture and field trip series, as well as many workshops and nature programs. Open year-round, Tuesday through Saturday.

Cable is in the heart of the Chequamegon Area Mountain Bike Association (CAMBA) off-road bike trail system. And there are three off-road events to challenge riders: the Cable Area Off-Road Classic, the Saturday before Memorial Day; the noncompetitive Fat Tire Poker Run guided tour the first Saturday in June; and the Chequamegon Fat Tire Festival the second weekend after Labor Day.

INFO & OPTIONS

Cable Area Chamber of Commerce
P.O. Box 217
Cable, WI 54821
800-533-7454
www.cable4fun.com

Hayward Lakes Visitor & Convention Bureau
P.O. Box 1055
Hayward, WI 54843
800-724-2992
www.haywardlakes.com

Hayward KOA
11544 North U.S. Hwy. 63
Hayward, WI 54843
800-562-7631
www.haywardcamping.com

Lake Chippewa Campground
8380 North County Hwy. CC
Hayward, WI 54843
715-462-3672
www.lakechip.com

River Road RV Campground
W449 East River Rd.
Hayward, WI 54843
715-634-2054

Twin Lakes RV Resort & Campground
12131 Hwy. 77
Hayward, WI 54843
715-462-3674
www.twinlakes-rvresort.com

Sunrise Bay Campground
16269 West Jolly Fisherman Rd.
Hayward, WI 54843
715-634-2213
www.nelsonlake.net/sunrisebay

Herbster

Population 195

The western Bayfield Peninsula towns of Herbster and Port Wing are accessed via Highway 13 from either Cornucopia to the north or off Highway 2 about 5 miles east of Superior. Like its neighboring community of Port Wing, the small Lake Superior village of Herbster captures the spirit of the commercial fishing industry of old. Herbster offers overnight camping and an

At the National Fresh Water Fishing Hall of Fame and Museum in Hayward, you can walk right through a 4½-story fish that features an observation deck in its open mouth.

excellent sand beach. Try trout fishing in the Cranberry River. The town has lodging and restaurant dining available. Northern Lights Gifts and Craft Shop offers items all made by local artists and crafters. One block outside of town on Lenawee Road, check the historic log gymnasium, built by the Works Progress Administration in 1940 from local timber.

The Apostles' famous Sea Caves are accessible from Herbster, offering spectacular ice formations in the winter and kayaking nooks and crannies in the summer.

What's Next

Depending on your route, up or down the road a bit, Port Wing has a claim to fame with its annual fish boil, which sounds strange but is absolutely enticing. (See separate listing)

INFO & OPTIONS

Woody's Food & Spirits
86985 Lenawee Rd.
Herbster, WI 54844
715-775-3338

Willow Motel
14935 Hwy. 13
Herbster, WI 54844
715-774-3385

Town of Clover Campgrounds (Herbster)
P.O. Box 94
86870 Lenawee Rd.
Herbster, WI 54844
715-774-3780
www.herbsterwisconsin.com

Hurley

Population 1,820

Hurley is the twin of Ironwood, Michigan (see city map, page 71), across the state border on the banks of the Montreal River. An integral part of the region's winter playground, Hurley is the western gateway to Big Snow Country and the ski area at Whitecap Mountains in nearby Montreal. It's the eastern gateway to Wisconsin for westbound travelers and is also home to some nice restaurants and more than 450 miles (724 kilometers) of snowmobile trails.

A Bit of History

Hurley's early days as a center of logging gave the town a reputation for having streets lined with barrooms, vice and wrongdoing. So notorious was the city that old-time lumberjacks often referred to northern Wisconsin's logging centers as being "Hurley, Hayward and Hell." Today, the city is much tamer and boasts fine restaurants, especially Italian.

Iron also helped make this a booming community. At the Plummer Mine Interpretive Park just west of Hurley stands the only remaining head frame from Wisconsin's old mining era in Wisconsin. The 80-foot head frame is listed on the National Register of Historic Places.

What to See and Do

Visitors with an interest in Finnish culture and history will want to visit nearby Little Finland, home of the National Finnish American Festival, with many artifacts and curios that came from Finland when their owners immigrated. The gift shop offers a large selection of glassware, linens, books and clothing, and is open 10 a.m. to 2 p.m. Wednesdays and Saturdays, April through December.

Just west of Hurley via U.S. 2, be sure to stop at Eagle's Bluff Golf Course for a panoramic view of the territory. Michigan's Copper Peak and the Porcupine Mountains are easily visible to the east, while, with a little imagination and a clear day, you can spot Lake Superior and the Apostle Islands to the west.

A couple of miles west beyond Eagle's Bluff on Highway 2, watch for a sign to Kimball Town Park. Turn left for a short drive to a delightfully pleasant little park and waterfall. You'll find a one-lane wood-decked bridge, a relaxing picnic area, restrooms, a small playground with swings and basketball court for the kids, and a rustic pavilion. The West Branch of the Montreal River gently cascades over a series of ledges in the riverbed, called Kimball Park Falls.

Mountain bikers will want to try the more than 200 miles (322 kilometers) of trails of the Pines and Mines Mountain Bike Trail System, accessible from Highway 77 near Hurley.

Kayakers and canoeists will be interested in paddling the "Rivers Through Time" route that follows the historic trek taken by native people, voyageurs and early pioneers along the Flambeau Trail and other waterways. A cooperative effort of Iron County Development Zone, the Wisconsin Humanities Council and National Endowment for the Humanities, there are "Rivers Through Time" maps and written descriptions available from the Information Center or the Development Zone office in Hurley.

Notable Museums

Iron County Historical Museum recalls Hurley's colorful past. The museum is in the old county courthouse, complete with bell tower. In downtown Hurley, the museum is open Monday, Wednesday, Friday and Saturday year-round. Closed holidays. Fee.

Notable Events

• In August, Hurley hosts the annual Paavo Nurmi Marathon, named after one of the greatest distance runners in the 1920s, and among the older marathons in the country.

• Iron County Heritage Festival is townwide in late July and early August.

What's Next

Before leaving the Hurley area, those heading west who have a bit of extra travel time will want to consider a side trip southward that takes an interesting and entertaining circular route to Ashland.

The Circle Tour Route follows Highway 2 east through Ironwood into the Michigan Upper Peninsula or west to Ashland within 5 miles (8 kilometers) of Lake Superior's shoreline, which can be accessed by turning north at the village of Saxon.

INFO & OPTIONS

Hurley Chamber of Commerce
316 Silver St.
Hurley, WI 54534
866-340-4334
www.hurleywi.com

Anton Walsh B & B
202 Copper St.
Hurley, WI 54534
715-561-2065
www.anton-walsh.com

Hurley Days Inn
13355 North U.S. Hwy. 51
Hurley, WI 54534
715-561-3500
www.hurleydaysinn.com

Hurley Inn
1000 10th Ave. North
Hurley, WI 54534
715-561-3030
www.hurleyinn.com

Liberty Bell Chalet
P.O. Box 55
109 Fifth Ave. South
Hurley, WI 54534
715-561-3753
www.libertybellchalet.com

Ino

Area Population 860

On Highway 2 in northern Wisconsin, you'll pass through the blink of a crossroad hamlet Ino (Dad always asked us kids, "Where are we?" And we answered, "INO!"), where you can jog south to visit the scenic Delta Lakes area. Hundreds of small lakes deep in the north woods are filled with fishing opportunities. This lovely forested and scenic area is well worth an hour side trip off Highway 2 south at Ino on County Highway E to County H, which angles northwest back to Highway 2 in Iron River. Several resorts do offer visitors a chance to stay in the Delta Lakes area. Stop at the Delta Diner for tasty food in a restored classic diner.

Follow the Moquah Barrens Auto Tour route, using a guide prepared by Chequamegon National Forest personnel. Moquah Barrens Wildlife Area is 5 miles (8 kilometers) north of Ino on Forest Road 236.

Delta Diner is a classic joint for a meal.

INFO & OPTIONS

Delta Diner
14385 County Hwy. H
Delta, WI 54856
715-372-6666
www.deltadiner.com

Iron River

Area Population 1,054

Iron River calls itself the "Blueberry Capital of the World" and proves it annually with its Blueberry Festival the fourth weekend of July. Wild blueberries grow on low bushes along roadsides and throughout the Chequamegon National Forest. For many, searching for the small sweet berries is as much fun as eating them.

What to See and Do

Iron River's 9-hole par 37 Northern Pines Golf Course is on Airport Road just west of town. The area offers more than 500 miles of groomed snowmobile trails.

Check out the Iron River National Fish Hatchery, which provides brook trout for Lake Superior tributaries. Off Highway A on Fairview Road, it's open year-round for self-guided tours.

Hikers will find a 60-mile (96.5-kilometer) section of the North Country National Scenic Trail beginning at County Highway A near Lake Ruth, approximately 5 miles (8 kilometers) south of Iron River. The North Country National Scenic Trail also extends westward 32 miles (51 kilometers) through the Brule River State Forest to St. Croix Lake near Solon Springs. More new trail begins at Lucius Woods County Park in Solon Springs and runs 11 miles (18 kilometers) southwest through the Douglas County Wildlife Area. There are eight backpacker campsites along the way, as well as dramatic overlooks of the Brule Valley, the historic Brule-St. Croix Portage, and a boardwalk through the cedar bog that forms the headwaters of the Brule and St. Croix.

For additional hiking opportunities, check with local information centers.

In downtown Iron River, the White Winter Winery provides a good sample of honey-based mead wines, which are made from the product of local bees. Scandia offers gifts and other items from the Norse traditions.

Notable Museums

A block south of the junction of Main Street and Highway 2, the Western Bayfield County Historical Museum has exhibits of photos, artifacts from early life in the area, a collection of wedding gowns, family Bibles (one dating from the 1700s) and a complete collection of a pioneer newspaper. Fee.

Notable Events

- Sled Dog Races have teams of dogs

and humans vying for honors in February.

• Summer Fest in June celebrates the full blush of the warm season.

• Blueberry Festival at the end of July gives everyone ample opportunity to sample this favorite regional fruit, while enjoying many other events.

What's Next

West from Iron River on Highway 2, the small outpost of Blueberry goes by in a blink, but slow down and pause to check out the antique shops, if they're open. Heading east on U.S. 2, you pass through the tiny hamlet of Ino on your way to Ashland.

Two interesting sidetrips off Highway 2 at Iron River follow county highways. County A heads north and picks up Highway 13 at Port Wing for a tour of the western Bayfield Peninsula. South from Iron River, Highway H angles southeasterly through the beautiful Delta Lakes region then picks up County E northward to reconnect to Highway 2 at Ino.

INFO & OPTIONS

Iron River Area Chamber of Commerce
7515 U.S. Hwy. 2
Iron River, WI 54847
800-345-0716
www.visitironriver.com

Wildwood Campground
9505 Wildwood Campground Rd.
Iron River, WI 54847
715-372-4072

Moon Lake Campground
County Hwy. H
Iron River, WI 54847
715-372-5457

Twin Bear
0370 County Hwy. H
Iron River, WI 54847
715-372-8610
www.twinbearcampground.com

Delta Lake Campground
62020 Delta Park Rd.
Iron River, WI 54847
715-372-8767, 715-209-6598
www.twinbearcampground.com

Madeline Island

Population 220 year-round/2,500 summer

Historic Madeline Island is the only one of the 22 Apostle Islands not in Apostle Islands National Lakeshore. The island is 14 miles long (22.5 kilometers) and 3 miles wide (5 kilometers). It is the only island with commercial development. It has sandy beaches, wooded trails, good fishing and sailing and breathtaking views no matter which way you turn, plus outstanding food and unique specialty shops. The village of La Pointe is the primary developed area of the island.

You can reach the island via a ride on one of the car ferries that carry passengers across 2.5 miles (4 kilometers) of Lake Superior to the island. Madeline Island Ferry Line offers regular service between Bayfield and La Pointe on one of four boats, *Madeline*, *Nichevo*, *Island Queen*, or the latest and largest addition to the fleet, the *Bayfield*. Take your vehicle or bicycle, or simply walk on board. There are more than two dozen 20-minute round trips daily between late June and Labor Day.

Tickets, schedules and information on island attractions are available during the summer at the ferry landing and other outlets in Bayfield, and year-round at the Madeline Island Chamber of Commerce and the ferry line offices on the island. Look for the chamber's island map.

Board the ferry on the Bayfield waterfront, one block north of the city dock at Washington Avenue.

During winter, after freeze-up, residents drive back and forth between the island and mainland on the thick ice. An ice road freezes (when conditions are right) and is plowed between Bayfield and La Pointe. The ice road has an official highway designation and is marked by recycled Christmas trees. Call ahead (715-747-5400) for ice conditions and crossing information. Caution is always advised. In the season between ice formation and breakup, a windsled transports passengers.

For pilots, Madeline Island has an uncontrolled, lighted 3,000-foot (915-meter) paved runway, Madeline Island Airstrip, 1.5 miles (2.4 kilometers) east of La Pointe.

What to See and Do

The 18-hole Madeline Island Golf Course was designed by Robert Trent Jones and offers breathtaking lake views, pine forests and the perfect challenge to any golfer. Sometimes dubbed "the St. Andrews of the North."

Snow Ryder Dogsled Adventures organizes adventure packages that teach mushing and offer visitors outdoor excitement as they mush a dog team around the island, on the lake ice and areas of the National Lakeshore. Check with Island Inn for details (800-899-1916).

The ferry line office, a half-block from the island ferry landing, offers a free guided one-hour walking tour twice daily during the summer. Many visitors arrive

Madeline Island Ferry Line can take you to Madeline Island for a day or more of adventure.

in their own boats and Madeline Island Yacht Club offers full service and transient dockage, with a launch ramp, fuel, pumpouts and a complete ship's store. Sail and power bare-boat or captained charter rentals are available at Apostle Islands Yacht Charters at the marina. It is in easy walking distance of all La Pointe attractions.

From early June to late July, the island is a magnet for musicians and budding performers, as Madeline Island Music Camp attracts students and master musicians who not only study but perform regular concerts open to the public.

Points of interest include St. Joseph's Catholic Church, built on the site of Bishop Frederic Baraga's third church; the La Pointe Post Office, part of the Old Mission built by Protestant missionaries in 1834; and the burial site of O-Shaka, son of Chief Buffalo and the chief speaker of the Ojibway on Lake Superior.

For those who choose not to walk, mo-peds or bicycles in a variety of styles can be rented from Motion to Go, which also sells island apparel. Most roads are newly paved, mainly flat and easy to ride. Blacktop shoulders on designated routes make for safer navigation.

Notable Museums

Discover La Pointe's varied history at the expanded Madeline Island Museum. The Wisconsin Historical Society operates the museum on the site of an early American Fur Company post, displaying lumbering, fur trading and fishing artifacts spanning three centuries. The important role of Native Americans, who influenced the development of this largest of the Apostle Islands, is told. The museum houses the Capser Center. Fee. Open Memorial Day weekend through early October.

A block east of Madeline Island Museum is the Madeline Island Heritage Center, which features three 100-year-old buildings offering a glimpse of island life from another time. One building is a restored one-room schoolhouse that was once on the north end of the Island. Open May through October on a limited schedule.

Parks and Public Areas

Drive or bike across Madeline Island and enjoy a day or an overnight at Big Bay State Park, which features hiking trails, sandstone cliffs, picnic areas and a sand beach that's great for swimming in Lake Superior in summer. A beach wheelchair is available. Pets and fires are prohibited on the beach. Contact the Wisconsin Department of Natural Resources for campground openings during the busy tourist season in July and August. Park sticker is required. In winter, the park provides a 5-mile (8-kilometer) loop for cross-country skiers.

Big Bay Town Park, operated by the town of La Pointe, has 40 rustic campsites, four with electricity. A picturesque picnic area overlooks a lagoon, and a wooden walking bridge leads to the sandy Big Bay Beach.

Ojibwa Memorial Park is next to the marina. The most famous people buried in the burial grounds are Ojibway Chief Buffalo and fur trader Michel Cadotte.

Where to Shop

Visitors searching for unique treasures of the island should stop at Island Thyme, near the ferry landing. Woods Hall Studios & Gallery is three blocks from the landing with hand-woven rugs, original designs, jewelry and pottery.

Island Carvers offers sculpture, relief carvings and classes. Other stops include Waterfront Gifts & Gallery, Cadotte's Gifts, Rendezvous Gift Shop at The Inn on Madeline Island and the Ships Store.

Don't miss Mission Hill Coffee House and Gift Shop, a year-round gathering place that caters to locals and visitors with coffee, breakfast rolls and sandwiches and a shop with books, wine and T-shirts.

INFO & OPTIONS

Madeline Island Chamber of Commerce
794 Main St.
La Pointe, WI 54850
888-475-3386
www.madelineisland.com

Ella's Island Cafe
858 Main St.
La Pointe, WI
715-747-2400

Lotta's Lakeside Cafe
794 Main St.
La Pointe, WI 54850
715-747-2033
www.lottascafe.com

Tom's Burned Down Cafe
Middle Rd.
La Pointe, WI 54850
715-747-6100
www.tomsburneddowncafe.com

The Inn on Madeline Island
P.O. Box 93
La Pointe, WI 54850
800-822-6315
www.madisland.com

Madeline Island Motel
P.O. Box 51
La Pointe, WI 54850
715-747-3000

Big Bay Town Park on Madeline Island
La Pointe, WI
715-747-2801

Big Bay State Park on Madeline Island
141 South Third St.
Bayfield, WI 54814
715-747-6425

Montreal

Population 810

Montreal on Wisconsin 77 a few miles southwest of Hurley is an old mining community that hasn't changed much over the years. The restored village with its quaint homes is listed on the National Register of Historic Places.

Whitecap Mountains in Montreal is on Lake Weber and offers 200 acres of alpine skiing terrain ranging from novice to expert slopes and trails. Located 11 miles (17.5 kilometers) west of Hurley on Wisconsin Highway 77, this is an especially attractive area in the summer. The resort offers hotel accommodations, and golfers will want to try Skye Golf in the Whitecap Mountains with its 18 holes of high-caliber challenges and views of the Apostle Islands.

INFO & OPTIONS

Whitecap Mountains Ski Resort
9106 West County Rd. E
Upson, WI 54565
715-561-2227
www.skiwhitecap.com

Oulu

Township Population 540

Oulu, a small hamlet just off Highway 2 east of Superior near Brule, is noted for its entry sign – a large painted rock with the name of the town on it. Visit the Oulu Glass Gallery and Studio for a display of blown, stained and fused glass. Jim and Sue Vojacek have made this a real family affair, one that will amaze you. Open daily, May until early January, with glass-blowing demonstrations from mid-November daily through early January. The studio also offers workshops on glass blowing in Oulu. Follow the signs; you'll get there, and the drive is worth it. Backtrack to Highway 2 to continue the Circle Tour either to the west or the east.

Poplar

Population 550

Poplar is the hometown of Richard Ira Bong, "America's Ace of Aces," a title he earned by shooting down the most enemy aircraft during World War II. The Richard I. Bong Veterans Historical Center (formerly Richard I. Bong World War II Heritage Center) honors Major Bong and the veterans of World War II and all later wars. It's in nearby Superior at Highway 2/53 near Barker's Island.

Also in Poplar, golfers will want to test their mettle against the 18-hole Poplar Golf Course and Campground on County Road D.

What's Next

On Highway 2 just east of Poplar is the small town of Maple, where you'll catch your first or last glimpse of the lake and Superior-Duluth in the distance from high along one of the ancient shorelines of Lake Superior. Night or day, the view is impressive.

A village and resort area about 5 miles (8 kilometers) south of Poplar on County Road P, Lake Nebagamon boasts a depot and post office that were built at the village site in 1896. The area is well-known for its summer recreation, which includes Botten's Green Acres Golf Course, a 9-hole par 35 course south of the townsite. Nearby at Lake Minnesuing is Norwood Golf Course, another 9-hole par 34 course. A few miles south at Solon Springs, Hidden Greens North offers an 18-hole par 72 challenge amid tranquil, tree-lined splendor. It's worth asking directions to get there. The clubhouse offers a bar and lounge for relaxation.

Port Wing

Population 430

The harbor at Port Wing opens the waters to prolific fishing opportunities. A boat launch and transient slips are available at the Port Wing Marina and Holiday Pines Resort. The marina has gas (no diesel), showers, a snack bar. Four charter services are located at the harbor for anglers wishing to get out on the big lake with an experienced captain. The drive from the marina east of town goes through the Port Wing Boreal Forest. There are two city parks to enjoy.

Reclaimed churches house Port Wing Pottery, with its local art and pottery, and Hoth Lee Gallery. Toward the marina, look for Trout Run Art and Ice Cream in a historic saloon, and the Lundgren Block Building with murals depicting local history.

Port Wing's claim to fame is its annual fish boil, which sounds strange but is absolutely enticing. The smells, outdoor ambiance and flavors of fish make it worth a special late summer trip. Held each year the Saturday before Labor Day.

If your route takes you north, Highway 13 passes through Herbster, Cornucopia and Red Cliff on the way to Bayfield. To the south and west are charming farms and farmland. This route offers occasional glimpses of Lake Superior and the Minnesota coastline over the trees. You'll pass through the small dairy communities of Cloverland and Lakeside. A bit farther along Wisconsin 13 at the Brule River, rest a bit at the canoe launch area or watch the river from the bridge. It's a chance to get right to the river's edge without having to bushwhack through the brush. Take the Brule River Road into the Brule River State Forest for beach access and fishing opportunities. Handicapped accessible. See details in listing for Brule.

INFO & OPTIONS

Ruxy's Cottage Cafe
8805 Hwy. 13
Port Wing, WI 54865
715-774-3565

Holiday Pines Resort
9130 Beach Rd.
Port Wing, WI 54865
715-774-3555

Johnson's Store & Campground
8875 Hwy. 13
Port Wing, WI 54865
715-774-3658

Red Cliff

Reservation Population 924

Red Cliff and the Red Cliff Indian Reservation are home of the Red Cliff Band of Lake Superior Chippewa. Nearby, Native Spirit Gifts and Indian Museum shop offers a delightful selection of Woodland Native crafts. The reservation, 3 miles (4.8 kilometers) north of Bayfield on Wisconsin Highway 13, operates the Red Cliff Fish Hatchery, where advance reservations allow visits.

The Red Cliff Entertainment Complex offers a variety of gaming fun at Isle Vista Casino, as well as live entertainment, bar and restaurant. The complex is open seven days a week, year-round. It's worth a stop just to see the beautiful wall-sized mural on native life by Rita Vanderventer. With completion of a new wastewater treatment plant, the tribe has approved a plan for a new $22 million casino, hotel, restaurant and marina complex. No timetable is set.

The view of the islands from the area around the center is spectacular. The 45-slip Buffalo Bay Marina provides services for those traveling by boat.

Sea kayakers will want to check on packages of instruction, as well as full-day or half-day tours of nearby sea caves, shipwrecks and Bass Island offered by Living Adventures.

Red Cliff's Fourth of July Powwow is a festival of traditional dance, song, food, arts and crafts. An outdoor concert in September is also a popular attraction.

Campers will find several options in the area: Point Detour Campground, which looks out on the Apostle Islands; the Town of Russell's Little Sand Bay Recreation Area; the Ranger Station and Hokenson Fishery.

WHAT'S NEXT

Just west of Red Cliff is an Apostle Islands National Lakeshore visitor center, with camping, boat launch and the restored Hokenson Brothers Fishery. Well worth the stop, you'll find it by taking County K to Little Sand Bay Road.

To the west 18 miles on Highway 13, Cornucopia has the state's northernmost post office. South on the highway takes you to Bayfield, Washburn and Ashland.

Saxon and Saxon Harbor

U.S. 2 between Ashland and Hurley travels within 5 miles (8 kilometers) of Lake Superior's shoreline, but it's possible to access the lake directly at Saxon Harbor via Wisconsin 122 approximately 12 miles (19 kilometers) west of Hurley, 5 miles (8 kilometers) north of Saxon off Highway 2.

Several charter fishing captains dock their boats in the harbor, offering a day of fishing or a cruise on the lake. Saxon Harbor offers transient docking, a public boat launch, fuel for visiting boaters, camping and a bar and restaurant. Saxon is also located on good snowmobile and cross-country ski trails.

INFO & OPTIONS

Frontier Campground & RV Park
11296 West U.S. Hwy. 2
Saxon, WI 54559
715-893-2461

Saxon Harbor Marina & Campground
County Rd. A (At Lake Superior, north of U.S. Hwy. 2 on Hwy. 122, turn left on County A to the harbor.)
715-561-2922
www.ironcountywi.com

Superior

Population 27,370

Superior, on the Wisconsin bank of the St. Louis River, was originally planned to be the primary city at the Head of the Lakes, but commerce and happenstance allowed Duluth, Minnesota, to dominate, though Superior's heritage is longer established.

This Wisconsin city exerts a strong influence on transportation. As part of the world port, its iron ore, coal facilities and grain elevators supply ships from around the world. With a much flatter terrain than its sister, Superior has captured many of the rail yards that serve the

Superior: Insider Tips

• Superior Municipal Forest covers 4,400 acres of wilderness in Billings Park on the southwest side of Superior. One of the city's true treasures, it's a great place for hiking, biking, birding, dog walking and canoeing in summer and cross-country skiing, snowshoeing, snowmobiling and riding ATVs in the winter. Look for the trailhead at 28th Street and Wyoming Avenue or off Billings Drive for parking.

• A World of Accordions Museum, basement of the Harrington Arts Center, 1401 Belknap Street, Superior. Here, Helmi Strahl Harrington, Ph.D., has chronicled the history of the sqeezebox with 1,000 accordions on display, along with related items such as figurines and artifacts. An accomplished accordion player with a doctorate in musicology, she leads many of the museum's tours.

• Wisconsin Point is an undeveloped finger of land that sits opposite Minnesota Point, offering a quiet place, beaches and generally few cars and people to contend with. It's a great spot for beach walking, picnicking and birdwatching.

• Among several well-done museums in Superior is the Old Fire House & Police Museum at Highway 2/53 and 23rd Avenue East. You'll find a fascinating array of historic (horse-drawn) and more modern firefighting equipment. One of the newer parts is the police room exhibit with examples of old-style mugshots and fingerprints, a jail cell, old photographs and interesting "compliance" devices, such as a"chain twister" that would seriously smart when placed around the wrist.

Superior, Wisconsin & Duluth, Minnesota

region. It is also a trucking center.

Superior has several neighborhoods with homes of classic design, including Billings Park, which overlooks the St. Louis River on the city's west end. Each neighborhood offers small shops with a friendly welcome to all visitors.

A Bit of History

The first trading post in the region was established in the 1790s on Conner's Point in Superior. The city was well established by 1855 and seemed sure to be the commercial center of the Upper Midwest, with the only natural entry to the protected harbor. The signing of the Treaty of La Pointe with the Ojibway opened northern Minnesota for settlement and exploration and Duluth came into existence. The 1871 opening of the Duluth Ship Canal removed Superior's dominance as a port and

Duluth soon supplanted Superior as the major settlement at the Head of the Lakes.

Today

Superior was one of the busiest ship construction ports on the Great Lakes. Today, Fraser Shipyards continues to repair and modify huge lake ships on the waterfront near the Blatnik Bridge. Its operations can be seen up close during a tour on the Vista Fleet tour boats.

The University of Wisconsin-Superior (UWS) is a major employer and has an outstanding curriculum of education with full four-year and advanced degrees in all major areas of concentration, including business, music, fine and applied arts and sciences. The university is involved in major Lake Superior environmental research. Through the Lake Superior Research Institute, it sponsors ecology cruises on the *L.L. Smith Jr.* out of Bayfield, Wisconsin, and Duluth and Two Harbors, Minnesota. UWS is also home to Wessman Arena, a year-round facility that hosts hockey and skating in winter and numerous community events during the rest of the year.

Wisconsin Indianhead Technical College offers nearly five dozen courses ranging from short term to two years for students seeking vocational skills that will give them entree to careers.

What to See and Do

Osaugie Trail, a paved pathway, opens a pleasant 5 miles for summer hiking, biking, 'boarding and 'blading along the Superior waterfront east to Moccasin Mike Road. There are four trailheads: Harbor View Park, 18th Avenue East, Loon's Foot Landing and Bear Creek Park (at Moccasin Mike Road). At the trail's halfway point at Loon's Foot Landing, motorized recreationists can connect to the unpaved Tri-County Corridor multiuse trail through Douglas, Bayfield and Ashland counties. In winter, the trail opens for snowmobiles.

Barker's Island is a recreational focal point, with a hotel complex, Barker's Island Inn and Conference Center. You'll find picnicking, shore fishing, a boat-launching site, mini golf and shopping. Barker's is home to the Superior Charter Dock Captains Association, with a boatload of licensed captains to find the big fish. Barker's Island Marina is a 420-slip facility with a ship's store, new boat showroom, charter service, sailing instruction and rental, and 24,000-square-foot heated winter storage. The marina is one of the largest in the Midwest.

The Vista Fleet runs a regular schedule of harbor cruises. In Superior, the boarding dock is at Barker's Island, where Vista Fleet operates its home for Vista Fleet Harbor Cruises and Gift Shop.

There is a new transient dock south of the Vista Fleet dock.

The impressive Superior Public Library is in a modern structure on the corner of Tower Avenue and Belknap Street. The library is home to 27 beautifully wrought wall-sized murals painted by well-known regional artist Carl Gawboy depicting early area history.

A favorite weekend destination of locals is the Lake Superior beach along Wisconsin Point Road, offering rustic picnicking spots, beach walking and driftwood gathering. Watch out for the occasional poison ivy plant. To reach the road, which is on the east side of the city, take U.S. 2/53 to Moccasin Mike Road to Wisconsin Point. There, Wisconsin Point Road runs along the point and extends to the Superior Entry of Lake Superior, then to Superior Harbor, where a lighthouse stands guard. Shortly before reaching the Superior Entry, watch for a 17th century Fond du Lac Ojibway burial ground beside the road, marked by a plaque 4.5 miles from U.S. 2/53. Although the remains were moved many years ago, native people still honor the location with ceremonial objects placed at the marker.

Burlington Northern Santa Fe Ore Docks in Superior are the largest in the world, loading taconite ore onto 1,000-foot (305-meter) lake vessels.

At the junction of highways 2 and 13 east of town, be sure to check out the unusual Finnish Windmill. Constructed by Jacob Davidson in the northern European style, the mill's arms had large "sails" to catch the wind. The mill no longer operates, but the building was preserved by Davidson's descendants, who presented the unique structure and grounds to the Old-Brule Heritage Society in 2001 for use as a public exhibit of early life and enterprise in the area. A turnoff allows you to stop, take photos and learn a bit of local history.

Fairlawn Mansion & Museum

Fairlawn Mansion and Museum faces Barker's Island and overlooks Superior Bay from across Highway 2/53. Built in 1890 as a private residence, this 42-room Victorian-style mansion is open year-round and epitomizes the lifestyle of early lumber-mining baron and Superior's second mayor, Martin Pattison, and his wife, Grace. It recalls the city's boomtown days with growth fueled by lumbering, mining and maritime commerce. Once again an opulent showplace on Superior's waterfront, Fairlawn Mansion had fallen into considerable disrepair before being rescued by Superior and Douglas County preservation groups. Extensively restored in 1997-98, the exterior and first floor display the elegant character of its early life. The third floor is also complete and is devoted to displays from the period when the mansion was a children's home. After restoration, the home was featured on the A&E series "American Castles." More recently, a series of Victorian-inspired gardens were being added to the grounds. Fee. Open year-round for guided tours, events and private parties.

Notable Museums

Richard I. Bong Veterans Historical Center (formerly Richard I. Bong World War II Heritage Center) honors Major Bong and the veterans of World War II as well as all later wars, including Korea, Vietnam and Desert Storm. The Bong Center, 305 Harbor View Parkway (U.S. 2/53) near Barker's Island, includes personal belongings of World War II vintage donated by veterans who served along with America's "Ace of Aces," Richard Ira Bong. A restored P-38 fighter plane similar to one flown by Major Bong is displayed, along with his many awards, including the Medal of Honor. Major Bong grew up on the family farm in Poplar, Wisconsin. He earned the "Ace of Aces" distinction in the Pacific Theater for shooting down more enemy planes than any other U.S. pilot, a record that still stands. Open daily mid-May to mid-October, with a limited schedule in winter. Fees apply. The Superior and Douglas County Visitor Information Center at the Bong Center is a dandy.

The SS *Meteor* Whaleback Ship Museum on Barker's Island displays the

The 42-room Victorian-style Fairlawn Mansion & Museum faces Barker's Island and is open year-round on U.S. 2/53 in Superior for guided tours, special events and private parties.

only remaining whaleback freighter, which resembles a submarine. These vessels were developed and built in Superior. Tours feature displays and a pictorial history on turn-of-the-century whaleback shipping. Open daily mid-May through mid-October. The *Meteor*, along with Fairlawn Mansion & Museum and the Old Fire House and Police Museum, are managed by Superior Public Museums.

Near the *Meteor* museum on Barker's Island are a covered concert stage, playground equipment, garden and mini golf course. A statue is "dedicated to the seamen of the Great Lakes." A small shopping complex has also been built here to house the Vista Fleet ticket office. Souvenirs, gifts and locally made dog treats are among the items that visitors will find.

Fairlawn Mansion and Museum served for 30 years as the family residence for Grace and Martin Pattison, who earned a fortune by prospecting and securing title on iron ore properties in northern Minnesota. Fairlawn (see side story) was donated to the Superior

Children's Home and Refuge Association and would house unfortunate children for 42 years. Renovations changed the original building, and by the early 1960s the association disbanded and abandoned the structure. The city assumed ownership and Douglas County Historical Society did considerable restoration and repair work, culminating in a major 1998 restoration. Once again the late-1800s elegance of Fairlawn wows visitors. Today, Fairlawn is operated by the city's Superior Public Museums. Fairlawn is open year-round seven days a week. Fees.

Historic and present-day firefighting equipment and police memorabilia are displayed at the Old Fire House and Police Museum, in the the last of Superior's turn-of-the-century firehouses. Station No. 4 was built in 1898 to replace the original East End Firehall that was destroyed by fire in 1896. The building is also a state Hall of Fame for those professionals. A recent addition upstairs is the police room exhibit featuring artifacts and photos from the police department's history. At Highway 2/53 and 23rd Avenue East. Open from mid-May through mid-October.

Parks and Public Areas

The city of Superior maintains 19 parks within its boundaries, as well as the Superior Municipal Forest, the third-largest city forest in the United States. The 4,400-acre forest has 19 miles (30.5 kilometers) of hiking and cross-country ski trails over beautiful rolling terrain, including the 1.6-mile paved Millennium Trail and the 6-mile Pokegama Multipurpose Trail, which was developed in natural surroundings and opened by the Cyclists of Gitchee Gummee Shores for hikers, bikers and snowshoers. The forest has 6 miles (9.7 kilometers) of snowmobile and winter ATV trails and a skijoring trail. An archery course has 14 targets.

Other hiking and cross-country ski opportunities can be found in Brule River State Forest and in Solon Springs.

At Pattison State Park, visit Wisconsin's highest waterfall, "Big Manitou," where the Black River plunges 165 feet (50 meters). The park, donated by and named after former Superior Mayor Martin Pattison, includes campsites, hiking trails, a picnic area and swimming beach, as well as ski and snowshoeing trails. A total of 9 miles of nature trails includes a 2-mile (3-kilometer) labeled trail. Interpretive programs and checklists of the park's birds and mammals are available. Brown and brook trout are native to the river; rainbow are stocked each year. The park is 12 miles (19 kilometers) south of Superior on Highway 35. Open all year. Many facilities, including two campsites, are handicapped accessible.

The Amnicon River is the focus of the 825-acre Amnicon Falls State Park. Named from Ojibway words meaning "where fish spawn," the Amnicon flows over a series of spectacular waterfalls and rapids within the park on the way to its mouth at Lake Superior. Interesting geologic formations along the riverbed are the result of an earthquake that occurred a half-billion years ago. Another attraction in the park is the 55-foot (17-meter) covered "bowstring" bridge, one of only five such bridges remaining in the United States. The bridge allows visitors to cross to an island in the Amnicon River. There are campsites, a 2-mile nature trail, a shelter in the picnic area and a playground. Anglers can catch trout, walleye and muskie. Located southeast of the city and 1 mile (1.6 kilometers) east of the junction of Highways 2 and 53 off U.S. Highway 2 on County U.

Downhill skiing is nearby at Mont du Lac Ski Area.

Douglas County offers a total of 325 miles of winter snowmobile/ATV trails.

If you're traveling with skateboarders, check out the skateboard park at 28th Street and Hammond Avenue near Mariner Mall.

Wisconsin Indianhead

Superior offers summer recreation at Nemadji Golf Course, a 36-hole full-service facility at 58th and Tower that has earned a 4-star rating by *Golf Digest.* Lessons available.

Nearby 9-hole courses are at Pattison Park, two in Gordon and two at Lake Nebagamon, with 18-hole courses at Poplar and Solon Springs, where it's worth asking directions to the excellent 18-hole Hidden Greens North Golf Course, which also offers a lounge and bar services.

About 20 miles east of town on Highway 2, the Brule River is excellent for canoeing/kayaking and fishing. It is known as the "River of Presidents" because Presidents Grant, Cleveland, Coolidge, Hoover and Eisenhower all cast lines there. President Calvin Coolidge, in fact, spent considerable summer time near the Brule in northwestern Wisconsin. During his presidency, the senior high school in Superior was called "the Summer White House" because he sometimes did business from there.

Notable Events

• Gitchee Gumee Brew Fest draws craft brewers from throughout the Midwest in April.

• Fourth of July Parade and Festival is a traditional, spectacular celebration of independence.

• Lake Superior Dragon Boat Festival in August involves paddling and is an exciting event benefitting local causes.

• Great Northern Rodeo in September brings the western tradition to Lake Superior.

Where to Shop

Superior Antique and Art Depot houses a collection of constantly changing antique and art dealer displays.

The historic building served as Superior's main railroad depot until the railroad yards were relocated out of the city. Situated at Oakes and Broadway, just off Tower Avenue and the downtown area. Open seven days a week. Globe News, at Tower Avenue and Belknap Street, is one of the few places to find a range of major newspapers, including *The New York Times*.

Mariner Mall contains a number of stores, including a department store, specialty shops, food and services and a multiscreen movie theater on the corner of Hill Avenue and North 28th Street.

Downtown Superior offers a variety of dining and shopping opportunities and is home to the Business Improvement District and the Development Association of Superior & Douglas County. Tower Avenue and Belknap Street are the main streets.

If you're looking for sporting or outdoor gear, Northwest Outlet on Belknap can supply most any need.

What's Next

If you're traveling from east to west on Highway 2, your next stop will be Duluth across either the Blatnik or the Bong bridge. If you're eastbound, follow Highway 2 through a series of small towns heading toward Ashland. If you plan to visit the Bayfield Peninsula, watch for the junction with Highway 13 east Superior or just west of Ashland.

INFO & OPTIONS

Superior/Douglas County Visitor Center, Wisconsin Travel Information
Hwy. 2/53 (in Veterans Historical Center)
305 Harbor View Parkway
Superior, WI 54880
715-392-2773, 800-942-5313

Superior/Douglas County Chamber of Commerce
205 Belkap St.
Superior, WI 54880
800-942-5313, 715-394-7716
www.visitsuperior.com

Gronk's Grill & Bar
4909 East Second St.
Superior, WI 54880
715-398-0333
www.gronksgrill.com

Hammond Steak House
1402 North Fifth St.
Superior, WI 54880
715-392-3269
www.hammondliquor.com

Barker's Island Inn and Conference Center
300 Marina Dr.
Superior, WI 54880
715-392-7152
www.barkersislandinn.com

Best Western Bridgeview
415 Hammond Ave.
Superior, WI 54880-1140
800-777-5572
www.bestwestern.com

Days Inn – Superior/Bayfront
110 Harborview Pkwy.
Superior, WI 54880
888-515-5040
www.daysinnsuperior.com

Holiday Inn Express Hotel & Suites
303 Second Ave. East
Superior, WI 54880
888-465-4329
www.ichotelsgroup.com

Super 8 Motel-Superior
4901 East Second St.
Superior, WI 54880-4303
800-800-8000
www.super8.com

Superior Inn
525 Hammond Ave.
Superior, WI 54880
800-777-8599
www.superiorinn.com

Amnicon Acres Campground
4505 East Tri Lakes Rd.
Superior, WI 54880
715-399-8443

Nemadji Campground
3132 East Fifth St.
Superior, WI 54880
715-398-6366

Pattison State Park
6294 South Hwy. 35
Superior, WI 54880
888-947-2757
www.dnr.state.wi.us/Org/land/parks

Amnicon Falls State Park
4279 South County Rd. U
South Range, WI 54874
715-398-3000 (summer)
715-399-3111 (winter)
www.wiparks.net

Brule River State Forest
6250 South Range Rd.
Brule, WI 54820
715-372-54820
www.dnr.wi.gov/

Manitou Valley Campground
3467 East Manitou Valley Rd.
Superior, WI 54880
715-399-8696
http://manitouvalley.samsbiz.com

Washburn

Population 2,105

Washburn, found on Highway 13 between Ashland and Bayfield, is a city of lakeside parks, with easy access to fishing, boating, snowmobiling and skiing.

What to See and Do

The city operates Memorial Park and Thompson's West End Park, each with camping, showers, sandy beaches, picnic tables, playgrounds and hookups. A boat launch is available at West End Park. Camping is available April 15 to October 15. A walking trail overlooking Chequamegon Bay runs from West End Park to the Washburn Marina, which is a pleasant haven for boaters and other visitors from around the lake. Full service, with diesel and gas. Boaters wishing to tie up awhile are advised to call the marina to ensure that space is available.

Anglers looking for action will want to check with Outdoor Allure bait, tackle and guide service for charter information.

Washburn's heyday saw it shipping enormous amounts of native brownstone from nearby quarries and explosives from a Dupont Corporation plant just outside of town, but the city has since evolved into a center for art.

There are two nice parks downtown that invite respite in their green and flowered expanses.

The impressive 145-seat StageNorth performing arts center opened in 2007, replacing its previous home in the former Swedish Lutheran Church. It offers a variety of live shows, entertainment and classic films, and a film festival in September.

Washburn claims the first "underground" Dairy Queen in the United States, constructed into a hillside.

Mt. Valhalla Recreation Area is on County Road C, northwest of Washburn and has scenic horseback riding trails, hiking and snowmobile trails and snowshoeing areas.

Eight miles (13 kilometers) toward Bayfield on Wisconsin 13, wax your skis and enjoy 40 miles (64 kilometers) of groomed cross-country trails at Mount Ashwabay, a ski area with an acronym name made from the first syllables of Ashland, Washburn and Bayfield. Turn west on Ski Hill Road off State Highway 13. Trails vary from old logging roads to hilly slopes.

Mt. Ashwabay has 14 downhill runs for all skill levels, snowmaking capability, ski rental, instruction, food and a chalet. It recently installed new lifts and is a family-friendly facility. Open Wednesday through Saturday for downhill and daily for cross-country skiing.

Also at Mt. Ashwabay, Lake Superior Big Top Chautauqua offers unique professional summer entertainment – culture under canvas.

The Big Top features popular historical musicals of Bayfield, Washburn and the Chequamegon region and many well-known national performers. The season runs from early June through Labor Day. Bay Area Rural Transit buses provide pickup from various locations in the area.

Daily self-guided tours of Bayfield State Fish Hatchery are available year-round. This is one of six northern Wisconsin hatcheries where visitors are welcome. A variety of game fish species are raised here.

Big Top Chautauqua

The cream of Bayfield Peninsula entertainment is found at the Lake Superior Big Top Chautauqua, which offers a summer-long schedule of musical performances ranging from top regional acts to nationally known performers like Willie Nelson, John Hiatt and Taj Mahal. Iowa native Greg Brown is an annual favorite. Big Top also features special regional house shows that spotlight the history and maritime traditions of the area. To avoid parking problems, Bay Area Regional Transit buses pick up passengers in a number of locations and deliver them to the Big Top, which is located at Mt. Ashwabay Ski Area.

Notable Museums

For a taste of local history and culture, stop at the historic Washburn Historical Museum and Cultural Center in the old Washburn Bank Building. It has displays on local historical families.

Notable Events

- Washburn holds a summer festival each year in late July. Every five years, a homecoming celebration is held concurrent with the summer fest.
- In February, the city is site of one end of the Book Across the Bay 10-kilometer ski and snowshoe race.
- West End Park is the site of the biannual Inland Sea Kayak Symposium, a mid-June event attracting fledgling and experienced paddlers from throughout the country.

Where to Shop

Visit Bloomquist Gallery on the shore of Lake Superior about a mile south of Washburn, where the local watercolor and pastel scenes of noted artist Art Bloomquist are displayed along with other art by David and Kathi Bloomquist.

In town, stop at Karlyn's Gallery, owned by artist Karlyn Holman, known for original designs in pottery and watercolors, as well as art by other area professionals.

Austin Miller Studio & Gallery on the Mt. Ashwabay road north of Washburn offers works about Lake Superior by France Austin Miller, a watercolorist. Her art and limited edition prints are available in many Lake Superior galleries and she also does framing of works at the studio.

Be sure to stop and visit with Richard Avol, owner of Chequamegon Book & Coffee Co., who deals in new and used books and in coffee, across from the Washburn Museum.

What's Next

You'll stay on Highway 13 to depart Washburn. Southward about 11 miles is Ashland. If your route is north toward Bayfield, you'll pass Port Superior Village on Chequamegon Bay as you begin your climb toward Bayfield.

This friendly marina provides accommodations and dining at the Portside Restaurant. Next door is Waterford by the Bay, a condo development, and Pikes Bay Marina, bringing the number of slips in these large complexes to more than 400.

Just prior to entering Bayfield, the Wild Rice Restaurant features upscale food and an extensive wine list during the summer months.

INFO & OPTIONS

Bayfield County Tourism
P.O. Box 878
Washburn, WI 54891
800-472-6338
www.travelbayfieldcounty.org

Washburn Area Chamber of Commerce
126 West Bayfield St.
P.O. Box 74
Washburn, WI 54891
800-253-4495
www.washburnchamber.com

Steak Pit
125 Harborview Dr.
Washburn, WI 54891
715-373-5492

North Coast Inn & Chalets
26 West Bayfield St.
Washburn, WI 54892
715-373-5512

Washburn Motel
800 West Bayfield St.
Washburn, WI 54891
715-373-5580

Memorial Park
P.O. Box 638
Washburn, WI 54891
715-373-6160

Thompson's West End Park
P.O. Box 638
Washburn, WI 54891
715-373-6160

Wanoka Lake
U.S. Hwy. 2
Washburn, WI 54891
715-373-2667

Page #p = photo; #m = map

C

From Lake Superior Port Cities Inc.
www.lakesuperior.com

Lake Superior Magazine
A bimonthly, regional publication covering the shores along Michigan, Minnesota, Wisconsin and Ontario

Lake Superior Travel Guide
An anually updated mile-by-mile guide

Lake Superior, The Ultimate Guide to the Region 2nd Edition
Softcover: ISBN 978-0-942235-97-5

Hugh E. Bishop:

The Night the Fitz *Went Down*
Softcover: ISBN 978-0-942235-37-1

By Water and Rail: A History of Lake County, Minnesota
Hardcover: ISBN 978-0-942235-48-7
Softcover: ISBN 978-0-942235-42-5

Haunted Lake Superior
Softcover: ISBN 978-0-942235-55-5

Haunted Minnesota
Softcover: ISBN 978-0-942235-71-5

Bonnie Dahl:

Bonnie Dahl's Superior Way, Fourth Edition
Softcover: ISBN 978-0-942235-92-0

Joy Morgan Dey, Nikki Johnson:

Agate: What Good Is a Moose?
Softcover: ISBN 978-0-942235-73-9

Daniel R. Fountain:

Michigan Gold, Mining in the Upper Peninsula
Softcover: ISBN 978-0-942235-15-9

Marvin G. Lamppa:

Minnesota's Iron Country
Softcover: ISBN 978-0-942235-56-2

Daniel Lenihan:

Shipwrecks of Isle Royale National Park
Softcover: ISBN 978-0-942235-18-0

Betty Lessard:

Betty's Pies Favorite Recipes
Softcover: ISBN 978-0-942235-50-0

James R. Marshall:

Shipwrecks of Lake Superior, Second Edition
Softcover: ISBN 978-0-942235-67-8

Lake Superior Journal: Views from the Bridge
Softcover: ISBN 978-0-942235-40-1

Howard Sivertson

Driftwood: Stories Picked Up Along the Shore
Hardcover: ISBN 978-0-942235-91-3

Schooners, Skiffs & Steamships: Stories along Lake Superior's Water Trails
Hardcover: ISBN 978-0-942235-51-7

Tales of the Old North Shore
Hardcover: ISBN 978-0-942235-29-6

The Illustrated Voyageur
Hardcover: ISBN 978-0-942235-43-2

Once Upon an Isle: The Story of Fishing Families on Isle Royale
Hardcover: ISBN 978-0-962436-93-2

Frederick Stonehouse:

Wreck Ashore: United States Life-Saving Service, Legendary Heroes of the Great Lakes
Softcover: ISBN 978-0-942235-58-6

Shipwreck of the Mesquite
Softcover: ISBN 978-0-942235-10-4

Haunted Lakes (the original)
Softcover: ISBN 978-0-942235-30-2

Haunted Lakes II
Softcover: ISBN 978-0-942235-39-5

Haunted Lake Michigan
Softcover: ISBN 978-0-942235-72-2

Haunted Lake Huron
Softcover: ISBN 978-0-942235-79-1

Julius F. Wolff Jr.:

Julius F. Wolff Jr.'s Lake Superior Shipwrecks
Hardcover: ISBN 978-0-942235-02-9
Softcover: ISBN 978-0-942235-01-2